A PRACTITIONER'S GUIDE TO THE FSA REGULATION OF INSURANCE

A PRACTITIONER'S GUIDE TO THE FSA REGULATION OF INSURANCE

Consultant Editor
John Young
Lovells

First Edition

City & Financial Publishing

City & Financial Publishing
8 Westminster Court, Hipley Street
Old Woking
Surrey GU22 9LG
United Kingdom
Tel: 00 44 (0)1483 720707 Fax: 00 44 (0)1483 727928
Web: www.cityandfinancial.com

ISBN 1 898830 57 6
© 2002 City & Financial Publishing and the named authors.

British Library Cataloguing-in-Publication Data. A catalogue record for this book is available from the British Library.

Typeset by Type Study, Scarborough and printed and bound in Great Britain by Biddles Limited, Guildford and King's Lynn

Biographies

John Young is a partner at Lovells. He spends the whole of his time advising on the regulation of insurance business and corporate transactions within the insurance industry, both in the UK and internationally. He manages the activities of the lawyers in Lovells' corporate insurance practice area who advise the insurance industry on a wide variety of non-contentious matters, including product development and marketing.

In the last few years John has advised on many of the most significant deals within the UK insurance industry. He was described in the 2000 edition of the UK's *Legal 500* directory as "the doyen of corporate insurance transactions", and was named in the 2000/2001 edition of *Chambers Guide to the Legal Profession* as the UK's leading solicitor in the field of non-contentious insurance.

James Bateson has been a partner with Norton Rose since 1995. He is a corporate finance lawyer, specialising in the insurance and financial services sectors. His experience includes mergers and acquisitions, capital raising and restructuring, demutualisation, flotations and advising on the establishment, regulation, sale and purchase of these businesses in the UK and Europe. James is also experienced in relation to Lloyd's matters and represents the firm in the Lloyds Market Association.

Katherine Coates has been a partner of the international law firm Clifford Chance since 1990, and heads the corporate insurance practice. She has advised on the establishment of new insurance companies, mergers, acquisitions and joint ventures, portfolio transfers of both life and non-life portfolios, demutualisations, distribution arrangements, a wide variety of regulatory issues, insurance securitisations and the development of insurance products and policy wordings.

Hilary Evenett is a partner within the corporate insurance practice of Clifford Chance. The corporate insurance group specialises in providing regulatory, corporate and product development advice to life and non-life insurers, mutual insurers, insurance brokers and participants in the Lloyd's market.

Hitesh Patel is a partner, insurance technical and regulatory services at KPMG. He is responsible for providing accounting and prudential regulatory advisory services to the insurance industry. He is also responsible for providing advice on the FSA's new senior management arrangements and approved persons regime. Hitesh provides technical support to the IASC's insurance steering committee and is a member of the ABI's working party on the revision of the SORP on accounting for insurance businesses.

Ian Poynton is a partner in Freshfields Bruckhaus Deringer, where he is a member of the London corporate department. His practice covers the range of corporate transactions with a particular focus on the insurance sector. He has worked on a number of proposals for the restructuring of life offices in the UK and elsewhere, including acting for Scottish Widows on its demutualisation into the Lloyds TSB Group.

Rob Stirling is a London-based corporate partner at Freshfields Bruckhaus Deringer. His experience includes both public and private M&A and a wide range of other corporate finance, securities and advisory work. He has particular experience in the insurance sector.

Geoffrey Maddock is a partner at the corporate department of Herbert Smith. He works principally on corporate finance transactions in the insurance sector and has experience of demutualisation of life assurance companies, acquisitions, disposals, joint ventures and related transactions in this sector. He also has particular experience of transfers of insurance business under the Insurance Companies Act.

Andrew Holderness is a partner within the corporate insurance department of Clyde & Co. He specialises in floatations, mergers, acquisitions and disposals, MBOs, MBIs, joint ventures and start ups for companies in both the Lloyd's and the insurance companies market.

Ambereen Salamat is a partner with DJ Freeman, having joined the firm in 1999. She has been involved in advising the insurance industry since 1988 and specialises in a wide range of non-contentious work, including regulatory and transactional, within the sector.

Claudia Monsanto is a senior associate in the Financial Institutions Group of Clifford Chance. Claudia joined Clifford Chance is 1997. She is experienced in mergers and acquisitions and joint ventures involving insurance companies and banks and transfers of insurance business and also specialised in advising on UK and EC insurance-related regulatory matters.

Philip Skerrett solicitor (1971) formerly head of the company department at Holborn firm Compton Carr. Formed the City Law Partnership (formerly the Brough Skerrett Law Partnership) of which he is the senior partner in January 1994 with Gordon Brough. He has been involved with the non-contentious aspects of the Life Insurance Industry since 1983 and lectures on matters in relation thereto.

Stephanie Fuller was admitted as a solicitor in January 1993. Formerly with DLA she joined the Lincoln Financial Group as a senior legal adviser in 1996. She has a broad background of commercial experience having represented a variety of blue chip companies in both contentious and non-contentious matters with a particular expertise in compliance and regulatory matters as well as life company and funds work.

Stephanie joined the City Law Partnership as an associate in July 2001.

John Gilbert is a partner at the international law firm, Lovells, where he combines a specialism in the law and regulation of friendly societies with his general banking law practice. He advises both incorporated and registered friendly societies and has been involved in most of the major developments in the friendly societies movement over the last decade. John is currently working in Lovells' Amsterdam office, but continues to be closely involved in UK friendly society matters from there.

Preface

John Young

Partner, Head of Corporate Insurance Group
Lovells

"The life of the law has not been logic; it has been experience." So wrote the great American jurist, Oliver Wendell-Holmes Jr, and nowhere is his comment truer than in relation to the development of English law relating to the regulation of insurance companies.

Even if it has not always been the largest, the UK's insurance market has historically been, and remains, the most important in Europe and arguably in the world. Yet insurance was barely controlled by any UK governmental authority before the mid-1960s. Such regulation as then existed, and most of that subsequently created, was almost always introduced as a reaction to financial scandals. There was little systematic philosophy behind it. The Life Assurance Act 1774 typified this reactive approach to regulation when it recited:

> "Whereas it hath been found by experience that the making insurances on lives or other events wherein the assured shall have no interest hath introduced a mischievous kind of gaming"

and went on to introduce the concept of insurable interest.

The first true insurance regulation was introduced by the Life Assurance Companies Act 1870, which merely required the making of deposits and the submission of annual accounts by life assurance companies. Perhaps the most lasting significance of the Act was the introduction of a court-supervised system of life assurance business portfolio transfers. Even this provision was not a socially useful measure introduced by a benevolent government, but simply a reaction to the unregulated portfolio transfers that were at the time common among life assurance companies, leading in particular to the collapse of the Albert Life Assurance Company.

The Assurance Companies Act 1909 broadly extended this degree of regulation to some classes of general insurance business and required different classes of business to be carried on in separate funds. The 1909 Act was amended in 1946 to include marine, aviation and transport business, and the legislation was further amended and consolidated in 1958. However, at a time when most of the world's sophisticated insurance jurisdictions boasted comprehensive regimes governing the licensing and supervision of insurance companies, the Insurance Companies Act 1958 still required merely the maintenance of a derisory minimum capital, the separation of funds, and the deposit of annual accounts with the Board of Trade.

It was only after the passing of the Companies Act 1967 that UK insurance companies had to be licensed in order to carry on business. This legislation was forced on the government of the day by the failure of Fire Auto & Marine, a short-lived company founded by the infamous Emil Savundra, who took advantage of the fact that even an insurance company did not, in practice, have to file its first accounts until at least two years after it had commenced business. Further legislation was introduced in the Insurance Companies Amendment Act 1973, largely as a consequence of the insolvency of Vehicle & General, which not only held about 10 per cent of the UK motor insurance market but was found to have borrowed heavily from its life assurance subsidiary in order to finance its motor insurance activities.

The regulation of the insurance industry was only addressed on a philosophical basis when the UK joined the European Economic Community ("the EEC" as it then was – subsequently the European Community ("the EC")). In the pursuit of the freedom of establishment and the freedom to provide cross-border services prescribed by the Treaty of Rome, the EEC struggled to adopt a series of directives which became, and remain, the dominant influence on the form and content of UK insurance legislation. Paradoxically, these directives ultimately imposed on EEC Member States a system that largely reflected the system that had evolved over the years in the UK. This resulted in the partial dismantling of much more comprehensive systems of regulation in a number of other states. The development and content of these directives are described in Chapter 1.

Insurance intermediaries have never been comprehensively regulated in the UK. Insurance brokers were thinly regulated via the Insurance Brokers Registration Act from 1977 until 2001. As this publication goes to print the regulation of general insurance intermediation is in practice governed on a voluntary self-regulatory basis by the General Insurance Standards Council ("GISC"), whose activities are outside the scope of this Guide.

The marketing of life assurance products has been regulated by statute since the 1980s. Financial scandals in the investment industry and, in particular, the publication of the Gower Report gave rise to the Financial Services Act 1986, which for the first time recognised that most life assurance products were appropriately categorised as "investments", and regulated them accordingly. For a period of just over a decade the 1986 Act gave rise to a system of selective regulation of the financial services industries via self-regulating organisations ("SROs") recognised by the Securities and Investments Board ("SIB").

In the field of prudential regulation, no domestically inspired legislation of any substance was passed in the UK between 1973 and 2000. However, 1997 saw the election of the UK's first Labour Government since 1979, and one of its stated priorities was the reform of the regulation and supervision of the UK's financial services industries. The Financial Services and Markets Act 2000 ("FSMA") brought together the regulation of the UK's insurance, investment and banking activities under a single regulator, a renamed SIB now called the Financial Services Authority ("FSA"). The FSMA introduced additional regulatory measures over and above those inherited from previous legislation and those prescribed by the EC directives. Whilst the UK will continue to be bound by the existing EC directives – and of course by new directives as and when they are adopted – it is clear that the FSA is likely to be more proactive than its predecessors in the adoption and modification of UK-specific legislation that it perceives to be required in the context of the UK insurance market.

This is not the place to attempt to describe the overall structure of the FSMA in any detail. It is a gargantuan piece of enabling legislation, pursuant to which the FSA became the single regulator of the UK's financial services industry on 1 December 2001. Under the FSMA the FSA has broad powers to make rules, conduct investigations and enforce both the law and its own decisions. The rules and guidance made by the FSA reside in its Handbook, which sets out in detail the manner in which it proposes to regulate the markets under its control. Three elements of the Handbook are particularly relevant for this publication.

First, the FSA has adopted 11 new principles, known as the "Principles for Business", which apply to all firms under its control. These are general statements regarding integrity; skill, care and diligence; management and control; financial prudence; market conduct; customers' interests; communications with clients; conflicts of interest; customers; relationships of trust; clients assets; and relations with regulators. They underlie the entirety of the more specific regulation described in the rest of this Guide. They are supported by further "High-Level Standards" in relation to (in particular) Senior Management Arrangements, Systems and Controls ("SYSC"), Statements of Principle and a Code of Practice for Authorised Persons ("APER"), and a Fit and Proper Test for Approved Persons ("FIT"). These standards are referred to in particular in Chapter 3.

Second, four manuals have been published covering regulatory processes in relation to authorisation ("AUTH"), supervision ("SUP"), enforcement ("ENF") and decision-making ("DEC"). The authorisation manual is referred to in particular in Chapter 2.

Finally, a variety of sourcebooks of rules and guidance have been published in relation both to the regulation of particular industries and to the conduct of investment business generally. An interim prudential sourcebook has been published in relation to insurers ("IPRU(INS)"). This contains most of the rules and guidance referred to in detail in Chapters 3 to 9 below. For the time being they are a thinly amended restatement of the legislation formerly contained in the Insurance Companies Act 1982 and its associated regulations and guidance. The Conduct of Business sourcebook ("COB") covers, *inter alia*, the marketing and distribution of life assurance products formerly covered by the Financial Services Act and the rules of the SROs and is referred to extensively in Chapter 10.

This Guide does not cover the FSA's involvement in Lloyd's, which is the subject of a companion volume. However, it does extend to the friendly societies movement. The UK friendly societies movement has frequently been the forgotten participant in publications purporting to cover the regulation of the UK insurance industry. For many individuals – especially those on lower incomes – friendly societies have historically provided their main access to the benefits of insurance, and indeed their main protection against misfortune. There are still around 250 friendly societies carrying on business in the UK, although many of them are inactive. Much of what is said in Chapters 2 to 10 below applies more or less to friendly societies but there are important differences and friendly societies have their own interim prudential sourcebook ("IPRU(FSOC)"). Accordingly Chapter 11 outlines the new regime covering the regulation of friendly societies by the FSA.

Table of Contents

11 The Regulation of Friendly Societies

John Gilbert

Partner, Lovells

Chapter 1

The Framework Established by the EC Directives

John Young
Partner
Head of Corporate Insurance Group
Lovells

1.1 The political background

The dominant influence on the form and content of UK insurance legislation is, and will for the foreseeable future remain, the provisions of the European Community ("EC") Insurance Directives, which influence (and, to a degree, harmonise) the regulation of insurance throughout the European Union ("EU") and the wider European Economic Area (the "EEA", comprising the 15 Member States of the EU plus Iceland, Liechtenstein and Norway). An understanding of the EC legislation is essential, not only as a backdrop to the domestic UK legislation but also as an indication of forthcoming developments.

Before the adoption of the directives described in the remainder of this Chapter, the regulation of insurance in the Member States of the EEA developed in an uncoordinated manner in a variety of directions. The Member States have always taken, and still do take, widely differing views on the purpose and relative importance of different means of insurance regulation.

There are, in broad terms, eight recognised methods of regulating insurance companies:

(a)   regulation of ownership;
(b)   review of managers and controllers;
(c)   prohibition of the placing of insurance or reinsurance with foreign insurance companies;
(d)   solvency requirements;
(e)   control of investments;
(f)   control of premium rates;

1

(g)   control of policy conditions;
(h)   regulation of marketing practices.

Regulation is usually explained in terms of consumer protection but in reality it has frequently had more to do with national politics and economics. Certain EEA States traditionally imposed the minimum possible restriction on insurers, whether domestic or foreign. Those notably included the Netherlands and the UK (the latter's approach has usually been described as "freedom with publicity"). By contrast, the Irish direct insurance market was effectively closed to foreign or foreign-owned insurance companies from 1936 to 1976. Some states have resorted to government domination or ownership of insurance. The Portuguese insurance market was almost completely nationalised in 1975 after the previous year's revolution. In France, post-war nationalisation put most of the market in the hands of a few state-owned companies.

In the insurance markets of most Member States other than the Netherlands and the UK, there has always been some measure of control over the extent to which potential insureds were free to place their business with overseas insurance companies. Typically these same Member States have also maintained regimes requiring to a greater or lesser degree the prior approval of policy terms and/or premium rates.

Such differences clearly nullified the concept of free competition. The triumph of EC insurance legislation has been to achieve a compromise between widely differing approaches to insurance regulation to the extent that, so far as can be achieved by regulatory means, a single market does now exist in the provision of insurance within the EEA. This has been achieved by the issue of directives addressed to the EU Member States (and adopted by the rest of the EEA) requiring them to amend their domestic legislation in certain ways. The flood of legislation of the 1980s and 1990s has now reduced, but the tap has not yet been turned off.

The institution now called the European Community (previously the European Economic Community), whose members are the same as those of the European Union, but in a different capacity, was formed by the Treaty of Rome (now officially the EC Treaty) in 1957. The EC Treaty provides only in very general terms for the creation of a common market in insurance. Article 52 provides that:

"Restrictions on the freedom of establishment of nationals of a Member State in the territory of another Member State shall be abolished by progressive stages in the course of the transitional period. Such progressive abolition shall also apply to restrictions on the setting up of agencies, branches or subsidiaries by nationals of any Member State established in the territory of any Member State."

This abolition is usually simply referred to as "freedom of establishment".

Article 59 provides that:

"Restrictions on freedom to provide services within the EEA shall be progressively abolished during the transitional period in respect of nationals of Member States who are established in a state of the EEA other than that of the person for whom the services are intended."

This abolition is designed to facilitate cross-border trade and is referred to as "freedom of services".

Article 61(2) provides that: "The liberalisation of banking and insurance services connected with movements of capital shall be effected in step with the progressive liberalisation of movement of capital."

Save for the purposes of Article 61(2), insurance is not mentioned specifically. The provision of those services that we know as insurance has been dealt with in subsequent legislation by way of crystallisation of the "freedoms" referred to in Articles 52 and 59.

Both Articles 52 and 59 are phrased in terms of "progressive" abolition of relevant restrictions. A timetable for the implementation of Articles 52 and 59 was set down in 1961. It was originally intended that the programme would be completed by 31 December 1969. However, the differential approaches to the regulation of insurance in the Member States proved so impenetrable that the programme was not substantially completed until 1992.

1.2   The principal directives

Insurance was approached incrementally through three "generations" of directives as follows:

(a)   The first generation, comprising principally the Reinsurance Directive of 1964, the First Non-Life Directive of 1973 and the First Life Directive of 1979 (also known as the Establishment Directives).

3

(b)   The second generation, comprising principally the Second Non-Life Directive of 1988 and the Second Life Directive of 1990 (also known as the Services Directives).

(c)   The third generation, comprising principally the Third Non-Life Directive of 1992, the Third Life Directive of 1992 (also known as the Framework Directives) and the Accounts Directive of 1990.

In addition, certain more specific themes have been followed in directives relating, *inter alia*, to intermediaries, co-insurance, tourist assistance insurance, credit and suretyship insurance, legal expenses insurance, motor insurance and insolvency.

The first real achievement was the First Non-Life Insurance Directive of 1973. This was mirrored six years later for the purposes of life assurance by the First Life Assurance Directive. The philosophy behind the legislation was that insurers incorporated in any Member State must be permitted to establish branches or agencies in other Member States and that no deposit or security could be required in exchange for the authorisation of any such establishment. As the price of these freedoms the directives prescribed that Member States must make establishment of a direct insurance company subject to the obtaining of prior authorisation. They defined and harmonised the classes of insurance business that were to be adopted by each Member State and the legal form to be adopted by an insurance company. They prescribed the form of application for authorisation and, of particular impact, they prohibited the authorisation of new "composite" insurers carrying on both non-life and life business. The greatest achievement of the directives was to provide that where an insurance company was incorporated in one Member State and had a branch in another Member State it need only demonstrate its solvency to one single regulator on the basis of one test applied to its worldwide business – a benefit yet to be achieved among the states of the USA after almost 200 years of intensive regulation.

As early as 1975 the EU Commission submitted a proposal for a second directive on non-life insurance. The purpose of the second generation of directives was to enable insurers incorporated in one Member State to cover risks situated in another Member State without establishing a branch there. Such operations were traditionally restrictively regulated or prohibited in virtually every EU Member State (the Netherlands and the UK being notable exceptions).

Discussions became bogged down until a decision of the European Court in 1986 in Case 205/84, *Commission* v *Germany* [1986] ECR 3755. This case,

4

which became known as the *Schleicher* case, concerned a German law which specifically prevented brokers from placing insurance with foreign insurance companies unless they were both established and authorised to carry on insurance business in Germany. The essence of the decision was that the German requirement was the "very negation" of the freedom to provide services.

The Second Non-Life Insurance Directive implementing "freedom of services" was accordingly adopted in 1988 and the Second Life Assurance Directive was adopted in 1990.

The lasting influence of the *Schleicher* case is twofold. First, the case distinguished between the level of regulation that might be justifiable in the case of "commercial insurance" by comparison with other insurance because of the different levels of concern over consumer protection. In the non-life directives the concept was invented of "large risks". This term was used to cover risks in respect of which it was felt that the policyholder was likely to be a sophisticated commercial operation needing less protection than was the case with other risks (which have become known colloquially, although not in the directive, as "mass risks"). This distinction continues to be reflected in the consumer protection provisions of both EC and UK legislation (*see* Chapter 7).

Second, the court stated in *Schleicher* that:

> "The freedom to provide services ... may be restricted ... by provisions which are justified by the 'general good' and which are applied to all persons and undertakings operating within the territory of the state in which the services are provided insofar as that interest is not safeguarded by the provisions to which the provider of a service is subject in the Member State of his establishment."

The concept of the "general good" has confused regulators and regulated companies ever since. The court held that any restrictions made "in the general good" must be objectively necessary, non-discriminatory and the least restrictive in the circumstances and should not duplicate any relevant legislation in the home state. The phrase was used several times without further clarification in the Framework Directives referred to immediately below. It was also the subject of a Commission interpretative communication in 2000 which is expected to be influential in guiding states who may be tempted to stretch the limits of the "general good" when drafting protective legislation.

The second generation of directives represented a philosophical triumph but they were superseded almost immediately in 1992 by the Third Non-Life and Life Directives. These directives complete the basis of the current law.

The theme of the directives was that the carrying on of insurance business within the EU, whether by way of establishment or by way of the provision of services, should only be subject to a prior authorisation from the regulatory authority of the Member State in which the insurer has its head office (usually called the "home Member State"). In pursuit of this goal the directives required Member States to repeal further restrictive legislation. There was a partial repeal of the prohibition of composites. At the same time a certain amount of additional harmonisation was introduced as the "price" of freedom in such areas as the establishment of technical provisions, the matching and localisation of assets, the calculation of margins of solvency and the regulation of control and management.

Some areas of regulation and numerous areas that are peripheral to the insurance industry have not yet been touched by specific EC legislation. The UK's legislation relating to the segregation of life assurance funds is, for example, wholly domestically inspired. The area likely to be covered next by an EC directive is the activities of insurance intermediaries (*see* 1.4 and 1.7.3 below). However, many areas, such as the activities of loss adjusters, have not yet commended themselves to the Commission as being sufficiently distinctive to require specific regulation.

1.3 The regulation of direct insurance

1.3.1 *The categories of insurance*

The directives relating to insurance do not define insurance. They leave the concept to be interpreted by the individual laws of individual states. Two separate series of directives deal with the categories of business known as "direct insurance other than life assurance" (usually called general insurance business) and the business of "direct life assurance" (known in the UK as long-term business).

General insurance business is divided by Article 1 of The First Non-Life Directive (as amended) into the following 18 classes:

- Accident (including industrial injury and occupational diseases)
- Sickness
- Land vehicles (other than railway rolling stock)
- Railway rolling stock
- Aircraft
- Ships
- Goods in transit
- Fire and natural forces
- Other damage to property
- Motor vehicle liability
- Aircraft liability
- Liability for ships
- General liability
- Credit
- Suretyship
- Miscellaneous financial loss
- Legal expenses
- Assistance (comprising assistance for persons who get into difficulties while travelling, while away from home or while away from their permanent residence).

By virtue of Article 2 of the First Non-Life Directive the directives relating to general insurance business do not apply to the type of on-the-spot breakdown service and ancillary services normally supplied by national motoring organisations unless they are carried out by a company that is governed by the directives for some other reason. By virtue of Articles 3 and 4 the directives do not apply to various organisations, including in particular:

(a)   small mutual insurance associations (most notably in the UK the smaller friendly societies); and

(b)   undertakings whose sole activity is Class 18 (assistance) business on a local basis consisting of the provision of benefits in kind whose annual income in respect of this activity does not exceed €200,000.

Long-term business is divided by Article 1 of the First Life Directive into the following Classes:

I: Life assurance, annuities and supplementary insurance carried on by life assurance undertakings, other than the types of life assurance referred to in Classes II and III

II: Marriage assurance and birth assurance

III: Life assurance and annuities that are linked to investment funds

7

IV: Permanent health insurance not subject to cancellation

V: Tontines (arrangements under which the proceeds of the premiums paid by policyholders are paid out to one or all of the last of them to survive – no UK insurer is authorised for this class of business)

VI: Capital redemption operations

VII: Managing the investments of group pension funds, whether or not accompanied by insurance covering conservation of capital or the payment of a minimum interest

VIII: The operations carried out by insurance companies such as those referred to in Chapter 1, Title 4 of Book IV of the French *"Code Des Assurances"* (relating to various quasi-insurance operations, particularly collective pension plans – no UK insurer is authorised for this class of business)

IX: Operations relating to the length of human life which are prescribed by or provided for in social insurance legislation when they are effected or managed at their own risk by insurers in accordance with the laws of a Member State – no UK insurer is authorised for this class of business.

By virtue of Article 2 of the First Life Directive the directives relating to long-term business do not apply to:

(a)   operations of mutual institutions funded by flat rate contributions of their members whose benefits vary according to the resources available;

(b)   operations carried out by trade unions and similar bodies providing life assurance, death or disability benefits; or

(c)   insurance forming part of a statutory system of social security.

By virtue of Articles 3 and 4 of the First Life Directive the directives do not apply to various organisations, including in particular:

(a)   small mutual assurance associations (again friendly societies are the best example in the UK); and

(b)   organisations providing funeral expenses coverage (although such organisations are now separately regulated in the UK by the FSA).

1.3.2   Authorisation to carry on insurance business

Each Member State is required by Article 6 of the First Non-Life Directive and by Article 6 of the First Life Directive to make the taking up of the business of direct insurance in its territory subject to an official authorisation. The type of authorisation required varies depending on whether the body has established its head office in a Member State or whether its head office is outside the EEA. The directives are now given effect in the UK in the manner set out in Chapter 2.

Once an authorisation has been granted pursuant to these provisions Article 7 of the First Non-Life Directive and Article 6 of the First Life Directive provide that the authorisation is valid for the entire EU. It permits an insurer to carry on business in the EU either through branches or on a cross-border basis under the freedom to provide services. However, there are administrative provisions that must be complied with before these freedoms may be exercised and these are described in Chapter 5.

Member States are not required to provide authorisation to insurers whose head offices are situated outside the EEA, but if they do so they must make access to the insurance market subject to an official authorisation and certain minimum standards. Again the provisions applicable in the UK are set out in Chapter 2.

1.3.3   Ownership and management

The three key focuses of the ongoing supervision of insurers within the EEA are the supervision of ownership and management, and financial supervision.

Ownership is controlled pursuant to Article 15 of the Third Non-Life Directive and Article 14 of the Third Life Directive by requiring advance approval by the home Member State of the direct or indirect acquisition of a "qualifying holding" in an insurer. Insurers are required by the authorisation procedures referred to above to be effectively run by persons of good repute with appropriate professional qualifications or experience, but there are no detailed procedures laid down as to how this condition is to be judged. The current system of control of ownership and management in the UK is described in Chapter 3.

1.3.4   Financial supervision

The financial supervision of an insurer, including its business carried out in the EEA through branches or on a cross-border basis, is the sole responsibility of its home Member State (Article 13 of the First Non-Life Directive and Article 15 of the First Life Directive). In the case of long-term business only, it is provided that if the regulatory authority of the

9

host Member State has "reason to consider that the activities of an assurance undertaking might affect its financial soundness" it should inform the regulatory authority in the home Member State, but any action is left to the latter regulatory authority. The regulatory authority in the home Member State is in turn required to ensure that an insurer has sound administrative and accounting procedures and adequate internal control mechanisms.

These responsibilities may be exercised through spot checks by the home Member State (after informing the authorities of the host Member State). More importantly (pursuant to Article 19 of the First Non-Life Directive and Article 23 of the First Life Directive), Member States must require each insurer to produce an annual return in relation to its financial situation and any other periodical returns that may be necessary for the purposes of financial supervision.

The result of this is that no regular financial supervision may be exercised by the regulators of the host Member State. However, Article 44 of the Third Non-Life Directive and Article 43 of the Third Life Directive provide for separate reporting to the home Member State of premiums and (in the case of general business) claims and European commissions accepted from or paid to insurers in each relevant host Member State. The regulatory authority of the home Member State is required "within a reasonable time and on an aggregate basis [to] forward this information to the competent authorities of each of the Member States concerned which so request".

Article 27 of the First Non-Life Directive and Article 31 of the First Life Directive provide that the financial supervisory powers of Member States also extend to branches of non-EEA insurers established in those states, including the powers to require the production of annual returns and other periodical returns. The most vital role of the returns is to demonstrate the maintenance of technical provisions, assets covering those provisions and assets constituting a margin of solvency over and above the technical provisions.

Article 15 of the First Non-Life Directive and Article 17 of the First Life Directive provide that each home Member State must require each insurer to establish adequate technical provisions in respect of its entire business. In the case of long-term business these provisions include mathematical provisions. In addition, insurers must cover their technical provisions by matching assets of an equivalent currency. The main rules are set out in Annex I to the Second Non-Life Directive (as amended) and Annex I to the Third Life Directive.

Article 20 of the Third Non-Life Directive and Article 20 of the Third Life Directive require that an insurer's assets covering technical provisions must:

> "take account of the type of business carried on by an undertaking in such a way as to secure the safety, yield and marketability of its investments, which the undertaking shall ensure are diversified and adequately spread."

More specifically, there is a finite list of assets in Article 21 of the Third Non-Life Directive and Article 21 of the Third Life Directive that an insurer may be permitted to use to cover its technical provisions.

In addition to the matching of technical reserves, each insurer that is authorised by a Member State must maintain a solvency margin. For an EEA insurer the solvency margin is defined by Article 16 of the First Non-Life Directive and Article 18 of the First Life Directive as "the assets of the undertaking, free of all foreseeable liabilities, less any intangible items". The directives prescribe a list of items that may be taken into account for this purpose.

The current solvency and accounting regimes applicable in the UK are described in detail in Chapter 4. Current proposals for the amendment of the EC solvency regime are described in 1.7 below. These provisions in relation to an insurer's finances are supported by the Accounts Directive, which makes provision for the harmonisation of the presentation and content of the annual accounts of insurers and reinsurers operating in the EU. The provisions of the Accounts Directive are reflected in the UK in the insurance company accounting provisions of the Companies Act 1985, which are outside the scope of this Guide.

1.3.5 Regulation of insurance contracts

Before the adoption of the Third Non-Life and Life Directives most Member States had some kind of control over policy documentation and premium rates. It is now provided by Articles 29 and 39 of the Third Non-Life Directive and Articles 29 and 39 of the Third Life Directive that neither home nor host Member States may adopt provisions requiring the prior approval or systematic notification of policy conditions, premium levels or other printed documents to be used in relation to policyholders. However, home or host Member States may still require non-systematic notification of policy conditions and other documents

11

with a view to verifying compliance with national provisions regarding insurance contracts. That requirement may not be a precondition for authorising an insurer to carry on insurance business.

In respect of general business, no Member State may require prior notification or approval of increases in premium rates except as part of general price-control systems. In the case of long-term business, the home Member State may require systematic communication of the technical bases used for calculating premium scales and technical provisions "for the sole purpose of verifying compliance with national provisions concerning actuarial principles". Again, that requirement may not be a precondition for the authorising of an insurer to carry on insurance business.

None of these limitations specifically benefit branches of non-EU insurers, in respect of which national regulatory authorities are still free to operate their previous regimes.

By contrast, because of the availability of insurance policies that may now emanate from anywhere in the EU, a certain amount of compulsory information must now be delivered to policyholders (*see* Chapter 7). In addition:

(a)   cancellation rights are prescribed by Article 15 of Directive 90/619 (as amended) in relation to long-term business (*see* Chapters 9 and 10); and

(b)   there are detailed provisions in Article 7 of the Second Non-Life Directive and Article 4 of the Second Life Directive regarding the law applicable to contracts of insurance (*see* Chapter 7).

Insurance companies are required by Article 41 of the Third Non-Life Directive and Article 41 of the Third Life Directive to be free to advertise their products in any place where they are entitled to form a branch or to conduct cross-border business, but they are subject to any local rules governing the form and content of such advertising adopted in the interest of the "general good". Non-EU insurers do not benefit from this provision.

Similarly, most Member States have premium taxes applicable at varying rates to most classes of general business and some classes of long-term business. The potential conflict between such taxes is resolved by Article 46 of the Third Non-Life Directive and Article 44 of the Third Life Directive on the basis that any insurance policy will be subject exclusively to the premium taxes levied by the host Member State.

1.3.6   Compulsory insurances

Under the First Non-Life Directive it was originally open to a Member State to require that compulsory insurances should be locally placed. By virtue of Article 8 of the Second Non-Life Directive, Member States may no longer require that compulsory insurance be placed with a company that has been locally established. However:

(a)   where a Member State imposes an obligation to take out compulsory insurance, a policy will not satisfy that obligation unless it complies with the provisions relating to that insurance laid down by the relevant Member State;

(b)   where any Member State makes a class of insurance compulsory, that Member State may dictate the law applicable to such classes; and

any Member State may require advance notification of the terms on which an insurer proposes to issue a compulsory policy before the policy is issued. In the UK a number of insurance coverages are compulsory, varying from third-party liability cover for motorists to cover for clients' money held by estate agents. The relevant legislation now complies with the requirements set out above.

1.3.7   Guarantee schemes

Most Member States have guarantee schemes designed to ensure the full or partial payment of insurance claims to insured persons and injured third parties, generally in the case of an insurance company becoming insolvent. It is provided by Article 45 of the Third Non-Life Directive that Member States are not prevented from requiring general business insurers from other Member States who are carrying on business either through a branch or on a cross-border basis to join any such guarantee scheme. In practice UK insurers were formerly required to contribute to the Policyholders Protection Fund and are now required to contribute to the combined Financial Services Compensation Scheme run by the FSA (*See* Chapter 7 below).

1.3.8   Portfolio transfers

One of the most helpful features of the directives is the codification of provisions for portfolio transfers of insurance business, both within Member States and from one Member State to another Member State. The concept is that there should be a mechanism whereby such portfolios may be transferred as a matter of law without the need for policy-by-policy novations. In this respect EU law is well ahead of the law in most other major insurance jurisdictions. The current provisions adopted in the UK in conformity with the directives are described in Chapter 6.

1.3.9 Motor insurance

The compulsory insurance of motor vehicles used in the EU is regulated by four generations of Motor Insurance Directives. The main theme of the directives is that each Member State is responsible for ensuring that vehicles normally based in its territory are insured against the risk of civil liability for damage to property and personal injury in other Member States and is in addition required to establish or authorise a body (a "Compensation Fund") to provide compensation for damage to property or personal injuries caused by a vehicle which is unidentified or not covered by the relevant Member State's compulsory insurance requirements. The provisions applicable in the UK in compliance with the directives are described in Chapter 8.

Providers of motor insurance are required to comply with certain additional requirements when benefiting from the right to provide services in accordance with the provisions of the Second Non-Life Directive (*see* Chapter 5).

1.3.10 Co-insurance

A co-insurance policy is one in which the risk is shared among two or more insurance companies who are severally (but not jointly) parties to the same policy. It is a direct way for insurance companies to share a single risk, having much the same economic effect as reinsurance but removing from any individual company the danger that a reinsurer may be unable to pay its debts. Co-insurance is typically used in major commercial risks, particularly in the marine and aviation markets, where risks are by convention and for good economic reasons shared in this manner. The principal terms of the policy are typically negotiated by a lead insurer, with the other "following" insurers taking a less detailed look at the risk in question. It is frequently appropriate for such risks to be shared on an international basis, and there was an early concern to enable insurers to share in such risks even if they were not authorised to carry on insurance business or established in the country in which the risk was primarily being placed.

The Co-insurance Directive of 1978 tackled the subject in relation to general business Classes 4, 5, 6, 7, 8, 9, 11, 12, 13 and 16 (*see* above) other than coverage for nuclear damage and damage from medicinal products. Risks under these Classes benefit from certain limited derogations from the authorisation provisions of the directives (*see* Chapter 8) but only so long as their nature or size require the participation of several insurers.

1.3.11 Miscellaneous directives

Until the adoption of the Third Non-Life and Life Directives in 1992 it was conventional in textbooks to study the insurance directives on a chronological basis, setting out each development in the order that it occurred. This approach included references to a number of specialised directives which have now ceased to have anything but historical significance because their terms consisted mainly of amendments to other directives already mentioned above. However, for completeness, and because their adoption explains some of the oddities of our current regulation, the main directives involved are as follows.

The provisions of the First Non-Life Directive in relation to freedom of establishment originally excluded legal expenses insurance (and credit and surety insurance) carried on in Germany because of the insistence in Germany that such classes of insurance should be carried out by an insurer carrying on no other insurance business (so as to avoid conflicts of interest). This situation was resolved by the adoption of the Legal Expenses Insurance Directive of 1987. This directive introduced Class 17 (legal expenses) general insurance business and gave rise to the slightly convoluted provisions in relation to legal expenses described in Chapter 8.

The Tourist Assistance Directive of 1984 recognised that some doubt was implicit in relation to the First Non-Life Directive over whether certain benefits in kind were to be regarded as insurance. It introduced into the First Non-Life Directive the provisions and exemptions relating to Class 18 (assistance) general insurance business and on-the-spot breakdown services and ancillary services that are referred to above and in Chapter 2.

The Credit and Suretyship Insurance Directive (87/343) was introduced in parallel with the Legal Expenses Insurance Directive referred to above. As with the Legal Expenses Insurance Directive, the Credit and Suretyship Insurance Directive was introduced in recognition of German sensitivity regarding the carrying on of credit and suretyship insurance by an insurer that was also carrying on other insurance business. The directive removed a previous exemption that had been accorded to Germany from making the benefits of the First Non-Life Directive available to this category of insurers. In exchange it introduced, *inter alia*, the high minimum guarantee fund required for credit business referred to in Chapter 4.

The Reinsurance Directive (64/225) is the only EU legislation directly affecting reinsurance activities. It abolished all restrictions, so far as they were based merely on nationality, on the freedom of reinsurers based in one Member State to form a branch in another Member State or on their freedom to supply cross-border reinsurance from one Member State to another. The directive did not require Member States to make the establishment of a reinsurance company subject to the obtaining of a licence. Because reinsurance is conducted between insurance professionals and not directly with members of the public, the view was taken that considerations of consumer protection and financial stability of pure reinsurers did not arise. Consequently reinsurance is still largely unregulated in many EEA Member States. The comprehensive legislation of reinsurance in the UK is almost entirely of domestic origin.

1.3.12   *The Prudential Supervision ("Post-BCCI") Directive*

In 1995 a directive was adopted to amend a number of directives applicable to financial institutions, including the First and Third Non-Life and Life Directives. Its purpose was to strengthen the powers of regulatory authorities following recent cases of fraud in the financial services sector, in particular the case of Bank of Credit and Commerce International. The First and Third Directives had envisaged the authorisation of an insurer as an entity in its own right without reference to the group of which it formed part. By virtue of the Prudential Supervision Directive it is now required that the group structure should be sufficiently transparent to enable the insurer to be supervised effectively. The effects of this directive are visible indirectly in a number of the provisions described in Chapters 2, 3 and 4.

1.4   Insurance intermediaries

The only EU legislation directly affecting insurance intermediaries the Intermediaries Directive of 1977. It sought to achieve its aims by providing that Member States who set requirements of professional knowledge for intermediaries must accept experience gained in another state as equivalent to experience gained in the host Member State. The method of regulating the activities of intermediaries was largely left in the hands of each Member State, provided that it did not discriminate against intermediaries from other Member States. In the absence of any directives requiring mutual recognition of professional qualifications of intermediaries, and given that some Member States hardly regulated the activities of intermediaries at all, the Intermediaries Directive was intended to be largely a transitional directive which would be superseded once directives were in place providing for mutual recognition of professional qualifications.

These were not in fact forthcoming, and in 1991 the European Commission issued an Intermediaries Recommendation which sought to encourage Member States to regulate the activities of insurance intermediaries and to establish minimum professional requirements for intermediaries. Current proposals are summarised in 1.7 below.

1.5   Liquidation and insolvency

As described above, the First Non-Life and Life Directives gave insurers of one Member State the right to establish themselves in another, subject to the satisfaction of certain requirements. Due to the great divergence of the insolvency laws in Member States and given the special features and needs of the insurance industry, the European Commission decided that a directive should be adopted to harmonise the laws and procedures for insurers and insurance contracts in the event of an insolvency.

A directive "on the reorganisation and winding-up of insurance undertakings" was finally adopted in 2001 and is due to be implemented in the UK by not later than 20 April 2003.

At one level, the directive is simply another example of "home state supervision", in that it resolves competing claims to supervise the winding-up of an insurer in favour of the insurer's home legal jurisdiction. However, its impact on the UK insurance market is likely to be more subtle in that it requires EU Member States to give insurance claims precedence over all other claims on the insurer, either by providing that insurance claims are to have priority over all other claims "with respect to assets representing the technical provisions", or by providing that insurance claims take absolute precedence over all other claims on the insurer apart from claims in relation to employees, tax, social security and charges.

The point about this formulation is that reinsurance claims are not "insurance claims" for this purpose, with the result that companies carrying on both direct insurance and reinsurance business will have to treat reinsurance claims as subordinated claims. Only time will tell precisely what effect this will have on UK insurance regulation – and, to a greater degree, on the structure of the insurance market as a whole.

1.6 Insurance groups

For some time there has been concern among those involved in the regulation and supervision of the financial services industries about the existence of "double gearing" within financial conglomerates. Double gearing arises where, for example, an insurer owns another insurer or a bank and the same assets are used to support the statutory solvency requirements of both bodies.

The Insurance Groups Directive was adopted in 1998. Its purpose was to enable insurance regulatory authorities to assess the solvency of each regulated insurer for which they are responsible in the wider context of the group of companies to which it belongs. The impact of the directive in the UK is addressed in Chapter 4.

1.7 Current proposals

A number of proposed modifications to EC insurance legislation are currently under consideration and, if pursued, will have an impact in due course on the FSA regulation of insurers in the UK. The following are the most important.

1.7.1 Solvency reform

The requirements of the directives in relation to the assessment of the solvency of insurance companies have been almost unchanged since the adoption of the First Non-Life Directive in 1973 and the adoption of the First Life Directive in 1979.

A European Commission report published in 1997 concluded that the current relatively simple system of solvency regulation was basically satisfactory and that more sophisticated systems (such as "risk based capital") remained unproved. However, it concluded that there was some localised scope for improvement. It also concluded that unnecessary additional costs for the insurance industry should be avoided.

Draft directives amending the solvency requirements for non-life and life insurers were published in October 2000, making substantially similar proposals in relation to the two sides of the industry. The following were common to both proposals:

(a) an acknowledgment that EC Member States should be free to establish solvency rules that were stronger than those required by the Insurance Directives (leaving scope, for example, for the introduction of some overlying measure of risk based capital);

(b) an increase and future indexation of certain financial amounts that had been prescribed in the First Insurance Directives but had never been subsequently amended (and were therefore now somewhat devalued); and

(c) the introduction of an explicit right for insurance regulators to intervene in the affairs of an insurer at a time when it was clear that policyholders' interests were threatened, rather than waiting until there was an actual breach of solvency requirements.

Certain changes are proposed in relation to the treatment of outwards reinsurance covering an insurer's liabilities, in particular, requiring regulators to reduce the amount of credit taken for reinsurance where the nature or quality of the insurer's reinsurance is impaired or where there is no real risk transfer. Finally, there is a proposed recategorisation and modification of the assets that may be used in order to cover an insurer's liabilities and solvency margin.

Additional measures are proposed affecting only non-life companies. The solvency margin requirement for marine, aviation and general liability policies is to be increased to 150 per cent of the normal requirement. Any discounting of technical provisions is to be reversed for the purpose of the calculation of solvency margins. Finally, special solvency margin requirements are to be introduced for run-off companies, where the application of the previous mechanical rule frequently resulted in an unnaturally low required solvency margin for such companies.

1.7.2 Financial conglomerates

Following the adoption of the Insurance Groups Directive referred to in 1.6 above, a further proposal on the same subject was introduced in April 2001. The proposal is still at an early stage, but seeks to ensure that a

19

complex financial group has adequate capital, proposing the introduction of methods for the calculation and monitoring of a conglomerate's overall solvency position and proposing the reporting and monitoring of intra-group transactions. If and when adopted, the directive will have a further significant impact on the financial supervision of insurers described in Chapter 4.

1.7.3   Insurance intermediaries

A proposal for a directive on "insurance mediation" was presented in September 2000. It followed the unsuccessful efforts to harmonise the approach to the regulation of insurance intermediaries throughout the EC referred to in 1.4 above, and is the third document to be issued on this subject since mid-1999.

If issued in the form currently proposed, the directive will have at least three important effects on insurance intermediaries:

(a)   they will be able to operate throughout the EU using freedom of services and establishment in much the same way as insurers under the Third Insurance Directives;

(b)   they will be subject to a common set of professional and financial requirements; and

(c)   they will be required to provide extensive precontractual disclosure for most personal lines and much commercial insurance business.

The draft proposal was agreed by the Council of Ministers in November 2001. Consequently it is only a matter of time before it becomes adopted as a directive. In the UK, the expected adoption of the directive was undoubtedly one of the factors influencing the FSA to announce, in December 2001, that it proposes to become more directly involved in the regulation of non-life insurance intermediaries. The precise nature of this involvement still remains unclear.

Chapter 2

Authorisation of UK, EU and Overseas Insurance Companies

James Bateson

Partner
Norton Rose

2.1 Introduction

The purpose of this Chapter is to give general guidance about the circumstances in which authorisation is required to carry on insurance business
(other than at Lloyd's) pursuant to the Financial Services and Markets
Act 2000 ("the Act"), the procedures applicable to applicants and the
FSA's powers in relation to authorisation. It is not and should not be
taken as a substitute for detailed professional advice and indeed the FSA
encourages all applicants to seek and obtain such advice in relation to
their application for authorisation to carry out a regulated activity. The
Act, the secondary legislation made under the Act and the Handbook of
Rules and Guidance are complex. For convenience certain provisions of
the legislation are summarised in this Chapter. In addition, the new regulatory framework makes considerable use of definitions the meaning of
which is not always obvious from the defined term. For precise details
of the legislation, reference should be made to the relevant source
materials and the glossary of definitions in the FSA Handbook. Cross-
references have been provided where appropriate.

The principal statutory sources for the authorisation of insurers are the
Act and the Financial Services and Markets Act Regulated Activities
Order 2001 ("the Regulated Activities Order") issued pursuant to the Act.
The authorisation process is set out in the Authorisation Manual
("AUTH") issued by the FSA. Other information relevant to the authoris-
ation process can be found in the Statements of Principle and Code of
Practice for Approved Persons ("APER") and the Fit and Proper Test for
Approved Persons ("FIT"), Threshold Conditions ("COND"), Principles
for Business ("PRIN"), and in Senior Management Arrangements
Systems and Controls ("SYSC"). Materials of continuing relevance after
authorisation can generally be found in the Supervision Manual ("SUP")

and the relevant Interim Prudential Sourcebook for insurers ("IPRU(INS)"). The Decision-Making Manual ("DEC") sets out the FSA's procedures for decisions that involve the giving of warning notices, decision notices or supervisory notices.

The new regime for authorisation replaces the provisions of the Insurance Companies Act 1982. Whilst much of the regime is familiar, there are some important differences which, at least initially, may cause some difficulties as the FSA, the professional advisory community and applicants themselves become accustomed to the new regulatory regime. All firms who were previously authorised to carry on insurance business under the Insurance Companies Act 1982 have been "grandfathered" under the new legislation, which means that they did not have to apply for a re-authorisation to carry out regulated activities of the equivalent type.

This Chapter addresses the two main routes for authorisation to carry on a regulated activity under the Act. They are:

(a)   through an application to the FSA for permission under Part IV of the Act (a "Part IV Permission"); or
(b)   by a person authorised in another EEA State exercising an EEA passport right.

Any person who is not otherwise exempt but who wishes to effect or carry out insurance contracts in the UK needs the prior authorisation of the FSA to do so. Under the Act there is a single process for authorisation which covers the whole of the financial services community. Because the scope of the information required to be submitted to the FSA as part of the authorisation process will vary depending on the nature and complexity of the activities undertaken, in accordance with the principle of proportionality set out in Section 2 of the Act, it is important that a person contemplating carrying out a regulated activity in the UK determines at the outset which type of authorisation is required.

Broadly, to become authorised an applicant must satisfy certain threshold conditions and the FSA's risk assessment process, which involves an assessment of the risks posed by an applicant against a number of probability and impact factors. These are discussed later in this Chapter. In reaching a decision on whether an applicant satisfies these conditions, the FSA will consider whether the applicant is ready, willing and organised so as to enable it to comply with the regulatory obligations that will apply to it if permission is given. This Chapter examines the requirements and procedures that became effective on 1 December 2001.

2.2   The general prohibition

The Act is the primary statute which regulates the carrying on of certain activities which the government has deemed appropriate for regulation. Section 19 of the Act contains the general prohibition against carrying on a regulated activity in the UK. The purpose of the general prohibition is to ensure that only persons who satisfy the necessary conditions engage in a regulated activity, and that only fit and proper persons perform key functions in the financial services industry.

Section 19(1) of the Act provides that:

> "No person may carry on a regulated activity in the UK, or purport to do so, unless he is:
> (a)   an authorised person; or
> (b)   an exempt person."

The prohibition is referred to as the general prohibition. It is worth noting that the scope of the general prohibition extends to purporting to carry on the activity concerned as well as carrying out the activity itself. This is wider than the prohibition under the Insurance Companies Act 1982, which provided in Section 2 that: "No person shall carry on insurance business in the UK unless authorised to do so".

Accordingly, someone purporting to carry on a regulated activity could infringe the Act even where no such activity is actually carried on.

An authorised person is defined by reference to Section 31 of the Act and it includes the following:

(a)   a person who has a Part IV Permission to carry out one or more regulated activities, including the Society of Lloyd's;
(b)   an incoming EEA firm;
(c)   an incoming Treaty firm;
(d)   a UCITS qualifier; and
(e)   an ICVC.

In relation to insurers, only the first three categories are likely to be relevant. The first category covers those persons who have obtained permission under the Act, and the second and third categories permit the exercise of passport rights and Treaty rights by EEA firms.

Exempt persons are defined in Section 417(1) of the Act as being persons falling within the following groups:

(a)   a person or class of persons specified in an Exemption Order;
(b)   an appointed representative;
(c)   a recognised investment exchange or a recognised clearing house as specified in Section 285 of the Act.

In granting a permission to carry out a regulated activity the FSA is required by Section 42(2) of the Act to specify the regulated activities for which permission has been granted. An authorised person who carries on a regulated activity otherwise than in accordance with its permission, or who purports to do so, will be taken to have contravened a requirement imposed on him by the FSA under the Act. However, Section 20 of the Act provides that such a contravention does not make the person concerned guilty of an offence, or make the transaction void or unenforceable, or give rise to any right of action for breach of statutory duty. In certain prescribed cases the contravention is actionable at the suit of a person who suffers loss as a result of the contravention. Contravention of Section 20 may also lead to the exercise by the FSA of its regulatory powers of intervention or to closer monitoring and supervision from the regulator.

Section 23 of the Act provides that a person who contravenes the general prohibition is guilty of an offence and is liable:

(a)   on summary conviction to imprisonment for a term not exceeding six months or a fine not exceeding the statutory maximum, or both;
(b)   on conviction on indictment, to imprisonment for a term not exceeding two years or a fine or both.

It is a defence for the accused to show that he took all reasonable precautions and exercised all due diligence to avoid committing an offence.

In addition to the commission of a criminal offence, Section 26 of the Act provides that an agreement entered into by a person in contravention of the general prohibition will be unenforceable against the other party, who will be able to recover any money or other property paid or transferred by him under the relevant agreement. Compensation will also be payable for any loss suffered as a result of having transferred the property concerned. Section 27 of the Act extends the scope of the restriction to contracts entered into by an authorised person through the intermediaryship of a person who is carrying on a regulated activity without authorisation.

2.3 Regulated activities

The list of regulated activities requiring authorisation is contained in the Regulated Activities Order. They include effecting contracts of insurance (Article 10(1)), and carrying out contracts of insurance (Article 10(2)). It is important to note that "effecting" and "carrying out" are regarded as separate activities under the Regulated Activities Order and that a separate authorisation is required for each.

The first stage in the application process is to establish whether the proposed activities will constitute the carrying on of regulated activities requiring Part IV Permission.

Section 22 of the Act provides that authorisation is necessary where it is proposed to carry on a regulated activity:

- by way of business;
- in the UK;
- which relates to an investment of a specified kind.

The three elements to be taken into account are discussed below. Before looking at the specified investments themselves, we need to examine the business element and geographical scope of the section.

2.3.1 The business element

For an activity to be a regulated activity under section 22 of the Act, it must be carried on "by way of business" – the so-called "business element". The Treasury has power under Section 419 of the Act to alter the scope of the business element so that different requirements will apply in respect of different activities. This in part reflects differences in the nature of each activity and the broad scope of the legislation over the financial services industry.

For those regulated activities most pertinent to insurers, however, there are, at present, no special rules for determining the meaning of "by way of business". Ultimately, therefore, the question of whether or not the business element is present will be a question of judgement taking into account several factors, none of which is likely to be conclusive. Such factors include the degree of continuity, the scale of the activity and the proportion which the activity bears to other activities carried on by the same person but which are not regulated. The nature of the particular regulated activity that is carried on will also be relevant to this analysis.

2.3.2   Link between the activities and the UK

The need to be authorised only arises if the activities are carried on in the UK. In most cases it is likely to be obvious whether or not an activity is being carried on in the UK. However, there will be occasions where the answer is not so apparent. For example, where services are carried out cross-border or where the transaction is multi-jurisdictional. Furthermore, Section 418 of the Act sets out four circumstances where a person who would not otherwise be regarded as carrying on a regulated activity in the UK is deemed to do so. In each of the four cases, for insurers it is irrelevant where the policyholder is situated.

The first case is where the registered or head office of the person concerned is in the UK, the person is entitled to exercise rights under a single market directive as a UK firm and he is carrying on in another EEA State a regulated activity to which that directive applies. This would catch, for example, a UK firm exercising a passport right to carry on insurance business in France irrespective of whether the firm is carrying on insurance business in the UK as well.

The second case arises where the registered or head office of the person concerned is in the UK, he is the manager of a scheme which is entitled to enjoy the rights conferred by an instrument which is a relevant community instrument for the purposes of Section 264 of the Act, and persons in another EEA State are invited to become participants in the scheme. This would apply to a collective investment scheme managed from the UK where the scheme is only promoted abroad and is not likely to be relevant to insurance business.

The third case is where the registered or head office is in the UK, and the day-to-day management of the carrying on of the regulated activity is the responsibility of:

- the head or registered office; or
- another establishment maintained by him in the UK.

This case would catch a UK firm carrying on insurance business overseas where the international business is managed from the UK, irrespective of whether any insurance business is also being carried on in the UK. This particular case is likely to be quite problematic, as it may not always be clear to what extent the day-to-day management of the regulated activity is being carried on from the UK where the management functions are split between several locations. In addition, it is important to note that there are two regulated activities, "effecting" and "carrying out" contracts of insurance. It will be necessary to assess Section 418 in the context of both regulated activities, and whilst the regulated activity of effecting contracts of insurance might be carried on outside the UK it may be that the separate activity of carrying them out is undertaken from the UK, triggering requirement for authorisation.

The fourth case is where the head or registered office is not in the UK but the activity is carried on from an establishment maintained in the UK. This case is also likely to cause practical difficulties, as it would catch the activities of any insurer where the activity is being carried on from an establishment maintained in the UK wherever the underlying risks are being written. Again the question of whether the activity is being carried on from one location or another is likely to be a matter of fine judgement in many cases, especially where the activity is carried on partly from one location and partly from another.

A person may also be carrying on an activity in the UK even if there is no permanent establishment there. For example the activities could constitute the carrying on of regulated activities where carried out over the internet, by telephone or during occasional visits to the UK from overseas.

2.3.3 *Specified investments*

A person needs an authorisation to carry out a regulated activity only if the activity relates to one of the specified investments laid down by the Regulated Activities Order. It is a requirement of the Act that both the investments themselves and the activities carried out in relation to those investments fall within the regulatory net. Both the investments and the activities are defined in the Regulated Activities Order. This Chapter focuses only on those specified investments and regulated activities likely to be relevant to insurance business.

2.3.3.1 *Rights under a contract of insurance*
Rights under contracts of insurance are specified investments by virtue of Article 75 of the Regulated Activities Order. Article 3 of the Regulated Activities Order defines a contract of insurance as: "any contract of insurance which is a contract of long-term insurance or a contract of general insurance" and the definition goes on to give examples of types of contract that are included as contracts of insurance, notwithstanding that they may not ordinarily be regarded as being so. Examples given include:

- fidelity bonds
- performance bonds
- administration bonds
- bail bonds
- customs bonds or similar contracts of guarantee
- tontines
- capital redemption contracts or pension fund management contracts
- contracts to pay annuities on human life
- collective insurance contracts
- social insurance contracts.

For more information about the circumstances in which these contracts are to be treated as insurance contracts, reference should be made to Article 3 of the Regulated Activities Order. The expressions "contract of general insurance" and "contract of long-term insurance" are also defined in Article 3 by reference to the various different classes of insurance contract in much the same way as under the Insurance Companies Act 1982. These are set out in Schedule 1 of the Regulated Activities Order.

The question of whether or not a contract is one of insurance is left open. There is much case law on this subject, the scope of which is outside this Chapter.

The insurance directives impose certain limitations on the combinations of regulated activities for which authorisation can be given. In particular, it is not generally possible to obtain authorisation to undertake regulated activities in respect of both contracts of general insurance and contracts of long-term insurance save in certain limited circumstances where accident and health may be written alongside life contracts (*see* below).

The Regulated Activities Order also provides that certain rights under qualifying contracts of insurance are treated as contractually based investments. In order to be a "qualifying contract of insurance" the contract concerned must be in respect of long-term insurance, other than a reinsurance contract, or a contract in respect of which certain specified conditions are met. The specified conditions are that:

(a) the benefits must be payable only on death or in respect of incapacity due to injury, sickness or infirmity;

(b) the benefits are payable on death (other than death due to an accident) only where death occurs within 10 years of the date on which the life of the person in question was first insured under the contract, or where death occurs before the person attains a specified age not exceeding 70 years;

(c)   the contract has no surrender value, or the consideration consists of a single premium and the surrender value does not exceed that premium; and

(d)   the contract makes no provision for its conversion or extension in a manner which would result in it ceasing to comply with any of the foregoing provisions.

The activities of agents arranging qualifying contracts of insurance may be regulated under the Act as carrying on the regulated activity of arranging (bringing about) deals in contractually based investments.

2.3.3.2 *Rights under a stakeholder pension scheme*
A stakeholder pension scheme is defined in Section 1 of the Welfare Reform and Pensions Act 1999. Rights under such schemes are specified investments for the purpose of the Regulated Activities Order.

2.3.3.3 *Lloyd's investments*
There are two types of specified investment in relation to Lloyd's:

- the underwriting capacity of a Lloyd's syndicate; and
- a person's membership (or prospective membership) of a Lloyd's syndicate.

Generally Lloyd's falls outside the scope of this Chapter.

2.3.3.4 *Rights under funeral plans*
Rights under a funeral plan are the rights to a funeral obtained by a person before the death of the person whose funeral it will be. These became specified investments with effect from 1 January 2002.

2.3.3.5 *Rights to or interests in investments*
Rights to, or interests in, all the specified investments are themselves treated as specified investments. This means that an activity carried on in relation to rights or interests derived from any specified investments is also a regulated activity if the activity would be regulated if carried on in relation to the investment itself.

2.3.4   *Regulated activities*

As referred to above, there are two elements to be taken into account when looking at regulated activities. The first concerns the specified investments, which are outlined above in so far as they relate to insurance. The second element concerns the activities that are undertaken in relation to the specified investments. These activities are referred to as regulated activities. A regulated activity is an activity specified in Part II of the Regulated Activities Order and carried on in relation to one or more specified investments. The Order sets out a wide range of regulated activities and describes any exclusion that is applicable to the regulated activity concerned. This Chapter concentrates on those activities and exclusions that are relevant to insurance.

2.3.4.1   *Effecting or carrying out contracts of insurance as a principal*
Article 10 of the Regulated Activities Order provides that effecting and carrying out contracts of insurance as a principal are regulated activities for the purposes of the Act. The activities of effecting and carrying out a contract of insurance are separate regulated activities, each requiring its own authorisation. This means that an insurance company in run off, for example, would not need to be authorised to effect new contracts of insurance, but would need authorisation to carry out those contracts of insurance already written.

Whilst generally an insurer must be authorised to effect and carry out contracts of insurance by reference to the various classes of insurance contract specified in the Regulated Activities Order, the permission to effect or carry out certain classes of insurance includes permission to effect or carry out certain classes of general insurance contracts on an ancillary or supplementary basis. Accordingly, in determining which classes to apply for, an applicant should have regard to whether the contracts he wishes to carry out would qualify to be effected or carried out on an ancillary basis. For example, permission relating to life and annuity contracts includes permission to effect or carry out accident or sickness contracts on a supplementary basis, and permission to effect or carry out any class of general insurance contract includes permission to carry out any other class of general insurance contract, other than credit, suretyship and (except in certain circumstances) legal expenses contracts, on an ancillary basis. For this reason, applicants seeking to carry on insurance business will additionally need to consider whether the class of specified investments qualifies to be carried out on an ancillary or supplementary basis.

A contract of insurance will qualify to be effected or carried out on an ancillary basis if:

(a)   the business in question is to be the subject of the same contract as the principal business and concerns the same object; and
(b)   the risks covered are connected to the principal risk.

Two activities, which might otherwise constitute the effecting or carrying out of contracts of insurance, are expressly excluded from the need for Part IV Permission:

(a)   in circumstances specified in Article 11 of the Regulated Activities Order, the activities of an EEA firm where participating in a community co-insurance operation other than as leading insurer; and
(b)   in circumstances specified in Article 12 of the Regulated Activities Order, activities that are carried out in connection with the provision of on-the-spot accident or breakdown assistance for cars and other vehicles.

Although activities requiring authorisation are those which consist of effecting and carrying out contracts of insurance as "a principal", the activities of some agents might also be caught. For example, the activities of certain agents carried on in relation to rights under qualifying contracts of insurance might be regulated because, as noted above, those rights are classified as "contractually based investments". The actions of agents in this regard will not strictly be effecting or carrying out contracts of insurance as principal but rather the separate regulated activity of bringing about deals in contractually based investments.

Accordingly, activities in relation to specified investments that will require permission to be carried on are as follows.

Dealing in investments (as a principal or an agent)
The activity of dealing in investments is a regulated activity by virtue of Article 14 of the Regulated Activities Order. It is defined in terms of "buying, selling, subscribing for, or underwriting securities or contractually based investments".

However, the scope of the activity of dealing in investments as a principal is reduced by further exclusions. In relation to life policies, for example, dealing as a principal is only a regulated activity if the person holds himself out as making a market in the relevant specified investments, or as being in the business of dealing with them, or he must regularly solicit members of the public with the purpose of inducing them into the deal.

Arranging deals in investments
Arranging deals in investments may be of relevance to insurers to the extent that it applies to arrangements that relate to contractually based investments, or the underwriting capacity of a Lloyd's syndicate or membership of a Lloyd's syndicate. Arranging is made up of two distinct regulated activities:

(a) making arrangements with a view to transactions in investments – this activity is described as "making arrangements for another person to buy, sell, subscribe for, or underwrite a particular investment". It is aimed at arrangements that would have the direct effect that a transaction is concluded;

(b) arranging (bringing about) deals in investments – this second activity is described as "making arrangements with a view to a person who participates in the arrangements buying, selling, subscribing for, or underwriting investments".

It is aimed at cases where it may be said that the transaction is "brought about" directly by the parties to it, but where this happens in a context set up by a third party specifically with a view to the conclusion by others of transactions through the use of that third party's facilities. A person may therefore be carrying on this activity even if it is only providing part of the facilities necessary before a transaction is brought about.

Safeguarding and administering investments
Safeguarding and administering investments covers the circumstances where a person undertakes to arrange on a continuing basis for others actually to carry out the safeguarding and administering. In each case, both elements of safeguarding and administering must be present before a person will be deemed to carry on such an activity. The property that is safeguarded and administered must belong beneficially to another person and consist of contractually based investments.

Establishing stakeholder pension schemes
The regulated activities carried on in relation to stakeholder pension schemes are their establishment, operation, or winding up. Managers of such schemes will require authorisation to operate the scheme.

Advising on investments
Advising on investments only applies to contractually based investments and does not include giving advice about rights under general insurance contracts or generally about things that are not specified investments in the Regulated Activities Order. Additionally, the advice must be given to someone who holds specified investments or is a prospective investor.

Entering into funeral plan contracts
Entering as a provider into a funeral plan contract is a regulated activity, the provider being the person to whom the prepayments are made and who undertakes to provide the funeral.

Lloyd's activities
The Regulated Activities Order expressly lays down three regulated activities in relation to Lloyd's:

(a) advising on syndicate participation at Lloyd's (i.e., advising a person to become, continue or cease to be a member of a particular syndicate) is a regulated activity. Giving advice about the syndicate participation (how to use capital within the Lloyd's market and arranging syndicate participation) is a separate regulated activity to that of providing advice in relation to securities and contractually based investments;

(b) managing the underwriting capacity of a Lloyd's syndicate as a managing agent;

(c) arranging deals in contracts of insurance written at Lloyd's.

Lloyd's is authorised for (c) under Section 315 of the Act. Section 316 provides that Lloyd's members do not breach the general prohibition (and consequently do not require authorisation for effecting and carrying out contracts of insurance) unless the FSA directs otherwise. Lloyd's is generally outside the scope of this Chapter.

2.4 Persons who do not need authorisation to carry on regulated activities

The general prohibition against carrying on regulated activities without permission and the regulated activities themselves are covered above. Before moving on to look at the authorisation process, it is necessary to address the matter of persons who do not need authorisation to undertake regulated activities. Although there is no general provision allowing persons to apply for exemption, certain specific persons may be exempted from the general prohibition in relation to one or more regulated activities. The Act provides that appointed representatives, recognised exchanges or clearing houses, members of the professions under particular conditions (laid down in Section 326 of the Act), and other particular exempt persons by Order made by the Treasury (under Section 38 of the Act) are exempted persons. None of these exemptions will be applicable to the regulated activities of effecting or carrying out contacts of insurance as a principal, but reference is made to them here for the sake of completeness.

2.5 Authorisation and regulated activities

The FSA has issued guidance in relation to the need for authorisation and in its guidance manual there are some helpful diagrams which show whether or not permission is required under the Act to carry on a regulated activity. The diagram relating to authorisation and regulated activities is reproduced here (Please *see* following page).

2.6 Part IV Permission

As we have seen, subject to certain exceptions most particularly in respect of EEA Firms or Treaty Firms wishing to exercise EU passporting rights, a person wishing to carry out regulated activities in the UK by way of business must apply to the FSA under Section 40 of the Act for permission under Part IV of the Act before commencing those activities. A permission under Part IV is referred to as a Part IV Permission. An applicant who is in receipt of such a permission will become an authorised person. Under the Act, there is a single process for all applications for Part IV Permission, irrespective of the regulated activity to which the application relates. However, the amount of detailed information that an applicant will have to provide as part of the application process will be proportionate to the risks posed to the FSA's regulatory objectives by the regulated and unregulated activities the applicant intends to carry on. Thus the information requested will depend on and be proportionate to the nature of the application.

Authorisation gives a firm the ability to carry on regulated activities without breaching the general prohibition and incurring criminal liability. A firm must have the necessary Part IV Permission for each regulated activity that it carries on and must carry on only those regulated activities for which it has Part IV Permission. The first step

Figure 1: Authorisation and regulated activities

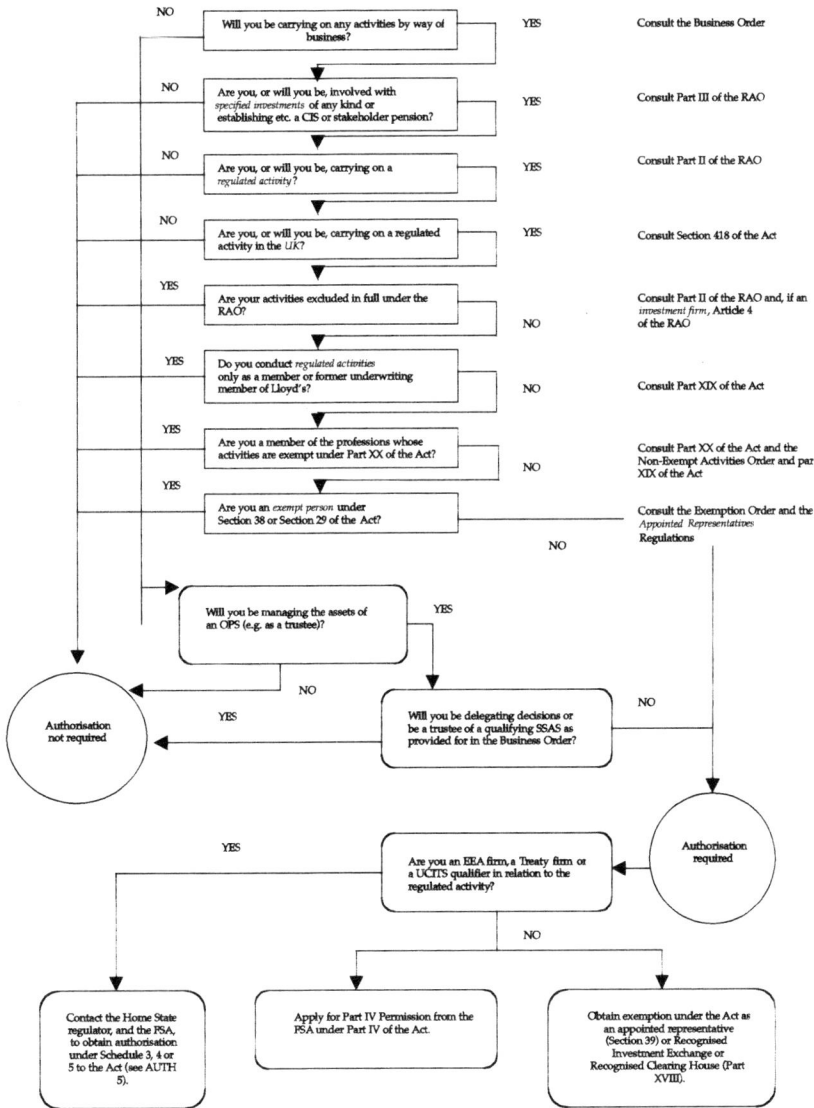

NO — Will you be carrying on any activities by way of business? — YES — Consult the Business Order

NO — Are you, or will you be, involved with *specified investments* of any kind or establishing etc. a CIS or stakeholder pension? — YES — Consult Part III of the RAO

NO — Are you, or will you be, carrying on a *regulated activity*? — YES — Consult Part II of the RAO

NO — Are you, or will you be, carrying on a regulated activity in the *UK*? — YES — Consult Section 418 of the Act

YES — Are your activities excluded in full under the RAO? — NO — Consult Part II of the RAO and, if an *investment firm*, Article 4 of the RAO

YES — Do you conduct *regulated activities* only as a member or former underwriting member of Lloyd's? — NO — Consult Part XIX of the Act

YES — Are you a member of the professions whose activities are exempt under Part XX of the Act? — NO — Consult Part XX of the Act and the Non-Exempt Activities Order and par XIX of the Act

YES — Are you an *exempt person* under Section 38 or Section 29 of the Act? — Consult the Exemption Order and the *Appointed Representatives* Regulations

NO

Will you be managing the assets of an OPS (e.g. as a trustee)? — YES

NO

Will you be delegating decisions or be a trustee of a qualifying SSAS as provided for in the Business Order? — NO

YES

Authorisation not required

Authorisation required

YES — Are you an EEA firm, a Treaty firm or a UCITS qualifier in relation to the regulated activity?

NO

Contact the Home State regulator, and the FSA, to obtain authorisation under Schedule 3, 4 or 5 to the Act (see AUTH 5).

Apply for Part IV Permission from the FSA under Part IV of the Act.

Obtain exemption under the Act as an appointed representative (Section 39) or Recognised Investment Exchange or Recognised Clearing House (Part XVIII).

Key to Abbreviations
CIS = collective investment scheme
RAO = Regulated Activities Order
OPS = occupational pension scheme
SSAS = small self-administered scheme

Business Order = The Financial Services and Markets Act 2001 (Carrying on Regulated Activities by Way of Business) Order 2001.

Non-Exempt Activities Order = The Financial Services and Markets Act 2001 (Professions) (Non-Exempt Activities) Order 2001.

Exemption Order = The Financial Services and Markets 2001 (Exemption) Order 2001.

therefore will be to identify the regulated activities that the applicant wishes to carry on and the specified investments associated with those activities for which Part IV Permission is required. These are referred to above.

2.6.1 Content of the permission

Section 42(6) of the Act requires the FSA to set out in the Part IV Permission the regulated activities for which a firm is given permission. Section 42(7) of the Act empowers the FSA to incorporate such limitations in respect of the regulated activities for which permission is given as the FSA deems appropriate and further empowers the FSA to grant a narrower or wider description of regulated activity than that applied for or to grant a permission to carry out a regulated activity for which no application has been made. The FSA may also exercise its powers under Section 43 of the Act, to include requirements to which the Part IV Permission will be subject where the FSA considers it appropriate.

Accordingly, a Part IV Permission will specify:

(a)   a description of the activities the firm can carry on, including any limitations to the scope of the permission;
(b)   the specified investments involved; and
(c)   if appropriate, any requirements imposed in relation to the Part IV Permission.

The specified investments and the regulated activities have already been discussed.

2.6.2 Limitations

The FSA may under Section 42(6) of the Act impose limitations on the scope of the regulated activities for which Part IV Permission is given if it decides it is appropriate to do so. Generally, a limitation is imposed to limit in some way the scope of the regulated activities in respect of which permission is given. Each limitation is specific to a particular regulated activity, either in relation to the regulated activity, the specified investments or both. For this reason the limitation is actually incorporated in the definition of the regulated activity itself, rather than being separately listed. An applicant may wish to apply for certain limitations to be imposed on the scope of its regulated activities at the outset, or alternatively the FSA may impose the limitation using its own initiative powers under Section 45 of the Act.

Examples of limitations include:

(a) a limit on the types of clients with whom the applicant may deal;
(b) a limit on the number of clients with whom the applicant may deal;
(c) a limit on the types of specified investments with which the applicant may deal;
(d) a limit on the type of insurance business that the applicant may carry on, for example reinsurance only.

Where the FSA intends to impose a limitation the applicant will be advised formally and given the opportunity to make representations before a final decision is made. Once a Part IV Permission has been given, a firm can apply at any time under Section 44 of the Act to have a limitation or requirement varied or removed.

2.6.3 Requirements

Section 43 of the Act gives the FSA power to include any requirement in a Part IV Permission that it considers appropriate.

The FSA can impose a requirement on a firm to:

• take a particular action, or
• refrain from taking a particular action.

A requirement can apply to unregulated activities as well as to regulated activities and accordingly can be used to control the performance of certain business activities that are not themselves regulated. The requirements can extend to the group of which the applicant is a member and to any member of such group. The FSA may set time limits on the imposition of a requirement.

Requirements can also be used to define the scope of a number of regulated activities carried out by a firm so that a particular differentiated regulatory regime applies.

If after reviewing an application the FSA proposes to impose a requirement, the applicant will be advised formally and given the opportunity to make representations before the FSA reaches its final decision. After being given permission, a firm can apply under Section 44 of the Act at any time to have a limitation or a requirement varied or removed following the procedures in Section 6 of the Supervision Manual.

As part of its application process, an applicant may wish to apply for certain requirements to be imposed or alternatively the FSA may impose the requirement using its own initiative powers under Section 45 of the Act. One of the advantages of applying for certain requirements is that, by reducing the scope of the permission requested, the firm will only be required to demonstrate that it will able to satisfy the threshold conditions in respect of this reduced scope.

2.6.4 Prudential categories

The FSA is moving towards the prudential supervision of financial services businesses in two stages. The objective will be to have a single Integrated Prudential Sourcebook containing the rules and regulations applying to all financial services businesses. Initially, however, separate prudential sourcebooks have been prepared on an interim basis, which apply to the various different segments of the financial services community. Accordingly, when applying for Part IV Permission it is necessary for a firm to identify the relevant prudential category. Appendix 1 to the Supervision Manual gives guidance as to the determination of the relevant prudential category. The relevant prudential category for an insurance company will be that of insurer. The relevant Interim Prudential Sourcebook will be IPRU(INS) and the provisions of the Supervision Manual applicable to firms in this prudential category will apply. As a consequence of falling within the prudential category of insurer, certain restrictions are imposed in IPRU(INS) on the other commercial business that the firm may wish to carry on in addition to an insurance business.

The assessment of a firm's prudential category can be made according to the following diagram, prepared by the FSA (*see* following page).

2.6.5 Risk assessment

In considering the application for Part IV Permission and whether to impose limitations and requirements, the FSA will adopt a risk based approach in order to concentrate the FSA's regulatory resources in the areas that most need attention. The approach to risk assessment is, according to Section 1 of the Supervision Manual, based on the extent to which a firm poses risks to the FSA in meeting its regulatory objectives. This involves an analysis of the impact of a risk materialising and the likelihood of it doing so. The probability of a risk materialising will depend on several factors including the inherent risks run by firms, the

Figure 2: Determination of an applicant's prudential category

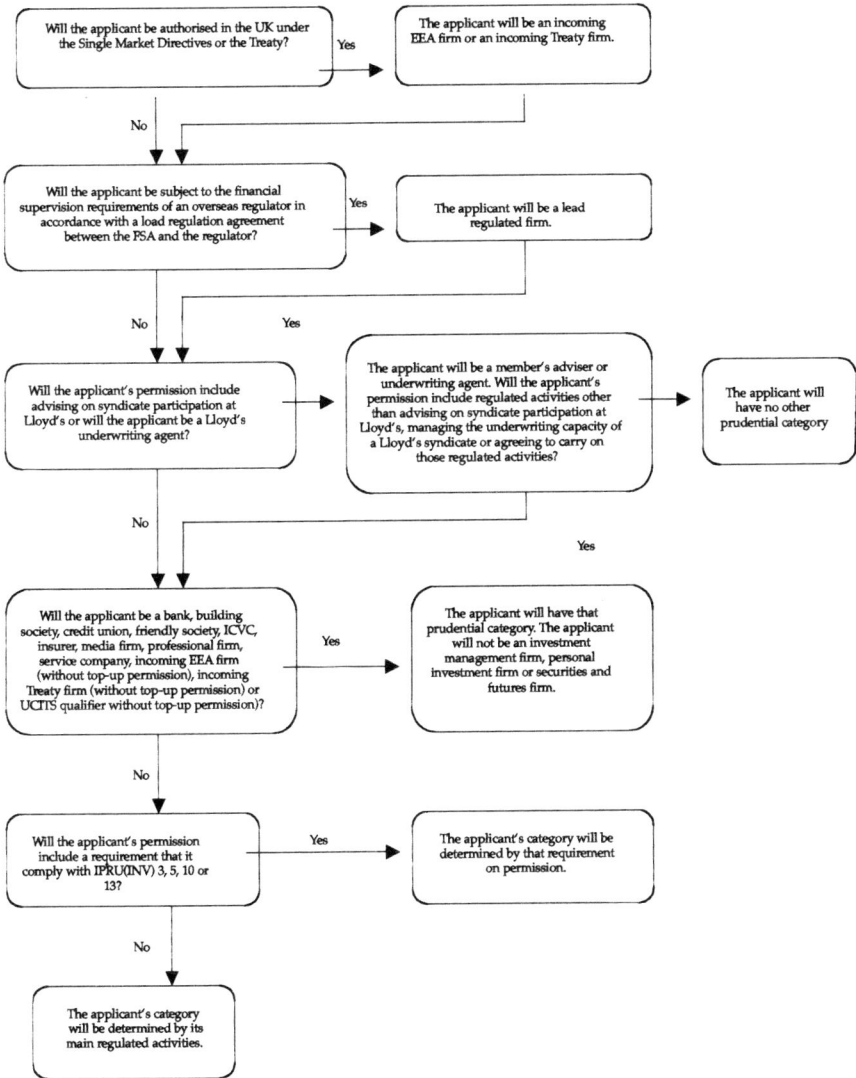

environment in which they operate and the firms' internal systems and controls.

The impact of a firm is assessed by reference to a range of factors derived from the regulatory objectives including:

(a)   the degree to which risks related to the firm, if they were to materialise, would damage market confidence;

(b)   the extent to which the firm may pose risks to the achievement of the objective of promoting public understanding;

(c)   the extent to which consumers may be adversely affected either directly or indirectly by the firm as a result of prudential failure, misconduct, market malfunction, market manipulation or the need to contribute to the financial reconstitution of compensation schemes;

(d)   the incidence and materiality of any financial crime which may be perpetrated through or by the firm.

The probability of a firm posing a risk to the regulatory objectives is, where applicable, assessed in terms of risk groups arising from the firm's:

(a)   strategy;

(b)   business risk (i.e. those risks, such as credit, market and operational risk) which are inherent in the business);

(c)   financial soundness;

(d)   customers and the products and services offered;

(e)   internal systems and controls and compliance culture;

(f)   organisation and the role played by the governing body, management and staff in effectively managing risk.

The FSA will take an overall view in reaching its assessment of the nature of the relationship that it will have with the firm and will take into account other relevant factors such as the level of confidence the FSA has in the risk assessment information available to it, the quality of the home state regulator (for firms with their head office overseas) and any anticipated material change in the impact or probability factors.

The risk assessment process will be applied to all firms although the details may vary from firm to firm. The FSA will communicate its risk assessment to firms and will also outline a programme intended to address any significant concerns. The FSA emphasises that the assessment is provided for specific regulatory purposes and as such encourages firms to keep their regulatory grading confidential.

2.7   The threshold conditions

Under Section 41(2) of the Act, the FSA is required, in giving Part IV Permission or in imposing any requirement, to ensure that the applicant satisfies and will continue to satisfy the threshold conditions in relation to all the regulated activities for which it has permission. The threshold conditions are set out in Schedule 6 to the Act and represent the minimum conditions that a firm is required to satisfy in order to become authorised. The statutory provisions are supplemented by a guidance section of the Handbook entitled Threshold Conditions. In considering whether an applicant meets the threshold conditions, the FSA is empowered to take such steps as are necessary for the preservation of the regulatory objective of protecting consumers. Once authorised, the obligation to meet these conditions is an ongoing one and if the FSA is concerned that a firm is not meeting one of these conditions, it may vary or even withdraw a firm's permission to carry out its regulated activities using its own initiative powers under Section 45 of the Act.

There are five threshold conditions specified in Schedule 6 to the Act, relating to the applicant's:

- legal status;
- location of office;
- close links;
- adequacy of resources; and
- suitability.

Each of the last three threshold conditions (close links, resources and suitability) will be viewed in the context of the regulated activities which the applicant wishes to carry on and in the light of the FSA's statutory objectives. The threshold conditions are applied in relation to each of the activities in respect of which Part IV Permission is sought, and it is not necessarily the case that the applicant will satisfy all the threshold conditions in relation to each. Where the FSA is not satisfied that an applicant will satisfy a threshold condition, the application will be denied in respect of that regulated activity. In making its determination, the FSA will consider whether the applicant can demonstrate that it is ready, willing and organised so as to enable it to comply with the specific regulatory obligations that will apply to the applicant if Part IV Permission is granted.

2.7.1   Legal status

If an applicant is seeking permission to effect or carry out contracts of insurance it must be a body corporate, a registered friendly society or a registered industrial and provident society, or a member of Lloyd's. This reflects the requirements of Article 8(1) of the First Life and Non-Life Directives.

2.7.2 Location of offices

Where the applicant is a body corporate constituted under UK law, its head office and registered office must be in the UK. If an applicant is not a body corporate but has its head office in the UK, it must also carry on business in the UK. This requirement is reflective of the Post BCCI Directive although the scope is extended somewhat. Whilst it is clear that this requirement does not necessarily mean the firm's registered office or indeed its principal place of business must be located in the UK, the expression "head office" is not defined in the Act or the Directive. The FSA has indicated that it regards the head office as the location at which the central management and control of the firm is undertaken. Whilst in some cases this will not be clear, the FSA guidance indicates that it will look at the location of the directors and senior management and the principal administrative functions in reaching its determination.

2.7.3 Close links

Close links must not prevent the FSA's supervision of the applicant. Close links are defined in paragraph 3(2) of Schedule 6 to the Act. Essentially the definition extends to links between the applicant and its parent undertaking, subsidiary undertaking and fellow subsidiary undertakings of the parent undertaking. It also extends to 20 per cent controllers.

In assessing whether this threshold condition is satisfied, the FSA will be primarily concerned to ensure that the information flow between the applicant and members of its group and those persons with whom the applicant has close links will be such as to enable the FSA to be satisfied that the applicant will be fulfilling its regulatory requirements and that the impact on the FSA's regulatory objectives is capable of being accurately assessed. The FSA will look at the structure and geographical spread of the group and will be especially concerned where the group has subsidiaries or branches located in jurisdictions which restrict the free flow of information. The FSA will also investigate how confident it can be that it can assess the overall financial position of the group at any particular time and will take into account factors such as whether the group prepares audited consolidated accounts, whether different members of the group have different financial periods or whether they share common auditors. The FSA must be satisfied that where the applicant has close links with a party which is not subject to the jurisdiction of a country in the EEA, the local regulatory regime, and its application, will not prevent the effective supervision of the applicant by the FSA.

Whilst the FSA will take into account these matters only in so far as they are significant in the context of the applicant viewed in the light of the FSA's regulatory objectives, the FSA will look at these issues as a package, so that although certain provisions may not be significant taken individually, when combined and taken together they may nevertheless prove to be significant.

2.7.4 Adequacy of resources

The resources of the applicant must, in the opinion of the FSA, be adequate with regard to the regulated activities it seeks to carry on. This requirement is not limited to financial resources and the FSA will look at all the resources available to the applicant. The FSA will look at the adequacy of the firm's resources in terms of quantity, quality and availability and will also be concerned to understand the means by which the firm is to manage its resources. The section of the handbook entitled Senior Management Arrangements, Systems and Controls ("SYSC") supplements this threshold condition and is described in more detail below.

The FSA will consider whether the firm is ready, willing and organised to comply with these requirements in assessing whether this threshold condition is satisfied. In reaching its opinion, the FSA may take into account the applicant's membership of a group and any effect which that membership may have on the applicant's resources. This reflects the provisions of Section 49 of the Act, which provides:

"In considering –
(a)   an application for a Part IV Permission . . .
the [FSA] may have regard to any person appearing to be or likely to be in a relationship with the applicant . . . which is relevant."

This Section also gives the FSA very wide powers to investigate the firm's controllers, directors and persons who have close links with the firm. It could also extend to other persons who are in a position to exert influence over the firm.

In assessing the adequacy of resources the FSA will act in accordance with the regulatory principle of proportionality but will look at the resources taken as a whole. Matters may not be of significance taken individually but may nevertheless be significant when combined with one or more matters in relation to the applicant.

2.7.5 *Financial requirements*

The detailed financial requirements for insurers are set out in the relevant Interim Prudential Sourcebook for insurers ("IPRU(INS)"). An applicant will be required to demonstrate that it has adequate financial resources to meet the financial resources requirement for its prudential category of being an insurance company. The Single Market and Capital Adequacy Directives set out minimum financial requirements for insurance businesses and these are reflected in IPRU(INS). Furthermore, when an applicant wishes to become an insurer the FSA will give it individual guidance (e.g. on its margin of solvency) during the preliminary application phase.

The FSA must also have regard to the provisions made by the applicant, or where relevant the group, in respect of liabilities including future or contingent liabilities. The FSA will also take into account the applicant's procedures, and where relevant the applicant's group's procedures for managing risk.

The FSA will be concerned to ensure that the business plans are well drawn up and robustly tested against a number of scenarios. The level of detail contained in the business plan will depend on the complexity of the business concerned. The Corporate Authorisation Department is available to provide guidance in this regard.

Other relevant matters may include:

(a)   the firm's ability to comply with the FSA's prudential rules;
(b)   ny indications that the firm may not be able to meet its debts as they fall due;
(c)   any implications that may be drawn from the firm's history;
(d)   the steps taken to identify and measure risks that may be of regulatory concern, including the systems and controls in place and the human resources available to manage and control them; and
(e)   the steps taken to investigate the sector in which the firm is to carry on business and that its resources are sufficient in terms of capital adequacy and consumer protection.

2.7.6 *Suitability*

The applicant must satisfy the FSA that it is a fit and proper person to perform the regulated activities for which application is made. In assessing whether the applicant is "fit and proper", the FSA will have regard to:

(a) the applicant's connection with any person;
(b) the nature of any activity which the applicant carries on or seeks to carry on; and
(c) the need to ensure that the applicant's affairs are conducted soundly and prudently.

Whilst the emphasis of this threshold condition is on the suitability of the firm itself, the suitability of the persons performing certain functions (known as "controlled functions", see below) may also be relevant, because where there are concerns raised about the suitability of an individual or management collectively, the FSA may determine that the candidate is not suitable for authorisation.

In assessing the suitability of a firm, the FSA is not confined geographically and the provisions of Section 49 of the Act confer on the FSA broad powers to investigate and take into account any person who appears or is likely to be relevant.

Matters that the FSA is likely to take into account in assessing the suitability of a candidate for authorisation include:

(a) the integrity and standards with which the firm will conduct its business;
(b) the competence and prudence of management; and
(c) the extent to which the firm is able to demonstrate that it will conduct its affairs with due skill care and diligence.

In determining whether the firm satisfies this threshold condition in so far as it relates to the firm's integrity and standards, the Handbook contains guidance as to the matters that the FSA will take into account. These matters include:

(a) the extent to which the firm has been open and cooperative in its dealings with the FSA and has demonstrated that it is ready, willing

and organised to comply with the applicable standards and requirements of the regulatory system;
(b)   whether the firm or any person connected with it has been
        convicted of any unspent criminal offence, including offences
        relating to consumer credit, consumer protection or significant tax
        offences;
(c)   whether the firm has been the subject of any regulatory investi-
        gation or enforcement proceedings by the FSA or any other relevant
        regulatory body;
(d)   whether the firm or any connected person has contravened the Act
        or any preceding legislation or the regulatory system or any other
        applicable rules and regulations of a regulatory nature;
(e)   whether the firm or any person connected with it has been refused
        registration, or any similar authorisation or permission to carry out
        any trade or business, or whether any such authorisation or per-
        mission has been withdrawn or terminated, or whether the firm or
        any person connected with it has been expelled from any relevant
        regulatory or governmental body;
(f)   the systems and controls that the firm has in place in order to ensure
        regulatory compliance;
(g)   the firm's procedures for ensuring that its employees, approved
        persons and subcontractors are aware of and comply with their
        regulatory obligations;
(h)   whether the firm or any person connected with the firm has ever
        been dismissed from employment or a position of trust or fiduciary
        or similar relationship, or has ever been asked to resign from such
        an appointment; and
(i)   whether the firm or any person connected with it has ever been
        disqualified from being a director.

In determining whether the firm satisfies the suitability threshold
condition with respect to the competence and prudence of management,
and the exercise of due skill, care and diligence of management, the
Handbook gives guidance as to the matters that the FSA will take into
account as follows:

(a)   whether there is a sufficient range of skills and experience in the
        firm's governing body to understand, operate and manage the
        firm's regulated activities;
(b)   whether the firm has sufficient non-executive directors and whether
        those non-executives are given appropriate responsibilities;

(c)   whether the systems and controls in place with regard to the governing body enable it to assess and control the firm's regulated activities;

(d)   the extent to which the persons performing controlled functions act with due skill and diligence in performing those functions;

(e)   the extent to which the firm has in place systems and controls to enable it to comply with SYSC;

(f)   whether the firm has approached financial control and other risks in a prudent manner and has taken reasonable steps to ensure that robust information and reporting systems have been developed, tested and installed;

(g)   whether the firm or any person connected with it has been concerned in the management of a company or other organisation that has become insolvent;

(h)   whether the firm has developed human resources policies and procedures that are designed to ensure that the firm only employs individuals who are honest and committed to high standards of integrity in the conduct of their activities;

(i)   the extent to which the firm has conducted enquiries that are sufficient to give it reasonable assurance that it will not be posing unacceptable risks to consumers or the financial system;

(j)   the firm's procedures for dealing with money laundering; and

(k)   the suitability of the firm's actuaries and auditors.

2.7.7   *Principles for business*

The fit and proper test is supplemented by the principles for business which form part of the Handbook. The principles for business apply to every firm, but are modified in respect of incoming EEA firms and incoming treaty firms. Compliance with the principles for business is therefore important in determining whether an applicant is ready, willing and organised to carry on regulated activities, and will be a crucial factor in assessing whether the firm satisfies the suitability condition.

There are eleven principles for business as follows:

1.   Integrity – a firm must conduct its business with integrity.
2.   Skill care and diligence – a firm must conduct its business with skill care and diligence.
3.   Management and control – a firm must take reasonable care to organise and control its affairs responsibly and effectively, with adequate risk management systems.

4.   Financial prudence – a firm must maintain adequate financial resources.
5.   Market conduct – a firm must observe proper standards of market conduct.
6.   Customers' interests – a firm must pay due regard to the interests of its customers and treat them fairly.
7.   Communications with clients – a firm must pay due regard to the information needs of its clients and communicate information to them in a way that is clear, fair and not misleading.
8.   Conflicts of interest – a firm must manage conflicts of interest fairly, both between itself and its customers and between a customer and another client.
9.   Customers: relationships of trust – a firm must take reasonable care to ensure the suitability of its advice and discretionary decisions for any customer who is entitled to rely upon its judgement.
10. Clients' assets – a firm must arrange adequate protection for clients' assets when it is responsible for them.
11. Relations with regulators – a firm must deal with its regulators in an open and cooperative way, and must disclose to the FSA appropriately anything relating to the firm of which the FSA would reasonably expect notice.

Principle 11 is the broadest principle and is one that is likely to be the most problematic with regard to ongoing compliance as it incorporates such a wide measure of discretion. Generally, however, once a problem arises, the FSA will expect to be the first to be told about it. As a result, there is a high burden on firms to report matters to the regulator as and when they arise. If a matter occurs which, for example, might have implications for a firm's solvency, the firm must tell the FSA as soon as it becomes aware of the matter concerned. It would not be sufficient to wait until the firm fills in its regulatory return in order to report a matter that might have an impact on solvency.

2.7.8   SYSC

The threshold condition relating to adequacy of resources is supplemented by a section of the Handbook dealing with Senior Management Arrangements, Systems and Controls, which amplifies the areas that the FSA will be examining in determining whether this threshold condition is satisfied. SYSC applies to every firm that carries on regulated activities in the UK but is modified in relation to incoming EEA firms and incoming Treaty firms. SYSC does not apply where services are provided cross-border only. The principal purpose of SYSC is to encourage management of regulated firms to take practical responsibility for their firm's arrangements for compliance with the regulatory system, that is to amplify Principle 3 under which a firm must take "reasonable care to organise and control its affairs responsibly and effectively with adequate risk management systems and to encourage firms to vest responsibility for effective and responsible organisation in specific managers and directors".

The principal requirement of SYSC is set out in Article 2.1.1, which provides:

> "A firm must take reasonable care to maintain a clear and appropriate apportionment of significant responsibilities among its directors and senior managers in such a way that:
> (a) it is clear who has which of those responsibilities; and
> (b) the business and affairs of the firm can be adequately monitored and controlled by the directors, relevant senior managers and governing body of the firm."

The firm is required to nominate one or more individuals to assume overall responsibility for ensuring compliance with the rule set out above in what is generally referred to as the "compliance and oversight function". SYSC specifies the individuals who may be appointed to perform this function, which will usually be undertaken by the chief executive.

Record keeping is an important part of SYSC. The firm is required to record and update regularly the arrangements that it has made for complying with the requirements of the regulatory system. The name of the person or persons appointed to perform the compliance and oversight functions must be recorded and, where responsibilities are shared, the division of responsibility should be clearly identified. Records must be kept for a minimum of six years. The FSA gives guidance in SYSC as to what might constitute appropriate records, including diagrams and organisational charts, project management documents, job descriptions and the constitution and terms of reference of committees. The guiding principle is that records must show a clear description of the firm's major functions. It will often be necessary to submit some or all of these diagrams and charts together with the application pack (*see* below).

Article 3.1.1 of SYSC provides that "A firm must take reasonable care to establish and maintain such systems and controls as are appropriate to its business". The nature and extent of the systems and controls that a firm is required to have in place will depend on the nature and complexity of the firm's business and its geographical spread. The volume of transactions undertaken and the degree of risk associated with its areas of operation will also be borne in mind. The FSA will expect a firm to review its systems and controls regularly and to update them as appropriate.

SYSC gives guidance as to the main areas that it expects firms to consider in establishing appropriate systems and controls, and investigation of these issues will form part of the authorisation process in determining whether the threshold condition relating to the adequacy of resources has been satisfied.

With regard to the organisation of its affairs, SYSC requires a firm to delegate and segregate the duties of individuals and departments responsibly. A firm's reporting lines should be clear and appropriate having regard to the nature, scale and complexity of its business. These reporting lines together with clear management responsibilities should be communicated throughout the firm and should be properly documented.

An insurance firm is likely to delegate many functions and tasks to more junior members of staff for the purpose of carrying on its business. When functions and tasks are delegated, appropriate safeguards should be put in place. For example, the firm should assess whether the person to whom the task has been delegated is suitably qualified to perform it, taking into account the degree of skill or responsibility concerned. Where appropriate, limits should be placed on the extent to which authority has been delegated and the scope of delegation should be made clear. Appropriate arrangements, such as review meetings, should be made to ensure that the delegation and the discharge of those functions are properly monitored. If cause for concern arises through the supervision and monitoring of the task there should be appropriate follow up action, at an appropriate level of seniority, and the steps taken should be documented.

Where tasks are delegated outside the firm to independent contractors, such as actuaries or accountants, similar issues will arise. In addition it will be necessary for the firm to obtain sufficient information from its external contractor to enable it to assess the impact of outsourcing on its systems and controls.

Compliance plays an important part in the new regulatory system and in appropriate circumstance the FSA may require the firm to have a separate compliance function. It is a requirement of SYSC that:

> "a firm must take reasonable care to establish and maintain effective systems and controls for compliance with applicable requirements and standards under the regulatory system for countering the risk that the firm might be used to further financial crime."

This is consistent with the regulatory objectives set out in Section 2 of the Act.

With regard to risk assessment, it may be necessary in large or complex firms to have a person or persons who have responsibility for assessing a firm's risk and advising management on risk. The organisation and responsibilities of the risk assessment function should be properly documented and the function should be adequately resourced by an appropriate number of suitably trained and competent staff who are sufficiently independent to perform their duties effectively. There should be regular reporting to line management and onwards to the board.

Risk management is an area likely to receive increasing attention from the FSA as a consequence of the Tiner Project. In future, in appropriate cases, risk management teams, including actuarial, legal and financial skills, will be required to be established in order to apply appropriate controls over the business. According to the FSA, legal risk has assumed an increased importance in recent years, arising principally from three sources:

(a) new legislation, such as that following the emergence of the new EU directives;
(b) legal precedents established by court judgments; and
(c) the emergence of increasingly complex transactions which contain inherent legal uncertainties.

The FSA believes that these situations can present significant risks to a firm's solvency, and consequently to policyholders, and that firms should be proactive in managing them. Firms should maintain the necessary resources to identify legal risks on a timely basis and should determine their strategy in respect of such risks. This will include seeking legal advice where relevant and at an early stage, generating test cases to determine precedents and carrying out scenario planning for possible adverse outcomes.

The FSA will also be requiring firms to determine and document policies for dealing with risk including credit, market group, operational, liquidity and insurance technical risks, together with matching and aggregating of risks between insurance and investment functions. Firms will also be required to demonstrate how combinations of these risks have been aggregated and mitigated; in particular, firms will be required to have written risk management plans that document the policies, methods and assumptions used. This would include, for example, a statement of how much risk the firm is prepared to accept and to what extent this is mitigated by reinsurance, hedging or other means. As a result of these changes, the FSA will place more emphasis on requesting information that it expects insurance companies to generate as part of their risk management processes.

With regard to management information, the FSA will expect the firm to ensure that the information flow to the governing body is sufficient to enable it to identify, measure, manage and control risk. It will be important that the systems that are put in place enable the board to consider all relevant information in a timely manner and that the information provided to the board is reliable. Again, the FSA would expect to see a greater level of documentation of these procedures, and where tasks have been delegated the competence of the delegate should be appropriate for the task allocated.

Larger or complex firms may need an audit committee or an internal audit function to examine the process implemented by management for ensuring that there are appropriate and effective systems and controls. Audit committees are not a new phenomenon and will already be in place in many well-run insurance firms. The audit committee will also be responsible for overseeing any internal audit function and will provide the interface between the management and the external auditors. Where established, the committees should have formal terms of reference and should include non-executive directors.

It will be important that the internal audit function is independent of the day-to-day activities of the firm and that members of internal audit have access to the firm's records. Again the internal audit committee should have formal terms of reference and the individuals charged with the internal audit function should be suitably trained and be able to operate with independence. To ensure that this is the case it may be appropriate for the internal audit function to have a direct reporting line to one of the non-executive directors in addition to reporting lines to executive management and the audit committee function.

Business strategy and business continuity will be areas of key import-ance to a firm's compliance with SYSC and hence the threshold condition relating to the adequacy of the firm's resources. Firms should have in place arrangements to ensure that they can continue to function in the event of interruption. Disaster recovery plans will obviously be key to the fulfilment of this, but there will be other less obvious steps that the firm can incorporate in its culture that will assist in ensuring business continuity. An example of this would be ensuring that knowledge is appropriately spread and documented throughout the organisation, to ensure that systems and controls impacting on solvency are not harmed by the loss of a single individual.

The need for the employees and agents of insurance firms to be competent to perform the tasks allocated to them has been mentioned several times already and the systems and controls put in place by a firm should enable the firm to satisfy itself that such is the case. The detailed requirements with respect to training and competence are set out in the Training and Competence section of the Handbook.

Once proper systems have been established these need to be reviewed regularly and the firm will need to ensure that it maintains adequate records of its matters and dealings.

2.7.9 Approved persons

The obligation to satisfy the threshold conditions is primarily an obligation of the firm. As mentioned above, when deciding on the suitability of the firm for Part IV Permission, the FSA will consider whether the persons performing certain specified functions in relation to the firm are fit and proper to perform those functions. The approved persons regime is derived from Section 59 of the Act which provides that firms must take reasonable care to ensure that certain individuals within authorised firms are approved by the FSA as being fit and proper to perform certain functions that they carry out. These people are known as approved persons and the functions they carry out are referred to as controlled functions. We have already seen that it is a requirement of SYSC that one or more individuals must be appointed to the "appor-tionment and oversight function" and must be individually approved by the FSA as being fit and proper for this role. Other controlled functions are divided in to three broad categories:

(a) the exercise of significant influence on the conduct of the firm's affairs in relation to regulated activities (Section 59(5));

(b) dealing with customers in connection with carrying out regulated activities (Section 59(6));

(c) dealing with customers' property in connection with the carrying on of regulated activities (Section 59(7)).

The full list of the controlled functions is set out below.

Table 1: Controlled functions

Type	CF	Description of controlled function
Governing functions*	1	Director function
	2	Non-executive director function
	3	Chief executive function
	4	Partner function
	5	Director of unincorporated association function
	6	Small friendly society function
	7	Sole trader function
Required functions*	8	Apportionment and oversight function
	9	EEA investment business oversight function
	10	Compliance oversight function
	11	Money-laundering reporting function
	12	Appointed actuary function
Systems and controls functions*	13	Finance function
	14	Risk assessment function
	15	Internal audit function
Significant management functions*	16	Significant management (designated investment business) function

Table 1: Continued

Type	CF	Description of controlled function
	17	Significant management (other business operations) function
	18	Significant management (insurance underwriting) function
	19	Significant management (financial resources) function
	20	Significant management (settlements) function
Customer functions	21	Investment adviser function
	22	Investment adviser (trainee) function
	23	Corporate finance adviser function
	24	Pension transfer specialist function
	25	Adviser on syndicate participation at Lloyd's function
	26	Customer trading function
	27	Investment management function

*significant influence functions

Each governing function (except non-executive director) includes systems and controls functions and significant management functions; a person approved for a governing function will not require separate approval for functions 13–20.

Customer functions do not apply to general insurers.

Functions 14 to 20 may only be necessary in larger or more complex firms.

The people approved to carry out these functions must comply with seven Statements of Principle for Approved Persons set out in the Code of Practice for Approved Persons issued under Section 64 of the Act, as follows:

(a)   an approved person must act with integrity in carrying out all his controlled functions;

(b)   an approved person must act with skill, care and diligence in carrying out his controlled functions;

(c)   an approved person must observe proper standards of market conduct in carrying out his controlled functions;

(d)   an approved person must deal with the FSA and with other regulators in an open and cooperative way and must disclose appropriately any information of which the FSA would reasonably expect notice;

(e)   an approved person performing a significant influence function must take reasonable steps to ensure that the business of the firm for which they are responsible in his controlled function is organised so that it can be controlled effectively;

(f)   an approved person in a significant influence function must exercise due skill, care and diligence in managing the business of the firm for which he is responsible in his controlled function; and

(g)   an approved person performing a significant influence function must take reasonable steps to ensure that the business of the firm for which he is responsible in his controlled function complies with the relevant requirements and standards of the regulatory system.

In assessing whether or not a person (referred to as a candidate) is fit and proper to perform a controlled function, the FSA will have regard to the section of the Handbook entitled The Fit and Proper Test for Approved Persons ("FIT"). FIT applies to every approved person and candidate and reflects the requirements of Section 61 of the Act which provides that the FSA may only grant an application for approval if it is satisfied that the candidate is a fit and proper person to perform the function to which the application relates. In dealing with that question, Section 61(2) provides that the FSA may have regard to whether the candidate or any person who may perform a function on his behalf has:

- obtained a qualification,
- undergone or is undergoing any training, or
- possesses a level of competence,

required by the rules relevant to the application. This list is not exhaustive and the FSA may have regard to other additional factors.

The guidance issued by the FSA and reflected in FIT indicates that the FSA will take into account several additional factors in assessing the suitability of a candidate for a controlled function. The most important are the candidate's:

- honesty, integrity and reputation;
- competence and capability; and
- financial soundness.

The FSA will look at the context in which the controlled functions are to be performed and will normally view any matter that comes to its attention in the light of its relevance and importance to the activities of the firm and the performance of the controlled function. The FSA would expect to discuss matters giving rise to concern with the firm as part of the application process.

FIT gives further examples of the matters that the FSA will take into account in assessing the honesty, integrity and reputation of a candidate as follows:

(a)   whether the person has been convicted of any criminal offence; this may include where relevant any spent convictions under the Rehabilitation of Offenders Act 1974. Particular consideration will be given to offences involving dishonesty, fraud, financial crime or other offences under legislation relating to banking and financial services, companies, insurance and consumer protection;

(b)   whether the person has been subject to adverse findings or any settlements in civil proceedings particularly in connection with investment or other financial business misconduct, fraud or the formation or management of a body corporate;

(c)   whether the person has been the subject of or interviewed in the course of any existing or previous investigation or disciplinary proceedings by the FSA by any other regulatory authorities (including any previous regulator), clearing houses and exchanges, professional bodies or governmental bodies or agencies;

(d)   whether the person is or has been the subject of any proceedings of a disciplinary or criminal nature or has been notified of any potential proceedings or of any investigation that might lead to those proceedings;

(e)   whether the person has contravened any of the requirements and standards of the regulatory system or the equivalent standards and requirements of other regulatory authorities (including any previous regulator), clearing houses and exchanges, professional bodies or government bodies or agencies;

(f)   whether the person has been the subject of any justified complaint relating to regulated activities;

(g)   whether the person has been involved with a company, partnership or other organisation that has been refused registration, authorisation, membership or a licence to carry out a trade, business or profession or has had that registration, authorisation, membership or licence revoked withdrawn or terminated or has been expelled by a regulatory or governmental body;

(h)   whether as a result of the removal of the relevant licence, registration or other authority the person has been refused the right to carry on a trade, business or profession requiring a licence, registration or other authority;

(i)   whether the person has been a director, partner or concerned in the management of a business that has gone into insolvency, liquidation or administration while that person has been connected with the organisation or within one year of that connection;

(j)   whether the person or any business with which the person has been involved has been investigated, disciplined, censured or suspended or criticised by a regulatory or professional body, a court or tribunal, whether publicly or privately;

(k)   whether the person has been dismissed or asked to resign and resigned from employment or a position of trust, fiduciary appointment or similar;

(l)   whether the person has ever been disqualified from acting as a director or disqualified from acting in any managerial capacity;

(m)   whether in the past the person has been candid and truthful in all his dealings with any regulatory body and whether the person demonstrates a readiness and willingness to comply with the requirements and standards of the regulatory system and with other legal regulatory and professional requirements and standards.

In assessing the competence and capability of a candidate, the FSA will consider a variety of factors including the extent to which the candidate has complied with the FSA's Training and Competence Sourcebook and the extent to which the candidate is able to demonstrate by experience and training that he is competent to perform the controlled function to which he is to be appointed.

The financial soundness of a candidate will be determined by reference to whether the candidate is the subject of any unsatisfied judgment or award or has been the subject of bankruptcy proceedings in each case on a global basis. The FSA will not normally require a statement of assets.

2.7.10 Controllers

As has been mentioned earlier in considering an application for Part IV Permission, the FSA will require to be satisfied that close links will not prevent the effective supervision of the applicant and that certain persons appointed to perform specified functions are fit and proper to perform those functions. The suitability of an applicant to receive authorisation to carry out regulated activities will also be viewed in the light of its controllers. The threshold conditions requiring the FSA to take account of an insurer's controllers are supplemented by Chapter 11 of the FSA's Supervision Manual and by Part XII of the Act which requires the FSA's approval before a person can become a controller of an insurer.

Section 422 of the Act defines what is meant by a "controller" as follows:

"(in relation to a firm or other undertaking ("A"))
a person who:
(a) holds 10 per cent or more of the shares in A;
(b) is able to exercise significant influence over the management of A through his shareholding in A;
(c) holds 10 per cent or more of the shares in a parent undertaking ("P") of A;
(d) is able to exercise significant influence over the management of P through his shareholding in P;
(e) is entitled to exercise, or control the exercise of, 10 per cent or more of the voting power in A;
(f) is able to exercise significant influence over the management of A through his voting power in A;
(g) is entitled to exercise, or control the exercise of, 10 per cent or more of the voting power in P; or
(h) is able to exercise significant influence over the management of P through his voting power in P."

The definition in Section 442 goes on the expand on the meaning of various expressions used in the definition.

Accordingly as part of the application process, the FSA may request information on an applicant's controllers to assess whether:

(a) the applicant's controller is a fit and proper person to have control over the firm;

(b) the applicant's directors, partners and members of the governing body who will be performing controlled functions are fit and proper persons to be granted approval under the approved persons regime.

Where a controller is not an authorised person, an applicant will be required to provide the information required in the Controllers Form A and Controllers Form B as applicable. In all other cases, the information required from the applicant is as set out in Controllers Form A, Sections 1, 5 and 6.

2.8   The application procedure

The Authorisation Manual sets out the formal procedure to be followed in relation to applications for Part IV Permission and derives its authority from Section 51(3) of the Act, which provides that:

"An application under [Part IV] must –
(a) be made in such manner as the Authority may direct;
(b) contain or be accompanied by such other information as the Authority may reasonably require."

The Authorisation Manual also gives guidance as to how the FSA will determine applications under Section 52 of the Act.

Application for a Part IV Permission must be made in writing to the Corporate Authorisation Department in the manner specified in the Authorisation Manual and with the information required in the Application Pack provided by the FSA. The up-to-date version of the Application Pack is available on the FSA's website at www.fsa. gov.uk/handbook/applicationpack.html. The nature of the information requested by the FSA will be proportionate to the nature of the business that the applicant seeks to carry on. The fee payable in connection with the application is payable on submission of the completed form. The application will not be deemed to be complete until the fee is paid.

Until the application has been determined, the applicant has an ongoing duty to disclose any significant change to the information given as soon as it becomes aware of the change. This is consistent with Principle for Business 11, which imposes an equivalent obligation following authorisation.

The Application Pack is divided into two Parts, each divided into several sections. Part A relates to information about the applicant and the regulated and unregulated activities it proposes to carry on. Part B relates to information about other persons, such as controllers, approved persons and appointed representatives. Not all the sections will be applicable to each applicant.

2.8.1 Application pack information

2.8.1.1 Part A
Part A of the application form deals with information about the applicant and will seek information in relation to six basic areas as follows:

- the formal application;
- core details about the applicant;
- regulatory business plan;
- compliance;
- systems; and
- financial resources.

Part A contains the formal request for Part IV Permission and accordingly must be signed on behalf of the applicant by a duly authorised director. Pursuant to Section 51(1)(b) of the Act, an application for Part IV permission must also give an address in the UK for service of any document required by the Act.

Part A also requires the applicant to provide certain core details about the application, including the name and contact details of the applicant; the name and details of any professional advisers, including bankers, auditors and actuaries; the legal status of the applicant; details of its group structure; the applicant's history and details of any close links. This is essentially the basic information needed to assess the requirements of threshold conditions 1, 2 and 3. The core details section will also require the applicant to submit information about its senior management, controllers, approved persons, appointed representatives and governing body. This information is required in connection with the assessment of the firm's suitability for authorisation. The core details section will also ask the applicant to provide details regarding the regulated activities in respect of which permission is sought and details of any limitations or requirements to be imposed. The applicant is also required to specify the appropriate prudential category.

The applicant will be requested to provide a business plan which describes the regulated activities and any unregulated activities that the applicant proposes to carry on, the management and organisational structure of the applicant and details of any proposed outsourcing agreements. The level of detail required will depend on the risks to consumers arising from those activities.

For an applicant seeking to carry on insurance business, the plan should include a scheme of operations prepared in accordance with Appendix 2 of the Supervision Manual. The scheme of operations will describe the applicant's business strategy and will include financial projections of the applicant's profit and loss account, a summary balance sheet and a solvency forecast, describing the assumptions underlying the forecasts and identifying any material transactions proposed to be entered into with any associate.

Detailed information will be required about the compliance systems and controls that the applicant has put in place in order to ensure that it complies with the regulatory system to assist the FSA to determine whether the applicant has the systems and controls necessary to carry out the regulated activities applied for. This section will include details of the applicant's compliance arrangements, procedures for accepting customers, procedures for dealing with complaints, money laundering procedures, training and competence arrangements and will require the applicant to specify and attach the supporting documentation.

Detailed information will also be required about the firm's systems and how they satisfy the requirements of SYSC and the threshold condition relating to the adequacy of resources. This section will include details of transaction reporting systems, settlement systems, accounting systems, position risk settlement, credit management, business usage, and will contain details of the firm's IT systems and the arrangements for their implementation, governance and infrastructure controls as well as details of the applicant's electronic commerce systems. An auditor's or independent reporting accountant's report into the adequacy of the systems and controls will accompany this information. The applicant will be required to attach appropriate supporting documentation in respect of this part of the application.

Financial resources will also form an important part of Part A of the Application Pack. The applicant will be required to give detailed information about its share capital, financial requirements, sources of income, external funding, details of any guarantees given, arrangements for insurance and indemnity, and a financial forecast accompanied by appropriate supporting documents.

2.8.1.2 Part B

Part B of the application pack contains the application forms in respect of persons who are to perform controlled functions under the approved persons and appointed representative regime. It also contains the form to be completed by an individual in respect of an applicant overseas firm.

The FSA will assess the applicant having regard to the regulatory objectives and threshold conditions and in accordance with the risk assessment principles referred to earlier.

In considering the application, the FSA may:

(a) carry out any enquiries which it considers appropriate, for example by holding discussions with other regulators or exchanges;
(b) ask the applicant, or any specified representative of the applicant, to attend meetings at the FSA to give further information and explain any matter the FSA considers relevant to the application;
(c) require any information given by the applicant to be verified in such a way as the FSA may specify;
(d) take into account any information which it considers appropriate in relation to the application, for example any unregulated activities which the applicant carries on or proposes to carry on;
(e) visit the premises that the applicant intends to use as its place of business.

In addition to the information in the application pack, the FSA may require the applicant to provide such further information as it reasonably considers necessary to enable it to determine the application and to verify it as the FSA directs. Should the FSA require further information on reviewing an application pack, the applicant will be advised in writing.

Applicants will often wish to discuss applications with the Corporate Authorisation Department during the application process; similarly, the FSA will often need to discuss and clarify information that has been submitted within the application pack. The exchange of information during the application process is viewed as important by the FSA since the final decision about an application needs to be based on as complete a picture of the application as possible.

2.8.2 Reports from third parties

Section 51(6) of the Act empowers the FSA to require the applicant to verify information provided in such a way as the FSA directs. Thus, as part of the application process, the FSA may require the applicant to provide, at its own expense, a report by an auditor, reporting accountant, actuary or other qualified person approved by the FSA. The report may be on such aspects of the information provided, or to be provided, by the applicant as the FSA may specify.

Applicants seeking to carry on long-term insurance business are also required to provide a certificate from an actuary confirming the appropriateness of the projections for the long-term insurance business and, in particular, the adequacy of premium rates, the technical provisions, margin of solvency and how quickly capital strains from effecting new business will be overcome.

If an applicant appoints a reporting accountant other than its own auditor or an actuary other than its own actuary to report on an application for Part IV Permission, the applicant is required to take reasonable steps to ensure that the reporting accountant or actuary satisfies the qualification and independence tests specified in the Supervision Manual.

Occasionally, the FSA may identify a need for an independent report on specific areas of an application, for example where the applicant's business plan is innovative, complex or raises concerns as a result of matrix management. Such reports will usually be discussed and agreed with the applicant as part of the pre-application meeting.

2.8.3 Connected persons

As has been mentioned earlier under Section 49 of the Act (persons connected with an application), in considering an application for Part IV Permission, the FSA may have regard to any person appearing to it to be, or likely to be, in a relationship with the applicant which is relevant.

A person in, or likely to be in, a relationship with an applicant that is relevant is known as a connected person. The FSA will assess whether a particular relationship is relevant in the light of the particular circumstances of each application. Examples of persons who might be considered connected with an applicant include, but are not limited to:

(a)   a controller of the applicant; or
(b)   an applicant's directors, partners or members of its governing body; or
(c)   a company in the same group as the applicant; or
(d)   a person with whom the applicant intends to enter into a material outsourcing agreement; or
(e)   any other person who may exert influence on the applicant, which might pose a risk to the applicant satisfying or continuing to satisfy the threshold conditions.

As a result, in addition to the specific information required to be submitted in respect of controllers, authorised persons and appointed representatives as part of the application process, the FSA may request information about any other person whom the FSA determines is in a relevant relationship with an applicant. The FSA may request information from the applicant on persons who are connected persons or are likely to become connected persons under any proposed transactions or relationships.

2.8.4   For applicants seeking to passport into another EEA State

If an applicant wants to exert an EEA right shortly after having permission, it should contact the Corporate Authorisation Department to discuss its plans. However, it may submit a separate notice of intention to passport with its application which will be reviewed with it. The business plans, financial projections and scheme of operations submitted with its application should in that case always reflect any passported activity that the firm plans to commence.

2.8.5   How long will an applicant have to wait?

Once the completed application has been received, the FSA has six months from the date of receipt to make its determination. This is a requirement of the Act specified in Section 52(1). However, the length of the process may vary with the complexity of the application. If the FSA receives an incomplete application, it has to determine it within 12 months of the initial receipt of the application. If material remains outstanding at the expiry of 12 months from the date of receipt of an incomplete application, the FSA must decline the application. The Act is silent as to what will happen if the FSA does not make a decision within this timeframe. There is no authorisation by default, but the FSA would be open to judicial review if it failed to make a decision within the required time period. The Act does not set out what constitutes a completed application. The application pack is designed to capture the information the FSA requires to assess the applicant's ability to meet the threshold conditions and, therefore, submission of a signed completed application pack with all required attachments should satisfy any quantitative test. However, the application and authorisation process is a dynamic one and information submitted or the regulatory vetting procedures may lead to a request for further information or reports. In assessing the quality of an application the FSA will need to be satisfied that the application demonstrates that the applicant is ready, willing and organised to become authorised to carry out each regulated activity for which application is made.

2.8.6 *Determining applications*

An application for Part IV Permission and approval of a candidate will be determined under Section 52 of the Act. As a general principle, when the FSA proposes or decides to take action in respect of an application it is required by the Act to follow specified procedures involving the issue of a warning notice or a decision notice.

A decision to determine an application might be taken in one of two ways according to the kind of decision reached. If the decision is to grant the application on the terms applied for, it will be taken by internal staff procedures involving FSA staff at an appropriate level of seniority.

In any other case, that is to say where FSA staff have recommended either:

(a) the refusal of an application; or
(b) they have proposed the grant of an application subject to a limitation or a requirement which was not applied for; or
(c) a narrower description of the regulated activity than that to which the application relates,

the FSA's Regulatory Decisions Committee ("RDC") will make the decision. The RDC is appointed by the FSA Board but is a body outside the FSA's management structure. The procedure followed where the

RDC is involved is therefore more formal than the internal staff procedures. Staff decisions to grant permission are commensurate with the degree of complexity (the manual distinguishes "routine" decisions from the others); RDC decisions involve statutory notices.

As outlined above, as part of the application process, an applicant may apply for a permission, which includes a limitation or a requirement. It should be aware that the decision-making process will vary according to the accuracy of its application. When the FSA staff review an application, if they consider that it should be refused or subject to a limitation or a requirement which was not applied for, or granted with a narrower description of a regulated activity, they will recommend to the RDC that a warning notice should be given. This warns the recipient that the FSA proposes to take certain action and gives the opportunity for representations to be made to the FSA before a decision is made within a period of time of not less than 28 business days from receipt. On receipt of a recommendation from the FSA staff, the RDC can then either decide to grant the application on the terms applied for or give the warning notice.

After representations have been made, the RDC will issue a decision notice which states the action that the FSA has decided to take and presents its determination of the application.

Any applicant or candidate who is in receipt of a decision notice is entitled to refer the decision to the Financial Services and Markets Tribunal within 28 days of the date when it has been given. A reference to the tribunal will be a full rehearing and not an appeal (appeals can be made to the Court of Appeal).

If the FSA takes the action set out in the decision notice, or takes action in accordance with any directions given by the tribunal or the court, a final notice will be given to state the action being taken and the date on which it is to be taken. The FSA's general policy is not normally to publish final notices in a way that would disclose confidential information or prejudice consumer interests.

The FSA Handbook includes a useful diagram which indicates how the FSA will deal with an application for a Part IV Permission, which is reproduced below:

Figure 3: Application for Part IV Permission

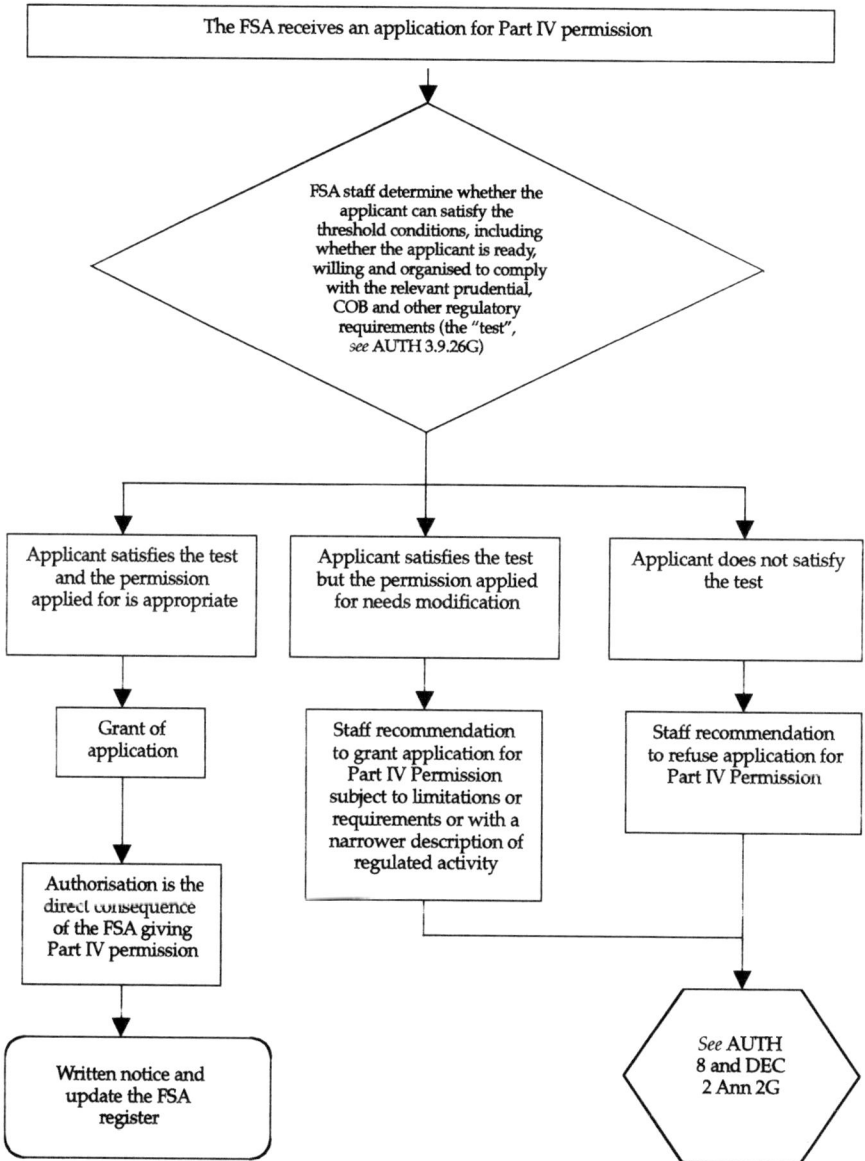

The FSA receives an application for Part IV permission

FSA staff determine whether the applicant can satisfy the threshold conditions, including whether the applicant is ready, willing and organised to comply with the relevant prudential, COB and other regulatory requirements (the "test", *see* AUTH 3.9.26G)

Applicant satisfies the test and the permission applied for is appropriate	Applicant satisfies the test but the permission applied for needs modification	Applicant does not satisfy the test

Grant of application

Staff recommendation to grant application for Part IV Permission subject to limitations or requirements or with a narrower description of regulated activity

Staff recommendation to refuse application for Part IV Permission

Authorisation is the direct consequence of the FSA giving Part IV permission

Written notice and update the FSA register

See AUTH 8 and DEC 2 Ann 2G

2.8.7   *Commencing regulated activities*

If Part IV Permission is given, the FSA will expect a firm to commence its regulated activity in line with its current business plan and the FSA may exercise its own initiative powers to vary or cancel a Part IV Permission once granted if it is redundant for 12 months from the date the permission was given or for a period of at least 12 months (irrespective of the date of the grant of permission).

If the FSA considers that it may be appropriate to exercise its own initiative powers to vary or cancel a firm's Part IV Permission, FSA staff will discuss the proposed action with the firm and ascertain the firm's reasons for not commencing or carrying on the regulated activities concerned.

Finally, an applicant seeking to carry on insurance business should be aware that specific reporting requirements apply during its first three years of operations.

2.8.8   The FSA register

The FSA is required to maintain a register pursuant to Section 347 of the Act containing details of all firms and the regulated activities for which they have Part IV Permission. The FSA register is open to public inspection and is available on the FSA website at www.fsa.gov.uk.

2.9   Applications to vary and cancel Part IV Permission and end authorisation

Sections 44 and 45 of the Act and Chapter 6 of the FSA's Supervision Manual specify the circumstances in which a Part IV Permission can be varied or cancelled at the initiative of the firm concerned or by the FSA on its own initiative.

Variation will occur where the regulated activities carried on in the UK under a Part IV Permission are varied either by adding new regulated activities to the permission or by removing certain categories from it. Cancellation will occur where a firm has ceased to carry on all of the regulated activities for which it has a Part IV Permission or expects to cease carrying on such activities. For insurers the cancellation of a Part IV Permission is not altogether straightforward because of the long-tail nature of some of the liabilities under insurance contracts that may have been written.

A firm which is seeking to vary or cancel its Part IV Permission, should, before applying to do so, discuss its plans with its supervision team at the FSA as the FSA has wide powers to apply different or additional prudential rules even where the varied or additional business proposed does not *per se* require a variation to its existing Part IV Permissions.

2.9.1 Variation of permission

Under Section 44 of the Act, a firm may apply to the FSA to vary its Part IV Permission in order to:

(a) allow it to carry on further regulated activities; or
(b) reduce the number of regulated activities it is permitted to carry on; or
(c) vary the FSA's description of its regulated activities (including by the removal or variation of any limitation); or
(d) cancel any requirement imposed by the FSA; or
(e) vary any requirement imposed by the FSA.

An application for variation may include any one or more of the above. In dealing with any application to vary, the FSA can impose new limitations and requirements as well as vary existing ones. It will consider the application against the threshold conditions and the FSA's regulatory objectives in much the same way as it would consider a new application for authorisation, but with due regard to the principle of proportionality.

A firm that wishes to apply for variation of its Part IV Permission must do so in writing to the FSA and explain the variation it seeks. There is an ongoing duty to update the information submitted in connection with an application to vary a Part IV Permission in accordance with Principle for Business 11 referred to earlier in this Chapter.

Section 51(2) of the Act requires that the application for variation must contain a statement of:

(a) the desired variation; and
(b) the regulated activity or activities which the firm proposes to carry on if its permission is varied.

Other than above, there is no prescribed application form for variation. Instead, the FSA, on receipt of the application, will advise the firm of any additional information which is required as part of its application. The FSA may at any time during the approval process require the applicant to provide additional information or documents. Information that may be requested includes business plans, financial projections, future regulatory compliance proposals and details of any changes in the persons performing controlled functions or in the functions they perform. Where an insurer is applying to add categories of insurance business to its Part IV Permission, it will also need to provide details of its existing business by submitting a scheme of operations in the current format specified in the Supervision Manual. Care will also need to be taken to ensure that the application for variation encompasses all the ancillary activities that may now need to be carried on. It will be necessary to make considerations similar to those specified in relation to a new authorisation.

Where the FSA considers that the variation constitutes a significant change in the firm's business or risk profile, it may require the firm to resubmit an application pack or certain sections of it.

Where a variation involves a change in the controlled functions of existing personnel or the appointment of new personnel to perform controlled functions, the firm should, at the same time as applying for variation, apply to the FSA for approval or transfer of its approved persons or notify the FSA of any approved person who has ceased to perform a controlled function.

In relation to a firm which is applying to vary its Part IV Permission by removing certain categories of specified investments in relation to insurance business, the application, if approved will mean that the applicant is no longer authorised to effect contracts of insurance in the relevant class, but will continue to be authorised to carry out contracts of insurance in the relevant class. This will enable the firm concerned to run off those contracts written in the former class. If, as a result of a variation, there are no longer any regulated activities for which the firm has permission, then under Section 45(3) of the Act, the FSA must cancel the permission using its own initiative powers. When the business has been run off completely, the firm should apply for removal of the permission to carry out the relevant regulated activity.

When varying a firm's Part IV Permission at the firm's request, the FSA has, under Section 44(5) of the Act, the same powers as those available to it when granting a new Part IV Permission in response to an authorisation application, including power to:

(a) specify in the description of a regulated activity a limitation; or
(b) specify a narrower or wider description of regulated activity than applied for; or

(c)   require the firm not to take a specified action (e.g. hold client money); or

(d)   require the firm to take a specified action (e.g. submit financial returns more frequently than normal).

However, the FSA will not use the power to grant a Part IV Permission for a regulated activity which was not included in the original application if the firm is applying to vary its Part IV Permission to carry on regulated activities that include insurance business.

Under Section 51(1) of the Act, the FSA has six months to consider a completed application. Where the FSA receives an application that is incomplete, Section 52(2) of the Act requires the FSA to determine that incomplete application within 12 months of the initial receipt of the application. Similar issues concerning the point at which an application for variation of a permission is complete arise as in respect of an original authorisation.

2.9.2   *Cancellation of permission*

A firm carrying on insurance business which ultimately intends to cease insurance business completely, will first need to apply for a variation of its Part IV Permission while it is running off its business. The firm should apply to remove the activity of effecting contracts of insurance from its Part IV Permission, thereby restricting its activities to carrying out insurance contracts to enable it to run off its business. Where an application is made for cancellation prior to the firm ceasing to carry on its regulated activities, the FSA will expect to review formal plans for the wind-down of the firm's activities in the period from the date of application.

If a firm wishes to cancel its Part IV Permission it must write to the FSA giving the reasons for its application and the date on which it ceased or intends to cease carrying on regulated activities. Cancellation applies to a firm's entire Part IV Permission and not to the individual elements such as specified investments, changes to which constitute a variation. The interests of consumers or any group of consumers are likely to be at the forefront of any decision to refuse an application to cancel a Part IV Permission.

The information concerning the circumstances of the application for cancellation and the confirmation that a firm is required to give to the

FSA will differ according to the nature of the firm and the activities it has a Part IV Permission to carry on. For insurers, the FSA will expect to see:

(a)   an audited closing balance sheet which demonstrates that the firm has no liabilities to policyholders;
(b)   a report from the auditors or reporting accountants; and
(c)   in some cases an opinion as to the likelihood of any remaining liabilities to policyholders.

If a firm is transferring business, the FSA may also require a professional opinion in respect of the transfer. The FSA may at any time during the approval process require the applicant to provide additional information or documents. The FSA will also expect to receive a copy of the board resolution of the applicant resolving to cancel the Part IV Permission.

At the same time as it applies for cancellation of its Part IV Permission the firm should notify the FSA of the persons ceasing to perform controlled functions.

Before the FSA cancels a firm's Part IV Permission the firm will be expected to be able to demonstrate that it has ceased or transferred all regulated activities under that permission. For example, the firm may be asked to provide evidence that a transfer of business is complete.

In deciding whether to cancel a firm's Part IV Permission, the FSA will take into account all relevant factors in relation to business carried on under that permission including whether there are unresolved or undischarged complaints and whether the firm has repaid all client deposits.

Where the FSA has granted an application for cancellation of a Part IV Permission and withdrawn a firm's status as an authorised person it will still retain certain investigative and enforcement powers in relation to the firm as a former authorised person.

Under Section 51(1) of the Act, the FSA has six months to consider a completed application. Where the FSA receives an application that is incomplete, Section 52(2) of the Act requires the FSA to determine that incomplete application within 12 months of the initial receipt of the application. Similar issues concerning the point at which an application for variation of a permission apply to a variation as apply in respect of an original authorisation.

2.9.3   Ending authorisation

Section 33 of the Act requires that where a firm's authorisation is cancelled, and as a result there are no regulated activities carried on by the firm in question, the FSA is required to give a direction withdrawing the firm's status as an authorised person. It must also update the firm's entry in the register to show that it has ceased to be authorised.

2.10   Applicants with a head office outside the EEA seeking to establish a branch in the UK

So far, this Chapter has addressed the provisions applicable to a UK entity applying for authorisation under the Act. It is permissible for an entity that is not incorporated in the UK or in the EEA to apply for authorisation under the Act by establishing a branch. This section looks at the provisions of the regulatory system applicable to such applicants.

The first and most important point to note is that in considering a branch application, the FSA will assess the applicant's application having regard to its situation as a whole (and not just to the circumstances of the proposed branch). This means that the regulatory requirements will apply to a firm in full and worldwide, and where necessary waivers, limitations and requirements will be used to ensure that appropriate prudential requirements apply to the branch. In making this assessment of the applicant for Part IV Permission as a whole, the FSA will take into account all relevant matters, including the extent to which the applicant is regulated in its home state. The FSA will seek to liase with any home state regulator and will take into account information from it with respect to, for example, the adequacy of the applicant's resources and the applicant's suitability, having regard to the need to ensure that the applicant's affairs are conducted soundly and prudently. Information with respect to the conduct of the applicant's affairs would extend in particular to the adequacy of the internal control systems under SYSC.

The Financial Services and Markets Act 2000 (Variation of Threshold Conditions) Order 2001 makes certain amendments to the applicable threshold conditions for non-EEA applicants. Under the order such an applicant must:

(a)   have a representative who is resident in the UK and who has authority to bind the applicant in its relations with third parties and

to represent it in its relations with the authority and in the courts of the UK;
(b)   be a body corporate entitled under the laws of the place where its head office is situated to effect and carry out contracts of insurance;
(c)   have assets of such value as may be specified located in the UK;
(d)   unless the regulated activity in question relates solely to reinsurance, it must have made a deposit (of money or securities as may be specified) of such an amount and with such a person as may be specified and on such terms and subject to such other provisions as may be specified.

The order makes certain additional amendments in relation to Swiss general insurance companies, which are not generally covered by this Chapter.

The FSA's regulatory requirements, including IPRU(INS), will apply to a branch applicant in full and worldwide, unless otherwise stated. In relation to the approved persons regime, there are three additional positions that for insurers require notification to the FSA rather than approval. These are:

(a)   the firm's worldwide chief executive where the person holding the position is situated outside the UK;
(b)   the person, if not the worldwide chief executive, within the overseas firm with a purely strategic responsibility for UK operations;
(c)   for a UK branch of an insurer, the authorised UK representative.

If the FSA considers that the applicant may be unable to satisfy the threshold conditions and that this cannot be addressed by the use of limitations and requirements, the FSA would have to conclude that a branch presence in the UK would be inappropriate. In such circumstances, the applicant may wish to consider forming a UK incorporated subsidiary as an alternative method of obtaining a presence in the UK.

2.11   Passporting of EEA and treaty firms

Much of the foregoing provisions of this Chapter relate to the first method of authorisation under the Act, namely by way of a Part IV Permission. The following sections of this Chapter relate to the second principal method of authorisation, which is by way of exercise or a passport right by an EEA firm. Specific provisions concerning the provision of services cross-border are dealt with elsewhere in this work. Schedule 3 to the Act deals with EEA firms qualifying for authorisation, and Schedule 4 to the Act deals with treaty firms.

2.11.1 EEA firms

Schedule 3, Part 1 applies to EEA firms seeking to exercise rights under the single market directives. Included within the definition of the single market directives are the insurance directives, namely the first, second and third life and non-life insurance directives. An EEA firm is defined in Schedule 3. The first requirement is that the firm must not have its head office in the UK. The definition includes "an undertaking pursuing the activity of direct insurance ... which has received authorisation under Article 6 from its home state regulator".

It is important to note that the directive applies to direct insurance only. Reinsurers will be treated as treaty firms and are discussed further below.

Schedule 3 also defines the expressions "EEA authorisation", "EEA right", "EEA State", "home state regulator", "UK firm" and "host state regulator".

The basic principle is set out in paragraph 12 of Schedule 3. Once a firm, which is seeking to establish a branch in the UK in exercise of an EEA right, satisfies the establishment conditions it qualifies for authorisation.

The establishment conditions are set out in paragraph 13(1) of Schedule 3 and state:

> "The establishment conditions are –
> (a) the Authority has received notice ("a consent notice") from the firm's home state regulator that it has given the firm consent to establish a branch in the UK;
> (b) the consent notice –
>   (i) is given in accordance with the relevant single market directive;
>   (ii) identifies the activities to which the consent relates; and
>   (iii) includes such other conditions as may be prescribed; and
> (c) the firm has been informed of the applicable provisions or two months have elapsed beginning with the date on which the Authority received the consent notice."

Where it has received a consent notice, the FSA is required to prepare for the firm's supervision, notify the firm of any applicable provisions and (because the firm will be an insurance firm) notify the home state regulator of any applicable provisions. Such a notification must be given within two months of the receipt of the consent notice. Applicable provisions mean the host state rules with which the firm is required to comply when carrying on a permitted activity identified in the consent notice. The host state rules will mean the rules made in accordance with the applicable single market directive and which are the responsibility of the UK both as to implementation and supervision of compliance in accordance with that directive.

Where an EEA firm has satisfied the requirements with regard to qualification, it is permitted to carry out the regulated activities referred to in the consent notice on terms equivalent to those contained in the consent notice. Where an EEA firm carries out a regulated activity for which it has not qualified for authorisation, Sections 26, 27 and 29 of the Act, relating to the enforceability of contracts entered into in breach of the general prohibition (*see* above), do not apply to agreements entered into by the firm.

2.11.2   Treaty firms

A treaty firm is defined in Schedule 4 to the Act as:

> "a person –
> (a)   whose head office is situated in an EEA state (its "home state") other than the UK; and
> (b)   which is recognised under the law of that state as its national."

Home state regulator is defined in relation to a treaty firm as "the competent authority of the firm's home state for the purpose of its home state authorisation".

Once a treaty firm has received authorisation under the law of its home state to carry on the regulated activity in question, it qualifies for authorisation provided:

(a)   the laws of the firm's home state provide equivalent protection or satisfy certain conditions laid down by a Community instrument for the coordination or approximation of laws, regulations or administrative provisions of Member States relating to the carrying on of that activity; and

(b)   the firm has no EEA right to carry on the activity concerned.

The home state regulator must inform the FSA that the firm has home state authorisation in order to qualify.

For the purposes of this requirement, provisions afford equivalent protection if, in relation to the firm's carrying on of the permitted activity they afford consumers protection which is at least equivalent to that afforded by or under the Act in relation to that activity. A certificate issued by the Treasury that the provisions of a law of a particular EEA State afford equivalent protection in relation to the activities specified in the certificate is conclusive evidence of that fact.

On qualifying in this manner, a firm has permission to carry on each permitted activity through its UK branch or by providing cross-border services on terms equivalent to those to which the firm's home state is subject.

In the context of insurers, this provision would normally be used to permit the carrying on of reinsurance activities by an EEA firm. Thus, for example, a firm authorised in another EEA State carrying on insurance and reinsurance business would exercise an EEA passporting right in respect of its insurance business and a treaty right in respect of its reinsurance business. This is dealt with in more detail elsewhere in this work, but reference is made here for the sake of completeness.

Figure 4: The application process

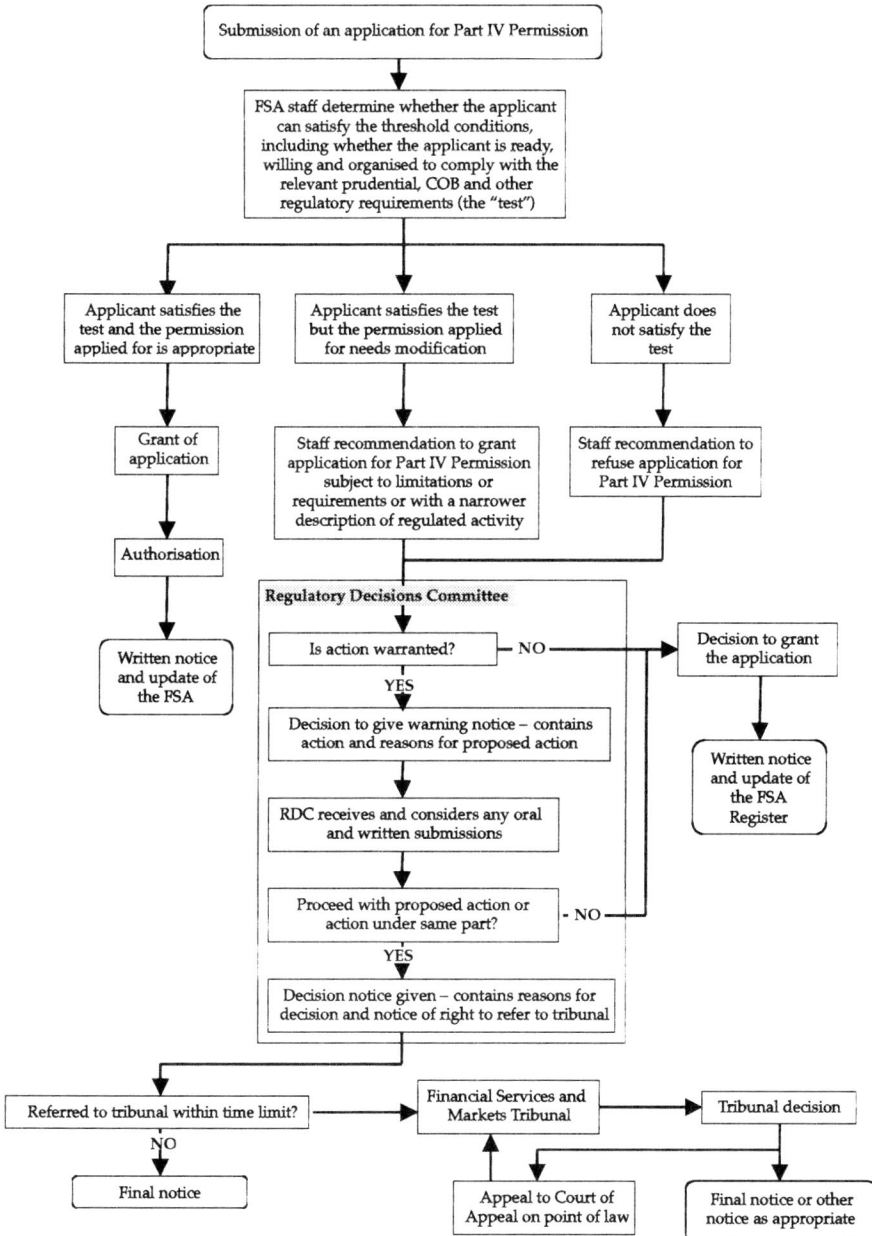

```
┌──────────────────────────────────────────┐
│ Submission of an application for Part IV Permission │
└──────────────────────────────────────────┘
                       │
┌──────────────────────────────────────────┐
│ FSA staff determine whether the applicant │
│ can satisfy the threshold conditions,     │
│ including whether the applicant is ready, │
│ willing and organised to comply with the  │
│ relevant prudential, COB and other        │
│ regulatory requirements (the "test")      │
└──────────────────────────────────────────┘
```

Applicant satisfies the test and the permission applied for is appropriate	Applicant satisfies the test but the permission applied for needs modification	Applicant does not satisfy the test

Grant of application → **Authorisation** → **Written notice and update of the FSA**

Staff recommendation to grant application for Part IV Permission subject to limitations or requirements or with a narrower description of regulated activity

Staff recommendation to refuse application for Part IV Permission

Regulatory Decisions Committee

- Is action warranted? — NO → **Decision to grant the application** → **Written notice and update of the FSA Register**
- YES
- Decision to give warning notice – contains action and reasons for proposed action
- RDC receives and considers any oral and written submissions
- Proceed with proposed action or action under same part? – NO →
- YES
- Decision notice given – contains reasons for decision and notice of right to refer to tribunal

Referred to tribunal within time limit? → **Financial Services and Markets Tribunal** → **Tribunal decision**

NO → **Final notice**

Appeal to Court of Appeal on point of law

Final notice or other notice as appropriate

Chapter 3

Ownership and Management of Insurance Companies

Katherine Coates, Hilary Evenett

Partners, Financial Institutions Group
Clifford Chance

3.1 Ownership of insurance companies

3.1.1 Introduction to the provisions of the Financial Services and Markets Act 2000

In relation to the acquisition of ownership and control of insurance companies, the Financial Services and Markets Act (the Act) has not substantially changed the core requirement of the regulatory regime established under the Insurance Companies Act 1982, that is to say the requirement for a person to obtain prior approval before becoming a controller (very broadly, a person who holds 10 per cent or more of the shares in an insurance company or one of its parents or the managing director of an insurer or one of its parents). However, there have been a number of changes to the detail of the controller regime. The provisions of Part XII of the Act establish the new framework under which persons are obliged to notify the FSA of intended acquisitions, and increases and reductions of control over authorised persons. Subsections 178(1) and 190(1) of the Act provide as follows:

> "178(1) If a step which a person proposes to take would result in his acquiring –
>
> (a) control over a UK authorised person;
> (b) an additional kind of control over a UK authorised person; or
> (c) an increase in a relevant kind of control which he already has over a UK authorised person,
>
> he must notify the Authority of his proposal.

190(1) If a step which a controller of a UK authorised person proposes to take would result in his –

(a) ceasing to have control of a relevant kind over the authorised person; or

(b) reducing a relevant kind of control over that person,

he must notify the Authority of his proposal."

Section 179 provides that a person (under Section 179(3) "a person" includes the person *or* any associates, or the person *and* any associates) acquires control over a firm where he:

(a) holds 10 per cent or more of the shares of the firm or its parent; or

(b) is able to exercise significant influence over the management of the firm or its parent by virtue of his shareholding in the firm or its parent respectively; or

(c) is entitled to exercise, or control the exercise of, 10 per cent or more of the voting power in the firm or its parent; or

(d) is able to exercise significant influence over the management of the firm or its parent by virtue of his voting power in the firm or its parent.

A person who is already a controller of one kind in relation to a firm requires approval if that person subsequently acquires another sort of control. For example, a person who is a controller by virtue of a shareholding in a firm's parent company would require prior approval if that person proposed to acquire a 15 per cent stake directly in the firm.

The Act establishes four percentage thresholds in respect of an increase or reduction in the firm's (or its parent's) shares or voting power which will trigger the notification requirements. These percentage thresholds are 10 per cent, 20 per cent, 33 per cent and 50 per cent.[1] Thus an increase or decrease of control passing through any of the thresholds requires consent.

For these purposes, the definition of controller includes any of the controller's associates or the controller and any of his associates.[2] However, it no longer includes the managing director of a parent company of a firm.

---

[1] Subsections 180(1) and (2) and 181(1) and (2).
[2] Subsections 180(3) and 181(3).

These provisions relate only to control over a UK-authorised person, which is defined in Section 178(4) (subject to certain exceptions) as a body incorporated in (or an unincorporated association formed under the law of) any part of the UK.

Accordingly, controllers or proposed controllers of entities which are not registered or formed in the UK will no longer require pre-approval.

Another change resulting from the new regime is that the pre-approval requirement no longer applies to a person who unintentionally acquires or ceases to have control of an insurer. Under Section 178(2) such persons are now simply required to notify the FSA within 14 days of the relevant event.

3.1.2 Requirements imposed on controllers and proposed controllers

3.1.2.1 Acquisitions and increases in control

Prior to a proposed controller acquiring control over (or an existing controller increasing its control over) a firm, it is required to notify the FSA, by means of a notice of control in the prescribed form, of its proposal to acquire or increase control as the case may be. Under Section 183(1) the FSA will then have three months from the date on which it receives the notice of control either to approve the proposal or to issue a warning notice notifying the proposed controller that it intends to issue a notice of objection to the proposals or that it intends to impose conditions on the proposed controller.

If the FSA receives notification from a firm as opposed to a controller, or becomes aware of a possible breach by a controller in relation to the obligation to notify under Section 178(1) or (2) of the Act, the FSA may require the person concerned to provide additional information under Section 188(4) of the Act. Upon receipt of this further information it will then be open to the FSA to either approve the notification as if it had been properly received from the controller, or, if there has been a breach and the approval requirements have not been met, to issue a warning notice.

There are two approval criteria set out in Section 186(2) of the Act. Firstly, the acquirer must be a fit and proper person to have control over the authorised person and, secondly, the interests of consumers must not be threatened by the acquirer's control or by his acquiring that control.

If the FSA fails to determine whether to approve or issue a warning notice in respect of a particular proposal within the three-month period then, under Section 184(2) of the Act, the FSA will be deemed to have approved the proposal.

Once the proposed controller or controller has either acquired or increased control as the case may be, he is again required to notify the FSA. This notification may be made jointly with the firm.

3.1.2.2 Improperly acquired shares

If a controller has acquired or continues to hold shares in contravention of a notice of objection issued by the FSA or a condition imposed on the FSA's approval, the FSA may issue a restriction notice to such controller restricting those shares in accordance with subsections 189(2)(a)–(d). Furthermore, the FSA may apply to court for an order for the sale of the shares concerned provided that either:

(a)   the time within which reference may be made to the Tribunal in respect of the notice of objection has expired; or

(b)   where a reference to the Tribunal has been made, the matter has either been determined or withdrawn.[3]

3.1.2.3 Reductions in control

Where a controller's control over a firm is reduced below one of the percentage thresholds mentioned above, the FSA must be notified in accordance with Section 190 of the Act. However, the FSA's formal approval is not required prior to the reduction taking place. Once the reduction has taken place, the FSA must again be notified in the prescribed form.

3.1.3 Requirements imposed on the controlled firm

There are two instances in which both UK domestic firms and overseas firms are required to notify the FSA of a change in control. Firstly, where a person is acquiring or ceasing to have control and secondly where an existing controller is becoming or ceasing to be a parent undertaking.[4] In addition, UK domestic firms are required to notify the FSA where an existing controller is acquiring an additional kind of control or ceasing to have a kind of control, or where an existing controller is increasing or decreasing a kind of control which he already has so that the percentage of shares or voting power concerned becomes or ceases to be equal to or greater than 20 per cent, 33 per cent or 50 per cent.[5] The firm's written

---

[3] Subsections 189(3) and (4)(a) and (b).

[4] SUP 11.4.2R(1) and (4); SUP 11.4.4.R(1) and (2).

[5] SUP 11.4.2.R (2) and (3).

notification must be in the prescribed form and must be made as soon as the firm becomes aware that a person is proposing to take a step that would result in the event concerned or, where the event takes place without the knowledge of the firm, within 14 days of the firm becoming aware of the event.[6]

A new requirement is that a firm must notify the FSA if it becomes aware of certain changes in the circumstances of its controller, namely if there is a significant deterioration in the financial position of the controller, if there is a substantial change to the controller's governing body, or if the controller is involved in legal proceedings or an investigation which may bring into question the integrity of the controller.[7]

The FSA's view (as set out in SUP 11.4.8G) is that firms should discuss at the earliest opportunity any prospective changes in controllers' or proposed controllers' shareholdings or voting power if such change is material:

"As a minimum ... such discussions should take place before a person:
(i)   enters into any formal agreement in respect of the purchase of shares or a proposed acquisition or merger which would result in a change in control (whether or not the agreement is conditional upon any matter, including the FSA's approval); or
(ii)   purchases any share options, warrants or other financial instruments, the exercise of which would result in the person acquiring control or any other change in control."

This Guidance codifies what was, in any event, always regarded as good practice.

The FSA requires firms to "take reasonable steps" to keep themselves informed about the identity of their controllers, and requires them to submit an annual report (within four months of their accounting reference date) as to who their controllers were on that date.[8]

Annex 1G to Chapter 11 of the Supervision Manual in the Handbook provides a useful summary of notifications required by both controllers and the firms controlled by the FSA.

---

[6] SUP 11.4.7R.
[7] SUP 11.8.1R.
[8] SUP 16.5.4R.

3.1.4 *Offences*

Section 191 of the Act provides that, *inter alia,* failure to notify the FSA in relation to an acquisition or increase or decrease in control is an offence and guilty persons will be liable on summary conviction to a fine. If a person to whom a notice of objection is given acquires the control to which the notice applies, he will be guilty of an offence and will be liable on summary conviction to a fine and/or on conviction on indictment to imprisonment for a term not exceeding two years.

3.2   Management of insurance companies

3.2.1   *Introduction to the "approved persons" regime*

The formal regulation of the management of insurance companies has been significantly altered by the Act which introduces an entirely new system under which certain individuals who carry out what the FSA refers to as "controlled functions" for an authorised person will need to be approved by the FSA. This new system is generally referred to as the "approved persons" regime (the AP regime). Approval requirements apply both to those in managerial positions (e.g. directors, service managers and compliance heads) and to those with customer responsibilities (e.g. advisers). Insurance firms regulated by the FSA will now be required to take a proactive approach in considering both the controlled functions performed within the firm and who will perform those functions. The pre-approval AP regime necessitates the establishment and maintenance by authorised insurance firms of appropriate internal controls which facilitate both organisational structuring and ongoing compliance with the provisions and rules contained in the Act and the FSA Handbook of rules and guidance ("the Handbook"), respectively. Firms will need to map the new categories of controlled functions onto their existing organisational structures and document the division of responsibilities and job descriptions. It is important that firms adequately consider the actual functions undertaken by an individual, as mere job title will not be sufficient to satisfy the requirements under the new regime. In particular, they will have to decide how to address the FSA's requirements relating to how certain of the managerial functions are allocated within the firm.

Concerns were raised during the consultation process preceding the finalisation of the Handbook that the AP regime could lead to increased levels of bureaucracy, external interference in the management of firms and generally an increase in the regulatory requirements to be complied with by the industry which is already subject to a relatively high level of regulation. Accordingly, the FSA has attempted to strike a balance:

> "between relying on those who manage the firm's affairs to employ appropriate staff, without intervention from the FSA, and seeking to ensure that such staff are fit and proper, in the interest of customers and potential customers."[9]

3.2.1.1 *The purpose of the AP regime*

The AP regime provides for the direct regulation of individuals (and in certain circumstances bodies corporate) which is intended by the FSA to complement the regulation of authorised firms.[10] The concept of risk-based regulation flows throughout the new regulatory regime established under the Act. The FSA adopts a "prevention is better than cure" approach and is clearly intending the AP regime to perform a central role in this approach. The main aim is to ensure that fit and proper persons with the appropriate qualifications undertake those functions within an insurance firm which are likely to have an impact on the integrity of the firm and the industry as a whole and are likely to affect consumers and potential consumers.

3.2.1.2 *The provisions of the Act*

Section 59 of the Act requires an authorised person to take "reasonable care to ensure" that no person performs a controlled function under an arrangement entered into by the authorised person (or a contractor of the authorised person) unless approval for the performance of that function has been obtained from the FSA. Accordingly, the authorised person must ensure that personnel are not performing controlled functions without the FSA's approval and should apply for approval of an individual who will be performing a controlled function prior to that function being assumed by the relevant individual. The person performing the function may not necessarily be an employee of the firm. For example, in a group there may be staff employed by one firm who carry out certain functions within other group firms. Those staff will require approval in relation to each firm for which they carry out the functions.

Under the Act the FSA has three months to consider an application for approval. This could cause practical problems for firms needing to make

---

[9] Consultation Paper 53: The Regulation of Approved Persons: Controlled Functions, June 2000, page 8.
[10] SUP 10.2.3G.

appointments in a timely fashion. The FSA have stated that they expect routine cases to be dealt with in a matter of days. There are also provisions which allow persons to carry out controlled functions for up to 12 weeks within a 12-month period without having to obtain the FSA's approval. This allows for emergency cover for sickness or holidays, for example.[11]

3.2.1.3   Notification of changes

If a person who has been approved to perform one particular function wishes to carry out another, different, function the firm must apply to the FSA for approval in relation to the second, new function, and the approved person must not carry out the second function before approval has been obtained. If there are any changes to the information previously submitted in respect of an approved person then the FSA must be notified. Lastly, the FSA must be notified within seven days of a person ceasing to perform a controlled function.

3.2.1.4   Fit and proper test for approved persons ("FIT")

FIT is the standard used by the FSA to assess whether or not to grant approval to a person to perform a controlled function. Once the FSA has approved an individual, that person must remain fit and proper to carry out his functions in addition to observing the standards of conduct set out in APER. Failure to do so could, *inter alia*, result in the FSA withdrawing its approval.

The FSA will have regard to a number of factors when assessing the fitness and propriety of a person to perform a particular controlled function. The most important factors are the person's honesty, integrity and reputation; competency and capability; and financial soundness. Further guidance in relation to the FSA's methods of assessing these factors are to be found at FIT 2.1.3G, 2.2G and 2.3G.

The FSA will also take into account the activities of the firm for which the controlled function is or is to be performed, the permission held by that firm and the markets within which it operates.

3.2.2   Application of the AP regime

3.2.2.1   To which firms does the AP regime apply?

The notes contained in Chapter 10 of the Supervision Manual of the Handbook set out the boundaries of application of the AP regime. The

---

[11] SUP 10.5.5.R.

general rule is that the AP regime applies to every firm, although there are certain exceptions. Chapter 10 does not apply to overseas firms (i.e. firms which have their registered office or head office outside the UK) unless the overseas firm concerned carries on regulated activities from an "establishment maintained by it or its appointed representative" in the UK.[12] Where this is the case the AP regime applies in a slightly restricted form and members of governing bodies of such firms, other than the chief executives, do not fall within the AP regime.

In relation to EEA firms, where the FSA is not responsible for prudential supervision, the AP regime does not apply to their governing bodies. However, the FSA is responsible for the supervision of the conduct of business of EEA firms, and therefore the FSA has included in the list of controlled functions a specific function (which is a required function) which is called the EEA Investment Business Oversight Function. This function is to be fulfilled by the individual who is responsible for an EEA firm's compliance with the UK conduct of business requirements in respect of designated investment business (which includes life assurance).

3.2.2.2   *To which persons does the AP regime apply?*
The AP regime will apply to those persons who perform controlled functions within an authorised insurance firm. The focus is on the functions performed by an individual as opposed to his job title.

The AP regime is essentially directed at the governing body and senior management of an authorised firm. Once approval has been obtained for the particular person to perform the controlled functions, and the relevant individual has been designated as an "approved person" by the FSA, personal culpability will attach to that person in certain circumstances if his conduct falls short of that required of approved persons.

3.2.3   *Controlled functions*

3.2.3.1   *Specification of the controlled functions*
The Act does not specify the controlled functions central to the AP regime but rather leaves it to the FSA to determine which functions are to be controlled functions necessitating prior approval for their performance. This approach is clearly adopted to allow the FSA flexibility in the specification process which is necessary in light of the

---

[12] SUP 10.1.6.R.

range of financial service industries regulated by it and the changing commercial and organisational structures of the firms authorised by it.

As explained above, individuals are required to be approved by the FSA in order to carry out a controlled function.

There are 27 controlled functions specified in the new regime and they are grouped into five categories: the governing functions, the required functions, the systems and control functions, the significant management functions, and the customer functions. They are set out at SUP 10.4.5R.

Table 1: Controlled functions

Type	CF	Description of controlled function
Governing functions*	1	Director function
	2	Non-executive director function
	3	Chief executive function
	4	Partner function
	5	Director of unincorporated association function
	6	Small friendly society function
	7	Sole trader function
Required functions*	8	Apportionment and oversight function
	9	EEA investment business oversight function
	10	Compliance oversight function
	11	Money laundering reporting function
	12	Appointed Actuary function
Systems and control functions*	13	Finance function
	14	Risk assessment function
	15	Internal audit function
Significant management functions*	16	Significant management (designated investment business) function
	17	Significant management (other business operations) function
	18	Significant management (insurance underwriting) function
	19	Significant management (financial resources) function

Table 1: *Continued*

Type	CF	Description of controlled function
	20	Significant management (settlements) function
Customer functions	21	Investment adviser function
	22	Investment adviser (trainee) function
	23	Corporate finance adviser function
	24	Pension transfer specialist function
	25	Adviser on syndicate participation at Lloyd's function
	26	Customer trading function
	27	Investment management function

*significant influence functions

3.2.3.2   Significant influence functions

The significant influence functions comprise the governing functions, the required functions, the systems and control functions and the significant management functions. As their title suggests, each significant influence function is one which is likely to result in the person responsible for its performance exercising a significant influence on the conduct of a firm's affairs, so far as they relate to a regulated activity of the firm. The persons performing these functions are likely to play an important part in ensuring that effective governance structures and systems and controls are developed and operated.[13]

As far as the directors of an insurance company are concerned, they will require approval to perform the governing function and, depending on the division of responsibility within the company, they may also perform (and hence require approval for) certain of the other significant influence functions. In relation to the governing function, every director (both executive and non-executive) of a body corporate will perform the governing function, that is he will be responsible for directing a firm's affairs and will therefore be required to be approved by the FSA. A person who is approved to perform a governing function (other than the non-executive function) will not have to be specifically approved to perform any of the systems and controls functions or the significant

---

[13] SUP 10.5.4R.

management functions, although additional approval will need to be obtained before he can perform any of the required functions or customer functions.[14]

3.2.4 High-level standards

3.2.4.1   Senior management arrangements, systems and controls ("SYSC")Purpose of SYSC

SYSC is a body of rules contained in the High-level Standards Manual of the Handbook, the stated purpose of the rules being:

(a)   to encourage firms' directors and senior managers to take practical responsibility for a firm's arrangements on matters which are likely to be of interest to the FSA because they impact on the FSA's functions under the Act;

(b)   to increase certainty by amplifying Principle 3, under which a firm is required to take reasonable care to organise and control its affairs responsibly, effectively and with adequate risk management systems; and

(c)   to encourage firms to vest responsibility for effective and responsible organisation in specific directors and senior managers.[15]

The FSA emphasised in the consultation process that in its view the rules contained in SYSC do not go beyond "accepted standards of good business practice".[16]

Senior management arrangements: apportionment and allocation
Firms are now required under the new regime to take reasonable care to maintain clear and appropriate apportionment of significant responsibilities among both its directors and senior managers. The apportionment must be effected such that "it is clear who has which of those responsibilities"[17] and "the business and affairs of the firm can be adequately monitored and controlled by the directors, relevant senior managers and governing body of the firm".[18] In order to monitor the apportionment of responsibilities, firms are required to appropriately

---

[14] SUP 10.6.3G.

[15] SYSC 1.2.1G.

[16] Consultation paper 35. Senior management arrangements, systems and controls, page 8.

[17] SYSC 2.1.1R(1).

[18] SYSC 2.1.1R(2).

allocate to one or more individuals (usually the firm's chief executive(s) or a director or senior manager responsible for the overall management of the group or a group division)[19] the functions of dealing with the apportionment of responsibilities and overseeing the establishment and maintenance of systems and controls. Furthermore, authorised firms are required by SYSC 2.2.1R(1) to ensure that they have adequate record-keeping controls in place recording the arrangements made to satisfy the rules in relation to appropriation and allocation.

Although the practical implications of the dual concepts of reasonableness and appropriateness are difficult to determine at this early stage, some guidance may be sought from the FSA's guidance note[20] in relation to the record-keeping requirement.

The FSA is of the view that appropriate records may include:

- organisational charts and diagrams,
- project management documents,
- job descriptions,
- committee constitutions, and
- terms of reference provided they show a clear description of the firm's major functions.

It is likely that most insurance firms will already have created this documentation and they will now need to build on it to reflect the apportionment and allocation within the firm. The FSA is aiming to enhance and enforce compliance culture within the firms it regulates. Central to this culture will be the requirement that firms establish and keep up-to-date and adequate records reflecting their internal compliance controls.

Systems and controls

SYSC 3.1.1R states that "[a] firm must take reasonable care to establish and maintain such systems and controls as are appropriate to its business". The FSA gives guidance[21] as to the factors which should be taken into account when determining the nature and extent of the systems and controls which a firm will need to maintain. These factors include the nature, scale and complexity of its business; the diversity of

---

[19] Firms must refer to the Allocation of Functions table at SYSC 2.1.4R to determine who in their organisation these functions must be allocated to.

[20] SYSC 2.2.2G(1).

[21] SYSC 3.1.2G.

its operations, including geographical diversity; the volume and size of its transactions; and the degree of risk associated with each area of its operation.

In determining which systems and controls are to be established in order to satisfy the FSA's requirements an insurance company will need to start by considering the areas listed and discussed by the FSA in paragraph 3.2 of SYSC in the High-level Standards Manual.

3.2.4.2   *Statements of principle and code of practice for approved persons ("APER")*

APER sets out Statements of Principle for approved persons and in accordance with Section 64(2) of the Act it also includes a code of practice in order to facilitate the FSA's determination of whether or not a person's conduct complies with the Statements of Principle.

Those approved persons who perform a significant influence function will be under a duty to comply with Statements of Principle 1–7; other approved persons will need to comply only with Statements of Principle 1–4 listed below.

Statements of Principle [22]
1. An approved person must act with integrity in carrying out his controlled function.
2. An approved person must act with due skill, care and diligence in carrying out his controlled function.
3. An approved person must observe proper standards of market conduct in carrying out his controlled function.
4. An approved person must deal with the FSA and with other regulators in an open and co-operative way and must disclose appropriately any information of which the FSA would reasonably expect notice.
5. An approved person performing a significant influence function must take reasonable steps to ensure that the business of the firm for which he is responsible in his controlled function is organised so that it can be controlled effectively.
6. An approved person performing a significant influence function must exercise due skill, care and diligence in managing the business of the firm for which he is responsible in his controlled function.
7. An approved person performing a significant influence function must take reasonable steps to ensure that the business of the firm for

---

[22] APER 2.1.2G.

which he is responsible in his controlled function complies with the relevant requirements and standards of the regulatory system.

The FSA considers[23] the following factors to be relevant when determining whether or not an approved person's conduct in relation to a controlled function complies with:

(a)   Statements of Principle 1, 2, 3 and 4:
    (i)   whether the conduct relates to activities that are subject to other provisions of the Handbook,
    (ii)   whether that conduct is consistent with the requirements and standards of the regulatory system relevant to the particular firm;

(b)   Statements of Principle 5 to 7:
    (i)   whether he exercised reasonable care when considering the information available to him,
    (ii)   whether he reached a reasonable conclusion which he acted on,
    (iii) the nature, scale and complexity of the firm's business,
    (iv) his role and responsibility as an approved person performing a significant influence function,
    (v)   the knowledge he had, or should have had, of regulatory concerns, if any, arising in the business under his control.

As would be expected, the principles to be complied with by an approved person performing a significant influence function are far wider in scope than those relating to other approved persons. In relation to the first two factors discussed under Statements of Principle 5–7, the concept of reasonableness once again emerges. In so far as practicable, it is advisable for approved persons to adequately document their consideration and consequent conclusions reached in relation to the controlled functions which they perform so that, if called upon to do so, they would be in a position to defend their decisions and actions on the basis of reasonableness. The last factor listed under Statements of Principle 5–7 is interesting in that it once again highlights the level of compliance culture which the FSA is aiming to introduce and in particular the need for approved persons to ensure that they understand the regulatory regime within which their controlled function is to be performed.

---

[23] APER 3.2.1E and 3.3.1E.

The Code of Practice for Approved Persons ("the Code")
The Code is framed in the negative, in that it describes conduct which would be regarded by the FSA to be a breach of a Statement of Principle. An approved person will only be in breach of a Statement of Principle where he is personally culpable. The Code is not exhaustive of the kinds of conduct that may contravene the Statements of Principle.

3.2.5 Enforcement of the AP regime

In addition to the power of the FSA to withdraw its approval from an individual to perform a controlled function in the event that the standards of conduct set out in APER are not complied with, the FSA may take action against an approved person if he is found to be guilty of misconduct. An approved person will be guilty of misconduct if he fails to comply with a Statement of Principle or if he has been knowingly involved in a contravention of a requirement imposed by the Act on the authorised person for whom he performs the controlled function.[24] If the FSA takes disciplinary action against an approved person guilty of misconduct it may impose a penalty on him in such amount as it considers appropriate or it may publish a statement of his misconduct. In extreme cases the FSA may seek a prohibition order which will effectively ban the individual from holding a post involving responsibility for regulated activities.[25]

It is important to note that the FSA will only take disciplinary action against an approved person where there is evidence of personal culpability on the part of that approved person.[26] Personal culpability only arises where the FSA considers the approved person's behaviour to be deliberate or where the approved person's standard of behaviour was below that which would be reasonable in all the circumstances.

---

[24] Section 66, the Act.
[25] ENF 8.1.2G.
[26] ENF 11.5.3G.

Chapter 4

Financial Supervision

Hitesh Patel
Partner, Insurance Regulatory Services
KPMG

4.1 Background

4.1.1 What is financial supervision?

Section 2 of the Financial Services & Markets Act ("FSMA") 2000 (the "FSMA") sets out the regulatory objectives of the FSA as follows:

- maintain market confidence;
- promote public awareness;
- protect consumers;
- reduce financial crime.

The key objective of the financial supervision of insurance companies is to protect consumers by ensuring that companies have adequate financial resources (Principle 4) to carry on insurance business and are soundly and prudently managed. (Principle 3).

The current supervisory regime for insurance companies is largely set out in the Interim Prudential Sourcebook: Insurers ("IPRU (INS)") which was issued in June 2001 and came into effect on 1 December 2001 (the date known as "N2"). Although the source of the rules and guidance relating to financial supervision is new, the supervisory regime is largely unchanged from previous years. The legislation in the Insurance Companies Act 1982 and related regulation has been collated and restated in the Sourcebook.

This Chapter summarises the key supervisory tools and gives more detailed description and analysis below.

4.1.2 The regulatory return

Historically, the principal tool in the supervision of insurance companies has been the regulatory return. All UK authorised insurance companies are required to complete and submit an audited return on an annual basis, although individual companies may be required to complete them more frequently, usually quarterly. The return consists of a series of forms which set out financial details of the company's performance and financial position.

The key purpose of the return is to allow the FSA to monitor the solvency of authorised insurance companies, and additionally to assess any other risks and exposures companies may face.

Further detail on the regulatory return is given in section two. Solvency and the various rules on asset valuation and admissibility and liability determination are discussed in 4.3 and 4.4 below respectively.

4.1.3   Insurance Groups Directive ("IGD")

The IGD (the EC directive on the Supervision of Insurance Undertakings in Insurance Groups) became compulsory for companies with accounting periods beginning on or after 1 January 2001.

The main impact of the directive is the extension (in some circumstances) of the requirement for solvency calculations beyond the single authorised insurance company to companies sitting above it in the group structure, as well as fellow subsidiaries and associates in the same group or sub group.

A further implication is increased reporting of intragroup transactions.

Further detail is included in 4.5 below.

4.1.4   FSA guidance

One of the FSA's stated aims is to introduce a regime which takes more account of the risks faced by an entity, and places more emphasis on ensuring that the directors and senior managers of insurance companies are "fit and proper" individuals.

Insurance companies must comply with prudential guidance which was originally issued as Prudential Guidance Notes (PGNs) during the 1990s. These set out a number of appropriate systems and controls over various areas which, in the view of the regulator, constitute a sound and prudent manner in which to run an insurance company.

As part of the regulatory return, the directors of an insurance company must submit a certificate which states *inter alia* that the company has complied with this published guidance.

Further detail is included in 4.6 below.

4.1.5   *Other supervisory tools and issues*

There are a number of other tools which the FSA uses as part of the supervisory regime. Further detail is given on some of these in 4.7 below. These include:

- Financial condition reports
- Applying limitations or requirements to the firm's permission
- On site visits by supervisory team
- Information requests
- Desk based reviews of regulatory returns or other information requested by the supervisor
- Liaison with other regulators or agencies
- Meetings with management or other representatives of firms
- Review of periodic returns and notifications
- Reviews of past business
- Transactions monitoring
- Use of skilled persons.

These generic activities will be employed by the FSA across the board. To supplement them, more "firm-specific" tools can also be employed where the FSA considers this necessary. These can include:

- making recommendations for preventative or remedial action;
- giving other individual guidance to a firm;
- imposing other individual requirements;
- in more extreme cases, varying or withdrawing a firm's permission.

4.2   The regulatory return

4.2.1   *The requirement to prepare*

The requirement to prepare and submit the regulatory return is set out in Chapter 9 of Volume 1 of IPRU(INS) (the "Accounts and Statements Rules"). This stipulates that each year insurance companies must prepare a revenue account, a profit and loss account and a balance sheet at the end of the year.

The form and content of the return, along with guidance on which forms different companies are required to prepare, is set out in the Accounts and Statements Rules and the accompanying appendices. The format of the return is unchanged from the previous regime.

The Accounts and Statements Rules in Chapter 9 (IPRU(INS)) apply to every insurer authorised under FSMA 2000, other than:

(a) an EEA deposit insurer in relation to the insurance business carried on by it outside the UK; or
(b) a Swiss general insurer in relation to the general insurance business carried on by it outside the UK.

4.2.2 Submission

Historically the return has been submitted in hard copy form within a period of six months following the insurer's financial year end.

This deadline has been reduced at N2, and companies are now encouraged to submit electronically (on FSA approved software). An important advantage of opting for electronic submission is that the filing deadline is extended by 15 days.

The submission deadlines (as set out in Chapter 9.6 of IPRU(INS)) can be summarised as follows.

Table 1: Submission deadlines

Year end between:	Hard-copy submission	Electronic submission
31 December 2001–30 December 2002	3 months 15 days	4 months
31 December 2002 onwards	2 months 15 days	3 months

It is likely that these reducing deadlines will have a significant impact on the resources of firms, and year end procedures may well have to be altered in order to enable companies to comply.

4.2.3 Structure of the return (set out in Appendices to IPRU(INS))

The principal purpose of the content of the return is to allow the FSA to monitor solvency and also other risks and significant exposures facing those companies required to submit returns.

The structure of the return differs for general and long-term business – with the number of forms being greater for long-term business, reflecting the differences in the nature and complexity of the business written.

4.2.3.1 General business solvency and balance sheet forms

The relationships between the general business solvency and balance sheet forms can be shown as follows.

Figure 1: Structure of general business solvency and balance sheet forms

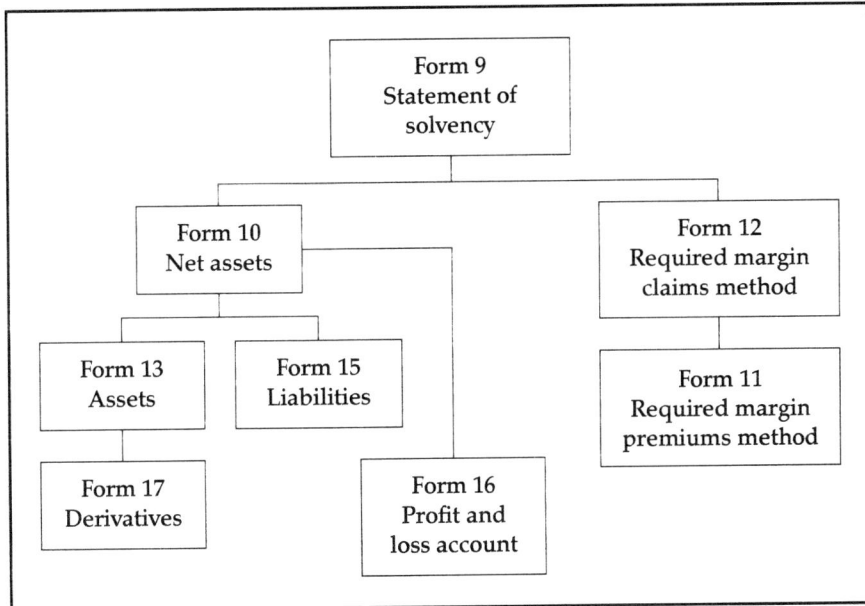

The solvency forms (9 and 10) summarise key solvency figures and compare the net assets available (derived from forms 13 and 15) with the required margin of solvency (calculated in forms 11 and 12). Forms 9 to 12 are generally considered the most critical forms as they contain the information pertaining to the key solvency monitoring objective of the regulatory return. Admissible assets are included in form 13 and technical provisions are set out in form 15.

4.2.3.2 *General business revenue forms*

The general business revenue forms (20 to 39) largely comprise analyses of premiums and claims by class of insurance business. This information is included as it allows the regulator to analyse the performance by class of business and to assess the adequacy of claims provisions by comparing actual claims movements with technical provisions when these were initially established.

The relationship between the various revenue forms is shown in Figure 2.

4.2.3.3 *Overview of long-term business forms*

An overview of the long-term business forms is set out in Figure 3.

As for general business, the long-term business solvency position is summarised on forms 9 and 10. In this case the solvency requirement is calculated in form 60. Details of technical provisions are set out on form 14, which is supplemented by an abstract of the Valuation Report of the Appointed Actuary (*see* 4.7.2 below). Long-term business revenue forms require significantly less detail than the general business equivalents as it is the valuation report which provides the detail on provisioning bases.

Due to the nature of the business there are additional forms required for long-term insurance, for example covering assets matching linked contracts and internal linked funds.

4.2.3.4 *Other content*

As well as the numerical forms which are outlined above there are a number of statements which must be provided to comply with the regulations included in Chapter 9 of IPRU(INS). A summary of the key statements are set out below.

(a) Information on major treaty (Regulation 9.25) and facultative (Regulation 9.26) reinsurers: Companies carrying on general insurance are required to prepare a statement of their major treaty and facultative reinsurers.

(b) Information on major general business reinsurance cedants (Regulation 9.27): General insurers are also required to provide a statement of their major cedants.

(c) Information on derivative and quasi-derivative contracts (Regulation 9.29): All insurers are required to provide a significant amount of information on the above, including an outline of investment guidelines on the use of derivatives.

Figure 2: General business revenue forms

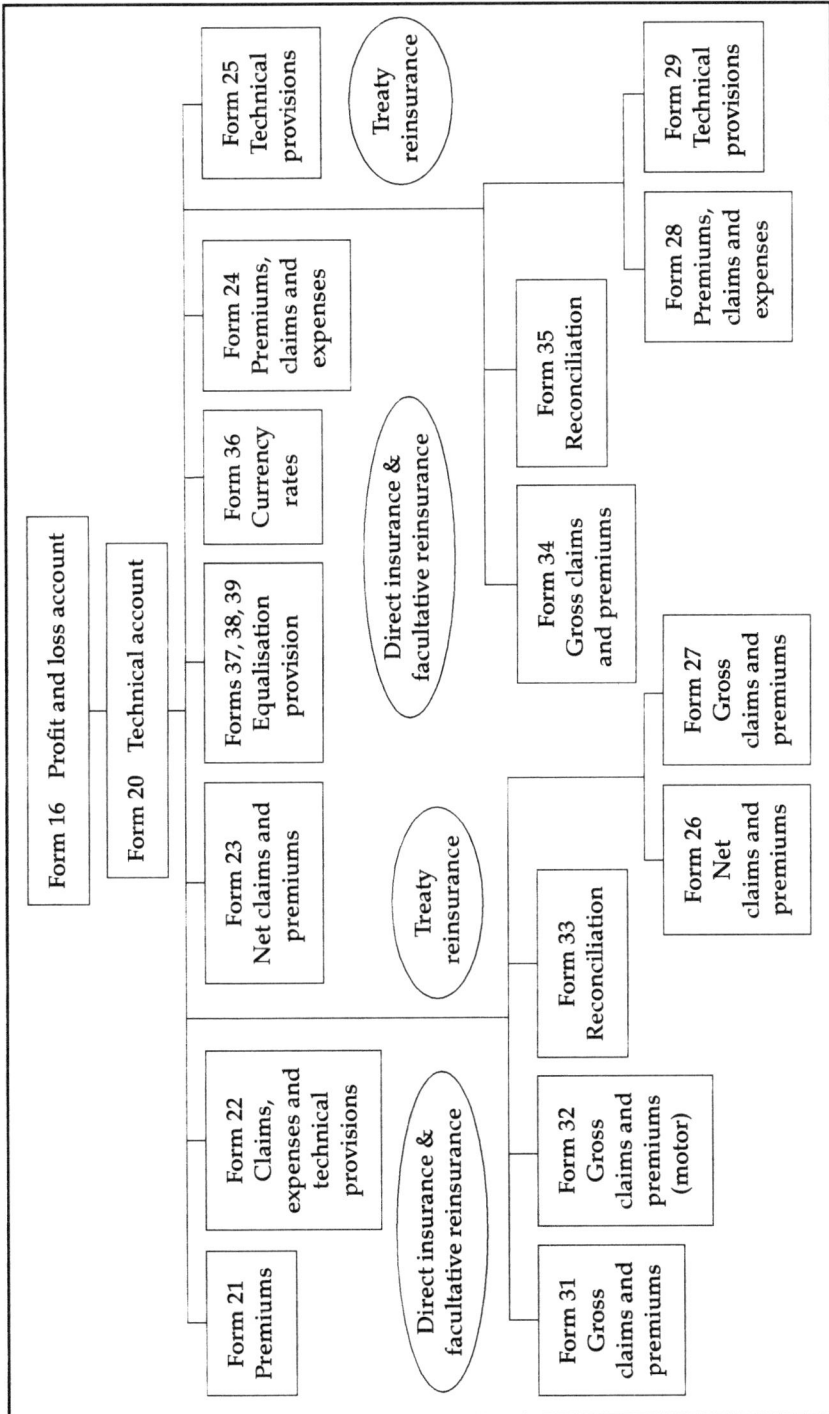

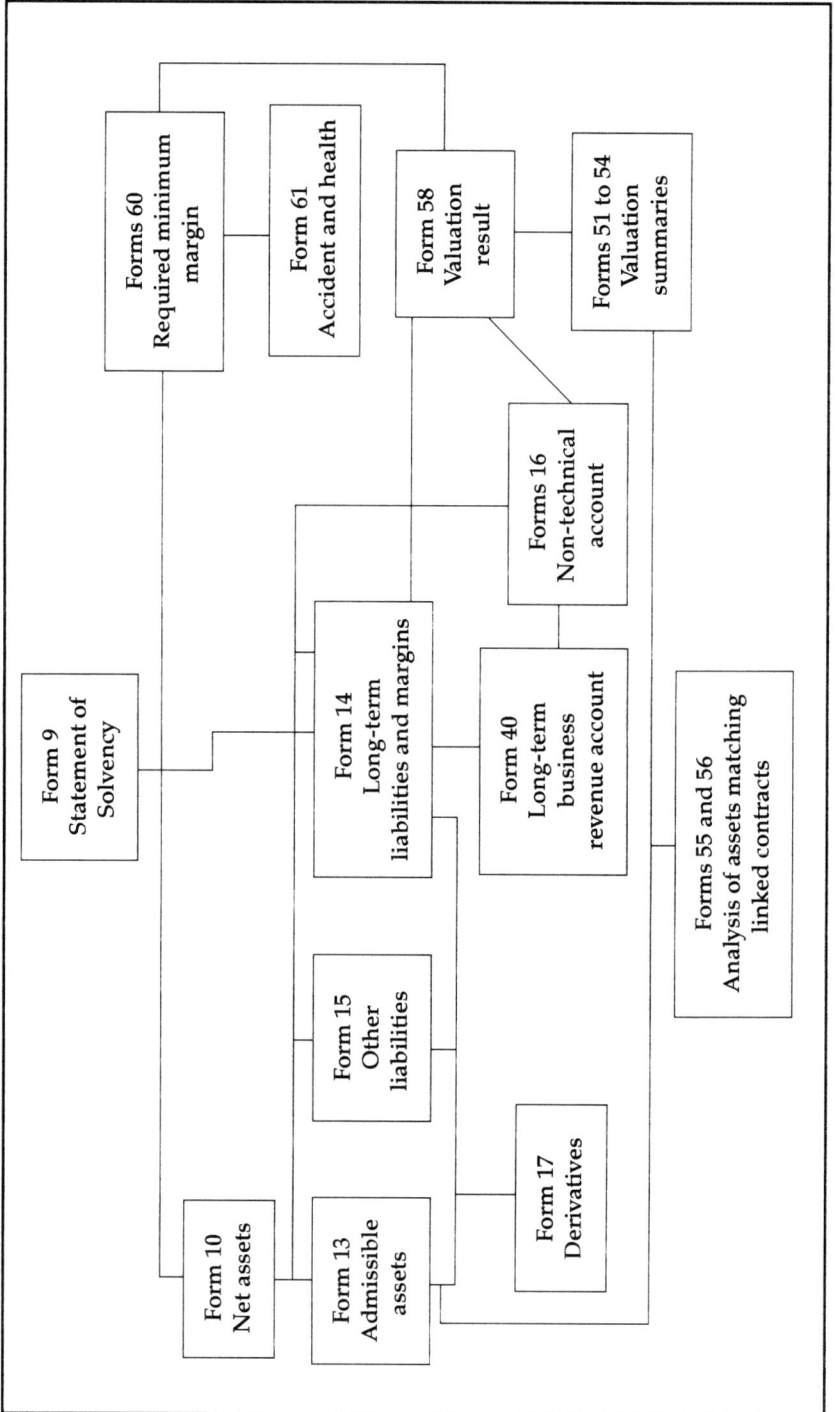

Figure 3: Long-term business – regulatory return overview

(d) Additional information on controllers (Regulation 9.30): All UK incorporated insurers must provide details of all controllers (definition set out in Chapter 11 of IPRU(INS)) of the company at any time during the year, including their name and the shareholding held.

(e) Additional information on general business ceded (Regulation 9.32): General insurers should provide an overview of the company's outward non-facultative reinsurance protections.

These statements (as appropriate to the type of insurer) must be appended to the numerical forms in the return and submitted to the FSA with them.

4.2.4   Uses and users of the return

A copy of the return must be filed with the company registrar in the UK, and hence the information is publicly available. The key users of the return can be summarised as follows.

4.2.4.1   The regulator
Despite being publicly available information, the key user of the return remains the FSA. As mentioned above, the key purpose of the return is to allow the regulator to monitor the solvency of the insurer. A key part of the regulatory review of the return is carried out by actuaries, particularly for life insurers.

4.2.4.2   Policyholders/brokers/financial advisors and analysts
Being publicly available information, the above parties have access to the same information as the regulator, and are thus able to form their own view as to the solvency and financial condition of insurers.

A large proportion of the policyholder base of insurers is the general public. The majority of these policyholders will not be aware of the existence of the return or be able to interpret or use it. As such, it is important that advisors and brokers have access to the information in order to provide appropriate advice.

Solvency disclosures, which make up the key element of the return, are not generally included in insurance companies' published financial statements. Statutory accounts are prepared on a different basis, and the net assets figure published therein is very unlikely to be the net assets figure as calculated in the return. The differences arise as the return takes into account the asset valuation rules ("AVRs") and the liability determination rules set out in Chapters 4 and 5 of IPRU(INS). (*See* 4.4 below for further detail on these rules.)

The return therefore provides crucial additional information relevant to assessing the financial condition of an insurer – information that could be of substantial importance to potential or existing policyholders.

4.2.5 The waiver regime

Under the previous regime an insurer could apply to the Treasury (under Section 68 of the Insurance Companies Act 1982) to disapply or modify specific rules where the application of those rules was inappropriate, unfair or resulted in excessive costs relative to the benefits of applying the rule.

This option has been carried forward into Section 148 of the FSMA 2000. Authorised insurers have to provide more information to support the request for a waiver than previously required for a Section 68 order. Fewer waivers are expected to be granted as a result.

4.2.6 Audit requirement

The majority of the return is subject to audit. The audited elements are:

(a) forms 9 to 17, and 20 to 45;
(b) any statement, analysis report or certificate furnished under Regulation 9.25, 9.26, 9.27 and 9.29.

In addition the directors' certificate, which is attached confirming that various requirements have been adhered to, is subject to a "not unreasonable" confirmation.

The unaudited sections are:

(a) statements furnished under Regulations 9.30 and 9.32;
(b) information on the Appointed Actuary (for long-term business insurers);
(c) the information provided in accordance with the requirement for a periodic actuarial valuation.

4.3   Solvency requirements

4.3.1   *Background*

Chapter 2 of IPRU(INS) (Margins of Solvency Rules) requires insurers authorised to carry on insurance business in the UK to maintain a margin of solvency. This is defined as the excess of the company's assets over its liabilities, calculated in accordance with the Valuation of Assets Rules (Chapter 4 IPRU(INS)) and Determination of Liabilities Rules (IPRU(INS)) (*see* 4.4 below).

The requirements for maintaining the margin depend on the type of insurer and can be summarised as follows:

(a)   All insurance companies with head offices in the UK, and overseas (non-EEA) insurance companies with UK branches whose business in the UK is restricted to reinsurance, are required to maintain a single margin of solvency based on the worldwide business of the company.

(b)   Companies with a UK branch whose head office is not in an EEA State and whose UK business is not restricted to reinsurance must, in addition to a worldwide margin of solvency, also maintain a UK margin of solvency based on business written in the UK.

(c)   Companies whose head offices are not in an EEA State and who have made a deposit in the UK must maintain a worldwide margin of solvency as well as a margin of solvency based on business written within the EEA.

(d)   Swiss general insurance companies carrying on business in the UK are not required to maintain either a UK or a worldwide margin of solvency but must maintain assets at least equal to liabilities for UK business.

The solvency position of the company is reported to the FSA annually through the regulatory return. However, companies are required to meet the solvency requirement at all times. The company's directors are required to confirm in their certificate accompanying the annual return that the required margin of solvency has been maintained throughout the year in question.

4.3.2   *Required minimum margin and minimum guarantee fund*

The required minimum margin ("RMM") is defined as the minimum margin of solvency that an insurance company must maintain. It is calculated as the higher of the required margin of solvency and the minimum guarantee fund ("MGF"). Details of the calculations of the RMM and MGF are set out in the Margins of Solvency Rules (Chapter 2 IPRU(INS)) and in Appendix 2.1 to 2.3 of IPRU(INS).

The MGF is a set amount dependent on the type of insurance business written (either general or long-term) and the class of business within each type of insurance.

For general insurance business, the MGF varies between 200,000 units of account (defined in Appendix 2.3 as the euro) and 1,400,000 units depending on the class of business and type of operation. For life business, the MGF is generally 800,000 units of account. For mutual organisations, the values may be reduced by 25 per cent for both general and long-term business.

With the exception of companies writing low levels of business, the calculated RMM is generally well in excess of the MGF.

Failure to maintain the RMM is considered to be a serious breach of the rules and the FSA has extensive powers of intervention available to it (as set out in the FSA Handbook) – including, in extreme cases, the ability to withdraw the company's authorisation to carry on insurance business. The regulator normally requires the directors to submit a plan for the restoration of solvency.

4.3.3 The calculations

4.3.3.1 General business
The general business RMM involves two calculations – the first based on premiums, the second on claims. Details are set out in Appendixes 9.1 and 9.2 to IPRU(INS) respectively.

The premium basis is a calculation based on the volume of gross premiums receivable. This is reduced for the effect of reinsurance by multiplying it by net claims and dividing by gross claims – subject to a maximum reduction of 50 per cent.

The claims basis is a calculation based on the level of claims incurred in the last three or seven years. In order to prevent the margin being distorted by abnormally high claims in any single year, a three-year average is taken (or seven years if more than half the gross premiums receivable were in respect of storm, hail or frost perils, or credit insurance).

The two calculations are compared and the higher result is taken. This is then compared with the MGF and the higher result is taken as the RMM.

4.3.3.2 Long-term business

The long-term RMM calculation (set out in Chapter 2 of IPRU(INS)) differs significantly from that applied for general business. The required margin is based on "mathematical reserves" (long-term insurance technical provisions) and also "capital at risk" (amounts payable at death less the mathematical reserves). The RMM is the aggregate of these two calculations.

The first calculation is 4 per cent (or 0 per cent or 1 per cent for certain business) of the mathematical reserves gross of reinsurance. This is then reduced to allow for reinsurance (subject to a maximum reduction of 15 per cent).

The second calculation is generally 0.3 per cent of the gross capital at risk (generally sums assured less the mathematical reserves), again reduced to allow for reinsurance (subject to a maximum reduction of 50 per cent).

In arriving at the required margin, "implicit items" (being future profits, zillmerisation (allowance for initial costs in the net premium valuation) and hidden reserves) can be taken into account provided the company has been granted an appropriate waiver by the FSA (*see* 4.2.5 above) permitting this. However, items that are not implicit items must be at least large enough to cover the greater of the MGF and 50 per cent of the guarantee fund (the latter being equal to one-third of the margin of solvency).

The RMM will be the higher of the required margin as calculated above and the MGF for long-term business.

4.3.3.3 Composite insurers

Companies writing both types of business must perform both of the calculations set out in 4.3.3.1 and 4.3.3.2 above. Long-term business net assets must be separately identified and compared with the long-term RMM. The remaining assets are then compared with the general RMM. (A company may, if it wishes, allocate general business assets to be counted towards the long-term margin.)

4.3.3.4 The parent undertaking solvency margin calculation

The Insurance Groups Directive has introduced a new requirement that, in some cases, the solvency margin calculation is required to be extended by a calculation covering the wider insurance group This requirement is dealt with further in 4.5 below.

4.3.3.5 *Free asset ratios*

The free asset ratio is a commonly used measure of the relative financial strength of life companies. Primarily it is the trend in the ratio over time that is important rather than the absolute value. The data to calculate the ratio is obtained from Form 9 of the FSA returns, hence its alternative name of the Form 9 ratio.

The free asset ratio is defined as the amount of free assets expressed as a proportion of the total assets that the company has disclosed in the regulatory return. For this purpose the total assets of the company include both policyholders and shareholder assets (in the case of proprietary companies). The amount of the free assets is determined by deducting the sum of the liabilities and required minimum solvency margin from the total assets and adding the amount of any implicit assets, as follows:

TOTAL ASSETS = Line 21 + Line 22

FREE ASSETS = Line 21 + Line 22 + Lines 31, 32 and 33 – Line 23 – Line 24 – Line 41

$$\text{FREE ASSET RATIO} = \frac{\text{FREE ASSETS}}{\text{TOTAL ASSETS}} \times 100\%$$

However, the measure should be used with care for the following reasons:

(a) the total assets exclude any inadmissible amounts and thus do not reflect the actual total assets of the company;

(b) the investment policy of the office will determine the assets held and hence values;

(c) the bonus policy will determine how much is included as a liability; companies with a higher proportion of reversionary bonus in the final payout will tend to have lower ratios;

(d) a low ratio could mean that the company has a particularly strong valuation basis;

(e) for a with profit company part of the free assets can be considered as a "liability" for accrued terminal bonus as these are not included in the liabilities shown on Form 9;

(f) the split between unit linked and with profit business will distort the ratio.

For unit linked business, assets and liabilities are closely matched and thus do not require the same level of free assets as with profit business. Hence a much clearer picture is obtained by considering the non-linked free asset ratio where the linked assets are deducted from the total assets figure before calculating the ratio.

4.4 Assets and liabilities – valuation, determination and admissibility rules

4.4.1 *Background*

Figure 4: RMM

Assets	
	Actual margin of solvency
	RMM
	LIABILITIES

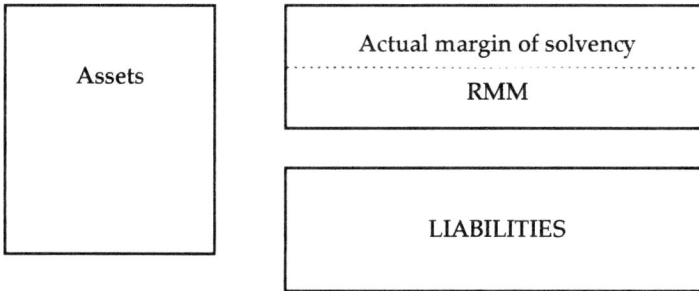

The RMM (shown above), calculated as outlined in 4.3, is compared to the available net assets for solvency purposes in order to ascertain the excess (or deficiency) of net admissible assets over the RMM. The regulatory return includes detailed forms which analyse the company's assets and liabilities, which are required to be valued in accordance with prescribed rules. The rules are set out in Chapters 4, 5 and 6 of IPRU(INS).

4.4.2 *Asset valuation*

4.4.2.1 *General*
Although insurance companies in the UK are not directly prohibited from investing in any particular type of asset, legislation requires that:

(a)   liabilities under contracts of insurance entered into are covered by
        assets of appropriate safety, yield and marketability having regard
        to the class of business carried on (IPRU(INS) rule 2.3); and
(b)   investments are appropriately diversified and adequately spread so
        that excessive reliance is not placed on investments of any particu-
        lar category or description.

The asset valuation rules ("AVRs") are contained in Chapter 4 of
IPRU(INS). These comprise a series of valuation methods for assets,
based largely on realisable value in the short term. The calculated asset
values may well differ from the statutory accounts values. The accounts
numbers will normally be based on the going concern assumption rather
than the more prudent valuation rules required for regulatory purposes.
There are specific rules in place for a large range of asset types including
(but not restricted to) debts, shares, land and other tangible assets, securities and other investments and derivatives.

If there is no explicit valuation rule in the AVRs for a particular asset type
then this asset must be valued at nil for the solvency calculation.

4.4.2.2   Admissibility
Once a company's assets have been valued according to the above rules,
the asset admissibility rules (set out in paragraph 4.14 of, and Appendix
4.2 to, IPRU(INS)) have to be applied. These rules are designed to
encourage companies to hold a prudent spread of relatively low-risk
assets. They contain a series of percentage limits which are applied by
reference to a benchmark amount representing the company's insurance
liabilities plus a notional margin of solvency. This benchmark is known
as the general insurance business amount or the long-term insurance
business amount dependent on the business written.

The general insurance business amount is the higher of:

(a)   the aggregate of the insurer's insurance liabilities (net of reinsur-
        ance) in respect of general insurance business and an amount equal
        to whichever is the greater of €400,000 or 20 per cent of the general
        insurance premium income (premium income receivable in the year
        net of reinsurance); or
(b)   such other amount as the insurer may select, not exceeding the
        value of its assets (other than long-term insurance business assets
        and excluding reinsurance recoveries) as determined in accordance
        with the AVRs (including admissibility testing).

The long-term insurance business amount is the higher of:

(a) the amount of the insurer's insurance liabilities in respect of long-term insurance business (net of reinsurance ceded and excluding property linked liabilities), together with:
  (i) the RMM or MGF (if greater) determined in accordance with IPRU(INS) 2.5 to 2.9 (or, in the case of an insurer whose head office is not in the UK, that amount which would apply if its head office were in the UK) less the amount of any implicit item valued in accordance with a waiver granted under Section 148 of the FSMA 2000, and
  (ii) the amount of any deposit-back in connection with a contract of reinsurance in respect of long-term insurance business; or
(b) such other amount as the insurer may select, not exceeding the value of its assets (other than general insurance business assets and excluding reinsurance recoveries and assets required to match property linked liabilities) in accordance with the AVRs (including admissibility testing).

Whilst these admissibility rules may not be a significant issue for an insurer with a significant excess of available assets, for a company with a much smaller margin careful attention must be paid to ensure that undue concentrations of assets in certain categories is avoided.

The limits set out in Appendix 4.2 to IPRU(INS) are then applied to:

• individual holdings of certain categories of assets;
• aggregate holdings of certain categories;
• exposure to individual counterparties;
• excess concentration exposure to a number of large counterparties.

The limits are graded according to the quality of the assets and counterparties. Not all assets are subject to the admissibility rules. Assets which are exempt from admissibility rules are as follows:

(a) approved securities, which include *inter alia*, any securities which are issued or guaranteed by any government or public or local authority (and accrued interest thereon);
(b) long-term debts secured on a policy of insurance issued by the company;
(c) rights under contracts of reinsurance to which the company is a party;
(d) general business salvage and subrogation rights;

(e)   debts in respect of premiums;

(f)   amounts due from, or guaranteed by, the government of any Zone A State;

(g)   shares in, or debts due to become due from, a dependant (not all subsidiaries will meet the revised definition which is now linked to the valuation basis applied);

(h)   holdings in a scheme falling within the UCITS (Undertaking for Collective Investments in Transferable Securities) Directive;

(i)   general business deferred acquisition costs.

Admissibility mechanics

Once the insurer has valued its assets in accordance with the AVRs, each category of asset must then be compared to the admissibility limits (IPRU(INS) Appendix 4.2) to determine the extent to which that asset may be included in the solvency calculation.

There are two types of exposure limit: one relates to the permitted exposure for an asset type and the other prescribes maximum exposures to particular counterparties. Details of the limits can be found in Appendix 4.2 IPRU(INS) and guidance on the valuation and admissibility rules can be found in Guidance Note 4.1.

4.4.2.3   New guidance

New rules were introduced in IPRU(INS) which modified the existing rules relating to the admissibility testing where the insurer has subsidiaries. The new rules are set out in IPRU(INS) Appendix 4.2, paragraphs 11A and 15A.

Paragraph 11A states that:

> "The amount arrived at under 4 to 11 [that is the total value of assets after applying the AVRs] must be increased by an amount representing the exposure, if any, of the insurer's dependants to assets of that description, calculating that exposure by applying 4 to 11 to each dependant as if it were an insurer (whether it is or not)."

Paragraph 15A states:

> "The amount arrived at in accordance with 13 to 15 [that is the value of exposure to counterparties after applying the AVRs] must be increased by the amount by which any dependant of the insurer is exposed to the same counterparty."

Dependant is defined as any subsidiary valued at its surplus asset number under rule 4.2 IPRU(INS).

4.4.3 Liabilities

The rules for determining liabilities are set out in Chapter 5 of IPRU(INS). These differ for general and long-term insurance business.

4.4.3.1 General business liabilities

The regulations require that the liabilities in respect of general business be determined in accordance with the Companies Act 1985 rules in relation to insurance companies' financial statements prepared under Schedule 9A. Liabilities set out on form 15 can be reconciled to the statutory accounts of the company.

4.4.3.2 Long-term business liabilities

Long-term insurance liabilities should be valued in accordance with actuarial principles having due regard to:

* the reasonable expectations of policyholders; and
* any relevant guidance of the Government Actuary.

The calculation must also include an appropriate margin for adverse deviations in the assumptions used.

The liabilities must be calculated in compliance with Rules 5.7 to 5.17 of IPRU(INS). Liabilities included in forms 14 and 15 will normally be different to the amounts included in the statutory accounts. This is largely due to the additional prudence built into the valuation of liabilities for the purpose of the regulatory return.

4.5 Insurance groups directive ("IGD")

4.5.1 Background

The EC directive on the Supervision of Insurance Undertakings in Insurance Groups (IGD) introduces new regulatory arrangements for supervising insurance companies which are part of a group. The earlier EC Life and Non-Life Directives (which were built into the UK regulatory regime many years ago) concentrated on regulation and supervision of insurers on an individual basis ("solo supervision"). The aim of the IGD is to extend supervision to the wider group.

The new rules included in IPRU(INS) which implement the IGD amend the solo supervision rules and introduce rules for "consolidated supervision". The requirements of the IGD came into effect for accounting periods beginning on or after 1 January 2001.

The IGD only applies to insurers, although the FSA has brought in the adjusted solo supervision rule and reporting of intragroup transactions for reinsurers. It intends to apply the consolidated supervision rules to all reinsurers in 2004 when the integrated prudential sourcebook comes into effect.

4.5.2 Key implications

The IGD introduces two major new requirements with which certain insurance undertakings in the UK must comply.

4.5.2.1 Parent company solvency margin calculation

An authorised insurer is required to perform a parent undertaking solvency margin calculation at the level of the highest EEA insurance parent undertaking and, if different, the ultimate worldwide insurance parent undertaking. An insurance parent undertaking is a parent undertaking which:

(a)   is an insurance holding company, a reinsurance company or a non-EEA insurance company; and
(b)   has a subsidiary which is a direct insurer whose head office is in a Member State.

This calculation should be submitted to the FSA with the authorised insurance company's own regulatory return. The calculation will not form part of the actual return and hence will not be publicly available information.

The group calculation will take account of participations (associates) as well as subsidiaries. Therefore, an insurance company which meets the definition of a participation will need to be included in the calculation on the basis of its surplus assets.

An important regulatory objective of the parent company solvency calculation is to highlight cases of "double gearing" between group companies. An example could be where a holding company has borrowed externally in order to invest in shares issued by its insurance subsidiary. It is possible that in some cases the group result could show a deficit position even if the authorised insurance company's result is positive.

There is currently no requirement for the group calculation to produce a positive result. However, the FSA is required to take action where it concludes that the solvency of the regulated insurance company is, or may be, jeopardised due to the group solvency margin calculation giving a negative result. The FSA has already announced that it will, at some stage, require a positive overall group solvency.

The directive prescribes three methods of calculation which may be adopted by Member States, which are described as "prudentially equivalent". The FSA has selected the "Deduction and Aggregation Method" (Method One), which the directive describes as the difference between:

(a)   the sum of:
  (i)   the elements eligible for the solvency margin of the partici-pating insurance undertaking, and
  (ii)   the proportional share of the participating insurance under-taking in the elements eligible for the solvency margin of the related insurance undertaking,

and
(b)   the sum of:
  (i)   the book value in the participating insurance undertaking of the related insurance undertaking, and
  (ii)   the solvency requirement of the participating insurance undertaking, and
  (iii) the proportional share of the solvency requirement of the related insurance undertaking.

Where a subsidiary is only partly owned, only the proportion of share capital held is taken into account in calculating its surplus net assets. However, where an insurance company is insolvent the whole of the deficit is to be taken into account unless the regulator is satisfied that the parent's liability is limited to its proportion of the subsidiary's share capital (in which case the appropriate proportion of the deficit is to be taken into account). The same rule also applies for the purpose of insurers valuing their own subsidiaries in their solo-solvency return.

4.5.2.2   Reporting of intragroup transactions:
The directive requires at least annual reporting to Member States (i.e. to the FSA in the UK) of the following transactions:

(a) Transactions between the insurance company and:
  (i) related undertakings (an undertaking in which a participation (generally the direct or indirect holding of 20 per cent of the voting capital) is held by another undertaking or which is a subsidiary undertaking);
  (ii) participating undertakings;
  (iii) related undertakings of participating undertakings;
  (iv) a natural person who holds a participation in any of the above.

A participating undertaking is defined as a parent undertaking or other undertaking which holds a participation. A parent undertaking is defined as any undertaking which exercises dominant influence (or under the Seventh Directive a company which in relation to another company has either a majority of the voting rights or which is a shareholder and has the right to appoint or remove a member of the board).

These definitions imply that the transactions to be disclosed will not be restricted to those with companies covered by the group solvency margin calculation.

The FSA has taken the view that existing UK requirements already meet those set out in the directive, with the exception of:

(a) intragroup transactions during the year (existing requirements only cover year end positions);
(b) agreements to share costs in respect of general business insurance (existing requirements only cover long-term insurance business).

The UK rules have been extended accordingly. All material (defined as more than 5 per cent of the business amount) intragroup transactions will be disclosed as a supplementary note to form 20 (general business) or form 40 (long-term business) and will therefore be publicly available information.

4.6 FSA guidance

4.6.1 Background

Insurers must comply with FSA guidance notes to the extent that they apply to that particular company.

The guidance was originally issued by the previous regulators as Prudential Guidance Notes ("PGNs"), and much of this original guidance has been subsumed into Volume 3 of IPRU(INS) – FSA Guidance Notes. The guidance notes that continue post N2 are set out below.

4.6.1.1 *Guidance Note P.1 – Systems and controls over investments (and counterparty exposure) of insurers (principles for business)*

The guidance states that suitable controls and management information must be in place to ensure *inter alia*:

(a) a suitable and appropriate investment strategy is in place;
(b) the creditworthiness of counterparties (including reinsurers) is appropriately considered;
(c) the investment strategy of the firm is communicated to the investment managers.

4.6.1.2 *Guidance Note P.2 – Systems and controls over general business claims provisions (principles for business)*

This guidance aims to set out, for insurers and reinsurers, appropriate:

"systems and controls which should be in place in order to ensure that the amounts set aside for claims outstanding and claims handling expenses are appropriately established, properly recorded and effectively monitored."

4.6.1.3 *Guidance Note 2.1 – Hybrid capital: admissibility for solvency*

As the FSA is able to modify or waive the rules in order to allow insurers to count the value of certain types of hybrid capital instruments towards the required margin of solvency, this guidance note sets out the types of instruments which would be eligible.

4.6.1.4 *Guidance Note 4.1 – Guidance for insurers and auditors on the valuation of assets rules*

This note sets out detailed assistance to directors of insurers, their auditors and any others who may be concerned regarding the application of the asset valuation rules (including admissibility testing).

4.6.1.5 *Guidance Note 4.2 – Use of derivative contracts in insurance funds*

Linked to Guidance Note 4.1 above, this guidance is concerned with the valuation of derivative contracts in an insurer's funds.

4.6.1.6 *Guidance Note 4.4 – Linked contracts*

This note provides guidance on the interpretation of Part II of Chapter 2 of IPRU(INS) which sets out rules on linked long-term contracts of insurance.

4.6.1.7 *Guidance Note 9.1 – Preparation of annual returns*

This is a detailed guidance note which provides the following:

- the statutory requirement to prepare returns;
- types of return;
- interpretation of the rules;
- completion convention;
- guidance on the forms;
- guidance on the Regulations Statements.

4.6.2 *Compliance with the guidance*

The directors' certificate, which forms part of the regulatory return, must state that the insurer has complied with certain guidance notes throughout the period. This certificate is subject to a "not unreasonable for the persons giving the certificate to have made the statements therein" audit opinion.

4.7 Other supervisory tools and aspects

4.7.1 *Financial condition report*

A further means of supervising long-term insurance business is the investigation (by the Appointed Actuary) into the financial condition of the long-term business of the regulated company.

There is currently no requirement in legislation for this report to be produced. However, many companies do produce this in accordance with the Institute of Actuaries Guidance Note 2.

This report considers the issues likely to be of greatest concern to an insurance company and assesses the potential strain that these issues could have on it, and whether the company would be able to meet such strains. It therefore provides useful information for risk assessment purposes.

4.7.2 *Actuarial abstract*

The report included in the regulatory return must contain adequate information to enable the FSA to form an opinion as to whether the minimum standards set out in the appropriate rules are met by the actuarial reserves.

The report, *inter alia*, must also contain:

(a) the date of current and previous actuarial investigations;
(b) a description of the benefits provided, and details of guarantees and options. For linked contracts this must also cover the nature of the link and details of the linked funds;
(c) general principles of valuation, including the manner of dealing with any asset mismatch, negative reserves, future bonuses, contingent liabilities, investment performance guarantees and other guarantees and options. Where a net premium method has been used, details must be given of any modifications made, such as zillmerising. Where a net premium valuation has not been carried out, additional information must be given to demonstrate that the reserves are at least as great as those required by the Regulations;
(d) for non-linked business, the method of providing for expenses after premiums have ceased, and for prospective methods, details of tests of adequacy;
(e) details of reinsurance;
(f) general principles on distribution of profit;
(g) particulars of bonus distribution;
(h) results of valuation for each fund;
(i) the amount of the required minimum margin of solvency;
(j) rates of interest and tables of mortality and morbidity assumed in the valuation of each category of contract, unless included in Forms 51 to 54 of the regulatory return, and details of the allowance made for future adverse changes in the mortality and morbidity experience;
(k) a description of the resilience tests undertaken, including details of the results of the most onerous test; and
(l) assumed levels of inflation of expenses and the bases used in the valuation to allow for such future inflation.

4.7.3 *Individual requirements*

When an insurer is granted a new permission to carry on insurance business it will be subject to specific reporting requirements (set out in

Appendix 2 of the Supervision Manual) during its first three years of operation. The FSA may also set additional requirements on an insurer in the form of limitations or requirements applied to the firm's permission. The powers available to the FSA are set out in the Supervision (SUP) Manual to the Handbook.

Insurers must adhere to these additional requirements as a condition of their permission, and the FSA may add or withdraw requirements as considered necessary throughout the course of its supervision of the insurer.

The main purpose of these additional requirements is to allow the FSA to monitor more closely certain aspects of an insurer's (or any other regulated company's) activities. A common example is where the FSA may require quarterly returns to be submitted if it considers the solvency position of the insurer to be under jeopardy.

4.7.4 Company supervisor and lead supervisor

Each authorised insurance company will be appointed a supervisor who will be responsible for overseeing the regulation and supervision of the company. The supervisor will also be the point of contact at the FSA for any queries the company may have from time to time.

In the case of groups which may have more than one supervisory contact at the FSA, a lead supervisor will be appointed. He will have three key responsibilities:

(a) to produce an overall assessment of the group (including consideration of the group's strengths and weaknesses, and also the risks faced by the group);
(b) to coordinate the supervision programme based on the above assessment; and
(c) to act as the central point of contact with the FSA to avoid duplication of communication.

The supervisor will have the power to issue information requests to the insurance companies supervised. The requests could be for information on exposures to unusual or potentially significant losses, for example in relation to asbestosis claims for general insurers.

In addition the supervisor can arrange for site visits where the supervisor and/or other FSA staff will visit the insurance company's premises in order to review records or conduct interviews with staff.

4.7.5   *Dear director/Dear Appointed Actuary letters*

Both of these forms of letter were issued under the old regime to provide additional guidance on the application of various rules. The former tended to address general business issues and the latter provided additional guidance on the valuation of liabilities. Typically these were matters that are not specifically covered in the Determination of Liabilities Rules (IPRU(INS) Chapter 5) and have covered subjects such as AIDS mortality, resilience reserves and guaranteed annuity options. The Appointed Actuary is expected to comply with the contents of the letters although there is no regulatory requirement to do so.

The existing letters have been carried forward into Volume 3 of IPRU(INS). The rules for issuing guidance have been changed post N2 and as such it is unlikely that future guidance will be issued in this manner.

Chapter 5

The Establishment of Branches and Cross-Border Provision of Services

Ian Poynton, Rob Stirling

Partners
Freshfields Bruckhaus Deringer

5.1 Overview

5.1.1 Concept of the insurance passport

When introduced, the insurance passport completed the framework for the single European market in insurance. European legislation established a common system for the authorisation and prudential supervision of an insurance undertaking by the Member State in which that undertaking has its head office, its "home Member State" (or "home state"). Such authorisation, in turn, enables that insurer to carry on insurance business anywhere in the European Union ("EU")[1] without the need for further authorisation, the so-called "insurance passport".

Insurers' rights to carry on business throughout Europe derive at a general level from the Treaty Establishing the European Community (as amended by the Treaty of Amsterdam) ("the Treaty"). In addition, a framework for the operation of the insurance passport is established by various EU directives which have been implemented into Member States' domestic law (*see* 5.2 below).

5.1.2 Origins of the concept of the insurance passport: the Treaty

The basic goals of the Treaty include establishing "an internal market characterised by the abolition, as between Member States, of obstacles to the free movement of goods, persons, services and capital" (Article 3(c)).

---

[1] By virtue of the EEA Agreement, the single passport regime extends to all EEA States (*see* 5.1.6 above).

In addition, Article 43[2] embodies the principle of the right of establishment; that is the right of an undertaking in any Member State to set up a branch or agency in another Member State. Article 49 of the Treaty[3] establishes the right of an undertaking in one Member State to provide services to customers in other Member States. This distinction between "branch" business and "services" business is an important one and is discussed further in paragraph 5.6 below.

5.1.3 Origins of the insurance passport: the directives

Based on the above provisions of the Treaty, the framework for the single insurance market was established in six stages by means of three directives in relation to life and non-life insurance respectively (together, the "Insurance Directives").

The First Non-Life Directive (73/239/EEC) and the First Life Directive (79/267/EEC) (the "First Insurance Directives") introduced a single set of standards for authorisation of insurers and also introduced some coordination of regulation compatible with Article 43 of the Treaty. The Second Non-Life Directive (88/357/EEC) and the Second Life Directive (90/619/EEC) removed some of the barriers to the cross-border supply of services. Finally, the Third Non-Life Directive (92/49/EC) and the Third Life Directive (92/96/EEC) (the "Third Insurance Directives"), which establish the passport, were introduced as part of the single market initiative in 1992. The Third Life Directive is modelled closely on the Third Non-Life Directive, but it contains certain more onerous provisions specific to the regulation of life insurance.

5.1.4 Mutual recognition

Because insurance is a heavily regulated industry, the single market is based on a system of mutual recognition. This has been achieved by harmonisation of national laws in accordance with the requirements of the EU directives described above and by giving primary responsibility to a single Member State to regulate the activity of an insurance undertaking, wherever that insurer carries on business.

Under the Insurance Directives, the home Member State has responsibility for authorisation and the financial supervision of an insurer. In

---

[2] Article 52 of the Treaty before amendment by the Treaty of Amsterdam.
[3] Article 59 of the Treaty before amendment by the Treaty of Amsterdam.

turn, an insurer's right to provide services into, or establish a branch in, another Member State (the "host Member State" or "host state") derives from its home state authorisation, which must be recognised as sufficient authorisation by the host state authorities.

5.1.5   Summary of the procedure

To establish a branch in, or provide services into, another Member State, an insurer must follow certain notification procedures prescribed by the Third Insurance Directives. Broadly, this involves providing the relevant home state regulator with certain information which that authority, in turn, passes on to the competent regulatory authority of the host state. The host state regulator may only impose conditions on business carried on in its territory (whether through a branch or by way of services) if they are in the interest of the "general good", as discussed further in paragraph 5.7 below.

5.1.6   Application of the insurance passport

The insurance passport applies throughout the Member States of the EU: Germany, France, Italy, Spain, Belgium, Luxembourg, The Netherlands, Portugal, Greece, Denmark, the UK, Ireland, Finland, Austria, Sweden. By virtue of the EEA Agreement[4] it also extends to Iceland, Norway and Liechtenstein. The insurance passport also extends to Gibraltar as if it were an EEA State.[5] The Financial Services and Markets Act 2000 (the "FSMA"), which implements the insurance passport in the UK, reflects this position.

As permitted by the First Non-Life Directive, in 1989 the EU and Switzerland (which is not a member of the EEA) entered into an agreement providing insurance companies with reciprocal rights to establish branches to carry on non-life business. The agreement, which entered into force on 1 January 1993, does not apply to life business and

---

[4] The agreement on the European Economic Area signed at Oporto on 2 May 1992. SI 2001/2511.

[5] The Financial Services and Markets Act 2000 (Gibraltar) Order 2001 (SI 2001/3084) treats Gibraltar as if it were an EEA State with regard to the use of the insurance passport by Gibraltar insurers and UK insurers (*see* Articles 2 and 4). But note that where an EEA insurer (other than a UK insurer) has already established a branch or provides services in the UK and wishes to do so in Gibraltar, it needs only to comply with the requirements for changing the details of its activities in the UK as if Gibraltar were part of the UK (*see* Article 3).

does not confer a right to provide cross-border services. Insurers who wish to establish an agency or branch in Switzerland must meet the same requirements as a Swiss insurer in respect of a minimum guarantee fund or minimum solvency margin. Their home state regulator must also certify that they have met the minimum requirements.

5.2   How EU legislation has been implemented in the UK

From 1 December 2001, the passporting requirements of the Third Insurance Directives are implemented in the UK by the FSMA, supplemented by the Financial Services and Markets Act 2000 (EEA Passport Rights) Regulations 2001 ("the Regulations"). The Insurance Companies Act 1982, which formerly implemented the regime, was repealed from that date. Various sections of the *Handbook of Rules and Guidance* ("the Handbook") issued by the Financial Services Authority (the "FSA") provide further guidance on the application of the passport under the FSMA regime, as indicated where relevant below.

Generally, by virtue of Section 19, FSMA 2000 an insurance company may not carry on its business in the UK without first obtaining authorisation from the FSA. It is this provision that imposes a requirement for FSA authorisation on insurers that have their head office in the UK. However, the position of non-UK EEA insurers is different – those that are entitled to the insurance passport and comply with certain conditions in Schedule 3, FSMA 2000 are granted automatic authorisation under the FSMA without any need to apply to the FSA.[6]

Schedule 3, in turn, reflects the notification requirements applying under the Third Insurance Directives to firms wishing to passport their business activities into an EEA State, covering both EEA insurers passporting into the UK and UK insurers passporting out.

Schedule 3 is not specific to insurance and also applies as appropriate to investment firms, credit institutions and financial institutions. The key difference in the application of the regime to insurance undertakings is that communications are made throughout the process through the home

---

[6] *See* Section 31 and Schedule 3, paragraph 12 FSMA 2000. NB Schedule 3 has been amended by the Financial Services and Markets Act 2000 (EEA Passport Rights) Regulations 2001 (SI 2001/1376).

state regulator. For other institutions, once initial notice has been sent to the home state regulator, passporting firms deal directly with the host state regulator.

Section 31, FSMA 2000 also confers authorisation under the FSMA on so-called "Treaty firms" qualifying for authorisation under Schedule 4 to that Act. The application of Schedule 4 to reinsurance business is considered briefly in 5.8 below, but this Chapter does not aim to describe in detail the exercise by firms of Treaty rights under that Schedule.

5.3 Procedure for establishment of branch or provision of services

5.3.1 Overview

Notification requirements that an insurer must follow in order to take advantage of the insurance passport are different in the following cases, each of which is considered separately below:

(a) establishment of a branch in the UK by an EEA firm (as defined *see* 5.3.2 below);
(b) provision of services into the UK by an EEA firm;
(c) establishment of a branch in an EEA State other than the UK by a UK firm (as defined *see* 5.3.5 below); and
(d) provision of services into an EEA State other than the UK by a UK firm.

The terms "EEA firm" and "UK firm" each have a technical meaning,[7] reflecting the fact that not all insurers are entitled to the rights conferred by the Insurance Directives. In particular, the directives only apply to insurers that carry on direct insurance, and the passport is not available to pure reinsurers.

5.3.2 General requirements – EEA firms

To qualify for the right to establish a branch in, or provide services into, the UK (the "inward passport") an insurer must:

---

[7] *See* Schedule 3, paragraphs 5 and 10 FSMA 2000.

(a)   have its head office in an EEA State other than the UK;
(b)   carry on direct insurance; and
(c)   have received authorisation under Article 6 of either of the First Insurance Directives from its home state regulator,

in which case it is an "EEA firm" (see Schedule 3, paragraph 5 FSMA 2000). An EEA firm must also satisfy certain conditions summarised below. Additional guidance for EEA firms wishing to establish a branch in the UK or provide services into the UK is contained in Chapter 5 of the FSA's Authorisation Manual. This includes guidance on how an EEA firm which qualifies for authorisation under Schedule 3 to FSMA 2000 and wishes to carry on extra activities for which it does not have an EEA right (broadly, the right to passport under the relevant directive) may apply for a "top-up" permission.

5.3.3 *Procedure for the establishment of a branch of an EEA firm in the UK*

An EEA firm which is seeking to establish a branch in the UK qualifies for authorisation under Section 31, FSMA 2000 once it satisfies certain "establishment conditions" (Schedule 3, paragraphs 12(1) and 13 FSMA 2000). The insurer's home state regulator must give the FSA notice that it has given the insurer its consent to establish a branch in the UK (a "consent notice"). The FSA must, in turn, have informed both the insurer and its home state regulator of any host state rules imposed in the "general good" (*see* 5.7 below) with which the insurer must comply when carrying on its branch activities, or two months must have elapsed from the date that the FSA received the consent notice.

The consent notice must:

(a)   be given in accordance with the relevant insurance directive;
(b)   identify the activities to which the consent relates;
(c)   include such other information as is prescribed by the Regulations,[8] being:
      (i)   a scheme of operations prepared in accordance with such requirements as may be imposed by the insurer's home state regulator setting out, amongst other things, the types of business to be carried on and the structural organisation of the branch;

---

[8] Information prescribed in the Regulations reflects the requirements of the Third Insurance Directives.

(ii)   the name of the insurer's authorised agent;

(iii) the address in the UK from which information about the business may be obtained and a statement that this is the address for service on the firm's authorised agent;

(iv)   a declaration of membership of the Motor Insurer's Bureau if the insurer intends to cover relevant motor vehicle risks; and

(v)   a statement by the home state regulator attesting that the insurer has the minimum margin of solvency calculated in accordance with the relevant provisions of the First Non-Life or the First Life Directive, as the case may be.[9]

Once a firm has satisfied each of the establishment conditions, it has permission pursuant to its branch authorisation to carry on each activity identified in the consent notice through its UK branch, on terms equivalent to those appearing in the notice (*see* Schedule 3, paragraph 15(1) and (2) FSMA 2000).

5.3.4 *Procedure for notifying provision of services by EEA firm into the UK*

An EEA firm which is seeking to provide services into the UK qualifies for authorisation under Section 31, FSMA 2000 once it satisfies certain "service conditions" (*see* Schedule 3, paragraphs 12(2) and 14 FSMA 2000).

The insurer must have given its home state regulator notice of its intention to provide services into the UK (a "notice of intention"). In turn, the FSA must have received notice from the home state regulator (a "regulator's notice") containing the information prescribed in the Regulations and the home state regulator must have informed the insurer that notice has been sent to the FSA. The FSA must then notify the firm of any host state rules imposed in the "general good" within two months of receipt of the regulator's notice.

The regulator's notice must contain (*see* Regulation 3(3)):

(a)   a statement of the classes of business which the firm is authorised to carry on in accordance with Article 6 of the First Non-Life or First Life Directive;

---

[9] *See* Articles 16 and 17 of the First Non-Life Directive and Articles 18 to 20 of the First Life Directive.

(b)   the name and address of the firm;
(c)   the nature of the risks or commitments which the firm proposes to cover in the UK;
(d)   in the case of an insurer which intends to cover relevant motor vehicle risks:
    (i)   the name and address of the claims representative; and
    (ii)   a declaration by the insurer that it has become a member of the Motor Insurer's Bureau;
(e)   a statement (in the same terms as in 5.3.3 above) in relation to the EEA firm's minimum margin of solvency.

Once a firm has satisfied the service conditions, it has permission to provide the services identified in the regulator's notice into the UK, on terms equivalent to those appearing in the notice (see Schedule 3, paragraph 15(1) and (2) FSMA 2000).

5.3.5   General requirements – UK firms

To qualify for the right to establish a branch in, or provide services into, an EEA State other than the UK (the so-called "outward passport"), a UK insurer must:

(a)   have its head office in the UK; and
(b)   have an "EEA right" to establish a branch in EEA States other than the UK (i.e. it must be an insurer which is entitled to the passport under the terms of the insurance directives),[10]

in which case it will satisfy the definition of "UK firm" for the purposes of the FSMA.[11]

Most UK-authorised insurers will therefore be entitled to passport their activities provided that they carry on some direct business and subject to limited exceptions (e.g. in the case of small mutuals).[12]

Chapter 13 of the FSA's Supervision Manual provides guidance on the exercise of passport rights by UK firms. It also gives guidance on the provisions in the Regulations that govern changes in the details of a UK firm's branches or cross-border services (*see* below).

---

[10] *See* Schedule 3, paragraph 10.
[11] *See* Schedule 3, paragraph 7 FSMA 2000.
[12] *See* the First Insurance Directives for further details.

It is a criminal offence for a UK firm to establish a branch in, or provide services into, another EEA State without first complying with the requirements as set out in 5.3.6 and 5.3.7 below (Schedule 3, paragraph 21 FSMA 2000).

5.3.6 *Procedure for establishment of branch of a UK firm in an EEA State*

For a UK firm to establish a branch in an EEA State other than the UK the following three conditions must be satisfied.[13]

(a) The UK firm must have given the FSA, in the specified way, notice of its intention to establish a branch (a "notice of intention"), which:
   (i) identifies the activities which it seeks to carry on through that branch (paragraph 19(3) specifically provides that unregulated activities may be included); and
   (ii) includes other specified information.
(b) The FSA must have given notice in specified terms (a "consent notice") to the host state regulator (and it must give written notice to the firm that it has given the notice).
(c) Either the host state regulator must have notified the FSA of any host state rules that will apply to the branch business (*see* 5.7 below on the "general good") or two months must have elapsed from the date the FSA gave the consent notice. In turn, the FSA must notify the insurer of those rules (but no time limit is provided for such notification).

The FSA has discretion to refuse to send a consent notice to the host state regulator if it has reason:

(a) to doubt the adequacy of the firm's resources or its administrative structure; or
(b) to question the reputation, qualifications or experience of the directors or managers of the firm or its proposed authorised agent in relation to the business that the firm intends to conduct through the branch (*see* Schedule 3, paragraph 19(7) FSMA 2000).

In this respect, the intention appears to be that the FSMA should reflect the provisions of the Third Insurance Directives and the FSA may in

---

[13] *See* Schedule 3, paragraph 19 FSMA 2000.

particular ask the firm for more information or require a report from a skilled person.

If the FSA proposes to refuse its consent it must issue a warning notice to the firm (*see* Schedule 3, paragraph 19(8) FSMA 2000). Subsequently, if the FSA decides to refuse to give a consent notice it must give the person who sent the notice of intention a decision notice to that effect within three months of receipt of the notice of intention (*see* Schedule 3, paragraph 19(12)(a) FSMA 2000).

Matters required to be "specified" for these purposes have been left under the relevant provisions of the FSMA for the FSA to prescribe in rules. These rules are contained in Chapter 13 of the FSA's Supervision Manual so that, for example, SUP 13.5.1R specifies the information to be included in a notice of intention (see SUP 13 Ann 1R and SUP 13 Ann 2R). SUP 13.5.3R in turn sets out the required manner for delivery of such a notice, including the various methods of delivery that may be used.

Finally, it is worth noting that the Regulations provide that where:

(a)   the activities identified in a notice of intention under Schedule 3, paragraph 19 FSMA 2000 include any activity which is not a regulated activity;[14] and
(b)   that activity is one which the UK firm in question is able to carry on in the EEA State in question without contravening any provision of the law of (any part of) the UK,

the UK firm is to be treated, for the purposes of its passported activities, as being authorised to carry on that activity.[15] This provision applies equally to services business.

5.3.7   *Procedure for notifying provision of services by UK firm into an EEA State*

For a UK firm to provide services into another EEA State it must have given the FSA, in the specified way, notice of its intention to provide services (a "notice of intention")[16] which:

---

[14] That is, regulated under FSMA 2000.
[15] *See* Regulation 19.
[16] *See* Schedule 3, paragraph 20 FSMA 2000.

(a) identifies the activities which it seeks to carry out (paragraph 20(2) specifically provides that unregulated activities may be included); and

(b) includes such other information as may be specified.

Within one month of receiving the notice of intention, the FSA must:[17]

(a) give notice in specified terms (a "consent notice") to the host state regulator (and inform the UK firm in writing that it has done so); or

(b) give written notice to the firm of:
     (i)   its refusal to give a consent notice; and
     (ii) its reasons for that refusal.

Again, "specified" requirements are contained in Chapter 13 of the FSA's Supervision Manual (see, in particular, SUP 13.5.2R and SUP 13 Ann 3R for contents of notice of intention and, again, SUP 13.5.3R for requirements as to delivery).

At SUP 13.4.4G the FSA provides guidance on the exercise of its powers to issue or refuse to give consent notices. In particular, in contrast to the position for branches (*see* 5.3.6 above), it notes that the consent notice in paragraph (a) above is not a statutory notice for the purpose of Section 395, FSMA 2000. This means that, in relation to services business, the Authority will follow the procedures set out in Chapter 1 of its Decision Making Manual.

5.3.8 Validity of policies

The European Commission regards the purpose of the notification procedures (both for branch and services business) described above to be the exchange of information between supervisory authorities. They are not consumer protection measures. As such, they should not be construed as conditions affecting the validity of insurance policies.

This position is reinforced by the FSMA. Under Section 26, agreements made by unauthorised persons are generally unenforceable against the other party. However, Schedule 3, paragraph 16 FSMA 2000 provides express derogation from this provision and its consequential provisions

---

[17] *See* Schedule 3, paragraph 20(3A).

for an EEA firm that does not qualify for authorisation under paragraph 12 of that Schedule.

5.3.9 *Cancellation of qualification for authorisation*

Section 34, FSMA 2000 provides that an EEA firm ceases to qualify for authorisation under Schedule 3 of that Act if, broadly, it ceases to be an EEA firm because its EEA authorisation has been withdrawn. In addition, Section 34(2) provides that, on request by an EEA firm, the FSA may give a direction cancelling its authorisation under Part II of Schedule 3. Regulation 8 of the Regulations[18] provides that where an EEA firm which is qualified for authorisation under Schedule 3:

(a) has ceased, or is to cease, to carry on regulated activities in the UK; and

(b) gives notice of that fact to the FSA,

the notice is to be treated as a request for cancellation of the firm's qualification for authorisation under Schedule 3 (and hence as a request under Section 34(2)). Among other things, Chapter 14 of the FSA's Supervision Manual provides for cancellation of EEA firms' qualification for authorisation (*see* SUP 14.6).

5.4 Changes in details

5.4.1 *General*

As stated above, an EEA firm that qualifies for authorisation to carry on insurance activities in the UK by satisfying the requirements of Schedule 3, FSMA 2000 becomes an authorised person by virtue of Section 31 of that Act. Its authorisation is treated as being on terms equivalent to those appearing on the consent notice or regulator's notice. Authorisation is withdrawn, by virtue of Section 34, if, broadly, the firm ceases to be authorised by its home state regulator.

If, therefore, the firm passports activities into the UK which exceed the scope of its authorisation, it will still be an authorised person but will be acting outside the terms of its permission for the purposes of Section 20 of the Act. Sections 194-199, FSMA 2000 set out the FSA's powers of

---

[18] *See* Schedule 3, paragraph 17(c) FSMA 2000.

intervention if it appears that an incoming firm has contravened a requirement of the Act.

Because of this, if an EEA firm intends to conduct business or provide services that are supplementary to those originally notified, it should consider whether it should notify the FSA of those changes. The Regulations set out detailed requirements in this respect and Chapter 14 of the Supervision Manual provides additional guidance. Similarly, UK firms are required to notify certain changes in details described below (Chapter 13 of the Supervision Manual is also relevant here), and failure to notify is a criminal offence.

5.4.2   Changes relating to EEA firms

The requirement to notify changes relating to UK branches of EEA firms arises if any of the details described in 5.3.3(c)(i)–(iii) above are to change.[19] Procedural requirements for giving effect to such a change are similar to the original notification procedures for establishment of that branch. Where the relevant requirements are complied with, the firm's permission is to be treated as varied accordingly. Broadly, except where the change is outside the insurer's control[20] the requirements are that:

(a)   the firm has given notice of the change to the FSA and to its home state regulator;

(b)   the FSA has received from the home state regulator a notice stating that it has approved the proposed change;

(c)   a period of one month beginning with the day on which the insurer gave the FSA the notice mentioned in subparagraph (a) has elapsed; and

(d)   either:
  (i)   a further month has elapsed; or
  (ii)   the FSA has informed the home state regulator of any consequential changes in the rules with which the insurer must comply when carrying on its branch activities in the UK.

In the case of services business, changes to any of the details described in 5.3.4(b), (c) or (d) above must be notified to the firm's home state

---

[19] *See* Regulation 6(1).

[20] In this case, the Regulations provide for notice to be given to the FSA and the firm's home state regulator as soon as practicable (whether before or after the change).

regulator as soon as practicable and then passed on by the home state regulator to the FSA for the permission to be treated as altered.[21]

5.4.3 Changes relating to UK firms

A UK firm must notify the FSA of any change to the "EEA details" with respect to a branch.[22] These details are, in summary:

(a) the address of the branch;

(b) the name of the firm's authorised agent;

(c) the classes or parts of classes of business carried on, or to be carried on, and the nature of the risks or commitments covered, or to be covered;

(d) details of the structural organisation of the branch;

(e) the guiding principles as to reinsurance of business carried on, or to be carried on;

(f) estimates of the costs of installing administrative services and the organisation for securing business and the resources available to cover those costs;

(g) for each of the first three years following the establishment of the branch:

    (i) estimates of the firm's margin of solvency and the margin of solvency required, and the method of calculation; and

    (ii) various other information and estimates, according to whether the firm carries on, or intends to carry on, general or long-term business through the branch.

A UK firm must also notify the FSA of any changes to the details which it is required to provide to the FSA by or under Schedule 3, paragraph 19(2) FSMA 2000 (see Chapter 13 of the FSA's Supervision Manual).

Notification procedures for changes of details in relation to the provision of services are similar to those in relation to branches. However, the procedures are triggered by changes to a list of details much less comprehensive than the EEA details. These include:

• the EEA State in which the activities are carried on;

• the nature of the risks or commitments covered; and

• certain details in relation to motor vehicle or health risks.

---

[21] *See* Regulation 7(1).

[22] *See* Regulation 13.

5.5 Transitional provisions

Grandfathering provisions contained in the Financial Services and Markets Act 2000 (Transitional Provisions) (Authorised Persons etc.) Order 2001[23] enable passporting insurers, as at the date that the new FSMA regime came into force, to continue passporting their activities. In addition, both UK and EEA firms that have begun, but not completed, notification procedures for the exercise of insurance passporting rights under the Insurance Companies Act regime are entitled to complete those procedures under the new FSMA regime as if they had been started under that Act.[24]

Finally, if before 1 December 2001 an EEA firm which was an EC company (as defined by the Insurance Companies Act[25] regime) gave notice under the relevant provision of that Act relating to changes in details, the Regulations provide that the notice is to be treated as being given in accordance with the Regulations if it was given in accordance with the requirements of the Insurance Companies Act. The same applies in relation to a UK firm, unless a notice of refusal was given to the firm.[26]

5.6 Right of establishment versus freedom to provide services

5.6.1 Interaction and analysis

As stated above, EU law makes an important distinction between the freedom of establishment and the freedom to provide services, which is reflected in Articles 43 and 49 of the Treaty.

As the original Treaty provisions suggest, the concept of provision of services is basically distinguished from that of establishment by its temporary character, to be assessed in the light of duration, regularity and continuity. This does not mean, however, that the provider of

---

[23] SI 2001/2636.

[24] *See* Part VIII of The Financial Services and Markets Act 2000 (Transitional Provisions) (Partly Completed Procedures) Order 2001.

[25] *See* Section 2(6) – broadly an EC company was intended to catch non-UK EEA insurers which were authorised in accordance with the First Non-Life or First Life Directive.

[26] *See* Regulations 21 and 22.

services may not provide himself with some form of infrastructure without coming under the right of establishment.

Grey areas in relation to the division between branch and services business (and, therefore, which notification procedure should apply) often arise where the undertaking has recourse to independent persons established in the host Member State or where it uses electronic machines to carry out insurance business. Case law has determined that if an independent person meets the following conditions it falls within the scope of the rules governing the right of establishment:

(a)   he must be subject to the direction and control of the insurance undertaking he represents;
(b)   he must be able to commit the insurance undertaking;
(c)   he must have received a permanent brief.

The Regulations define an "authorised agent" for the purposes of the FSMA as:

"an agent or employee of the firm who has the authority to bind the firm in its relations with third parties and to represent the firm in its relations with the [FSA] or the host state regulator (as the case may be) and with the courts in the UK or the EEA State concerned (as the case may be)."

This definition suggests that the authorised agent falls within the scope of the right of establishment (particularly as the term is only used in the FSMA in relation to the establishment of branches).

The FSA has indicated that it expects to issue guidance on what constitutes a branch and on where a cross-border service is provided (*see* SUP 13.3.1G and SUP 13.4.1G), although it had not done so at the time of writing.

5.6.2   *Consequences of setting up a branch or providing services*

Key reasons why it is important to identify accurately whether particular activities fall to be treated as services or branch business are as follows:

(a)   The procedure to establish a branch, while similar, is more onerous than for the provision of services. For example, a consent notice in respect of a UK branch will have to include a scheme of operations.

(b)   Timing: it takes considerably longer to comply with notification provisions for branch business than to comply with the relevant requirements for services business.

(c)   An undertaking that establishes a branch should comply with branch registration requirements in Sections 690A to 699 of the Companies Act 1985.

(d)   Taxation: the holder of an EEA passport who can provide services in another EEA State without the use of a local branch may not be taxable locally owing to the operation of double tax treaties.

(e)   Cost: the administrative costs of setting up a branch may be marginally higher but there is no difference in the solvency margin required for services or branch business.

Under the Third Insurance Directives an insurer can carry on both services and branch business simultaneously, but it should be able to relate a particular activity to one or the other. This was originally prohibited (in certain cases) under the Second Life and the Second Non-Life Directives.

5.7   Conditions imposed by host Member State in the "general good"

5.7.1   Background to the concept of the "general good"

Insurers operating under the single passport must comply with host state rules imposed in the interest of the "general good". The Insurance Directives refer to the "general good" in the following places:

(a)   Under the procedure for establishing a branch, a host Member State has two months from receipt of notice from the home Member State to notify the passporting insurer of any conditions imposed on the activities of the proposed branch in the "general good". There is no corresponding express provision relating to services (Article 10 of the First Non-Life and First Life Directives).

(b)   The host state should not prevent policyholders from concluding a contract with an insurer authorised under the First Insurance Directives, provided that to do so does not conflict with legal provisions protecting the general good in the host state (Article 28 of the Third Non-Life and Third Life Directives).

(c)   Recital 21 to both the Third Non-Life and Third Life Directives refer to the "general good" in relation to both the establishment of branches and the provision of services as follows:

> "Whereas the Member States must be able to ensure that the assurance products and contract documents used, under *the right of establishment or the freedom to provide services,* to cover commitments within their territories comply with such specific legal provisions protecting the general good as are applicable." (emphasis added)

(d)   Recital 24 to the Third Non-Life Directive, in relation to health insurance taken out as an alternative cover to that provided by a statutory system of social security, refers to Member State rules adopted to protect the general good.

(e)   Recital 19 of the Third Non-Life Directive and recital 24 of the Third Life Directive explicitly mention advertising or marketing of insurance policies and Article 41 of both directives states:

> "Nothing in this Directive shall prevent insurance undertakings with head offices in Member States from advertising their services, through all available means of communication, in the Member State of the branch or the Member State of the provision of services, subject to any rules governing the form and content of such advertising adopted in the interest of the general good."

This Article, taken with the recitals, suggests that the ability of the host state to govern marketing and promotion is one of the key reasons for introducing the "general good" concept into EU legislation.

5.7.2   *"General good" under the FSMA*

As noted above, the First Insurance Directives only expressly confer authority on the host state to impose "general good" conditions in relation to branch business. However, the recitals to the First Insurance Directives extend the concept to the provision of services. In addition, Article 28 of the Third Insurance Directives is not specific to establishment or services business. Unlike the earlier Insurance Companies Act regime, the new FSMA regime gives the FSA explicit power to impose provisions in the interest of the "general good" on EEA firms wishing to provide services into the UK (as well as establishing a branch). Arguably, it does so, therefore, on the basis of these provisions.

Article 40 of both of the Third Insurance Directives gives the host state regulator power to remedy the situation if a passporting firm is not complying with legal provisions applicable to it in that state. After informing the home state competent authority, the regulator may, in certain circumstances, take steps to prevent or penalise further infringements. Under the FSMA the FSA has powers of intervention in respect of passported EEA firms, which it may exercise if it appears that:[27]

(a)   the firm has contravened, or is likely to contravene, a requirement imposed on it by or under the FSMA; or
(b)   the firm has, in purported compliance with a requirement under the FSMA, knowingly or recklessly given the FSA false or misleading information; or
(c)   it is desirable to exercise the power in order to protect the interests of actual or potential customers; or
(d)   there have been certain contraventions of the Consumer Credit Act 1974.

The FSA may also exercise its powers of intervention at the request of, or for the purpose of assisting, an overseas regulator. This primarily means a home state regulator, although it can also cover other regulators in certain specified circumstances.

The power of intervention is a power to impose any requirement in relation to the firm that the FSA could impose if the firm had permissions under the FSMA and if the FSA were entitled to exercise its power to impose requirements in relation to UK regulated insurers. This means that the FSA can impose on incoming firms the same types of requirements as it can impose on UK regulated insurers.[28]

5.7.3   *Interpretation/case law*

Recital 19 to the Third Non-Life Directive and recital 20 to the Third Life Directive provide that conditions imposed in the interest of the general good should only be applied:

"insofar as the general good *is not safeguarded by the rules of the home Member State,*[29] provided that such provisions must be applied *without discrimination* to all undertakings operating in that Member

---

[27] Section 194.
[28] In relation to such a firm it cannot add, remove, or vary the description of a regulated activity.
[29] It could be argued that this statement is only relevant when the home country has rules governing the provision of cross-border insurance.

State and *be objectively necessary* and in *proportion* to the objective pursued." (emphasis added)

The concept of the general good has been subjected to further qualification by European case law. In particular, the European Court of Justice requires that a national provision must satisfy the following requirements.

(a)   It must come within a field that has not been harmonised.
(b)   It must pursue an objective of the general good.
(c)   It must be non-discriminatory.
(d)   It must be objectively necessary.
(e)   It must be proportionate to the objective pursued.
(f)   It is also necessary for the "general good" objective not to be safe-guarded by rules to which the provider of services is already subject in its home state.

These conditions are analysed in more detail in the EU Commission's Interpretative Communication 2000/C/43/03 ("the Interpretative Communication").

5.7.4   Examples

The Interpretative Communication sets out the following possible problem areas:

(a)   prior notification of policy conditions;
(b)   capital redemption operations of insurance undertakings;
(c)   uniform no-claims bonus systems;
(d)   language of the policy;
(e)   professional codes of conduct;
(f)   maximum technical interest rates for life insurance;
(g)   imposition of standard clauses or minimum insurance conditions;
(h)   clauses imposing mandatory levels of excess in insurance policies;
(i)   compulsory stipulation of a surrender value in life assurance policies;
(j)   prohibition of cold calling;
(k)   arrangements for charging indirect taxes on insurance premiums for policies concluded under the freedom to provide services;
(l)   appointment of a tax representative of the insurer.

Of these, the Commission's view is that the requirement to appoint a tax representative of an insurer doing business under the freedom to provide services pursues an objective that is justified under community law.

However, the host state may not reject a notification on the ground that no tax representative has been appointed. The tax representative should be appointed only once the activities have effectively begun.

Of the other possible "general good" conditions, the Interpretative Communication concludes, for the most part, that there is no justification for their imposition, either because the area has already been harmonised or because the host Member State has no competence for financial supervision of an insurer authorised in, and supervised by, its home Member State.

5.7.5 *Typical FSA conditions*

The UK's approach to the imposition of conditions on incoming firms in the general good has not been entirely straightforward. Its usual approach to insurance notifications under the former Insurance Companies Act regime seemed to be merely to send out a notice incorporating a list of insurance legislation applying in the UK (headed "Measures imposed in the interest of the general good and other provisions applicable to insurers authorised in other EEA States which propose to offer insurance in the United Kingdom"). Although the notice was carefully worded, stressing that applicants should take their own legal advice as to what rules and regulations should be followed, and it stating that the interpretation of the law is a matter for the courts, the FSA's approach in this respect seemed to be at odds with the narrow meaning given to the "general good" in the Interpretative Communication. The position under the FSMA regime appears to remain unclear, even though the FSA has issued some guidance in its Authorisation Manual (*see* AUTH 5.6). In addition to including a table summarising the application of the Handbook to incoming EEA firms, the FSA states, at AUTH 5.6.2G, that such a firm must comply with the applicable provisions (i.e. host state rules which are notified to it by the FSA). It is not clear from the guidance what form such notification will take and whether it will differ significantly from that provided under the old regime.

Still more confusing though, the FSA states that incoming firms must comply with "other relevant UK legislation" (e.g. where relevant, the Consumer Credit Act 1974). The basis for requiring firms to comply with UK legislation other than that which has been notified to them by the FSA (i.e. "applicable provisions" for the purposes of the FSMA regime) is not clear and may be subject to future challenge.

145

5.8   Reinsurance

5.8.1   Reinsurance and Retrocession Directive of 1964

This Directive establishes the right of reinsurance companies from one Member State to establish themselves in another (but it goes no further).

5.8.2   Third Insurance Directives only apply to direct insurance

Pure reinsurers are not covered by the insurance directives and cannot therefore utilise the EEA passport rights to establish branches or provide services in other Member States. This is reflected in the drafting of Schedule 3 to FSMA 2000.

The Insurance Companies Act 1982 contained a provision allowing direct insurers that also carried on reinsurance business to passport their reinsurance business alongside their direct business.[30] The FSMA has not carried forward this specific provision. It does, however, contain provisions allowing firms to passport using "Treaty rights"[31] (broadly, rights deriving directly from the Treaty rather than from a specific single market directive). In order to take advantage of Treaty rights the following conditions apply:

(a)   a firm must be authorised in its home state;
(b)   the relevant provisions of the law of the firm's home state must either:
  (i)   afford equivalent protection to that provided to consumers under the FSMA, or
  (ii)   satisfy conditions laid down in an EU instrument for the coordination of laws, regulations or administrative provisions applying to the particular activity;
(c)   there must be no single market directive which applies to the particular activity.

In relation to the "equivalent protection" condition, a certificate from the Treasury is conclusive evidence of the fact that the home state laws provide equivalent protection. This condition is likely to limit the application of Treaty rights for pure reinsurers, since it is not clear whether the Treasury has in fact assessed the equivalence of protections provided

---

[30] Schedule 2F, paragraph 4 Insurance Companies Act 1982.
[31] Schedule 4, FSMA 2000.

in other Member States. For mixed direct and reinsurance business, however, Treaty rights form the basis of the ability to passport the reinsurance business element. The FSA has indicated that it regards the equivalent protection requirement as satisfied for a mixed direct and reinsurance business on the grounds that, by virtue of the insurance directives, the reinsurance element would be subject to the same solvency requirements in the home state as the direct business.

The FSA suggests (*see* SUP 13.2.3.G) that UK insurers wishing to take advantage of Treaty rights in relation to reinsurance might like to consult with the FSA on their particular circumstances.

5.8.3 UK regime compared to other EEA States

Reinsurance is not directly affected by the Third Insurance Directives because, while reinsurers in the UK and some other countries (such as Sweden) are licensed under the same rules as direct insurers, they are not licensed at all in some other European countries (such as Germany).

Some participants in the insurance industry believe that insurance companies, as the customers of reinsurance companies, are sophisticated and therefore do not require the same level of protection as individual customers. So far, proposals for common minimum standards of supervision of reinsurance across the EU have been consistently rejected.

5.9 Approved Persons regime

The new Approved Persons regime under the FSMA has a "controlled function" test (Section 59), requiring prior approval by the FSA of persons performing significant influence functions. This would apply to key people of a UK branch of an EEA firm. Section 59(8) exempts this requirement where the question of whether a person is fit and proper is reserved under *any of the single market directives* to an authority in a country or territory outside the UK.

Section 10 of the Regulations explicitly subjects EEA firms seeking an inward passport to the Approved Persons regime.

Chapter 6
Portfolio Transfers

Geoffrey Maddock

Partner
Herbert Smith

6.1   Introduction

Part VII of the Financial Services and Markets Act 2000 ("the FSMA";
"the Act") deals with the control of transfers of insurance business and
banking business. Legislation controlling the transfer of insurance
business was first introduced in the Life Assurance Companies Act 1870
and was most recently contained in Section 49 (for long-term business)
or Section 51 (for general business) and, in each case, Schedule 2C of the
Insurance Companies Act 1982. The new regime makes a number of
significant changes to the Schedule 2C regime, and has for the first time
resulted in substantially similar law and practice for both long-term and
general business.

The rules are set out in Part VII of the Act, Schedule 12 to the Act, The
Financial Services and Markets Act 2000 (Control of Business Transfers)
(Requirements on Applicants) Regulations 2001 (the "Regulations"), and
guidance from the FSA in Chapter 18 of the Supervision Manual (the
"Guidance"). Further regulations may in future be made under Section
108 and/or Section 117 of the Act.

Sections 115 and 116 and Part III of Schedule 12 to the Act replace the
provisions previously in Sections 52A and 52B of the Insurance
Companies Act 1982, and deal with insurance business transfers which
take place outside the UK, in accordance with the requirements of the
Third Life Directive and the Third Non-Life Directive.

6.2   Scope of insurance business transfer provisions

6.2.1   *Meaning of insurance business transfer scheme*

The expression used in Section 105 of the Act is "insurance business
transfer scheme". No such scheme is to have effect unless an order of the

court has been made in relation to it under Section 111. With the exception of the four excluded cases referred to below (*see* 6.2.6), the expression covers any scheme to transfer the whole or part of the business carried on by an authorised person, including a member of Lloyd's, if:

(a)   the transferor is a "UK authorised person" (i.e. an authorised person which is incorporated in the UK or is an unincorporated association formed under the law of any part of the UK) and the business is being carried on in one or more EEA States; or

(b)   the business is reinsurance carried on in the UK; or

(c)   the business is carried on in the UK and the transferor is neither a UK authorised person nor an EEA firm (a term defined in Schedule 3 to the Act to mean, essentially, an insurance company authorised in an EEA State to carry on direct insurance business); and

in each case, the transferred business will be carried on by the transferee from an establishment in an EEA State.

It was held in *Re Eagle Star Insurance Co. Ltd and Eagle Star Life Assurance Co Ltd* [1990] *The Times* December 7 that where a single scheme proposed the transfer of all insurance business wherever carried on, the court could sanction the scheme only so far as it related to insurance business which it had jurisdiction to transfer notwithstanding that the same document also proposed a transfer of business which was outside the court's jurisdiction. However, it is more normal to document the scheme so that it covers only business which the court has jurisdiction to transfer, and propose a separate scheme for other jurisdictions.

Although this is not apparent from the legislation, it is clear from practice under Schedule 2C to the Insurance Companies Act 1982 and its predecessors that a single scheme, court application and court hearing can be used to transfer the insurance business of one or more transferors to one or more transferees.

6.2.2   The transferee

Section 111(2) of the Act provides that the transferee must have the authorisation required (if any) to enable the business which is to be transferred to be carried on in the place to which it is to be transferred not later than the date on which the scheme is to take effect. Subject to this requirement and to the solvency requirement in Schedule 12, however, there is no restriction on the legal nature or of the transferee or the country in which it is established. For the first time, therefore, it is possible (subject to any limitation in the relevant local law) to transfer insurance business carried on by a UK authorised person to a body which has neither a UK nor an EEA authorisation.

6.2.3 UK and EEA States

For this purpose "UK" means England, Wales, Scotland and Northern Ireland; the Channel Islands, the Isle of Man and Gibraltar do not form part of the UK. Gibraltar is treated as an EEA State by virtue of paragraph 4(3) of The Financial Services and Markets Act 2000 (Gibraltar) Order 2001, made under Section 409 of the Act, at least so far as relates to UK firms.

The term "EEA State" is defined by Schedule 3 to the Act, and at N2 the EEA States (other than the UK) are:

* Austria
* Belgium
* Denmark
* Finland
* France
* Germany
* Gibraltar
* Greece
* Holland
* Iceland
* Italy
* Liechtenstein
* Luxembourg
* Norway
* Portugal
* Republic of Ireland
* Spain
* Sweden.

6.2.4 Where is insurance business carried on?

The test of whether insurance business is "carried on" in the UK or in any other particular location is not exhaustively set out in the Act but should be determined by reference to the tests set out in Section 418 of the Act (a new provision which sets out certain circumstances in which business not otherwise treated as being carried on in the UK is to be so treated for the purpose of the Act) and, to the extent not in conflict with Section 418, by reference to the case law in Section 2 of the Insurance Companies Act 1982 and its predecessors. The most recent relevant case is *Re Great Western Assurance* [1997] 2 BCLC 685 (CA).

6.2.5   Reinsurance

The expression "insurance" in the context of this part of the Act includes reinsurance and retrocession (although some provisions specifically relate only to direct insurance or to reinsurance). This is clear both from the language in the Act, such as the fourth excluded case described below, and from the continued relevance of decisions on this point under Schedule 2C (such as *Re NRG Victory Reinsurance Ltd* [1995] 1 AER 533 and the first instance decision (not overruled on this point) in *Re Friends' Provident Life Office* [1999] 1 AER (Comm) 28).

6.2.6   Excluded cases

There are four categories of excluded scheme, being situations where (except in the first case) use of the court procedure is permitted but not compulsory. The first such case refers to transfers by a friendly society, which must be carried out under separate provisions described at 6.9 below. Cases two and three concern transfers approved by certain overseas courts or overseas regulators. Case four is where the business to be transferred under the scheme is the whole of the business of the authorised person concerned and either:

(a)   the business consists solely of the effecting or carrying out of contracts of reinsurance; or

(b)   all the policyholders are controllers (as defined in Section 422 of the Act) of the transferee or of companies within the same group (which is defined in Section 421) as the transferee,

and, in either case, all of the policyholders who will be affected by the transfer have consented to it.

Although the fourth case is apparently useful, it is rather more limited than it might be and is likely to apply to relatively few proposed transfers. Even where it does apply, there may be good reasons for using the court procedure (such as the fact that, despite the time and costs associated with a court application, it provides much greater certainty of outcome).

6.2.7   What is a transfer?

The expression "transfer" denotes an arrangement under which primary liability for the insurance policies forming part of the business transferred is moved from the transferor to the transferee. For practical purposes, the policyholders are thereafter treated as if their contracts had always been with the transferee. A transfer is therefore to be distinguished from reinsurance; even though reinsurance can, as between transferor and transferee, pass economic responsibility in relation to the underlying contracts, it has no effect on legal responsibility to the policyholder.

What the legislation deals with is transfers of insurance business, not merely transfers of insurance policies. Thus, it is possible to have a transfer of an insurance business even where there is only one policy. In *Re Friends' Provident Life Office* [1999] 2 AER (Comm) 437, Chadwick LJ said:

> "The transfer of long-term business from one company to another may (and usually will) involve the transfer of the legal rights and obligations which have arisen, or which will arise, under existing contracts of insurance; but it will also involve the transfer of the functions which have to be performed by the insurer in "carrying out" those contracts and, usually, a transfer of the business of "effecting" future contracts of the same class."

The result was that even though there was in that case only a single contract of reinsurance being transferred, and it was being "transferred" from the reinsurer to the ceding company, there was nevertheless a transfer capable of sanction by the court because the transferor had a number of other facets of its "insurance business" which were to be transferred.

6.2.8   Other matters

Although the term "scheme" is used in Section 105, this is not felt in this context to have any particular meaning or to denote any particular form of transfer instrument. For example, the FSA states in the Guidance at paragraph 18.1.5 that a novation or a number of novations could constitute an insurance business transfer regulated by the legislation if their number or value were such that the novation was to be regarded as a transfer of part of the business.

153

It is not clear what the scope of the expression "whole or part of the business" is intended to be. The Guidance does not assist in understanding the scope of this expression and none of the reported cases on Schedule 2C or its predecessors has explained the expression further. It is therefore sensible to assume that the expression has a very wide meaning and any portion of the business identifiable by reference to any particular criteria is likely to be caught by the legislation.

6.3   Uses of insurance business transfers

Most insurance business transfers fall into one of the following three categories:

(a)   Where one authorised person wishes to transfer the assets and liabilities of its insurance business to another, for example on an intra-group rationalisation, a "domestication" of a branch business, or as part of the sale of the business, an insurance business transfer scheme is the only means of doing this unless one of the excluded cases outlined above applies. Subject to these excluded cases, use of the court procedure is mandatory. It is often possible to achieve a similar commercial result to a transfer of insurance business through reinsurance, but this does not have the effect of physically merging funds, nor of actually transferring liabilities so that the transferee becomes liable to the policyholders and the transferor is released from liability.

(b)   Where a mutual insurance company established in the UK wishes to demutualise, the accepted means of doing so is by transferring its insurance business to a successor company, either a third-party acquiring company or a company which (or the holding company of which) issues shares to the former members of the mutual. The transfer procedure has therefore been applied to achieve what in a number of other countries is achieved by a specific demutualisation statute.

(c)   An insurance business transfer scheme can be a useful tool to obtain the sanction of the court, and so make enforceable, what is essentially a fund restructuring such as a reorganisation of the inherited estate of a life insurance company.

An insurance business transfer is also the means envisaged in Section 376(2) of the Act by which an insurance business which is in the process of being wound up could be transferred as a going concern to a solvent insurance company. There are, however, no examples of this occurring in recent years.

6.4   Procedure

6.4.1   Introduction

Until N2 the procedure for transfers of long-term business and general business had been quite different. The latter had involved approval by the regulator alone and had not required production of an expert's report on the effect of the scheme. The procedure has now been unified for the two types of business and is substantially similar to the former procedure for long-term business, although a number of changes have been made.

6.4.2   Timetable

Set out below is an indicative timetable for a transfer of insurance business. This contemplates that the nature of the business or the policies to be transferred gives rise to a requirement to consult regulatory authorities in EEA States as described below and assumes that the transaction is not a demutualisation and so no vote is required. It also assumes that the procedure is being carried out through the High Court in England rather than the Court of Session in Scotland (as to which *see* 6.4.13 below).

Table 1: Timetable for transfer of insurance business

End July	Initial meeting with FSA. Independent expert and all advisers to have been instructed
During August and September	Develop proposals and key documents, in discussion with FSA
Mid September	Proposals substantially final and key documents sufficiently advanced, so three-month EEA State notification can be made
Mid September to early October	Finalise key documents: scheme, reports, circular (if applicable), claim form, affidavits
Early October	File application notice, claim form (including scheme), affidavits (including

Table 1: Continued

	independent expert's report and draft circular, if applicable) Submit tax clearance applications
Mid October	First court hearing on application notice
Late October	Documents given to FSA. Notice advertised in Gazettes and newspapers Despatch of documents (notice and, if applicable, circular) to policyholders and those other persons requesting them (this to continue until final court hearing in mid December)
Mid December	Expiry of three-month EEA State consultation period Receipt of tax clearances All other evidence and certificates filed in court
31 December	Court hearing to sanction scheme Unless already held, authorisation of transferee to have been received Effective date of transfer

6.4.3 Involvement of the FSA

The first formal step in planning an insurance business transfer is to notify the FSA of the proposal. Paragraph 18.2.12 of the Guidance states that the promoters should discuss a proposed insurance business transfer scheme with the FSA as soon as reasonably practical, to enable the FSA to consider what issues are likely to arise, such as issues relating to policyholder rights or security, and to agree a practical timetable for the scheme. The FSA will also need to consider what skills are required to make a proper report on the scheme and what criteria should therefore be applied to the choice of independent expert to be appointed under Section 109. The scheme report may only be made by a person who appears to the FSA to have the skills necessary to enable him to make a proper report and who has been nominated or approved for that purpose by the FSA.

The Guidance sets out at paragraphs 18.2.14 to 18.2.22 the criteria which the FSA expects to apply to nomination or approval of an independent expert. Transfers of long-term business have long required the production of a report by an independent actuary, but transfers of general business have never previously required any such report. The Guidance indicates that the expert should continue to be an actuary for transfers of long-term business but need not be for a transfer of general business, where the main test will be competence in assessing technical provisions and the uncertainties of the liabilities they represent. The suitability of a particular individual will depend on the nature of the scheme and the firms concerned. The FSA will indicate the criteria it expects the promoters to apply in choosing an independent expert and, unless the FSA wishes to make its own nomination, the companies will then select an individual and notify the FSA.

Although the FSA is not required formally to approve the scheme, it will expect to be kept fully informed as the proposal develops and to review a number of drafts of the formal scheme document, any circular which is to be made available for sending to policyholders, and the scheme report. The FSA will indicate to the promoters how closely it wishes to monitor the progress of the scheme, including the extent to which it wishes to see draft documentation (see paragraph 18.2.13 of the Guidance). The length of time which this initial phase will take depends on the complexities inherent in the proposal and the issues which it raises for policyholder rights and security, but will rarely be less than six weeks to two months.

6.4.4 Consultation of regulatory authorities in EEA States

One of the major determinants of the likely timetable is whether any consultation with regulatory authorities in other EEA States is required in order that one or more of the appropriate certificates under Section 111(2) of and Schedule 12 to the Act can be given.

This might be required for a number of reasons:

(a) because the business to be transferred includes business carried on from a branch located in another EEA State;

(b) because the transferee is (or will be) an EEA firm authorised in an EEA State to carry on the relevant class of insurance business; or

(c) because the contracts proposed to be transferred include one or more policies of direct insurance for which another EEA State is the "state of the commitment" (in the case of long-term business) or the

157

state "in which the risk is situated" (in the case of a general business).

In such cases the regulatory authority in that EEA State must be consulted about the scheme and, in general, has three months to indicate whether or not it consents to the proposed transfer. The detailed provisions are set out in Schedule 12 to the Act. If no response is received during that time, the transfer of a branch business cannot proceed, but transfers of the contracts described above can proceed as consent is assumed.

The expression "state of the commitment" is defined by Schedule 12 to mean:

(a) where the policyholder is an individual, the EEA State in which he had his habitual residence at the date that he took out the contract; and
(b) if the policyholder is not an individual, the EEA State in which the establishment of the policyholder to which the policy relates was situated at the date on which the policy was taken out.

Paragraph 6(3) of Schedule 12 provides a means of identifying the EEA State in which a general insurance risk is situated, which will depend on the nature of the insurance but may also depend on the "habitual residence" of the policyholder when the policy was taken out.

The references to "habitual residence" are unfortunate: this is a European law concept and there is no single reliable test or set of rules which can be applied to define the meaning of the expression. There are, however, certain indicators and factors which can be taken into account when deciding whether a person has habitual residence in a certain state, such as:

(a) external appearances such as making a home, location of one's "centre of interest", the development of "normal social relations" and the obtaining of stable employment;
(b) length and continuity of residence; and
(c) intention to reside in the relevant state in the future.

It will be obvious from the nature of these criteria that an insurance company is very unlikely to have gathered information as to habitual residence when a policy was taken out, and indeed prior to the introduction of these requirements in the Third Insurance Directives on 1 July 1994 there would have been no reason for it to do so.

Practice since 1994 has shown that the court and the FSA (and its predecessors) are prepared to be pragmatic in the application of these requirements. Companies typically consult their computer records to identify the number of policyholders with a current residential or registered address in a particular EEA State and, depending on that number, conduct an examination of original paper files to investigate whether the policyholder was resident in that EEA State when the contract was taken out. In order to invoke the requirement for consultation in relation to a particular EEA State, it is necessary to find only one policy to which the requirements apply, so it is customary to err on the side of caution and consult unless it is fairly clear that the requirement cannot apply to the relevant EEA State. Once a certificate has been given by the FSA in relation to a particular EEA State under paragraph 6(4) or (5) of Schedule 12 it does not matter that there may in fact have been many more policies subject to the requirement in that EEA State than were identified to the overseas regulatory authority. It is usual to include wording in the scheme document which excludes from the transfer any policy to which these requirements apply and in respect of which the relevant certificate has not been given by the FSA. The interests of holders of these "excluded policies" are protected by means of a reinsurance contract entered into between the transferor and transferee.

The Guidance sets out (at paragraph 18.2.29) only very brief details of the FSA's requirements before it will agree to commence the three-month notification period. In practice, it will be necessary to confirm with the FSA at the outset what exactly they will require.

6.4.5 *Application to court*

Once the documents are finalised, the process is commenced by an application notice and claim form issued in the relevant court as determined under Section 107. In England this is the Companies Court of the Chancery Division of the High Court and the procedure is governed by Parts 8 and 49 of the Civil Procedure Rules 1998 and the related Practice Directions. At this stage the scheme will be in final form (subject only to any amendment provision specified in the scheme itself), as will be the scheme report. The form of any circular to be sent to policyholders (if required by the FSA and in any event on request) will be substantially final, as will the form of notice to be placed in Gazettes and newspapers following its approval by the FSA.

6.4.6 Scheme report

Section 109(3) of the Act provides that the scheme report must be made in a form approved by the FSA. This is a new provision and the Guidance sets out the FSA's requirements, which are to be assumed to supersede the previous requirements for independent actuaries reporting on transfers of long-term business under Guidance Note 15 issued by the Institute and Faculty of Actuaries. The main areas to be covered include a description of the purpose of the scheme, a summary of the terms of the scheme (so far as relevant to the report), the expert's opinion of the likely effects of the scheme on all relevant classes of policyholders (both as to the security of their contractual rights and, for long-term business, their reasonable expectations) and an outline of the reasons for that opinion. The amount of detail that it will be appropriate to include in the scheme report will depend on the complexity of the scheme, the materiality of the details themselves and the circumstances. The principal objective behind the scheme report is to inform the court on those matters on which it will require specialist advice (notably, in the case of a transfer of long-term business, actuarial matters) and the Guidance indicates that the report must comply with the rules on expert evidence (which are set out in Part 35 of the Civil Procedure Rules 1998). In addition reliance will be placed on it by policyholders, other persons affected by the scheme and by the FSA. In developing the scheme report, the independent expert will have extensive discussions with the FSA and will endeavour to agree its terms (even though it is his own report and not the FSA's, and the FSA is only required to approve its form not its contents). In considering any possible area of disagreement, the independent expert and the promoters of the scheme should have regard to the statement by Evans-Lombe J in *Re AXA Equity & Law Life Assurance Society plc* [2001] 1 AER 1010 that in any case where the view of the expert differs from that of the FSA on a particular point, the court will tend to prefer the view of the FSA.

6.4.7 Report by Appointed Actuary

Although it is not a requirement of the Act or the Regulations that a report be prepared by the Appointed Actuary of either the transferor or the transferee on the terms of a scheme for the transfer of long-term business, this has become customary and the Guidance indicates in paragraph 18.5.58 that the FSA would expect to receive such a report at an early stage. It is also likely that the independent expert will wish to rely on statements in the Appointed Actuaries" reports as to matters such as future interpretation of policyholders" reasonable expectations and exercise of any discretions contained in the scheme.

6.4.8   Circular to policyholders

Until N2 it had been a requirement of Schedule 2C in the case of transfers of long-term business that, subject to any direction to the contrary by the court, the policyholders and members of the transferor and, if applicable, transferee be sent a document including a "statement setting out the terms of the scheme" and containing a summary of the independent actuary's report. It has never been clear, as a legal matter, what the expression "statement setting out the terms of the scheme" means and it has been customary to apply to the court at the hearing on the application notice for a direction that this requirement be disapplied on the basis that the companies send out a circular in the form produced to the court. This disapplication had the effect that it was not necessary to establish definitively what the expression meant and also recognised that there will almost inevitably be some policyholders and/or members with whom a company has lost touch. The requirement to send any circular has not been reproduced by the Regulations but is replaced by a requirement, which again may be disapplied by the court, to send to policyholders (but not members) a notice in a form approved by the FSA and as published in newspapers (Regulation 3(3)). Companies are still required to give a statement setting out the terms of the scheme, together with a copy of the scheme report and a summary of the scheme report, to any person who requests them (Regulation 3(4)). Notwithstanding this apparent relaxation of the requirements by Parliament, the Guidance states that it would normally be appropriate to send to policyholders a statement setting out the terms of the scheme and containing a summary of the scheme report. The Regulations state that the summary of the scheme report must be sufficient to indicate the opinion of the expert of the likely effects of the scheme on the policyholders of both the transferor and the transferee, and the Guidance contains the FSA's views on this requirement. However, neither the Regulations nor the Guidance assists in understanding the meaning of the expression "a statement setting out the terms of the scheme". Neither Regulation 3(4) nor the requirement under Regulation 3(5) to give a copy of the application (i.e. claim form and scheme), expert's report and statement to the FSA may be disapplied by the court. The combined effect of the Regulations and the Guidance, as compared with the position under Schedule 2C, is therefore to add greater uncertainty than before as to the scope of the requirements with which companies must comply if the court is to have jurisdiction under Section 108(2) of the Act to sanction a scheme.

The uncertainty as to the meaning of the expression "a statement setting out the terms of the scheme" needs to be seen in the context of the fact that (unlike under Schedule 2C) the full text of the petition and scheme is neither required to be on display nor made available on request. Any objector who requires the full terms in order to be able to frame his objection properly will, unless the parties are prepared to provide these documents voluntarily, need to apply to the court for it to provide a copy under its general jurisdiction.

Until a judge gives clear guidance on the meaning of this expression most companies will be likely to wish to prepare a fuller summary of the terms of the scheme in the same manner as has been customary under Schedule 2C. In addition, the circular is likely to contain other related information and disclosures. If the circular is being published in advance of a vote or other choice to be made by policyholders or members, such as on a demutualisation, it will be necessary under the general law to provide sufficient information to enable that decision to be taken (see for example *Baillie* v *Oriental Telephone and Electronic Company Limited* [1915] 1 Ch 503 and *Pacific Coast Coal Mines Ltd* v *Arbuthnot* [1917] AC 607 (PC)).

6.4.9   Initial affidavit evidence

The affidavits filed in court at the time of commencement of proceedings will include information about the transferor and the transferee and their insurance business, the purposes of the scheme, and the companies" proposals as to notification to policyholders of the proposals. This will include details of any categories of policyholder to whom it is not proposed to send documents, such as persons with whom the companies have lost touch. It will also include details of any policies or business to which the requirement to consult with regulatory authorities in EEA States applies. The documents to be exhibited to the affidavits will include the claim form itself with the proposed scheme annexed, the scheme report, appointed actuaries" reports in the case of a transfer of long-term business, the form of notice and any circular to be sent or made available to policyholders.

6.4.10   Directions hearing

Approximately seven days after the papers are filed in court a hearing will be held before a registrar in chambers at which directions will be sought as to publication of notices to policyholders, advertisements in UK newspapers and, if applicable, newspapers in EEA States and as to the date for the final hearing to sanction the scheme. The requirement under Schedule 2C to place copies of documents on display at offices of the companies concerned and in relevant EEA States has not been reproduced and so directions on that subject are no longer required.

6.4.11 *Notification to policyholders and others*

Following the directions hearing, the companies will arrange for the dispatch of notices and, if applicable, circulars to policyholders. The Guidance indicates that it may also be appropriate to notify other persons affected, in particular reinsurers of the transferor (where it is proposed that benefits or liabilities under their contracts should pass to the transferee), and any other person with an interest in the policies being transferred who has notified the transferor of their interest. It will also be necessary to comply with any further notification requirements as a result of any order made under Section 414 of the Act. Although this is not specified in the Regulations, the Guidance indicates that the FSA would normally expect this notification to occur at least six weeks before the date set for the final court hearing. The only formal requirement under the Regulations is that a copy of the scheme report, a statement setting out the terms of the scheme and a summary of the scheme report should have been given to the FSA at least 21 days prior to the final court hearing. In *Re Sun Life of Canada Assurance Company* [1999] (unreported), Neuberger J (following guidance given by the Court of Appeal in *R v Immigration Appeal Tribunal ex parte Jayantha* [1999] 3 AER 231) held that the equivalent provision in Schedule 2C to the Insurance Companies Act 1982 was not a mandatory requirement but was instead for the benefit of the FSA, who could if it wished waive non-compliance. Even if the FSA were to take the point that insufficient notice had been given, it would still be open to the court to consider whether any real prejudice had been suffered by the FSA as a result of the non-compliance and, if satisfied that no prejudice had been suffered, it would be open to the court to hold that there had been substantive compliance with the requirement. It is unlikely that a different conclusion would be reached on the new wording.

6.4.12 *Final court hearing*

Assuming that matters have proceeded satisfactorily, the companies will prepare and file a final set of affidavits approximately seven days in advance of the final court hearing. These affidavits will typically:

(a) prove the various matters set out in the order made on the directions hearing, such as due posting of notices to policyholders and publication of the notice in the Gazettes and newspapers;

(b) produce the appropriate certificates as required under Section 111(2)(a) of the Act;

(c) confirm the position regarding the authorisation required by the transferee for the purpose of Section 111(2)(b) of the Act;

(d) prove that any conditions to which the scheme was made subject, such as the receipt of tax clearances or confirmations, have been satisfied or waived. Although the court generally expects all conditions to have been satisfied or waived before the hearing, a scheme may sometimes be subject to conditions which by their nature cannot be satisfied until a later date, such as a listing condition. Section 111(2)(b) of the Act makes it clear that authorisation of the transferee to carry on the business need only be in place by the time the scheme is to become effective;

(e) deal with the content of any material objections to the scheme which have been intimated to the companies;

(f) contain such further argument as may be necessary as to why it is appropriate for the court to sanction the scheme; and

(g) summarise any views expressed by the FSA, as required by the Guidance (unless the FSA has indicated that it intends to attend and be heard at the court hearing).

The final hearing will be before a judge in open court, as described at 6.5 below. It is usual for evidence to be given exclusively by affidavit, rather than in person. Any objector who wishes to do so may appear and argue his case in person or by counsel. In determining whether it should order that the promoters meet the objectors" costs, it appears from the decision of the Vice Chancellor in *Re The Royal London Mutual Insurance Society Limited* [2000] (unreported) that the court is likely to apply the principle in *Re National Bank Limited* [1966] 1WLR 819, namely that a person who, in answer to the publicity given to a scheme, appears and raises objections which are not frivolous in nature should ordinarily receive his costs from the promoters as his argument had been helpful to the court.

Following the hearing, assuming an order has been made sanctioning the scheme, the companies must deposit two office copies of the order with the FSA within 10 days of the making of the order (Section 112(10) of the Act) and comply with any directions made by the court in relation to the publication of notice of the making of the order in EEA States as required under Section 114 of the Act. In many cases the regulatory authorities in the EEA States will indicate how such publication should be made and in other cases it will be necessary to ask the court for a direction as to how publication should be effected.

6.4.13   *Insurance business transfers in Scotland*

Section 107 of the Act provides that if a transferor and a transferee are registered or have their head offices in the same jurisdiction, the application for an order sanctioning a transfer scheme must be made to the court in that jurisdiction. If a transferor and a transferee are registered or have their head offices in different jurisdictions such an application may be made to the court in either jurisdiction. Section 107 of the Act defines "court" as the High Court or the Court of Session. The term "High Court" is not defined in the Act but is defined in Schedule 1 to the Interpretation Act 1978 as Her Majesty's High Court of Justice in England and Wales, in relation to England and Wales, and Her Majesty's High Court of Justice in Northern Ireland, in relation to Northern Ireland.

Procedure in the Court of Session, so far as it relates to insurance business transfers, differs materially from that in the High Court in two respects, as described below:

(a)   any person wishing to object to an application for an order sanction-ing the proposed transfer is required to submit an objection in the appropriate form to the Court of Session within 21 days of the publication of the last of the notices posted in the Gazettes and the newspapers under paragraph 3 of the Regulations; and

(b)   the Court of Session appoints a Reporter (being a senior solicitor in private practice who is independent of the transferor and the transferee) to review compliance by the transferor and transferee with the legislation governing the transfer of insurance business. Prior to the final court hearing, the Reporter produces a report addressed to the court which considers whether each of the require-ments of the legislation has been met and draws any defects in compliance to the attention of the Court of Session. The Reporter's remit does not extend to considering the terms or the merits of the scheme.

6.5   The decision of the court

Section 110 of the Act provides that both the FSA and any person (including an employee of the transferor or the transferee) who alleges that he would be adversely affected by the carrying out of the scheme is entitled to be heard at the court hearing to sanction the scheme. Section 111(3) of the Act provides that, if it is to sanction an insurance business transfer scheme, the court (having satisfied itself that the procedural and jurisdictional requirements described above have been satisfied) must consider that, in all the circumstances of the case, it is appropriate to sanction the scheme. This latter requirement was not included in Schedule 2C but is not expected to give rise to any material change to the test which the court will apply in a typical case, although it is likely to be used by the FSA to justify any objections it has which are of a procedural nature, as described below.

The Guidance contains a considerable amount of information about how the FSA would expect to exercise its discretion in deciding whether to attend the court hearing. The matters it will take into account include both substantive matters such as the effect of the scheme on the security of policyholders" rights and (in the case of long-term business) reasonable expectations and procedural matters such as whether policyholders have been properly notified, and have had adequate information and adequate time to consider that information. The FSA is not required under its regulatory objectives set out in Section 2(2) of the Act to object to a scheme merely because some other scheme might have been in the better interests of policyholders, if the scheme itself is not adverse to their interests. However, the Guidance indicates that there may be circumstances where the requirement to treat customers fairly would require the parties to consider or to implement an alternative scheme.

There is no reason why a scheme may not be proposed even though the parties know that the FSA will object. However, before doing so, regard should be had to the principles which the court will apply in exercising its discretion.

The leading case under the law prior to N2 was the decision of Hoffmann J in *Re London Life Association Limited* [1989]. Curiously, this decision has never been reported, although it has been followed by judges ever since. In *Re AXA Equity & Law Life Assurance Society plc* [2001] 1 AER 1010 Evans-Lombe J summarised the *London Life* decision in eight "London Life Principles" which (with minor updates to reflect the language in the Act) were as follows:

(a)   First, the Act confers an absolute discretion on the court whether or not to sanction the scheme, but this is a discretion which must be exercised by giving due recognition to the commercial judgment entrusted by the company's constitution to its directors.

(b)   The court is concerned with whether a policyholder, employee or other interested person, or any group of them, will be adversely affected by the scheme.

(c)   This is primarily a matter of actuarial judgment involving a comparison of the security and reasonable expectations of policy-holders without the scheme with what would be the result if the scheme were implemented. For the purpose of this comparison, the Act assigns an important role to the independent expert, to whose report the court will give close attention.

(d)   The FSA, by reason of its regulatory powers, can also be expected to have the necessary material and expertise to express an informed opinion on whether policyholders are likely to be adversely affected. Again, the court will pay close attention to any views expressed by the FSA.

(e)   The fact that individual policyholders, or groups of policyholders, may be adversely affected does not mean that the scheme has to be rejected by the court. The fundamental question is whether the scheme as a whole is fair as between the interests of the different classes of persons affected.

(f)   It is not the function of the court to produce what, in its view, is the best possible scheme. As between different schemes, all of which the court may deem fair, it is the company directors" choice which to pursue.

(g)   Under the same principle, the details of the scheme are not a matter for the court provided that the scheme as a whole is found to be fair. Thus, the court will not amend the scheme because it thinks that individual provisions could be improved upon.

(h)   The court, in arriving at its conclusion, should first determine what the contractual rights and reasonable expectations of policyholders were before the scheme was promulgated and then compare those with the likely effect on the rights and expectations of the policy-holders if the scheme is implemented.

Whilst this provides a very convenient summary of the principles estab-lished by the *London Life* decision, it was prepared in the context of the particular question before Evans-Lombe J and is therefore not compre-hensive as to the criteria which might be applied by the court in other cases. The following further principles can be deduced from the cases:

(a)   it appears to be acceptable, in determining the question set out at point (e), to take into account the advantages which would be secured by implementation of the scheme for a particular class of persons as a counter weight to potential disadvantages which other groups of persons may suffer. What is required is a balancing exercise. This is clear both from the decision in *Re The Royal London Mutual Insurance Society Limited* [2000] (unreported) and from paragraph 2.3.2 of the FSA's feedback on CP110;

(b)   in relation to point (g), Hoffmann J had suggested in *London Life* that if the court was of the view that the scheme was unfair, it could indicate that it thought the vice lay in some particular term and that a fresh scheme without that term was likely to be acceptable;

(c)   although Evans-Lombe J in *AXA* referred only to policyholders, the court will apply the same tests to objections raised by any other category of objector claiming to be adversely affected; and

(d)   Evans-Lombe J stated that in any actuarial matter the court's approach should be to accept the views of the independent expert and the FSA in preference to those of the companies and any objectors where they are in conflict, except where there is a compelling reason, based on proven fact, or demonstrable mistake in calculation or forecast, which points to a contrary view. Where the views of the FSA conflict with those of the independent expert, the court is likely to prefer those of the FSA.

It will be apparent that the *London Life* principles and the additional statements set out above are not all necessarily applicable to transfers of general business. However, it is to be expected that the same broad principles will be applied.

The principles described above should be used as a guide in deciding how to deal with policyholder or other objections to the scheme. Matters extraneous to the scheme such as complaints about service, mis-selling, unpaid claims or lack of membership on a demutualisation should, in principle, all be treated by the court as not amounting to a reason why the scheme should not be sanctioned. In contrast, complaints alleging that the scheme would have a material adverse effect on security or policyholders" reasonable expectations as to benefits would potentially lead the court to decline to sanction the scheme. Given the views of the FSA set out in the Guidance, however, it is unlikely that a scheme which gave rise to serious concerns on these points would reach the court.

6.6 The effect of the court's order

6.6.1 *Effect generally*

The powers of the court when sanctioning an insurance business transfer scheme are dealt with in Section 112 of the Act. A typical transfer scheme will take advantage of many of these powers and accordingly a typical court order will have the following effects:

(a)   policy rights and liabilities transfer without any requirement for consent by the relevant policyholder so that the transferee becomes directly liable to the policyholder and the transferor ceases to be so liable – indeed this is the principal objective of the order;

(b)   all other assets, rights, contracts and liabilities within the scope of the order also transfer, subject in certain cases to consents as described at 6.6.2 below – this power is new in relation to transfers of general business;

(c)   the court order is the only instrument needed to effect the transfer (albeit in any case where registration is needed to perfect a transfer, e.g. real property and shares, the registration requirement is not dispensed with);

(d)   the transaction is a transfer by operation of law, as a result of the court's order, of the assets and liabilities within the scope of the order. It is not a transaction of assignment nor of novation (novation would, in law, give rise to a new contract, whereas the transfer does not); and

(e)   as the authority is given by virtue of statute, it does not extend to foreign assets or liabilities which an order of a UK court cannot transfer for want of jurisdiction; such assets or liabilities will need to be transferred by separate documents in accordance with local laws (and may give rise to foreign stamp duties or other consent requirements).

6.6.2 *Third party consents*

A question which typically arises is the scope of the court's ability to make an order which transfers assets and contracts which by their terms or nature require the counterparty's consent to their transfer. This is particularly an issue in relation to reinsurance contracts: while reinsurers have generally been content to transfer or novate contracts in the context of transfers of long-term business, they may be reluctant to do so on a transfer of general business. Prior to N2 the procedure under Schedule 2C gave companies no power to include reinsurance contracts within the

169

scope of a transfer of general business. The Guidance states that in the opinion of the FSA, the court has the power to transfer, on such terms as may be appropriate, the benefit of reinsurance contracts protecting the transferring business and to make such amendments to the terms of those contracts as may be necessary to give effect to that transfer of benefits. It remains to be seen whether a court will agree with this view in the face of opposition from a reinsurer. It must be very unlikely that a court would override any clause in a reinsurance contract which explicitly requires the reinsurer's consent to a transfer of the underlying business.

As regards consent in relation to other contracts, the view is generally taken that although transfer of assets and contractual arrangements (both rights and liabilities) occurs by operation of law under the court's order, subject to de minimis limits (it is never proposed that consent be sought from casual suppliers, e.g. of office stationery), third party consents should be sought before the court will be content to transfer assets and contracts which contain an explicit requirement for consent to assignment or transfer. This view is based on two principal considerations. First, an analogy is drawn from the decision in *Nokes* v *Doncaster Amalgamated Colliery Limited* [1940] AC 1014. This case related to the predecessor of what is now Section 427 of the Companies Act 1985, which contains virtually identical wording to that in Section 112(1) of the Act. Although the decision related to a contract of employment and has now been superseded by the Transfer of Undertakings (Protection of Employment) Regulations 1981 (SI 1981/1794), the decision can be treated as authority for the proposition that the court ought not to make an order which overrides third-party rights which, whether expressly or impliedly, contain restrictions on transfer. Examples of such restrictions are clauses providing:

(a) expressly against transfers taking effect by operation of law or assignment; such provisions may be found in contracts of debt, shareholders" agreements and other joint venture arrangements, limited partnerships and leases; or

(b) impliedly against transfers occurring by operation of law or assignments; typically such a construction will be implied where the contract has a personal nature and the identity of the contracting parties is deemed by law to be fundamental to the contract.

The second reason for seeking consent is merely a consideration of fairness, to notify the third party of the proposal and give them an opportunity to express a view.

There may be some third party consents that, despite the best endeavours of the parties, are not forthcoming prior to the transfer date. The scheme language will therefore typically contain a category of "residual assets" (and the associated category of "residual liabilities") designed to cater for these cases. In summary, these are assets and contracts the transfer of which requires either the consent of the third party or the waiver of rights arising as a result of a proposed transfer or its implementation, such as rights of pre-emption or rights of termination. The scheme will normally provide for these assets to remain behind in the transferor and held for the benefit of the transferee until the necessary consent, waiver or other event has occurred, whereupon the order of the court will automatically transfer the assets.

Section 112(2) of the Act provides that the court order may transfer property or liabilities whether or not the transferor otherwise has the capacity to effect the transfer in question. It is not entirely clear what the scope of this provision is intended to be, but it is probably safe to assume that it is not intended to override the requirements for consents, but merely to cure any lack of corporate capacity to effect the transfer and so reverse the decision in *Re Sovereign Life Assurance Company* [1889] L.R.42 ch. D.540.

6.6.3 Supplemental provisions

Under Section 112(1)(d) of the Act the court order may make such provision (if any) as the court thinks fit with respect to such incidental, consequential and supplementary matters as are, in its opinion, necessary to secure that the scheme is fully and effectively carried out. The equivalent provision (but without the words "in its opinion") in Schedule 2C has been considered in a number of judgments, including *Re Hill Samuel Life Assurance Limited* [1998] 3 AER 176 and *Re Sun Life of Canada Assurance Company* [1999] (unreported). Concern had been expressed in an earlier decision of Rattee J in *Re Lincoln Assurance Limited* [1996] (unreported) that certain provisions of a scheme unrelated to the policies which were transferring did not fall within the court's jurisdiction because they could not be said to be necessary. Very shortly after that decision, Harman J in *Re Consolidated Life Assurance Co Ltd* [1996] (unreported) said:

"Although 'necessary' is somewhere in the middle between 'vital' on the one hand, and 'desirable' on the other, when it is used in the phrase 'necessary to secure that the scheme shall be fully and effectively carried out' and it extends to 'consequential and supplementary matters', it seems to me legitimate for the court to include within the ambit of the scheme which it approves something which will give the full benefit of the scheme for one or other of the two units that are being amalgamated."

This test was preferred in the later *Re Hill Samuel* and *Re Sun Life of Canada* decisions. Nevertheless, it will always be necessary to consider critically in the light of this line of cases any provision of the scheme which does not relate to the transferring policies or their future management within the transferee or, even if it does, which interferes with the contractual rights of policyholders.

6.6.4   Companies in financial difficulty

Section 112(8)(c) and Section 113 of the Act contain provisions dealing with the potential reduction of benefits payable under policies transferred by the scheme. These provisions are intended to apply to companies experiencing financial difficulty and will not be relevant in other contexts.

6.7   Taxation

6.7.1   Introduction

An insurance business transfer will by its nature involve the disposal by the transferor of its assets, both investment portfolios and operational assets (and, to the extent that it exists, goodwill) to the transferee. Application of general UK tax principles would give rise to the following consequences:

(a)   the transferor would be regarded as making a disposal, probably at market value, of its assets for the purpose of corporation tax on chargeable gains ("CGT");

(b)   any capital losses claimed and losses or excess management expenses incurred by the transferor would not be available for offset against income of the transferee for periods after the transfer and/or the transferor would incur a balancing charge in respect of capital allowances;

(c)   if the transferor conducts pension business or overseas life assurance business the excess of the liabilities assumed by the transferee (or market value, if different) over the acquisition costs of investments might give rise to a Schedule D, Case VI charge; and

(d)   since the effect of the order of the court would be that the trans-
      feror ceases to be liable to policyholders under, and the transferee
      becomes liable to policyholders under, all life insurance policies
      extant at the date of the order, that policyholders who have effected
      policies before 13 March 1984, or before 19 March 1968 in the case
      of non-qualifying policies, might lose their entitlement to relief.

In practice, in most cases, insurance business transfers are most unlikely
to have such dramatic results.

6.7.2   CGT

As far as CGT is concerned, comprehensive relief is provided for by
Section 139 of the Taxation of Chargeable Gains Act ("TCGA") 1992 as
modified in relation to the transfer of long-term business by Section 211.
This relief is only available if certain conditions are satisfied, as described
below. Where the relief is available, the transfer of assets subject to CGT
is treated as being for a sum equal to the transferor's base cost so that no
gain accrues to the transferor but the transferee "inherits" the base cost
of the transferor. Relief will be available in relation to the operational
assets including goodwill of the transferor, and to that part of its business
as is referable to basic life and general annuity business. In a Statement
of Practice (SP7/93) issued by the Inland Revenue on 11 June 1993, the
Inland Revenue have confirmed that the relief will be available to a
company which carries on basic life assurance and general annuity
business on the one hand and pension business on the other hand where
the assets backing basic life assurance and general annuity business are
not segregated from those backing other categories of business.

The conditions that must be satisfied for relief under Section 139, TCGA
1992 as modified by Section 211, TCGA 1992 to be available are as
follows:

(a)   the transfer is of a business which consists of the effecting or
      carrying out of contracts of long-term insurance;
(b)   the transfer is to another person whether resident in the UK or not;
(c)   the transfer is in accordance with a scheme falling within Section
      105 of the Act (including an excluded scheme falling within Case
      2, 3 or 4 of Section 105(3)) or is a "qualifying overseas transfer" (*see*
      6.7.11 below);
(d)   the transferee is either resident in the UK at the time of the acqui-
      sition of the assets, or if the transferee were to dispose of the assets
      immediately after that time, any gain accruing to the transferee

would be a chargeable gain forming part of its chargeable profits for corporation tax purposes;

(e) the transferor is either resident in the UK at the time of the acquisition of the assets, or if the transferor were to dispose of the assets immediately before that time, any gain accruing to the transferee would be a chargeable gain forming part of its chargeable profits for corporation tax purposes;

(f) no gain of the type mentioned in (d) or (e) above would be a gain exempted from UK tax under any double taxation arrangement; and

(g) the transferor receives no part of the consideration for the transfer (otherwise than by the transferee taking over the whole or part of the liabilities of the business).

An application for clearance that the transfer is for bona fide commercial reasons and does not form part of a scheme or arrangement of which the main purpose, or one of the main purposes, is the avoidance of liability to corporation tax and that Section 211, TCGA 1992 may therefore apply can be made to the Inland Revenue in advance of the transfer.

The relief will not be available in relation to the transfer of an asset which prior to the transfer backed one category of business (e.g. basic life and general annuity business) and after the transfer backs another category of business (e.g. pension business). In that case, the transferor is treated as having disposed of and immediately reacquired the asset for a consideration equal to the market value immediately before the transfer (Section 440, Income and Corporation Taxes Act ("ICTA") 1988). In practice, however, this provision is only applied where the change of category is part of an arrangement to which both the transferor and the transferee are party. If this is not the case, the asset is treated as having been transferred between categories by the transferee immediately after the transfer with the result that any gain or loss accrues to the transferee and not the transferor.

6.7.3 Capital allowances

Section 560 of the Capital Allowances Act 2001 (previously in Section 152A of the Capital Allowances Act 1990) provides that where assets are transferred as part of, or in connection with, a transfer of the whole or part of the long-term business of an insurance company to another company and the transfer is in accordance with a scheme falling within Section 105 of the Act (including an excluded scheme within Case 2, 3 or 4 of Section 105(3)) to transfer business which consists of the effecting or carrying out of contracts of long-term insurance or a "qualifying overseas transfer", the transferee shall be entitled to any allowances and charges as would have fallen to be made to or on the transferor. The amount of the allowances or charges are computed as if everything done to or by the transferor had been done to or by the transferee. In other words there is a complete continuity of the capital allowances position of the transferor and the transfer itself will occasion no balancing charge.

6.7.4 *Expenses of management and losses available for carry forward*

Expenses of management which would have been deductible by the transferor under general principles for the accounting period following that in which the transfer takes place will be treated as expenses of management of the transferee and deductible in accordance with general principles provided that there is a transfer of long-term business from one person to another in accordance with a scheme falling within Section 105 of the Act (including an excluded scheme within Case 2, 3 or 4 of Section 105(3)) or a "qualifying overseas transfer").

Similarly, losses which would have been available to the transferor for the accounting period following that in which the transfer takes place shall be treated as a loss of the transferee and available to be set off against profits of the same class of business as that in which it arose in accordance with ordinary principles.

The relief for carry forward of management expenses and losses is contained in Section 444A, ICTA 1988. It is only available if the transfer has been effected for bona fide commercial reasons and does not form part of a scheme or arrangement of which the main purpose, or one of the main purposes, is the avoidance of liability to corporation tax. An application for clearance to that effect may be made to the Inland Revenue in advance of the transfer.

6.7.5 *Charges to tax on an income basis*

Section 211, TCGA 1992 does not apply to exclude any Case VI charge that might arise in respect of the transfer, as it applies only to the CGT. The current insurance companies tax legislation (in particular Section 432E, ICTA 1988 and Section 83, FA 1989) imposes a charge to taxation on any increase in value (whether realised or not) of the assets of the long-term business fund which are brought into account in the Revenue Account of the FSA Return prepared for the purposes of Rule 9.6 of the Interim Prudential Sourcebook for Insurers (i.e. the increase in value brought into account in Form 40 of that Return). If the transfer takes place at a year end, there may therefore be no substantial effect. In the case of a mutual, moreover, it is only "unallocated surplus" of the relevant category that is charged (subject to the "floor" basis) in Section 432(3)); and it will be rare, in the case of a mutual, for there to be any such surplus brought into account in Form 40. Thus an insurance business transfer is unlikely of itself to create a major Case VI charge. It is, however, prudent to confirm with the Revenue that, in the context of the particular scheme, this will be the case. Careful consideration would also be necessary, where permanent health insurance business is significant, of any potential Case I charge in respect of the assets of such business.

6.7.6   Life assurance premium relief

It is quite likely that the transferor will have issued polices which confer on their holders the right to life assurance premium relief ("LAPR") under Section 266, ICTA 1988. However, premiums paid under policies issued after 13 March 1984, or after 19 March 1968 in the case of non-qualifying policies, will not normally qualify. Such relief can, in certain circumstances, be lost if a new policy is issued in substitution of the existing one or the terms of the existing policy are varied. A possible analysis of the effect of an order under Section 111 might be that policies issued by the transferor are "novated", that is to say, cancelled and substituted by new policies in appropriate terms issued by the transferee, and if this analysis were appropriate, LAPR could in certain circumstances be lost. It is therefore important to ensure that the scheme is drafted in such a way as not to constitute a novation (i.e. release and recreation) of liabilities but a transfer of liabilities by operation of law. In these circumstances the Revenue are normally prepared to confirm that LAPR will remain undisturbed by the transfer.

Likewise, the Revenue are normally prepared to confirm that other reliefs available to policyholders and annuitants, such as retirement benefit scheme relief, retirement annuity relief and personal pension scheme relief, will be unaffected by the transfer.

6.7.7   Distribution

It may be the case that, either deliberately or fortuitously, the transferee may around the time of the insurance business transfer be or become a member of the transferor. In such cases it may be argued by the Revenue that the excess of the value of the transferor's assets over the liabilities assumed by the transferee constitutes a distribution. It is considered that treatment of that excess as a distribution, even where the transferee is a member of the transferor, is not inevitable, but it is clearly a matter to be borne in mind by those devising the scheme. It may well be advisable, depending on the circumstances, for appropriate confirmation to be obtained from the Revenue. If shares are offered on a demutualisation to former members of the mutual, their value might (depending on the exact terms of the scheme) constitute a distribution.

6.7.8 VAT

Provided what is being transferred is the whole of a business or, where part of a business is being transferred, that the part business is capable of separate operation, VAT does not pose any particular problems since the transfer will be of a business as a going concern and the transfer will be treated as neither a supply of goods nor a supply of services for VAT purposes (under paragraph 5 the VAT (Special Provisions) Order 1995).

However, where the assets being transferred include land and buildings in relation to which the transferor has made an election to waive its exemption from VAT, then the transferee must make an election in relation to those properties with effect from the transfer date.

6.7.9 Stamp duty

A significant issue is whether the order of the court, transferring the various assets of the transferring company, attracts UK stamp duty. The potentially relevant heads of charge are:

(a) Schedule 13, paragraph 1 FA 1999 – "conveyance or transfer on sale [of any property or any interest in any property]" ("Property" in the Stamp Acts is not confined to real property, i.e. land and buildings). The amount of the duty is a percentage of the "amount or value of the consideration for the sale", and such duty is called *ad valorem* duty. This duty is charged at different rates for different types of asset (0.5 per cent on equity securities including convertible and other special kinds of debt; a maximum of 4 per cent on goodwill, cash on deposit and UK or foreign land and buildings; nil on corporate and government debt, intellectual property (including trade marks), cash on current account and the benefit of mortgages); or

(b) Schedule 13, paragraph 16 FA 1999 – "conveyance or transfer of property otherwise than on sale". The amount of the duty is a fixed amount of £5 per instrument.

In the straightforward case of a transfer of long-term business where the transferee is subjected to liabilities but no price (either cash or stocks and shares) is payable or to be issued as consideration for the transferred business, whether to the transferor or, on a demutualisation, its members, the court order will be a "conveyance or transfer otherwise than on sale" and hence will not attract *ad valorem* stamp duty but will be subject to £5 fixed duty.

Equally, where there is an agreed price for the transfer of the business, *ad valorem* duty will be payable and Section 139, TCGA 1992 relief for gains arising on the transfer will be lost (*see* above). Then the question is how the duty should be calculated, given the different rates of duty. There appears to be no settled Stamp Office practice but most commentators agree that the correct approach in such a case is to calculate a "blended rate" (between nil and 4 per cent) by reference to the aggregate value of the assets of each kind transferred by the court order.

Certain types of demutualisation involve the making of payments to members (policyholders) of the transferor under the scheme. It is a question of construction of the scheme whether the payments are consideration for anything and if so what. The Stamp Office have in the past sometimes argued that *ad valorem* duty is payable, calculated on the value of payments made to members on the basis that these represent consideration for the property transferred. If, however, the correct construction of the scheme (which, of course, needs to be consistent on this point with the circular to policy holders and any press release) is that the payments are being made to members to cancel their membership rights, this is not the purchase price of the business transferred so no *ad valorem* duty should in any event be payable. However, the position is sometimes open to doubt and it is understood that the Stamp Office are currently taking advice from external counsel on the issue.

Where special bonuses have been or are to be declared in favour of the transferor's policyholders, such bonuses do not of course amount to "consideration" and the practice of the Stamp Office reflects this.

Relief from *ad valorem* stamp duty (where the Order does amount to a conveyance or transfer on sale) under Section 42, Finance Act 1930 may (subject to the potential application of elaborate anti-avoidance provisions) be available where the transfer is between associated companies.

The Finance Act 1997 introduced a specific relief intended for "pure" demutualisations, although it is possible to structure a demutualisation which is in substance an acquisition so as to benefit from the relief. The relief is contained in Section 96. In very brief terms, the relief is available where at least 90 per cent of the members of the transferor are offered shares in the transferee (or the parent of the transferee) and where any other shares issued by the transferee (or its parent) go to employees or pensioners of the transferor or are issued as a result of an offer to the public.

In addition, the question of stamp duty reserve tax ('sDRT") needs to be considered. Where the order is appropriately stamped, no question of SDRT should arise.

In view of the fact that any consideration, no matter how small, may mean that the order will be a conveyance or transfer on sale and hence trigger stamp duty on the basis of all the consideration including the liabilities assumed by the transferee, it is prudent to obtain prior confirmation from the Inland Revenue as to the stamp duty treatment.

The above remarks address UK duty only. There will often be assets of the transferor situated outside the UK and the question of overseas duties should not be overlooked.

6.7.10 Policyholders" personal position

The tax position of the policyholders themselves will need careful consideration. The extent to which problems arise will clearly depend upon what is offered to them, and in what capacity they receive it (whether as policyholder or, in the case of a mutual, as member).

It is sometimes questioned whether there is any liability to capital gains tax in relation to members of a mutual company which is the transferor under an insurance business transfer scheme where, as is not unusual, the scheme provides for them to become members of the transferee. It is normally very difficult to ascribe any monetary value to the membership rights. Furthermore, Section 136, TCGA 1992 provides that in the case of a reconstruction or amalgamation (an insurance business transfer is likely to fall within one or other category) the issue by the transferee of "shares" – which is expressly declared in this context to include the interest of a member in a company such as the interest of a policyholder in a mutual company – against the cancellation of "shares" in the transferor does not of itself give rise to a disposal by members of the transferor of their interest.

179

6.7.11   The Third Life Coordination Directive (92/96/EEC)

Article 11 of the Third Directive permits the relevant authorities in the country in which the head office of an insurer is situated to authorise the transfer of the portfolio of polices to another life office in the Community.

A "qualifying overseas transfer" is so much of the transfer of the whole or part of the business of an overseas life insurance company carried on through a branch or agency in the UK as takes place in accordance with any authorisation granted outside the UK for the purposes of Article 11 (Schedule 19AC, paragraph 4A ICTA 1988).

6.7.12   Taxation of friendly society transfers

The reliefs available for transferors of long-term business as described above apply equally to transfers of long-term business by a friendly society or to a friendly society notwithstanding that (in the former case) the transfer is an excluded scheme within Case 1 of Section 105(3) of the Act (Section 463, ICTA 1988 and the Friendly Societies (Taxation of Transfers of Business) Regulations 1995).

6.7.13   General insurance business

Although the procedure for transfers of long-term business and general business has been unified, the special tax provisions explained above (with the exception of stamp duty) apply only to transfers of long-term business. The tax legislation will require amendment if the tax treatment for long-term business transfers is to apply to transfers of general insurance business.

All general insurance business carried on by a company is a trade, and a transfer of general insurance business will be governed by general tax principles as underlined in 6.7.1 above.

The paragraphs below elaborate on these general principles.

6.7.13.1   CGT
Section 211, TCGA 1992 applies only to the transfer of long-term business and so there is no modification to Section 139 where general insurance business is being transferred. Section 139 TCGA 1992 will not apply to a transfer of general insurance business to the extent that the assets being transferred are trading stock or if there is no reconstruction or amalgamation.

There is a deemed disposal for market value under Section 100, ICTA 1988 of trading stock of the general insurance business. The transferor may therefore be charged tax on the deemed trading profits.

If the transferor and the transferee are in the same chargeable gains group, Section 171, TCGA 1992 will apply so that the transfer will be for no gain/no loss to the extent that the assets transferred are chargeable assets.

6.7.13.2   Capital allowances, trading losses and management expenses

Where the transferor and the transferee are not under common ownership (*see* 6.7.13.3 below for the meaning of common ownership) the transferor is treated as having ceased to carry on the general insurance business and the transferee is treated as having commenced the general insurance business. This means that capital allowances, trading losses and management expenses of the transferor are not available to the transferee.

A balancing adjustment will be made on the transferor in respect of any assets of the general insurance business on which capital allowances have been claimed.

The trade charges and losses of the final 12 months of trading can be carried back by the transferor for three years under Section 393A(1)(b), ICTA 1988.

6.7.13.3   Common ownership

If the conditions for Section 343, ICTA 1988 are satisfied, the general insurance business shall not be treated as ceased by the transferor and commenced by the transferee for capital allowances purposes. The transferee will stand in the shoes of the transferor as respects capital allowances, losses and charges.

The conditions for Section 343 to apply are:

(a)   a company ceases to carry on a trade and another company begins to carry on the same trade;

(b)   on or at any time within two years of the transfer of trade, the trade or an interest in the trade amounting to not less than 75 per cent in it belongs to the same persons as the trade or such an interest belonged to at some time within a year before that event; and

(c)   the trade is not within the period of two years before and one year after the transfer carried on otherwise than by a company which is within the charge to tax in respect of it.

181

6.7.13.4   VAT

The analysis at 6.7.8 above applies equally to the transfer of general insurance business.

6.7.13.5   Stamp duty

The analysis at 6.7.9 above applies equally to the transfer of general insurance business, although the discussion concerning compensation payments to members is less likely to be applicable as most companies which carry on general insurance business are proprietary companies. It should be noted, however, that if the transferor is a mutual company, the relief under Section 96 of the Finance Act 1997 will also cover a demutualisation in connection with a transfer of general insurance business under a scheme which is an insurance business transfer scheme for the purposes of the Act.

6.8   Miscellaneous points on insurance business transfers

6.8.1   Amendment of schemes

Once a scheme has been sanctioned it cannot be amended except in accordance with its terms. It is customary for the scheme to include words permitting its amendment with the further sanction of the court given at a hearing at which the FSA is entitled to be heard. There is no reason in principle why the right to propose any such amendment should be further constrained, although the FSA will typically require the right to appoint an independent expert to consider the effect of the amendments.

6.8.2   Appeal against the court's order

There is no specific provision in the Act, the Regulations or Guidance dealing with the possibility of appeal against an order of the court sanctioning the scheme. Objectors will therefore have the same ability to appeal against an order as exists under the general law in relation to any other court order. If this is a real possibility, the parties to the scheme may prefer to delay the effective date of the transfer until it has become clear whether such an appeal will be made.

The court is able to set aside a judgment obtained by fraud even if the scheme has already become effective and even if the result of setting aside the order would require the scheme to be unravelled and the transfer of policies, assets and liabilities to have been deemed never to have occurred. However, it will not do so if on investigation the court is satisfied that the result would have been the same even if the fraud had not been perpetrated. These two propositions follow from the judgment of Neuberger J in *Fletcher* v *Royal Automobile Club Limited* [2000] 1 BCLC 331, a decision on a scheme of arrangement under Section 425 of the Companies Act 1985.

6.8.3 Enforcement of scheme provisions

After the transfer, the transferor will, unless the transfer does not encompass the whole of its business, be left as a shell company, usually with no incentive to take steps to enforce provisions of the scheme. Failure to observe the terms of the scheme is, in principle, a contempt of court and may be treated accordingly. In practice, however, it is necessary for the Appointed Actuary of the transferee, or the FSA, to seek to bring such breaches to the attention of the court. The scheme will generally disapply the provisions of the Contracts (Rights of Third Parties) Act 1999, which, if the scheme is a contract for the purposes of that Act, probably has the effect that an individual policyholder cannot take enforcement action. It is likely, in practice, for it to be simpler for a policy-holder to complain to the FSA, who would then consider exercising its general supervisory powers.

6.8.4 Section 427A of the Companies Act 1985

If an insurance business transfer scheme involves a compromise or an arrangement falling within Section 427A of the Companies Act 1985, then Sections 425 to 427 of the Companies Act have effect, as modified by Section 427A, in relation to that compromise or arrangement. Section 427A applies, for example, to a transfer by a public company to another public company which already has a business of its own where the consideration for the transfer includes shares in the transferee receivable by members of the transferor. In such a case, the meetings required by Section 425 and the other procedural requirements of Schedule 15B to the Companies Act 1985 will apply. There does not, however, appear to have been a scheme under these provisions since they were first introduced in 1987 in order to comply with EC directives on mergers and divisions of public companies (78/855/EEC and 82/891/EEC).

6.8.5   *Application of company law principles*

Nothing in the Act or the Regulations disapply provisions of the general law or the Companies Act 1985 relating to maintenance of capital, financial assistance, dividends or transactions having the effect of dividends (such as the rule in *Aveling Barford* v *Perion* [1989] BCLC 626). It is therefore important to consider at an early stage the way in which these rules apply to any given proposal. It is probable that the correct analysis of Section 151 of the Companies Act 1985, which will often need to be considered in circumstances where a transfer is made following an earlier acquisition of an insurance company or its holding company, is that the transfer occurs by order of the court rather than by action of the company itself, and that on this basis the Section does not apply. However, there are mixed views on this point.

An insurance business transfer scheme will generally amount to a transfer of an undertaking within the meaning of the Transfer of Undertakings (Protection of Employment) Regulations 1981 (SI 1981/1794) with the result that contracts of employment with any employees of the transferor will pass to the transferee as a result of the court's order.

6.8.6   *Certificates in relation to transfers outside the UK*

Sections 115 and 116 of the Act, Part III of Schedule 12 to the Act and paragraph 18.3 of the Guidance implement obligations of the UK under EU directives in relation to transfers of insurance business occurring outside the UK. These provisions have the following broad effects:

(a)   the FSA may give a certificate confirming that a UK authorised person possesses the required minimum margin of solvency to facilitate an insurance business transfer to the firm under relevant legislation in another EEA State (or from a Swiss general insurance company). The Guidance indicates how that power will be exercised; and

(b)   Section 116 enables the FSA to publish notice of a transfer authorised in another EEA State and therefore make that transfer effective in law to transfer obligations under the UK policies, and any legal proceedings, within the scope of that transfer.

6.8.7 *Insurance business transfers in the Channel Islands and the Isle of Man*

The Channel Islands do not form part of the UK and are not EEA States. Accordingly transfers of insurance business carried on by an authorised person from branches in those jurisdictions will be subject to the applicable local legal regime for the transfer of insurance business. In Jersey, Guernsey and the Isle of Man a separate scheme document will be required for the transfer of long-term insurance business although this will in most cases be similar to, and conditional upon court sanction of, the scheme in respect of which application has been made to the court under the Act. It is also likely that the reports produced by the independent expert and, if applicable, Appointed Actuary and any notices or circulars sent to long-term policyholders by the authorised person or transferee concerned will suffice for the purposes of the relevant local courts in these jurisdictions, provided the position of policyholders with long-term insurance policies written from the relevant branch is specifically addressed. There is no specific legislation governing the transfer of general insurance business in Jersey, Guernsey or the Isle of Man.

6.9 Friendly society amalgamations, transfers and conversions

6.9.1 *Introduction*

Although the continued existence of two Acts of Parliament on the subject (the Friendly Societies Act 1974 and the Friendly Societies Act 1992) gives rise to a number of complexities in other areas, the position in relation to transfers of insurance business by friendly societies is relatively straightforward.

The relevant provision in the 1974 Act (Section 82) does not apply to the amalgamation of, or transfer of engagements by, a "registered friendly society", which is defined by Section 7(i)(a) of that Act and Section 116 of the 1992 Act to mean a friendly society registered under the 1974 Act.

Part VIII of, and Schedule 15 to, the 1992 Act contain provisions applying to "friendly societies" as defined for the purposes of that Act, namely societies incorporated under the 1992 Act and registered friendly societies (as referred to above). The consequence is that it is only the 1992 Act which applies to any transfer of insurance business by a friendly society, however it may be registered.

185

6.9.2   *Part VIII of the 1992 Act*

Part VIII of the 1992 Act deals with three different transactions:

(a)   an amalgamation of two or more friendly societies by means of establishment of an incorporated friendly society as their successor, to which all the property, rights and liabilities of each amalgamating society are transferred;

(b)   a transfer by a friendly society of all or part of its engagements to another friendly society, an industrial and provident society, a company or any other insurance company; and

(c)   the conversion of a friendly society into a company registered under the Companies Act 1985.

Part VIII and Schedule 15 also include requirements to be fulfilled by a friendly society which proposes to accept a transfer of business from another friendly society, an industrial and provident society or any other insurance company, notably a requirement that the transfer should be approved by a special resolution of the members of the transferee (with one limited exception where the transfer is between friendly societies and the FSA consents to the approval being given by the committee of management of the transferee).

The Guidance (at SUP 18.4) gives further information as to the way in which the FSA (as successor to the Friendly Societies Commission) will exercise its powers in relation to these three types of transactions. The court is not involved in approving any such transaction.

6.9.3   *Differences between the amalgamation and transfer provisions*

Part VIII and Schedule 15 of the 1992 Act, together with the Guidance, set out in detail the requirements for each of the three transactions mentioned above, and it is not necessary to repeat them here. It will sometimes be clear which of the three transactions is the most appropriate, but sometimes more than one would be suitable. The notable differences are as follows:

(a)   an amalgamation can only involve two or more friendly societies, whereas a transfer can involve a friendly society and a number of other types of entity, as described above;

(b)   an amalgamation leads to the dissolution of the previous societies, and is therefore not suitable where only part of the business is to be transferred, whereas a transfer may relate to all or any part of a friendly society's business;

(c)   an amalgamation requires the parties to establish a new incorporated friendly society as the successor to the amalgamating societies;

(d)   an amalgamation takes effect simply by virtue of the special resolution and does not require the further instrument of transfer required for a transfer. In both cases, the terms on which the amalgamation or the transfer of engagements is to be made would normally be expected to be set out in the statement sent to members;

(e)   it is only on a transfer of engagements, not an amalgamation, that an actuarial report is required under Section 87 of the 1992 Act as to the margin of solvency (or, in the case of long-term business, the extent of any excess of assets over liabilities) of the transferee;

(f)   further, it is only upon a transfer of long-term business, not an amalgamation of two friendly societies each carrying on long-term business, that the FSA may require under Section 88 of the 1992 Act the production of a report by an independent actuary on the terms of the proposed transfer and the likely effects of the transfer on the members of the society who are long-term policyholders; and

(g)   the jurisdictional requirements before the FSA can confirm an amalgamation are substantially more straightforward than the requirements for a transfer. In particular it is necessary on a transfer to notify regulatory authorities in EEA States in similar circumstances to those applicable to insurance companies (*see* 6.4.4 above) and in the case of general business, the FSA only has power to transfer the contracts entered into before the date of the application, not all contracts entered into up to the transfer date (this was also the position in relation to general business under Schedule 2C to the Insurance Companies Act 1982).

The requirements as to statements to members and as to the right to make representations at the hearing are substantially similar whether the transaction is proposed to take effect as an amalgamation or as a transfer.

The procedural requirements in relation to a conversion of a friendly society into a company, which might be appropriate in the event of the proposed demutualisation of a friendly society, are similar to the simpler requirements applicable to amalgamations.

Chapter 7

Miscellaneous Issues Relating to Contract Law etc.

Andrew Holderness
Partner, Corporate Insurance Department
Clyde & Co.

With the introduction by the Financial Services and Markets Act 2000 (the "FSMA") of a "super regulator" and other regulatory provisions flowing from this, much of the commentary on the FSMA 2000 has focused on how this will affect those insurance companies active in the financial services field.

This Chapter focuses on those issues that are relevant to policyholders, with the knock-on effect that these will have on insurers. It concentrates on five areas:

(a) policyholders' rights to cancel policies during a "cooling off" period;
(b) restrictions on advertising to policyholders and potential policy-holders by insurers;
(c) the compensation structure in place for policyholders who find that their insurer is unable to meet their liabilities;
(d) choice of law for insurance contracts; and
(e) compulsory information that must be provided to policyholders in certain circumstances.

Each of these areas is reviewed in turn to ascertain the current position and to see what, if any, effect the FSMA 2000 will have for policyholders in the situations described.

7.1 Specific rights to cancel insurance policies after a "cooling off" period

"Cooling off" rights are an important part of consumer protection designed to protect policyholders and investors against high-pressure selling tactics and "cold calling". There are already protections for consumers in the Consumer Credit Act 1974 which allows debtors or hirers to cancel consumer credit and customer hire agreements regulated by that Act within a specified period of time. Also, the Consumer Protection (Cancellation of Contracts Concluded Away from Business Premises) Regulations 1987 deal with contracts concluded in those circumstances as a result of unsolicited visits, or visits where the consumer did not know such goods and services formed part of the trader's business activities.

In addition, various EU directives contain the right to cancel a contract. An example is Directive 97/7/EC, which has been enacted into UK law by the Consumer Protection (Distance Selling) Regulations 2000. These Regulations apply to services supplied to a consumer where the contract is made by means of distance communication (e.g. over the internet) and provides for a cooling off period to enable the consumer to cancel the contract by giving notice of cancellation to the supplier within a specified period.

In these cases "investment agreements" and insurance and reinsurance operations respectively are exempt from the provisions of the Regulations. So what protections are there for policyholders?

7.1.1 *The position under the Financial Services Act 1986*

The principle that parties to particular insurance and other contracts should have the right to cancel them within a short period of signing was incorporated into Section 51 of the Financial Services Act 1986 ("FS Act 1986"). This stated that the Secretary of State (later the Securities and Investments Board) might:

> "make rules for enabling a person who has entered or offered to enter into an investment agreement with an authorised person to rescind the agreement or withdraw the offer within such period and in such manner as may be prescribed."

This right could also include the return of any payments made by the person cancelling the agreement.

These rules mean that individuals and others entering, or agreeing to enter, into a long-term insurance contract with a company or firm authorised to carry on insurance business which is investment business or with a person authorised under the FS Act 1986, would be able to take advantage of the "cooling off" provisions legislated for by Section 51 of the FS Act 1986. "Investments" were defined in Schedule 1 to the FS Act 1986 and included long-term insurance contracts as well as shares, debentures, government and public securities, and units in collective investment schemes, among other things.

The Insurance Companies Regulations 1994 deal with the notices to be provided by insurers to policyholders in relation to long-term insurance agreements at Section 41 and Schedules 8 and 9 (*see* 7.5.1 below). These "cooling off" rights are embodied in the form of notice of cancellation, which must be sent to policyholders when or before the long-term insurance contract is entered into. As set out above, such notice is required to state that the policyholder has 14 days (or 10 days in the case of non-EC contracts) in which to cancel the contract with the insurer.

If such a cancellation right is exercised within the appropriate time scale, the contract would then be treated as if it had not been entered into. Any premiums or other monies paid by the policyholder to the insurer would then fall to be repaid.

7.1.2 The impact of the FSMA 2000

Like the FS Act 1986, the FSMA 2000 contains provisions in Section 139(4) to enable the Financial Services Authority ("FSA") to draw up rules which:

"may:

(a) confer rights on persons to rescind agreements with, or withdraw offers to, authorised persons within a specified period; and

(b) make provision, in respect of authorised persons and persons exercising those rights, for the restitution of property and the making or recovery of payments where those rights are exercised."

These provisions require the FSA to draw up cancellation rules similar to those provisions under the FS Act 1986, to override a contract between an insurance company authorised for the purpose of the FSMA 2000 and their customer, by granting the policyholder unilateral "cooling off" rights to cancel or withdraw from an insurance contract within a certain period of its having been entered into. In such cases, any premiums or other monies paid would be recoverable.

These provisions carry forward the principle that parties to insurance and other contracts will have time after signing such a contract to change their minds, as was embodied in Section 51 of the FS Act 1986. As under those provisions, if the rights contained in the rules to be drawn up by the FSA under the directions in the FSMA 2000 are invoked, the contract will be treated as if it was never made. Again, like the FS Act 1986, these provisions only relate to insurance contracts with authorised insurers.

The FSA has set these rules out in its Conduct of Business Sourcebook ("COB"). Chapter 6.7 sets out the cancellation periods for certain investments. In some cases these rights arise only if the insurer provided advice, for example, in relation to packaged products and ISAs. In the case of certain products (e.g. a life policy for a term of less than six months or where the insured entering a non-life policy is not a private customer) there is no right of cancellation.

Chapter 6.7 also sets out that, as under the FS Act 1986 and the Insurance Companies Regulations 1994, an insurer must give notice of cancellation rights. Such notice must be in writing and clear and prominent notice of this right must be given:

- before the agreement is concluded (a "pre-sale notice"); and
- after the agreement has been concluded (a "post-sale notice").

Section 6.7.36 details the information which must be contained in such a notice, which includes a statement that such a cancellation rights exists, the duration of that right and the steps the customer must take to cancel the agreement. If an insurer fails to send a post-sale notice when required, the customer is entitled to cancel the agreement at any time within two years of the agreement (and will not be liable for any shortfall, that is, market loss).

7.2   Restrictions on advertising

7.2.1   *The restrictions on advertising contained in the FS Act 1986*

The FS Act 1986 established a framework of rules governing advertisements that relate to "investment agreements". Certain insurance agreements were caught by this, as long-term insurance contracts constituted investments under Section 130 of the FS Act 1986.

An advertisement was defined by Section 207(2) to include "every form of advertising, whether . . . by means of circulars, . . . price lists or other documents, . . . or in any other manner".

Under Section 57(1) of the FS Act 1986, no insurer other than an "authorised person" (a person authorised under the FS Act 1986) can issue, or cause to be issued, an advertisement in relation to long-term insurance in the UK unless its contents have first been approved by an authorised person. Investment advertisements are defined in Section 57(2) as:

> "any advertisement inviting person to enter or offer to enter into an investment agreement or to exercise any rights conferred by an investment to acquire, dispose of, underwrite or convert an investment or containing information calculated to lead directly or indirectly to persons doing so."

The meaning of "issue" should be interpreted liberally; and advertisement would include oral or visual communications and publications on the internet. Whether an advertisement is "calculated" to lead someone into entering into a long-term insurance contract would be judged on an objective basis to see if it was likely, or intended, to lead to that particular result, irrespective of whether or not such a result was intended by the insurer or other person issuing the advertisement.

There are a number of exemptions that could be used to avoid the need to have the advertisement approved by an authorised person, including those set out in the FS Act 1986 itself or in various statutory instruments. However, these did not immediately lend themselves to exempting long-term insurance contracts.

Under Section 57(5) and (6) of the FS Act 1986 an insurance agreement entered into as a result of a non-compliant advertisement might be unenforceable and the policyholder or investor might be entitled to recover any premium or monies paid, and perhaps to compensation for any loss sustained. Section 61 of the FS Act 1986 provided that the court could order restitution as it saw fit.

Breach of the provisions dealing with investment advertisements was a criminal offence, punishable on indictment by up to two years in prison and/or a fine, and on summary conviction by up to six months imprisonment.

In addition, Section 47 of the FS Act 1986 dealt with cases where misleading or inaccurate statements were made. Any insurance company which made (recklessly or otherwise) a statement, promise or forecast which it knew to be misleading, or dishonestly concealed any material fact if it did so for the purpose of inducing someone to enter, or offer to enter into, an insurance contract, committed a criminal offence. Again, this was punishable by imprisonment and/or a fine.

7.2.2 Advertisements by insurers regulated outside of the EC

Regulations stemming from the ICA 1982 and the FS Act 1986 require advertisements and invitations to enter into insurance contracts to make certain statements where the relevant insurer is not regulated within the EC, or where the issuer of the advertisement or invitation is connected with the insurance company. These requirements do not apply to advertisements in relation to reinsurance contracts.

Section 36 of the Insurance Companies Regulations 1994 requires advertisements by insurers whose head office is not in a European Economic Area ("EEA") State and which are not authorised under the ICA 1982 to include a paragraph warning potential policyholders and investors that:

> "the management and solvency of this company are not supervised by Her Majesty's Government and you will not be protected by the Policyholder Protection Act 1975 if the company should be unable to meet its liabilities to you."

Such advertisements must also state the full name of the insurance company, the country where the insurance company is registered and the country where its principal office is situated (if different).

A statement that an insurer's head office is not in an EEA State and that it is not authorised under the ICA 1982 to carry on long-term business (which is not related to a contract of insurance) will be required under Section 36(4) where this is the case.

7.2.3 How these restrictions are changed by the FSMA 2000's provisions

The FSMA 2000 sets out in Sections 19 and 21 that an insurance company must not, in the course of business, communicate an invitation or inducement to effect an insurance contract or engage in investment activity unless:

- he or it is an authorised person; or
- the contents of the communication are approved by an authorised person; or
- the communication is covered by an exemption.

"Communicate" is stated at Section 21(13) of the FSMA 2000 to include "causing a communication to be made". This seems to be intended to catch a broader range of activities than "issue". The words "invitation or inducement" indicate a degree of incitement, so purely factual communications should not be caught by these provisions. However, the Explanatory Notes on the FSMA 2000 give no guidance as to how "inducement" will be construed: whether it will be objective or subjective, or whether it will be judged as to how it will be seen from the insurer or the policyholder's perspective.

Under Section 21(8) "engaging in an investment activity" means:

(a)   entering or offering to enter into an agreement the making or performance of which by either party constitutes a controlled activity; or
(b)   exercising any rights conferred by a controlled investment to acquire, dispose or underwrite or convert a controlled investment.

"Controlled activities" are stated at Section 21(9) to be an "activity of a specified kind". These activities are defined in Part I, Schedule 1 to the Financial Services and Markets Act 2000 (Financial Promotion) Order 2001 and Section 10 of the Financial Services and Markets Act 2000 (Regulated Activities) Order 2001 to include:

- effecting a contract of insurance as principal; and
- carrying out a contract of insurance as principal.

"Rights under a contract of insurance" are defined as "controlled investments" in Part II, Schedule 1 to the Financial Promotion Order 2001. Article 12 of the Regulated Activities Order 2001 excludes from this, however, insurance contracts which are "exclusively or primarily benefits in kind in the event of accident to or breakdown of a vehicle".

The FSMA 2000 does not make a distinction between investment advertisements and unsolicited/solicited calls, as the FS Act 1986 did. This is intended to reflect the fact that the line between advertisements and unsolicited calls has become blurred. The wording is also more media neutral than the provisions of the FS Act 1986, as it has been drafted to cope with changing technologies and the various new forms of communication.

As drafted, the FSMA 2000 states that communications are now caught whether they are made in the UK, into the UK from elsewhere, or from the UK to another country. Communications from the UK to another country were not previously caught by the FS Act 1986, although it is likely that a future order may provide that the FSMA 2000's provisions do not apply to such communications. Under Section 21(3) of the FSMA 2000, communications made from outside the UK will only be caught if they are capable of "having an effect" in the UK. Until such further regulations are made, the FSMA 2000's requirements in respect of communications will catch insurers regulated outside of the EC where the communication is intended to have an effect in the UK.

It would appear, however, that promotion of long-term insurance contracts by unauthorised persons is not specifically subject to any special restrictions.

Breach of the above communication requirements of the FSMA 2000 is a criminal offence, as was the case under the provisions of the FS Act 1986. This is also the case for unsolicited calls, which were not subject to the FS Act 1986.

7.3 The provisions of the Policyholders Protection Acts and the scheme that is intended to replace them

7.3.1 *The current compensatory system for policyholders*

The Policyholder Protection Acts 1975 (the "PPA 1975") and 1977 (the "PPA 1977") make provision through the Policyholders Protection Scheme for the protection of policyholders who have been or may be prejudiced by the inability of authorised insurance companies to meet their liabilities. A policyholder is a person who is for the time being the legal holder of a policy for securing a contract with an insurance company and this includes an annuitant and a person to whom, under a policy, a sum is due or contingently due or a periodic payment is payable (defined in Section 96, ICA 1982 as amended by Section 16 of the PPA 1997).

The Policyholders Protection Scheme was run by the Policyholders Protection Board, established by Section 1 and Schedule 1 to the PPA 1975. The functions of the Board were exercised in relation to authorised insurance companies and UK insurance policies and it had power to impose levies on the insurance industry to finance the performance by the Board of their functions. Compensation was available for all insured: 100 per cent of compulsory insurance claims; 90 per cent of long-term insurance claims; and, for individuals, 90 per cent of other general insurance claims (with no upper limit to the level of compensation, and to include making arrangements for continuing cover).

7.3.2 The new compensatory scheme established by the FSMA 2000

Replacing this and the four other financial services compensation schemes is the Financial Services Compensation Scheme ("FSCS") to be set up by the FSA. Described by Part XV of the FSMA 2000, it is designed to be the body that consumers complain to or seek compensation from in respect of financial services generally. Like the Policyholders Protection Scheme, this scheme is designed to inspire consumer confidence, as well as providing a degree of protection to policyholders and investors.

A company, the Financial Ombudsman Scheme Limited ("FOSL"), has already been set up to act as the FSCS's scheme manager, whose board has been appointed by the FSA with, in the case of its chairman, the Treasury's approval.

Under Section 213(3) of the FSMA 2000, the FSCS:

"must, in particular, provide for the scheme manager:

(a) to assess and pay compensation, in accordance with the scheme, to claimants in respect of claims made in connection with regulated activities carried on (whether or not with permission) by relevant persons; and

(b) to have power to impose levies on authorised persons, or any class of authorised person, for the purpose of meeting its expenses (including in particular expenses incurred, or expected to be incurred, in paying compensation, borrowing or insuring risks)."

The FSCS is to take effect "for compensating persons in cases where relevant persons are unable, or are likely to be unable to satisfy claims against them" (Section 213(1), FSMA 2000). "Relevant persons" are defined quite specifically as those insurers who were authorised at the time the act or omission giving rise to the claim against them took place, or that were an authorised representative at such time.

The FSMA 2000 contains at Part XV a framework of guidelines that set out the issues and points on which the FSCS may make rules or provisions to govern. Provisions dealing specifically with long-term insurance policies and insurers in financial difficulties are set out in Sections 216 and 217 of Part XV of the FSMA 2000.

7.3.3 Long-term insurance policies

In respect of long-term insurance policies:

> "The compensation scheme may, in particular, include provision requiring the scheme manager to make arrangements for securing continuity of insurance for policyholders, or policyholders of a specified class, of relevant long-term insurers." (Section 216(1))

"Long-term insurers" are defined as insurers who are authorised to effect or carry out long-term insurance contracts, but which are unable, or likely to be unable, to satisfy claims made against them. "Eligible policy-holders" are to be defined (Section 217(8)).

Section 216(3) sets out that, in the first place, the scheme manager may take such measures as seem appropriate to him to ensure the transfer of all or part of a relevant long-term insurer's business (so far as it consists of carrying out long-term insurance contracts). This will include taking measures to ensure that other authorised persons issue policies to the policyholders in question in substitution for their existing policies.

As a second choice in such cases, Section 216(4) sets out that the FSCS manager may make payments to policyholders where it is not "reasonably practical" for a transfer to be made under Section 216(3). He may also make payments to policyholders while he is arranging for the long-term insurance contract to transfer and continue with some other authorised insurer.

These arrangements reflect the fact that long-term insurance policies are difficult to place a compensation value on, for example a life policy where the insured is still alive at the time that the insurance company suffers financial difficulties.

7.3.4 Insurers in financial difficulties

Section 217 of the FSMA 2000 is concerned with insurers in financial diffi-culties. The Section provides that the FSCS may allow the scheme manager to take measures to protect all, or a specified class of, policy-holders of an insurer who is permitted to effect or carry out insurance contracts but who is in financial difficulties. "Financial difficulties" are to be defined (Section 217(8)).

These measures may include (as the scheme manager considers) appro-priate):

(a) transferring that insurer's insurance-related business to another authorised insurer; and
(b) assisting that insurer so that it can carry on effecting or carrying out insurance contracts.

If the scheme manager decides to transfer the insurance-related business of an insurer in financial difficulties to another insurer, such a transfer shall be on terms that the scheme manager considers appropriate, including reduced terms or deferring payment to which the eligible policyholders are entitled (Section 216(4)(a)). A provision of the FSCS may permit the scheme manager to make interim payments to eligible policyholders of relevant insurers, or indemnify any person who makes such payments.

If the scheme manager decides to assist an insurer in financial difficulties so that it can continue effecting or carrying on insurance contracts, such assistance will be conditional upon reduction or deferment of payments to which eligible policyholders are entitled (Section 216(4)(b)). The scheme manager may also ensure that such measures do not benefit to any material extent those who were members of the insurer when it began to have financial difficulties, or anyone who may have been responsible for, or profited from, the circumstances giving rise to the insurer's financial difficulties.

In either case, the measures that the scheme manager proposes to take must be likely to cost less than the compensation which would be payable if the insurer became unable (or likely to be unable) to satisfy claims made against it.

In addition to these provisions, of FSCS may also allow the FSA to:

(a)   give assistance to the scheme manager to help him decide what measures are practicable or desirable in relation to an insurer;

(b)   impose constraints on measures that the scheme manager can take in relation to particular insurers; and

(c)   require the scheme manager to give it information about the measures it proposes to take.

As was the case under the Policyholders Protection Board, it is intended that the compensation measures or expenses incurred by the scheme manager will be met by levies on authorised insurers and other authorised persons.

7.4   Provisions restricting the choice of law applicable to certain contracts of insurance

The Contracts (Applicable Law) Act 1990 ("CALA 1990") sets out a framework of rules to apply to contractual obligations in any situation involving a choice between the laws of different countries. These rules do not apply to contracts of insurance which cover risks situated in the territories of the Member States of the EEC: in order to determine whether a risk is situated in these territories, the court shall apply its internal law. However, these provisions do not apply to contracts of reinsurance.

7.4.1   Choice of law

The initial position is that parties have the freedom to choose which law will govern the insurance contract. This choice must be expressed or demonstrated with reasonable certainty by the terms of the contract. It is possible to select the law applicable to whole or part only of a contract and to agree to change the law to which a contract is subject.

7.4.2   Where the parties do not choose which law shall govern the contract

Where the parties have not expressly chosen a particular law, nor can a choice be "demonstrated with reasonable certainty", the presumptions in Article 4 of the Rome Convention will be used to decide which law will apply. The general rule is that "the contract shall be governed by the law of the country with which it was most closely connected" (Article 4(1)).

The Articles go on to state that there is generally a presumption that this is the law of the party who is to effect "characteristic performance". This is a concept borrowed from Swiss law and it refers to the party who performs the obligation which characterises the contract. In an insurance contract, this would be the party who provides the insurance cover rather than the party who pays the premiums. Payment under a contract is only rarely characteristic performance. However, this presumption can be rebutted if the court considers that the contract is more closely connected with another country.

One of the circumstances in which the above presumption is rebutted is when the insurance contract is with a consumer and the parties have made no choice as to law. The court will in almost all circumstances apply the law of the country of the consumer's habitual residence in such cases.

7.4.3 Disputes over the choice of law

Where the presumptions in Article 4 do not apply, or are rebutted, or the agreement does not involve a consumer, any dispute about the "proper law" of the contract which fall to be determined in the UK shall, under the CALA 1990, be determined in accordance with the Rome Convention. This Convention aims to establish uniform choice of law rules for contractual obligations throughout the EC. Article 1 provides that "the rules of this Convention shall apply to contractual obligations in any situation involving a choice between the laws of different countries".

This provision has the effect that, whenever a Contracting State (including the UK) is called upon to determine the law applicable to a contract, it shall do so in accordance with the rules of the Convention even if neither of the competing laws is that of a Contracting State. However, there are certain circumstances when the rules of law of the particular country cannot be derogated from by the contract, which are described as "mandatory rules".

Mandatory rules are defined in Article 3(3) as rules of a particular country "which cannot be derogated from by contract". These would be applicable to insurance contracts between insurance companies and individuals as Article 5 provides that the consumer cannot be deprived of the protection of the mandatory rules of his country of habitual residence.

7.4.4   What the FSMA 2000 says about choice of law

The FSMA 2000 states that:

> "The law applicable to a contract of insurance, the effecting of which constitutes the carrying on of a regulated activity, is to be determined, if it is of a prescribed description, in accordance with regulations made by the Treasury." (Section 424(3))

The Financial Services and Markets Act 2000 (Law Applicable to Contracts of Insurance) Regulations 2001 sets out these provisions, which again do not apply to contracts of reinsurance.

In the case of general insurance contracts, the Law Applicable to Contracts of Insurance Regulations 2001 deals with the choice of applicable law where the insurance contract relates to risks situated in an EEA State. Where the policyholder lives in the EEA State where the risk is also situated, the applicable law will be the law of that EEA State (unless the law of that state allows parties to choose the law of another country, and they choose to do so). If the policyholder lives in a different EEA State to the one where the risk is situated, or carries on a business which has risks (which the insurance contract covers) in more than one other EEA State, the parties will have a choice of the laws of those states. Again, if the risks covered by a general insurance contract are limited to events occurring in an EEA State other than the one where the risk is situated, that state's law may also be chosen by the parties as the applicable law for that insurance contract.

However, the Law Applicable to Contracts of Insurance Regulations 2001 states that if the insurance contract covers "a large risk" (with the meaning given by Article 5(d) of the First Non-life Insurance Directive) the parties may choose any law as the applicable law of that insurance contract.

If no choice of law is made, or the parties' choice is not "expressed or demonstrated with reasonable certainty by the terms of the contract or the circumstances of the case" (regulation 6(1)), the applicable law will be that law most closely connected with the insurance contract. This will be the EEA State where the risk is situated, although this presumption is rebuttable (regulation 4(9)). Regulation 4(8) provides that severable parts of an insurance contract, with a closer connection with another EEA State, may have the law of that state as its applicable law instead of the law applicable to the rest of the contract.

Mandatory rules (defined in the Law Applicable to Contracts of Insurance Regulations 2001 as "rules from which the law allows no derogation by way of contract") of any part of the UK will apply to general insurance contracts regardless of the applicable law of that contract (regulation 5(1)). In addition, where the choice of law relates to one EEA State only, "the application of the mandatory rules of that EEA State is not prejudiced" (regulation 5(2)).

The CALA 1990 applies to contracts of general insurance, subject to the specific provisions outlined above, and will apply where the parties have chosen the law of any part of the UK as the applicable law and may also apply to determine what freedom of choice they have under that UK law.

Part II of the Law Applicable to Contracts of Insurance Regulations 2001 deals with long-term insurance contracts. It will apply where the policyholder is an individual living in an EEA State, or where the policyholder is not an individual and is based in an EEA State.

The scope to choose an applicable law is narrower in the case of long-term insurance contracts and, as might be expected, favours the law of the EEA State in which the policyholder lives (or the country of which he is a national, if different) or is situated (unless the law of that state permits the parties to choose another EEA State's law and they do so choose).

Again, the mandatory rules of any part of the UK will apply, regardless of the applicable law of the insurance contract; and the CALA 1990 will also apply, subject to the above provisions, to determine the applicable law and to determine the freedom of choice of the parties under the law of any part of the UK.

The Law Applicable to Contracts of Insurance Regulations 2001 applies with some modifications (set out in regulation 3(2)) to insurance contracts entered into by friendly societies.

7.5 Provisions regarding compulsory information that must be given to policyholders in certain circumstances

Currently, under the Insurance Companies Act 1982 ("ICA 1982"), certain information must be given to a policyholder by insurance companies before and/or after agreements relating to "long-term insurance" business are entered into. For example "key features documents" and details of cancellation rights must be provided by the insurer either before the insured signs or within three days of entering into the agreement if this was done without a written application (e.g. where it was concluded over the phone). Further details of the information to be provided, and when this must be provided, are set out below.

The ICA 1982 divides insurance business into long-term business (e.g. life and annuity, marriage and birth, linked and long term, permanent health, tontines, capital redemption, pension fund management, collective insurance and social insurance) and general business (e.g. accident, sickness and land vehicles insurance). The provisions governing the supplying of information to policyholders set out below are concerned with the supply of data to individuals and others entering into insurance contracts for long-term business.

7.5.1   Statutory notices

When insurance companies, EC companies and members of Lloyd's enter into a contract relating to long-term insurance business in the UK they are required by ICA 1982 to send a "statutory notice" in relation to the contract (Section 75 ICA 1982) to the other party to that contract. The "statutory notice" must be sent by post when or before the contract is entered into, it must contain the information prescribed and be easily legible.

An outline example of the form that the statutory notice should take is set out in Schedule 8 to the Insurance Companies Regulations 1994. This Schedule requires the insurer to provide certain information to its policyholder under the headings "Points you should consider", "Your right to withdraw from the transaction" and "Financial consequences of withdrawal".

This statutory notice should be sent to policyholders with a form of notice of cancellation in the standard format annexed to it, as required by Section 76 of the ICA 1982. The form of this notice of cancellation is set out in Schedule 9 to the Insurance Companies Regulations 1994. The notice of cancellation must state that the policyholder has 14 days (or 10 days in the case of a non-EC contract) in which to cancel the contract. An "EC contract" is one where the insurer is a UK, EC or European Free Trade Association company or a member of Lloyd's, and the insured is habitually resident in the UK.

Where the statutory notice is sent to the policyholder before the contract is entered into, the insurer must inform that policyholder in writing that it did so, not later than 14 days after the contract becomes binding.

An insurer which breaches the requirement contained in Section 75, ICA 1982 to send out the statutory notice to policyholders will be guilty of an offence, but the contract will remain valid.

These provisions do not apply to non-EC contracts or industrial assurance business and they do not apply to contracts if the insured is non-UK resident.

7.5.2 Information to be provided before and during contracts of long-term insurance

Schedule 2(E) to ICA 1982 sets out the information that must be provided before and during a contract of long-term insurance. Before the contract is entered into, the insurer must provide to the policyholder in writing certain information, including but not limited to:

(a) the definition of each benefit and option;
(b) the term of the contract and the means by which it may be terminated;
(c) the method of paying premiums and the duration of payments;
(d) the method of calculating bonuses and the distribution of bonuses;
(e) an indication of surrendered and paid-up values and the extent to which such values are guaranteed;
(f) information about any compensation or guarantee arrangements which will be available if the insurer is unable to meet its liabilities under the contract; and
(g) whether the parties to the contract are entitled to choose the law applicable to it; and if so, which law the insurer proposes to choose, and if not, which law will apply.

The insurer is also required to provide details of its name and legal form, its home state (and, where appropriate, the Member State of the branch through which the contract is to be entered into), the address of its head office and (where appropriate) the address of the branch through which the insurer will enter into the contract.

Information to be provided during the contract of long-term insurance must be provided to the policyholder in writing. Where, for example, the contract provides for the payment of bonuses, the insurer shall at least once in every calendar year (except the first) inform the other party to the contract in writing of the amount of any bonus that has become payable. Insurance companies must also notify the policyholder if there are any changes in the information previously supplied.

7.5.3   The impact of the FSMA 2000

The provisions of ICA 1982 have been replaced by the FSA's COB and are specifically dealt with in Chapter 6.

Before pure protection policies are entered into, the insurer (or its authorised intermediary) must provide various information of the type which was required to be provided under Schedule 2(E) of ICA 1982 (*see* Section 7.5.2 above). This information must be provided in writing and if contact is made by telephone and the customer commits to enter into the agreement, a written version of the information provided must be sent out to the customer within five days. An insurer is not required to provide such information if the customer is not present in the UK and if the customer is habitually resident outside the UK.

The information an insurer is to provide during the life of a pure protection contract is also the same as was required to be provided under Schedule 2(E) of ICA 1982 (*see* Section 7.5.2 above) and is now to be found at Sections 6.8.6–6.8.10 of COB.

In relation to general insurance contracts, if the risk covered is situated in the UK, insurers are required by Sections 6.8.11–6.8.14 to provide customers with:

(a)   details of their complaints procedure; and
(b)   a statement saying whether the insurer or customer is entitled to choose the law applicable to that contract and, if so, the law the insurer proposes to choose for it.

The insurer will not have to provide this information where the contract is submitted for the customer by an intermediary who is either authorised or is a member of the General Insurance Council. Insurers are required to keep a record of the information provided to customers for six years in the case of pure protection contracts and three years for general insurance agreements (Section 6.8.18).

Under Chapter 6 of COB, where an insurer:

(a)   sells, recommends or arranges the sale of packaged products to private customers or to trustees or managers of occupational or stakeholder pension schemes; or
(b)   sells or recommends cash deposit ISAs to private customers; or
(c)   effects, recommends or arranges to vary a life policy for a private customer;

then key features must be provided to customers in relation to packaged products and life policies and an information document (containing details including the minimum needed to open an account, the maximum yearly deposit and the interest earned and if and how it may vary) must be provided in relation to ISAs. This information must be provided in writing before the customer completes the application for the policy or, in the case of packaged products and life policies, within five days of having provided such information orally. There are certain limited exemptions to the requirement to provide this information (set out at Sections 6.2.24-6.2.25). As before, insurance companies must also notify the policyholder if there are any changes in the information previously supplied.

Chapter 8

Special Rules Relating to Certain Categories of Insurance Business (Motor, Health, Legal Expenses and Export Credit Insurance)

Ambereen Salamat

Partner
DJ Freeman

Whether as a result of membership of the European Union or due to domestic reasons, certain categories of insurance business in the UK are subject to special rules. In this Chapter we consider the special rules that apply to motor, health, legal expenses and export credit insurance.

8.1 Motor insurance

8.1.1 *Compulsory cover*

The insurance of motor vehicles against the risk of liability for injury to, or the death of, third parties caused by the driver's negligence has been compulsory since 1930. The scope of compulsory cover has expanded since that time as a result of case law and also European law.

To date, three Council Directives have influenced motor insurance. The chief aim of Council Directive 72/166/EEC[1] was to ensure that all insurers in individual Member States provided the minimum compulsory

---

[1] Council Directive 72/166/EEC, as amended by Council Directive 72/430/EEC, was implemented in the UK by the Motor Vehicles (Compulsory Insurance) Regulations 1973 SI 1973/1820, as subsequently replaced by the Motor Vehicles (Compulsory Insurance) (No. 2) Regulations 1973 SI 1973/2143.

indemnity against third-party liability required by the national law of that state. However, under the Directive it was not necessary for the same levels of compulsory third-party cover to be set by the individual Member States. By the Second Council Directive 84/5/EEC,[2] each Member State was obliged to put in place a similar form of compulsory third-party cover, giving protection not only against personal injury but also against material damage to third-party property. This Directive also set minimum indemnity limits and required every Member State to establish a body tasked with providing compensation for injuries caused by uninsured or unidentified drivers. Finally, the Third Council Directive 90/232/EEC[3] required insurers to give third-party cover anywhere within the European Union on the basis of a single premium.

8.1.2 Road Traffic Act 1988

The relevant provisions relating to compulsory insurance in the UK are set out in Part VI of the Road Traffic Act 1988, Sections 143 to 161. Section 143 is the key operative provision. It makes it compulsory to insure against liability in respect of death or bodily injury to third parties, including passengers, and in respect of liability for damage to a third party's property. The Section makes it an offence for any person to use, or to cause or permit any other person to use, a motor vehicle on a road unless there is in force, in relation to such use, a policy of insurance or such security in respect of third-party risks as complies with the requirements of the Act.

To comply with the Act, policies must be issued by an authorised insurer (i.e. a person or body of persons carrying on insurance business within Group 2 in Part II of Annex 11.2 of the *Prudential Sourcebook for Insurers* and being a member of the Motor Insurers' Bureau)[4] and must insure the person specified in it:

(a)   against liability in respect of death or bodily injury to any person or damage to property caused by, or arising out of, the use of the

---

[2] Second Council Directive 84/5/EEC was implemented in the UK by the Motor Vehicles (Compulsory Insurance) Regulations 1987 SI 1987/2171.
[3] Third Council Directive 90/232/EEC was implemented in the UK by the Motor Vehicles (Compulsory Insurance) Regulations 1992 SI 1992/3036 by way of amendments to Section 143 of the Road Traffic Act 1988.
[4] Section 145(2) and (5) of the Road Traffic Act 1988.

vehicle on a road in Great Britain. The term "person" includes any passenger but not the driver;[5] and

(b)   in the case of a vehicle normally based in the territory of another Member State, against any civil liability occurring as a result of an event related to the use of the vehicle in Great Britain if:

   (i)   the law of that Member State would require such insurance in respect of an event occurring in that country; and

   (ii)   the cover required by that law would be higher than that required by (a) above;[6] and

(c)   in the case of a vehicle normally based in Great Britain, against any liability in respect of the use of the vehicle in the territory other than Great Britain of each of the Member States according to:

   (i)   the law on compulsory motor insurance of the state where the event occurred; or

   (ii)   if it would give higher cover, the law which would apply if the place where the event occurred was Great Britain;[7] and

(d)   against the statutory liabilities for payment for emergency treatment.

Reference has been made above to the three Council Directives concerning compulsory motor insurance that have been implemented into legislation in the UK. In this context, two further Directives require mention.

8.1.3   Fourth Motor Insurance Directive

The Fourth Motor Insurance Directive[8] is required to be implemented by Member States on or before 20 January 2003. This Directive provides for improved information, easier procedures and quicker settlement of claims. It applies not only to accidents occurring in a Member State other than that of the injured party's residence, but also to accidents occurring in third countries covered by the green card system,[9] affecting injured

---

[5]   *R v Secretary of State for Transport ex parte National Insurance Guarantee Corporation Plc*, (1996) *The Times* June 3.

[6]   Section 145(3)(aa) of the Road Traffic Act 1988, inserted by Regulation 2(1) of the Motor Vehicles (Compulsory Insurance) Regulations 1992 SI 1992/3036.

[7]   Section 145(3)(b) of the Road Traffic Act 1988, as amended by Regulation 2(2) of the Motor Vehicles (Compulsory Insurance) Regulations 1992 SI 1992/3036.

[8]   2000/26/EC.

[9]   By virtue of agreements between Motor Insurance Bureaux, the green card provides that compulsory motor insurance in one participating country will be effective in another. The victim of an accident is to be compensated by the Motor Insurance Bureau in the country in which he is injured following which that Motor Insurance

parties resident in the European Union ("EU") and involving vehicles insured and normally based in a Member State.

Should an accident take place that falls within the scope of the Directive, injured parties are given a direct right of action against the insurer of the party responsible for the accident. Further, injured parties suffering loss or injury shall be entitled to claim in their Member State of residence against a claims representative appointed there by the insurer of the responsible party. Therefore, damage suffered by such injured parties would be dealt with by procedures familiar to them. The claims representatives resident or established in the various Member States (who may represent more than one insurer) are required to collect all necessary information and to take appropriate action to settle such claims on behalf of the insurer concerned.

The Directive aims to achieve the speedy settlement of claims. Where liability is not contested and damages have been quantified, insurers are given a period of three months after presentation of a claim to respond with a reasoned offer of compensation. Otherwise, they have three months in which to provide a reasoned reply to the points made in the claim. Appropriate sanctions are to be imposed for failure to comply with the prescribed time limits.

The Directive also requires Member States to set up information centres to collect data such as the name and address of the owner or usual driver, the number of the policy, the registration number of the vehicle and other information, and to supply injured parties with the name of the insurer of the party responsible for the accident or its claims representative or, in certain instances, the owner or usual driver or registered keeper of the vehicle. In the UK this task is being undertaken by the Motor Insurers' Information Centre, a subsidiary of the Motor Insurers' Bureau. From 16 July 2001[10] motor insurers agreed to supply to the Information Centre details of all their motor policies, on a daily or weekly basis. Initially, only the details relating to private cars will be supplied and the information will be the same as that contained in the proposal form (e.g. name, address, age, type of vehicle and other details).

Bureau is able to seek an indemnity from either the foreign insurer or the Bureau which provided the green card. The green card operates simply as an international insurance certificate valid for the dates mentioned in it and the countries referred to in it.

[10] Motor Vehicles (Third Party Risks) (Amendment) Regulations 2001 SI 2001/2266 amending the Motor Vehicles (Third Party Risks) Regulations 1972 SI 1972/1217.

Where an insurer fails to appoint a claims representative or is manifestly dilatory in settling a claim or cannot be identified, the injured party shall be entitled to apply to a compensation body. The compensation body is required to take action if, within two months of presentation of a claim, the insurer concerned or its claims representative does not make a reasoned reply.

The compensation body shall have a right of subrogation insofar as it compensates an injured party. Further, where a compensation body compensates an injured party in his Member State of residence, that compensation body shall enjoy an automatic right of reimbursement with subrogation to the rights of the injured party on the part of the corresponding compensation body in the Member State of the insurer which issued the policy.

8.1.4 *Proposed Fifth Motor Insurance Directive*

A Fifth Motor Insurance Directive, aimed at improving the legal protection of accident victims, is currently being proposed.[11] Its main recommendations include:

(a)   requiring insurers to provide either an offer of compensation or an explanation of why an offer is not provided within three months of receiving a claim (along the lines of the Fourth Motor Insurance Directive);

(b)   requiring a uniform minimum sum insured for compulsory cover of €2,000,000 throughout the EU whatever the number of injured parties or the nature of damage, with future increases in line with inflation;

(c)   making it permissible for insurers to provide insurance for a maximum period of 30 days in respect of a vehicle purchased and registered in one Member State provided there is an intention to reregister in the Member State of residence;

(d)   harmonising the different periods for compulsory reregistration of all vehicles with foreign number plates, with three months as the new standard; and

(e)   obliging insurers to extend home state cover for citizens who take up temporary residence for up to 12 months in another Member

---

11 European Parliament resolution with recommendations to the Commission on a Fifth European Parliament and Council Directive on motor vehicle liability insurance to improve the legal protection of accident victims (2000/2126 (INI)).

State. After the 12-month period, citizens would need to reregister their vehicles and take out local insurance cover.

8.2   Health insurance

8.2.1   *Types of cover*

Health insurance is conventionally divided into four types, as follows:

(a)   Private Medical Insurance ("PMI") insures against the cost of short-term acute conditions in a private hospital or as a private patient in an NHS ward. It does not normally cover the cost of routine health, dental and eye checks but some policies include additional benefits such as payment for home nursing or alternative medicine;

(b)   Permanent Health Insurance ("PHI") replaces some or all of the income lost when a person becomes sick or disabled or unable to work. This replacement income is normally paid up to retirement age;

(c)   Critical Illness Insurance ("CII") provides a lump sum in the event of a serious illness. It can be used to pay for medical care, to repay a mortgage or to provide replacement income. Although some policies are stand alone, others are linked to life insurance or to mortgage protection policies; and

(d)   Long-Term Care Insurance ("LTCI") covers the cost of long-term care for those who become unable to look after themselves. This is most likely to happen in old age.

As will be seen below, although different regulatory regimes apply to the marketing and sale of each type of health insurance product, providers of such products are all subject to prudential regulation by the FSA. Generally, PMI is classified as general insurance business whereas PHI, CII and LTCI are regarded as long-term insurance business within Parts I and II respectively of Schedule 1 to the Financial Services and Markets Act 2000 (Regulated Activities) Order 2001.

Where a PHI, CII or LTCI product contains an investment element, full conduct of business regulation for providers and independent financial advisers or salesmen means that these need specific permission from the FSA to sell such products. This Section, however, focuses on those long-term insurance products that do not have an investment element.

8.2.2 Reports of the Office of Fair Trading

By way of background, the Office of Fair Trading ("OFT") announced an investigation into health insurance in May 1995 which culminated in a first report in July 1996 and a second one in May 1998. These reports have, to an extent, influenced the way health insurance products are regulated and it may be useful to summarise the main recommendations.

Given the complexity of health insurance products which made comparisons difficult, in its report of 1996 the OFT recommended the introduction of "benchmark" products. The OFT went on, in its report of 1998, to identify the essential features of core term products for PMI, PHI and CII.

In 1998 the OFT reviewed its earlier recommendation that moratorium underwriting of health insurance products should be discontinued (i.e. where customers' medical history is not checked and existing conditions are not covered for (typically) two years after the policy starts). The OFT concluded that moratorium underwriting may be acceptable provided there is effective regulation requiring the insurer to:

(a)   establish the customer's need for the policy;
(b)   explain orally, and then in writing, the essential features of moratorium underwriting of health insurance, paying particular attention to the extent to which pre-existing conditions are covered, before the customer enters into a contract;
(c)   stress the inadvisability of foregoing medical advice in the period before the pre-existing conditions are covered; and
(d)   monitor the sales process to ensure that the above procedures are adhered to and to provide evidence in case of dispute.

In the OFT's view, the regulator should monitor the experience of customers following a purchase and carry out research into the extent to which medical advice may systematically be foregone by customers during the moratorium period.

The OFT re-affirmed its earlier recommendation that the selling of LTCI should be regulated in a way analogous to regulation under the Financial Services Act 1986. It further recommended that every health insurance policy should be accompanied by a clear summary, in standard form, showing what the policy does and does not cover, and that the terms and text of the policy itself should be expressed in plain and intelligible language in line with the Unfair Terms in Consumer Contracts Regulations 1994 (now the Unfair Terms in Consumer Contracts Regulations

1999). Customers should receive more comprehensive warnings about likely increases in PMI premiums, supported by reliable data on average increases over the last five years. Moreover, the need for clarity in the presentation of possible premium increases extended to any health insurance product where premiums are reviewable or guaranteed only for a fixed period, as in many PHI and LTCI contracts.

8.2.3   Marketing and sale

Turning now to the manner in which the marketing and sale of health insurance products is regulated, each of the four types is considered below.

8.2.3.1   PMI
There is no statutory regulatory regime that applies specifically to the marketing and sale of PMI products, which is largely self-regulated. As a condition of membership, members of the Association of British Insurers ("ABI") and their intermediaries are expected to comply with the ABI General Insurance Business Code of Practice[12] (supplemented by the Selling Private Medical Insurance to Individual Purchasers information sheet). This covers areas such as recruitment of intermediaries, their training and competence, explanation of products to customers, processing of information, complaints procedures and monitoring.

Members of the General Insurance Standards Council will need to comply with the Rules of that organisation in the marketing and sale of PMI products as well as with their other obligations of membership.

8.2.3.2   PHI
As with PMI, the sale of PHI products is not subject to statutory regulation. Members of the ABI, their intermediaries and introducers are, however, required to comply with the ABI Life Insurance (Non-Investment Business) Selling Code of Practice.

8.2.3.3   CII
The regime governing the marketing and sale of CII products is the same as that applying to PHI products. In addition to ABI members being required to comply with the Life Insurance (Non-Investment Business)

---

[12] For all intermediaries (including employees of insurance companies) other than registered insurance brokers (introduced January 1989).

Selling Code of Practice, the ABI have issued a Statement of Best Practice for Critical Illness Cover which includes the use of generic terms in CII documentation, the use of the standard Key Features format for all long-term products featuring CII and sets out model wordings for medical conditions, surgical procedures, disabilities and model exclusions.

8.2.3.4 LTCI

Currently the marketing and sale of LTCI products is not the subject of statutory regulation but ABI members are required to comply with the Statement of Best Practice for Long-Term Care Insurance which outlines good marketing and selling principles in addition to complying with the Life Insurance (Non-Investment Business) Selling Code of Practice.

8.2.4 Regulation by the FSA

As mentioned above, the OFT in both of its reports recommended that the marketing and sale of LTCI products should be regulated. Following this, in its report in March 1999, the Royal Commission on Long-Term Care for the Elderly made a number of recommendations, including the need for the Treasury and the FSA to begin work to bring all LTCI under the full conduct of business regulation. In addition, the Treasury Committee and the Joint Scrutiny Committee on the Financial Services and Markets Bill both recommended that the marketing and sale of LTCI be regulated.

In its response to the Royal Commission, the government made a number of decisions that may help reduce the cost of LTCI. As a result, LTCI may be more attractive to consumers due to premiums being cheaper and thus the insurance being more affordable. In December 2000 the government consulted on whether LTCI should be regulated by the FSA on this basis.

Having completed the consultation process, the government announced[13] that the FSA is to have responsibility for regulating the marketing and sale of these products. The next stage is for the government to consult on the definition of the LTCI product to be regulated and for the FSA to consult on its rules before inviting firms to seek authorisation.

---

13 HM Treasury press release of 22 October 2001.

8.3   Legal expenses insurance

8.3.1   *Insurance Companies (Legal Expenses Insurance) Regulations 1990*

The Insurance Companies (Legal Expenses Insurance) Regulations 1990[14] impose specific requirements on insurers carrying on legal expenses insurance[15] in the UK. Prior to the adoption of these Regulations, insurers writing policies that contained provision for the payment of the insured's or a third party's legal costs incurred in connection with a claim were regarded as writing an ancillary risk. Since the adoption of the Regulations, insurers are no longer entitled to treat such risks as ancillary to other classes.

The Regulations do not apply to:[16]

(a)   legal expenses insurance contracts concerning disputes or risks relating to the use of seagoing vessels;

(b)   anything done by a person providing civil liability cover for the purpose of representing the insured in an enquiry or proceedings which is at the same time done in the insurer's own interest under such cover; or

(c)   legal expenses cover provided by an assistance insurer where that cover is provided under a contract of which the principal object is the provision of assistance for persons who fall into difficulties while travelling, while away from home or their permanent residence and where the costs are incurred outside the state in which the insured normally resides. In this event, the contract must clearly state that the cover in question is limited to the circumstances referred to and is ancillary to that assistance.

The Regulations provide that legal expenses cover must be the subject of a separate policy, or dealt with in a separate section of a single policy in which the nature of the cover is specified.[17] Further, an insurer carrying

---

[14]   SI 1990/1159 implementing Council Directive 87/344/EEC.

[15]   Falling within general business class 17 in Part I of Schedule 1 to the Financial Services and Markets Act 2000 (Regulated Activities) Order 2001 (i.e. "contracts of insurance against risks of loss to the persons insured attributable to their incurring legal expenses (including costs of litigation)").

[16]   Regulation 3 of the Insurance Companies (Legal Expenses Insurance) Regulations 1990.

[17]   Regulation 4 of the Insurance Companies (Legal Expenses Insurance) Regulations 1990.

on legal expenses business[18] must adopt at least one of the following arrangements to avoid conflicts of interest:[19]

(a)   it must ensure that no member of staff engaged in the management of claims under legal expenses insurance contracts, or with legal advice in respect of such claims, carries on at the same time any similar activity:
   (i)   in relation to another class of general insurance business carried on by that insurer; or
   (ii)   in another insurer having financial, commercial or administrative links with the first insurer, which carries on one or more classes of general insurance business;
(b)   it must entrust the management of claims in respect of legal expenses insurance to an undertaking having separate legal personality. This undertaking will need to be mentioned in the separate policy or section of the policy, as the case may be;
(c)   it must afford the insured, in the policy, the right to entrust the defence of his interests, from the moment that he has the right to claim from the insurer under the policy, to a lawyer of his choice.

The legal expenses insurance policy must expressly recognise[20] that, where under the policy recourse is had to a lawyer to represent the interests of the insured in any enquiry or proceedings, the insured shall be free to choose that lawyer. Further, the policy must also expressly recognise that the insured shall be free to choose a lawyer to serve his interests whenever a conflict of interests arises.[21]

The Regulations require that any dispute between the insurer and the insured may be referred to arbitration and the policy must expressly mention the right of the insured to have recourse to such a procedure.[22]

---

[18] Defined in the 1990 Regulations as "the business of effecting or carrying out contracts of insurance (other than contracts of reinsurance) which insure against a risk arising from legal expense."
[19] Regulation 5 of the Insurance Companies (Legal Expenses Insurance) Regulations 1990.
[20] Regulation 6 of the Insurance Companies (Legal Expenses Insurance) Regulations 1990.
[21] Exemptions set out in Regulation 7 of the Insurance Companies (Legal Expenses Insurance) Regulations 1990.
[22] Regulation 8 of the Insurance Companies (Legal Expenses Insurance) Regulations 1990.

8.3.2 Administration of Justice Act 1999

In the context of legal expenses insurance, mention should be made of the Administration of Justice Act 1999 as this Act is responsible for a new burgeoning type of insurance policy known as "after the event" insurance where legal expenses cover is purchased after a specified event.

The 1999 Act is the government's attempt to increase access to the legal system and to make it more affordable through the use of conditional fee agreements and after the event insurance. The Act reforms the law relating to these matters.[23]

Conditional fee agreements allow clients to agree with their lawyers that the lawyer will not receive all or part of his usual fees if the case is lost; but that, if it is won, the client will pay an uplift to the lawyer in addition to the usual fee. In July 1995 conditional fee agreements were allowed for a limited number of cases (i.e. personal injury, insolvency and cases before the European Commission of Human Rights). As a result of the 1999 Act (together with the Conditional Fee Agreements Order 2000), the enforceability of conditional fee agreements that provide for an uplift has been extended to all civil cases except specified family proceedings. Section 27 of the 1999 Act enables a court to order a losing party to pay any uplift on the successful party's lawyers' normal fees. The maximum uplift that can be charged if a lawyer is successful remains at 100 per cent.

After-the-event policies that are available make it possible for a person contemplating litigation to purchase cover providing, in the event that the case is lost, both the costs of the other party and his own legal costs (including the solicitor's fees if these are not subject to a conditional fee agreement). Some of these policies have been developed to support conditional fee agreements but others are used to meet lawyers' fees charged in the traditional way. Section 29 of the 1999 Act now enables the court to order a losing party to pay any premium paid by the successful party for such cover.

---

[23] Section 27 of the 1999 Act substitutes Section 58 of the Courts and Legal Services Act 1990.

There is very little guidance in the legislation or as a result of case law[24] as to the amount of premium that a court would order a losing party to pay. As is the case with any uplift, the amount of any recoverable premium would need to be reasonable. Section 11 of the Practice Direction about Costs (supplementing Rule 44.5 of the Civil Procedure Rules) sets out the relevant factors to be taken into account in deciding whether the premium is reasonable.

These include:

(a)   where the insurance cover is not purchased in support of a conditional fee agreement with an uplift, how its cost compares with the likely cost of funding the case with a conditional fee agreement with an uplift and supporting insurance cover;
(b)   the level and extent of the cover provided;
(c)   the availability of any pre-existing insurance cover;
(d)   whether any part of the premium would be rebated in the event of early settlement; and
(e)   the amount of commission payable to the receiving party or his legal representatives or other agents.

8.4   Export credit insurance

8.4.1   *What is export credit insurance?*

Export credit is included in insurance business classified under general business class 14 by the First Council Directive 73/239/EEC as follows:

"14.Credit
– insolvency (general)
– export credit
– instalment credit
– mortgages
– agricultural credit."

The UK has implemented this directive and defined the same class of general business as:

---

[24] *Callery* v *Gray, Russell* v *Pal Pak Corrugated Limited* [2001] NLJ 1129; *Sawar* v *Alam* Times Law Reports (11 October 2001).

"contracts of insurance against risks of loss to the persons insured arising from the insolvency of debtors of theirs or from the failure (other than through insolvency) of debtors of theirs to pay their debts when due."[25]

There is clearly a divergence between the wording of the directive and that of the legislation in the UK. It can be argued that the manner in which class 14 has been defined in the UK is capable of a different, and narrower, meaning than in the directive. It should be noted that where "the wording of a Directive is sufficiently precise and unambiguous, [it will] have direct effect and be relied upon before the national Courts".[26]

There appears to be no comprehensive definition of "export credit" under either European or English law. Witherby's *Dictionary of Insurance* defines export credit insurance as "insurance for exporters against the risk of non-payment for political and/or commercial reasons". Council Directive 98/29/EC on harmonisation of the main provisions concerning export credit insurance for transactions with medium- and long-term cover[27] sets out in its Annex the common principles for export credit insurance. Pursuant to this directive, the covered risks relate to risks of loss arising from the manufacturing or credit risk. The covered causes of loss are as follows:[28]

(a)   insolvency of the private debtor[29] and, if any, its guarantor, either de jure or de facto;

(b)   default of the debtor and, if any, its guarantor;

(c)   decision of the buyer under a supplier credit[30] to interrupt or cancel

---

[25] Now contained in Part I of Schedule 1 to the Financial Services and Markets Act 2000 (Regulated Activities) Order 2001.

[26] *Association Basco-Béarnaise des Opticiens Indépendants* v *Préfet des Pyrénées-Atlantiques* Case C-109/99.

[27] Council Directive 98/29/EC was not required to be implemented by the UK as the Export and Investment Guarantees Act 1991 was considered to make provision for the requirements of the directive.

[28] The causes of loss set out are reflected in the Export Credit Guarantee Department's Export Insurance Policy.

[29] A private debtor is any debtor that is not a public debtor. A public debtor is any entity which, in whatever form, represents a public authority and which cannot, either judicially or administratively, be declared insolvent.

[30] The term "supplier credit" is said to apply to a commercial contract providing for an export of goods and/or services originating in a Member State between one or more suppliers and one or more buyers, whereby the buyer(s) undertake to pay the supplier(s) on cash terms or on credit terms.

the commercial contract, or to refuse to accept the goods and/or services without being entitled to do so;

(d) any measure or decision of the government of a country other than the country of the insurer, or that of the policyholder, which prevents performance of the loan agreement or the commercial contract respectively;

(e) general moratorium decreed either by the government of the country of the debtor, or by that of a third country through which payment in respect of the loan agreement or the commercial contract is to be effected;

(f) political events, economic difficulties, or legislative or administrative measures which occur or are taken outside the country of the insurer, and which prevent or delay the transfer of funds paid in respect of the loan agreement or the commercial contract;

(g) legal provisions adopted in the country of the debtor declaring payments made by the debtor in local currency to be valid discharge of the debt, notwithstanding that, as a result of fluctuations in exchange rates, such payments, when converted into the currency of the commercial contract or the loan agreement, no longer cover the amount of the debt at the date of transfer of funds;

(h) any measure or decision of the government of the country of the insurer or of the policyholder, including measures and decisions of the EU, relating to trade between a Member State and third countries, such as a ban on exports, insofar as its effects are not covered otherwise by the government concerned; and

(i) cases of *force majeure* occurring outside the country of the insurer, which could include war, including civil war, revolution, riot, civil disturbance, cyclone, flood, earthquake, volcanic eruption, tidal wave and nuclear accident, insofar as its effects are not insured otherwise.

The aim of Directive 98/29/EC is to ensure that export policy is based on uniform principles and that competition between enterprises in the EU is not distorted. The directive applies to insurance for transactions related to the export of goods and/or services originating in a Member State insofar as this support is provided directly or indirectly for the account of, or with the support of, one or more Member States involving a total risk period of two years or more. Member States must ensure that those institutions providing cover for such transactions directly or indirectly in the form of export credit insurance for the account of the Member State or with the support of the Member State must do so in accordance with the provisions of the directive if destined for countries outside the EU and financed by buyer credit,[31] supplier credit[32] or paid on cash terms.

8.4.2   Equalisation reserve

Part III of Chapter 6, Volume 1 of the *Interim Prudential Sourcebook for Insurers* applies to all insurance business classified under general business class 14 that is not reinsurance.[33] Every UK insurer[34] carrying on credit insurance business and every non-EEA insurer[35] carrying on credit insurance business in the UK is required to maintain an equalisation reserve for the purpose of providing against above average fluctuations in claims in respect of general business of that description.

In the case of a UK insurer, the requirement to maintain an equalisation reserve does not apply where the net premiums written in any financial year in respect of its credit insurance business are less than four per cent of the total net premiums written by it in that financial year and less than €2,500,000. In the case of a non-EEA insurer, the same thresholds relate to business being carried on through a branch in the UK.

8.4.3   OECD Arrangement

By virtue of Council Decision 2001/76/EC, the OECD Arrangement on Guidelines for Officially Supported Export Credits[36] has been implemented into European law. The main purpose of the Arrangement is to provide a framework for the orderly use of officially supported[37] credits.

---

[31] The term "buyer credit" is said to apply to a loan agreement between one or more financial institutions and one or more borrowers financing a commercial contract providing for an export of goods and/or services originating in a Member State, whereby the lending institution(s) undertake to pay the supplier(s) under the underlying transaction on cash terms on behalf of the buyer(s)/borrower(s), while the buyer(s)/borrower(s) will reimburse the lending institution(s) on credit terms.

[32] *See* footnote 30.

[33] Implements Council Directive 87/343/EEC.

[34] A "UK insurer" is defined as an insurer, other than a pure reinsurer or a non-directive insurer, whose head office is in the UK.

[35] A "non-EEA insurer" is defined as an insurer, other than a pure reinsurer, whose head office is not in an EEA State.

[36] The Arrangement came into being in April 1978 and is a "Gentlemen's Agreement" between its participants.

[37] Official support can take the form of direct credit/financing, refinancing, interest rate support, aid financing (credits and grants), export credit insurance and guarantees.

The Arrangement seeks to encourage competition among exporters from the OECD-exporting countries based on quality and price of goods and services exported rather than on the most favourable officially supported terms. It applies to officially supported credits with repayment terms of two years or more, relating to exports of goods and/or services or to financial leases. Official support is not prohibited but certain limitations on the terms and conditions of export credits that benefit from it are laid down (e.g. minimum premium benchmarks, the minimum cash payments to be made at or before the starting point of credit, maximum repayment terms, and minimum interest rates which benefit from official financial support).

8.4.4 Commission Communication

The Communication of the Commission to Member States relating to short-term export credit insurance (OJ 97/C281/03), which takes effect for a period of five years from 1 January 1998, aims to remove distortions of competition which arise from the financial advantages due to state aid given to public or publicly supported export credit insurers[38] who export within and beyond the EU. Member States were requested to amend, where necessary, their export credit insurance systems for marketable risks[39] so that the granting of different forms of state aid (including state guarantees for borrowing or losses, relief or exemption from taxes) to public or publicly supported export credit insurers in respect of those risks ended within one year of publication of the Communication. Further, public or publicly supported export credit insurers were to be required, as a minimum, to keep a separate administration and account to show that they did not enjoy state aid in their insurance of marketable risks.

---

[38] Defined as those export credit agencies which are supported by the government through guarantees or equivalent reinsurance arrangements for certain parts of their business.

[39] "Marketable risks" are defined as commercial risks on non-public debtors established in Member States and certain other countries. "Commercial risks" include:
   (a) arbitrary repudiation of contract by a debtor;
   (b) arbitrary refusal by a non-public debtor to accept the goods covered;
   (c) insolvency of a non-public debtor or his guarantor; and
   (d) protracted default.

The maximum risk period is two years.

Chapter 9

The Prudential Regulation of Long-term Insurance

Katherine Coates

Partner

Claudia Monsanto

Associate
Clifford Chance LLP

The reason for regulating insurers is essentially to protect policyholders against the risk of companies being unable to pay valid claims and to promote confidence in the insurance industry. This aim is reflected in the statutory objectives of the Financial Services Authority ("FSA") set out in Sections 2–6 of the Financial Services and Markets Act 2000 ("FSMA 2000"):

- maintaining confidence in the financial system;
- promoting public understanding of the financial system;
- securing the appropriate degree of protection for consumers; and
- the reduction of financial crime.

In the context of direct long-term insurance business, the need for policyholder protection is enhanced by the fact that long-term insurance contracts are, by their nature, long-term and can involve substantial investments, sometimes of an individual's life savings. Moreover, securing public understanding of long-term products can be a difficult objective to achieve. This is especially the case where the insurance contract in question is a complex investment product which is far removed from a traditional life policy providing a cash payment in the event of death of the insured – for example, a policy permitting the policyholder to invest through an "insurance wrapper" in pooled investments such as unit trusts, collective investment schemes and other investments, featuring complicated options or benefits, such as annuities, guaranteed options, unit-linked benefits or with-profits entitlements.

For the purpose of achieving the above objectives in relation to the long-term insurance industry, insurers carrying on direct long-term insurance business are subject to two types of regulation:

(a) prudential regulation, which constitutes the subject of this Chapter and focuses mainly on the suitability, solvency and internal systems and controls of the insurer; and

(b) conduct of business regulation, which deals mainly with communications with customers, including the marketing of products, disclosure of product information and provision of investment advice.

Reinsurers that carry on long-term insurance business are subject only to prudential regulation, as they deal with sophisticated counterparties (i.e., other insurers) as opposed to individual investors.

Prudential rules and standards are usually implemented by imposing on the insurer regulatory requirements regarding its authorisation, financial position, reporting and internal systems and controls, and through the regulator's exercise of its powers of supervision and enforcement.

This Chapter covers the following aspects of the prudential regulatory regime applicable to long-term insurance business in the UK:

(a) the framework for regulation;
(b) certain features of authorisation;
(c) internal systems and controls;
(d) supervision and enforcement by the FSA;
(e) rules relating to long-term insurance funds and transactions with connected persons;
(f) linked long-term contracts;
(g) with-profits policies; and
(h) the inherited estate.

Financial requirements applicable to long-term insurers are described in Chapter 4. Conduct of business regulation is dealt with in Chapter 10.

References in this Chapter to a "rule" refer to a rule of the Interim Prudential Sourcebook for Insurers, unless otherwise indicated.

9.1 The framework for prudential regulation

9.1.1 From 1990 to N2

Historically, prudential regulation and conduct of business regulation of long-term insurance business in the UK have been carried out by separate regulators. The prudential function was carried out by the Insurance Directorate of the Department of Trade and Industry ("DTI") until 31 December 1997 and then by Her Majesty's Treasury ("HMT") from 1 January 1998.

With effect from 1 January 1999, following the government's announcement in May 1997 of its intention to establish the FSA as a single regulator, HMT contracted out its prudential function in respect of insurance companies to the FSA. The FSA therefore carried out most aspects of the role of insurance regulator under the statutory regime established under the Insurance Companies Act 1982 ("ICA 1982") for an interim period before the FSMA 2000 came into force.

At the time, prudential standards for long-term insurers were set out in the ICA 1982 and the various regulations made thereunder, supplemented by guidance contained in a series of Prudential Guidance Notes issued by the DTI. In 1994, the ICA 1982 and related regulations were substantially amended to implement the European Community ("EC") Third Life Insurance Directive. This heralded the creation of an European Economic Area ("EEA") market in long-term insurance, including the recognition of the principles of home state regulation, freedom of establishment and freedom of services.

For long-term insurers carrying on direct business, conduct of business regulation was governed under a system of self-regulation established under the Financial Services Act 1986 ("FS Act 1986"). Such long-term insurers were required to either join the FSA's predecessor, the Securities and Investment Board or "SIB" (as was opted for by one insurer) or an appropriate self-regulatory organisation or "SRO". As members of an SRO, long-term insurers carrying on direct business had a duty to comply not only with the provisions of the FS Act 1986 and relevant regulations but also with the rules of the SRO. Until 1994, most long-term insurers were members of an SRO called the Life Assurance and Unit Trusts Regulatory Organisation Limited ("LAUTRO").

In 1994, the Personal Investment Authority Limited ("PIA") replaced LAUTRO. While most long-term insurers were members of PIA and subject to the rules of PIA, a few long-term insurers that wrote pensions policies were members of another SRO, the Investment Management Regulatory Organisation Limited ("IMRO"), and subject to the IMRO Rules. PIA and IMRO contracted out their regulatory functions to the FSA with effect from 1 June 1998.

9.1.2 Post N2

On 30 November 2001 (also known as date "N2"), the FSA became the single regulator responsible for insurance, banking and other financial services sectors in the UK. It also assumed responsibility for both prudential and conduct of business regulations in relation to long-term insurers (among other financial services firms).

The legislation, regulations and rules described in 9.1.3 below were repealed and replaced by a single legislative framework comprising the FSMA 2000 and various orders made thereunder.

Pursuant to its rule-making powers under the FSMA 2000, the FSA set out detailed rules and guidance in the FSA Handbook of rules and guidance (the "Handbook"). Of particular relevance to the prudential regulation of long-term insurance are:

(a) the Interim Prudential Sourcebook for Insurers ("IPRU(INS)"), which is part of the Business Standards block of the Handbook;

(b) relevant provisions in the Authorisation, Supervision and Enforcement Manuals, which are part of the Regulatory Processes block of the Handbook; and

(c) within the High-Level Standards block of the Handbook, the Principles for Businesses ("PRIN"), Threshold Conditions ("COND"), and Senior Management, System and Controls ("SYSC") modules as well as the modules dealing with Statements of Principle and Code of Practice and the Fit and Proper Test for Approved Persons ("APER" and "FIT" respectively).

9.1.2.1 The Interim Prudential Sourcebook for Insurers

The stated intention of the FSA in creating the IPRU(INS) was to enable the existing prudential regime applicable to insurers to continue for an interim period, until its replacement by an Integrated Prudential Sourcebook. The Integrated Prudential Sourcebook is to be the single sourcebook which will contain the prudential rules applicable to firms across all financial services sectors in the UK and is expected to come into force for insurers only in 2004/2005.

The IPRU(INS) therefore contains many provisions which repeat in substance the corresponding provisions in the ICA 1982 or regulations made thereunder. There have been some minor changes in terminology. Other changes are described by the FSA as amendments considered necessary or desirable to reflect recent statutory or international developments, such as the recent implementation of the EC Directive on Insurance Groups.

The prudential standards and requirements previously set out in the ICA 1982 or relevant regulations that have been substantially reproduced in the IPRU(INS) are no longer statutory provisions (or provisions in a statutory instrument). They are now rules adopted by the FSA under its rule-making powers under the FSMA 2000. However, with few exceptions, they are generally given the same effect as the corresponding provisions in the ICA 1982.

The effect of a provision in the Handbook depends on whether it is designated as a rule or guidance (or evidentiary provision) and, in the case of a rule, whether it can give rise to an action for damages by a private person under Section 150, FSMA 2000.

A breach of any rule in the IPRU(INS) will not be actionable at the suit of a private person, as stated in rule 11.4 which disapplies Section 150, FSMA 2000. Furthermore, as is the case for rules in other modules of the Handbook, breach of a rule in the IPRU(INS) is not a criminal offence and will not render any transaction void or unenforceable (Section 151 FSMA 2000).

However a breach of a rule in the IPRU(INS) (or a rule in another part of the Handbook) may give rise to disciplinary action by the FSA. As briefly outlined in 9.4.2 below, the FSA now has a wider range of investigation and enforcement powers than was the case with previous insurance regulators under the ICA 1982.

9.1.2.2 *Recent changes in regulatory approach*

Although the provisions in the IPRU(INS) are similar to those in the ICA 1982, since N2 there have been some changes in regulatory approach in relation to long-term insurers. For instance:

(a)   the FSA now adopts a "risk-based" approach to regulation, which broadly means that it will aim to allocate its resources in a way which is proportional to the risk posed by the insurer to the FSA's regulatory objectives. As part of this approach, the FSA has been carrying out risk-assessments of insurers and financial services groups. The intention is for the FSA to develop closer supervision and a continuous relationship with higher-risk insurers, while maintaining merely routine oversight of the lowest impact insurers. (*See: A Regulator for the New Millennium* (FSA, January 2000) and *Building the New Regulator: Progress Report 1* (FSA, December 2000)); and

(b)   there is greater emphasis on the supervision of financial services groups, across all financial services sectors, as opposed to the supervision of insurers or other financial services firms on an individual basis. This is reflected not only in the provisions in the IPRU(INS) implementing the EC Directive on Insurance Groups but also in other rules and guidance in the Handbook which confirm that the circumstances of another member of an insurer's group may affect the insurer's ability to satisfy the Principles or Threshold Conditions.

9.1.3   The future of long-term insurance regulation

9.1.3.1   Trend towards harmonisation
A number of imminent changes to the prudential regulation of long-term insurance in the UK will result from the movement towards the harmonisation of prudential standards across financial services sectors and among different jurisdictions.

Within the UK, as mentioned above, the FSA intends to eventually issue an Integrated Prudential Sourcebook consolidating prudential standards across different financial services sectors. The timetable for the issue of the Integrated Prudential Sourcebook is being reconsidered, following delays in the implementation of the new Basel Accord and related European Union ("EU") legislation. New timetable proposals, including the possibility of implementing certain provisions of the Integrated Prudential Sourcebook in 2004 with other provisions coming into force in 2005, are currently under consultation. (*See* Consultation Paper 115, *Integrated Prudential Sourcebook – timetable for implementation* (FSA, November 2001)).

At an international level, major changes are currently being considered mainly in connection with the harmonisation of solvency requirements and financial reporting standards. Proposals for other new EC directives, including a reinsurance directive and additional directives relating to insurance intermediaries, are still under consideration. If an EC reinsurance directive were to be adopted it is likely that EU authorisation requirements for long-term reinsurers would be more harmonised. At present, UK reinsurers are subject to prudential regulation, but this is not the case in certain other EEA States. Long-term reinsurance is not currently covered under the EC Life Insurance Directives and long-term reinsurers do not therefore benefit from freedom of establishment and services across the EEA in the same way as insurers in the EEA.

9.1.3.2   FSA review of insurance regulation

In direct contrast with the trend towards harmonisation and integration is the FSA's recent recognition that special considerations apply to the insurance sector. The regulation of insurance generally, and of with-profits policies in particular, are the subject of several recent reports and ongoing FSA reviews.

The problems recently faced by Equitable Life Assurance Society ("Equitable Life"), described in more detail in 9.7.3 below, and those revealed by the pensions and endowment misselling reviews, were among the factors that led the FSA to undertake a comprehensive review of UK insurance regulation, including a specialised review of the regulation of with-profits policies. This review of insurance regulation, which is being led by the FSA's Managing Director of the Consumer, Investment and Insurance Directorate, John Tiner, is also known as the "Tiner Project". The ongoing specialised review of the regulation of with-profits policies (the "With-Profits Review") was first announced by the FSA in February 2001.

Following a ruling by the House of Lords that Equitable Life had treated certain policyholders unfairly and its resulting financial difficulties, the board of the FSA commissioned an independent report on the FSA's regulation of Equitable Life. This report (the "Baird Report") was issued in October 2001. The Baird Report identified certain problem areas and made certain recommendations for changes to regulation of the insurance sector.

In response to the Baird Report, the FSA has issued a report setting out the actions that it has already taken or plans to take to implement the recommendations made in the report. (*See: The Future Regulation of Insurance*, FSA, November 2001.)

The recommendations made in the Baird Report include the following:

(a)   the FSA should adopt a more proactive approach, with more access
        to information regarding the insurers it regulates and the insurance
        industry;
(b)   appointed actuaries should be subject to independent external
        reviews;
(c)   the use of financial reinsurance within the insurance market needs
        to be reviewed;
(d)   there should be improvements in relation to disclosure in regu-
        latory returns and making these returns more accessible to the
        public (e.g. possibly by having them available on the FSA website);
(e)   the FSA should develop policies to ensure consistency of interpre-
        tation on vague concepts such as "policyholders' reasonable expec-
        tations" (or "PRE") and clarifying the meaning of "customer
        interests" (which replaces the concept of "PRE" in the Handbook);
        and
(f)   the current solvency framework needs to be changed.

The Tiner Project, which will take into consideration the Baird Report
recommendations, is due to be completed in September 2002. The With-
Profits Review is set for completion in Spring 2002.

9.2   Authorisation

9.2.1   *The general prohibition and Part IV Permission*

Effecting and carrying out of contracts of long-term insurance, if carried
on by way of business, is a regulated activity under the FSMA 2000 (*see*
FSMA 2000 (Regulated Activities) Order 2001, SI 2001/544). As was the
case under the ICA 1982, an insurer or reinsurer intending to carry on
long-term insurance business in the UK can do so only if it is an authorised person or exempt from the authorisation requirement (Section 19,
FSMA 2000). The authorisation takes the form of a permission under Part
IV, FSMA 2000 to carry on the relevant regulated activities. Contravention of the general prohibition in Section 19, FSMA 2000 is a criminal
offence and insurance contracts entered into by the unauthorised person
are unenforceable (Sections 23, 26, FSMA 2000).

The territorial scope of the general prohibition in Section 19, FSMA 2000
is slightly wider than that under the ICA 1982. Case law prior to N2
suggests that an insurer may not need to be authorised in the UK if its
insurance contracts are written and negotiated outside the UK, even if it
carried out certain activities leading up to the negotiation of the contract

234

in the UK. This no longer appears to be the case. Section 418, FSMA 2000 now provides that as long as the day-to-day management of regulated activities by a company having its registered office (or head office) in the UK is the responsibility of the registered office (or head office) or another establishment maintained by it in the UK, that activity will be regarded as being carried on in the UK for the purposes of the FSMA 2000.

9.2.2 Classes of long-term insurance business

Within the IPRU(INS), long-term insurance business is divided into the same classes as those previously set out in Schedule 1, ICA 1982 (*see* IPRU(INS) Ann 11.1.), namely:

- I (life and annuity);
- II (marriage and birth);
- III (linked long-term);
- IV (permanent health);
- V (tontines);
- VI (capital redemption);
- VII (pension fund management);
- VIII (collective insurance); and
- IX (social insurance).

Part IV Permissions granted to long-term insurers will cover one or more of these classes.

Pursuant to rule 11.8, an insurance contract issued by an insurer authorised to carry on class I (life and annuity) business that also provides supplementary general insurance (accident and sickness) cover will be considered to be a long-term contract if it has the principal object of a long-term insurance contract.

9.2.3 Approved persons regime

The Handbook introduces a new approved persons regime for long-term (and general) insurers whereby individuals who carry out specified "controlled functions" within an insurer must pass the "fit and proper" test at the time of their initial application to the FSA for approval and on an ongoing basis. They are also required to comply with, among other things, some or (if they exercise "significant functions") all of certain Statements of Principle for approved persons and rules in the Code of Conduct for approved persons. *See* Chapter 10 for further details.

9.2.4 Appointed actuary

As was the case pursuant to Section 19, ICA 1982, long-term insurers have an obligation to appoint an appointed actuary (SUP 4.3.1R). The difference since N2 is that the appointed actuary exercises a controlled function and must be an approved person. Moreover, the Handbook includes provisions setting out his rights and duties as appointed actuary (see SUP 4). These include the duty to identify and monitor the insurer's risks, to perform actuarial investigations and to inform management of any material concerns regarding the firm's financial resources and its ability to meet policyholder liabilities when due (SUP 4.3.13R).

Certain duties in relation to the appointed actuary are imposed on the insurer. For example, the Supervision Manual requires an insurer to take reasonable steps to ensure that a proposed appointed actuary has the requisite qualifications, skill and experience to perform his functions, given the nature, scale and complexity of the insurer's business (SUP 4.3.9R, 4.3.10G).

Furthermore, the appointed actuary now has an express duty to inform the FSA of material matters, similar to the duty which previously applied only to auditors of the insurer. Statement of Principle 4 and guidance on the Code of Practice for Approved Persons (APER 4.4.4G) suggest that the appointed actuary's duty, as an approved person, to "disclose appropriately any information of which the FSA would reasonably expect notice" includes the duty to report promptly to the FSA information which could be reasonably assumed to be of material significance to the FSA, whether in response to questions or otherwise.

9.2.5 Restriction of business to insurance

Rule 1.3(1) states that an authorised insurer "must not carry on any commercial business in the United Kingdom or elsewhere other than insurance business and activities directly arising from that business". This rule is specific to insurers; similar restrictions do not apply to banks or other financial services firms.

The rule 1.3 restriction is similar to that previously found in Section 16, ICA 1982, but the language, and its effect, are very different. Section 16, ICA 1982 stated that any insurance company carrying on insurance business in the UK or (if a UK authorised insurer) in the EEA "shall not carry on any activities, in the United Kingdom or elsewhere, otherwise than in connection with or for the purposes of its insurance business".

Rule 1.3(1) is arguably a narrower restriction. Unlike Section 16, ICA 1982, it implicitly permits insurers to carry on activities of any nature so long as they do not constitute a "commercial business"; "commercial business" is not defined. No guidance has been issued on this point but if "commercial business" requires frequency or regularity of the activities in question, and possibly an intention to make a profit from such activities, insurers will arguably have more latitude under rule 1.3(1) to enter into certain arrangements that would be caught under Section 16, ICA 1982.

It remains to be seen whether the words "arising directly from" in rule 1.3 will be considered to have a meaning similar to the words "in connection with or for the purposes of" in Section 16, ICA 1982.

Prior to N2, a contravention of Section 16, ICA 1982 was not a criminal offence, but it was unclear whether a contract entered into in contravention of Section 16 was void and unenforceable. The Court of Appeal considered the question in *Fuji Finance Inc. v Aetna Life Insurance Co Ltd*, (1996) 4 All ER 608, but with two differing dicta at the Court of Appeal level and an out-of-court settlement despite permissions to appeal to the House of Lords, the issue was never resolved. Pursuant to Section 150, FSMA 2000, it is now established that a contravention of rule 1.3 is not an offence and will not render such a contract null and void.

9.3   Internal systems and controls

The Handbook includes detailed rules and guidance on the internal systems and controls required to be maintained by all authorised firms. For long-term insurers, this codified approach presents a marked departure from the regime before N2, despite the fact that certain principles and detailed requirements already applied to long-term insurers (mainly in the context of conduct of business regulation) under the FS Act 1986, its regulations and the rules of the PIA.

Under the ICA 1982, insurers had to fulfil the criteria of sound and prudent management (Section 5(1A), ICA 1982). However, the description of the systems and controls required to be in place to satisfy the sound and prudent management requirement were relegated to a few lines in Schedule 2A, ICA 1982 and guidance which focused on controls over investments and counterparty risk. (*See* Prudential Guidance Note 1994/6, "Guidance systems of control over investments (and counterparty exposure) of insurance companies with particular reference to the use of derivatives", since reproduced as Guidance Note P1.)

The relevant Handbook provisions include those summarised below.

9.3.1 Principles

Most elements of the "sound and prudent management" criteria previously applicable to insurers are reflected in the Principles for business contained in the High-Level Standards module of the Handbook, in particular:

(a) Principle 1 (integrity) – a firm must conduct its business with integrity;
(b) Principle 2 (skill, care and diligence) – a firm must conduct its business with due skill, care and diligence;
(c) Principle 3 (management and control) – a firm must take reasonable care to organise its affairs responsibly and effectively, with adequate risk management systems; and
(d) Principle 6 (customers' interests) – a firm must pay due regard to the interests of customers and treat them fairly.

As before, the rules focus on the fitness and properness of management and the presence of effective internal controls and resources. What differs from the regime in place before N2 is the level of detail set out in the rules and guidance in relation to internal structure and process requirements. Also, the rules now emphasise the importance of the firm's group, including group activities outside the UK, in assessing the firm's suitability.

9.3.2 Management

Like the Principles, the Threshold Conditions must be complied with by firms on an ongoing basis. Threshold Condition 5 (suitability) states that a firm must satisfy the FSA that it is a fit and proper person having regard to all the circumstances, including (among other factors) the need to ensure that its affairs are conducted soundly and prudently. Guidance on this Threshold Condition states that the governing body of a firm is to be made up of individuals with an appropriate range of skills and experience to understand, operate and manage the firm's regulated activities. If appropriate, the governing body is to include non-executive representation at a level which is appropriate for the control of the regulated activities (COND 2.5.7G(2)).

Firms also have a duty to maintain a clear and appropriate apportionment of responsibilities among its directors and senior managers (SYSC 2.1.1G).

9.3.3 Internal controls

The Senior Management Arrangements, Systems and Controls module of the Handbook sets out firms' duties to take reasonable care to:

(a) establish and maintain such systems and controls as are appropriate to its business (SYSC 3.1.1R);
(b) establish and maintain effective systems and controls for regulatory compliance and to counter the risk that the firm may be used for financial crime (SYSC 3.2.6R); and
(c) make and retain adequate records of relevant matters and dealings, in a form that is capable of being reproduced on paper (SYSC 3.2.20R).

Detailed guidance in SYSC refers to, among other points, the importance of maintaining clear reporting lines and considering in each case (depending on the nature, scale and complexity of the business) whether it is appropriate for the firm to have a separate risk assessment function, an audit committee with an appropriate number of non-executive directors and possibly an internal audit function. Guidance provides that the functions must be adequately resourced and staffed by competent and sufficiently independent staff.

9.3.4 Importance of risk assessment

The need for proper risk management is emphasised throughout the guidance. For example, guidance on Threshold Condition 5 (suitability) states that the firm is to have approached the control of financial and other risk in a prudent manner (for example, by not assuming risks without taking due account of the possible consequences) and taken reasonable care to ensure that robust information and reporting systems have been developed, tested and properly installed (COND 2.5.7G).

Guidance in SYSC 3.2.11 states that a firm's arrangements should be such as to furnish its governing body with the information it needs to play its part in identifying, measuring, managing and controlling risks of a regulatory concern.

239

9.3.5 Relevance of the insurer's group

The activities of other members of a firm's group will be relevant in assessing whether an authorised insurer satisfies Principles 3 (management and control), 4 (financial prudence) and 11 (relations with regulators, in so far as it relates to the duty of disclosure to the FSA). Guidance specifies that the inadequacy of a group member's risk management or resources would not necessarily mean contravention of Principles 3 or 4 by the firm in question, but the potential impact of the group member's activities (e.g. group-wide risk assessment systems) will be relevant in determining the adequacy of the firm's own resources (PRIN 1.1.5G).

Threshold Condition 3 (close links) requires that the FSA is satisfied that any close links between a firm and another person are not likely to prevent the FSA's effective supervision of the firm.

Threshold Condition 4 (adequate resources) requires that the firm's resources be adequate in relation to its regulated activities. Guidance on this Threshold Condition states that the FSA may take into account the firm's membership of a group and have regard, among other factors, to the means by which the firm, or members of its group manage the incidence of risk in connection with its business. In this context, "resources" refers not only to financial resources but also to non-financial resources (such as human resources) and the means of managing its resources (COND 2.4.2G).

9.3.6 Relevance of activities outside the UK

Principles 1 (integrity), 2 (skill, care and diligence) and 3 (management and control) apply to worldwide activities "in a prudential context". In considering whether it will take regulatory action in relation to any activities outside the UK, the FSA will take into account the standard expected in the market in which the firm is operating (PRIN 1.1.6G).

9.3.7 Application of Principle 3 to reinsurance business

Principle 3 (management and control) applies to the activities of long-term business "involving reinsurance contracts" (presumably long-term reinsurance business) only "in a prudential context". In this context, this means that the FSA would not expect to exercise any disciplinary or enforcement powers unless the contravention amounted to a serious or persistent violation which had implications for confidence in the financial system or for the fitness and propriety of the firm or the adequacy of the firm's resources (PRIN 1.1.3G).

9.4 FSA supervision and enforcement

Consistent with its stated intention to adopt a more proactive approach to prudential regulation, the FSA has stated that it is planning to develop more effective working relationships with insurers (especially higher impact firms), in part by conducting reviews of control processes, making greater use of on-site visits and placing more reliance on skilled persons. (*See*: *The Future Regulation of Insurance* (FSA, November 2001)).

Provisions in the FSMA 2000 and the Handbook give it the tools to supervise long-term insurers (and other financial services firms) more closely. These include:

(a) extensive requirements regarding notification of relevant information to the FSA; and
(b) increased powers of investigation and enforcement, by comparison with the regime in place before N2.

9.4.1 Duty to inform the FSA

The Principles and the provisions in Chapter 15 of the Supervision Manual impose new duties on long-term insurers (and other authorised firms) to provide the FSA with a wide range of information, in addition to formal reporting and transaction reporting requirements. For long-term insurers, this differs substantially from the provisions of the ICA 1982 regime.

The ICA 1982 did not explicitly impose a general duty on insurers to disclose new, material circumstances to the regulator. Information was required to be provided in specific circumstances. These included:

(a) disclosure on an application for authorisation;
(b) provision of any additional notification as required by the regulator in a "notice of requirements" issued to a newly authorised insurer;
(c) reporting prescribed information on the submission of annual regulatory returns;
(d) required notification of any proposed change of directors or change of controllers;

241

(e)   required disclosure of the intention to open a branch or provide cross-border services in another EEA State; and

(f)   the correction of inaccuracies in information previously provided to the regulator.

The flow of information between the insurer and the regulator concerning the company's affairs relied, to some extent, on the recognition by insurers of the importance of maintaining a good, open relationship with their regulator and of keeping their supervisor promptly informed of any material, potentially adverse event.

The Handbook adopts an approach that is more similar to the system of "notifiable events" in the rules of the PIA but the notification requirements are potentially much more extensive.

9.4.1.1   Duty to cooperate with regulators

Principle 11 (relations with regulators) states that:

> "a firm must deal with its regulators in an open and cooperative way, and must disclose to the FSA appropriately anything relating to the firm of which the FSA would reasonably expect notice."

For the purposes of Principle 11, "information relating to the firm" can consist of information relating either to the insurer or to other members of its group and to information about either regulated and unregulated activities. The insurer's duty of cooperation and disclosure under Principle 11 is in relation to the FSA and any other regulators to which the insurer is subject worldwide (PRIN 3.4.5 R). A breach of Principle 11 could lead to disciplinary action by the FSA.

9.4.1.2   Important notifiable events

Chapter 15 of the Supervision Manual contains rules and guidance which supplement Principle 11, most of which require notification of important matters which should obviously be brought to the attention of the FSA. These include immediate notification as soon as the firm becomes aware that any of the following may have occurred or may occur:

(a)   the insurer failing to satisfy a Threshold Condition or a significant breach of a rule or Statement of Principle;

(b)   any matter which could have a significant adverse impact on the insurer's reputation;

(c)   a matter which could affect the firm's ability to continue to provide adequate services to its customers and result in serious detriment to a customer;

(d)   a matter which could result in serious financial consequences to the financial system or to other firms;

(e)   criminal prosecution or conviction of the firm for an offence involving fraud or dishonesty or penalties for tax evasion or disciplinary investigations or sanctions imposed on the firm; or

(f)   insolvency, bankruptcy or winding-up proceedings.

According to guidance, the duty to notify also arises in the event of:

(a)   any proposed restructuring, reorganisation or business expansion which could have a significant impact on the firm's risk profile or resources;

(b)   any proposed action which would result in a material change in a firm's capital adequacy or solvency, including a material change resulting from the payment of a special or unusual dividend; or

(c)   a significant failure in the firm's systems or controls, including those reported to the firm by its auditor.

(*See* SUP 15.3.1R, 15.3.8G, 15.3.17R and 15.3.21R.)

9.4.1.3   *Less obvious notifiable events*

Certain notifiable events referred to in guidance are events (some of which would not necessarily have required notification prior to N2) where it may be difficult for the insurer to assess whether notification in any given case to the regulator would be appropriate or not. For example, the duty to notify arises on the following events:

(a)   the firm identifies irregularities in its accounting or other records, whether or not there is evidence of fraud and the event is "significant" (SUP 15.3.17R);

(b)   the firm becomes aware that an employee may have committed fraud against a customer and the event is "significant" (SUP 15.3.17R);

(c)   civil proceedings are brought against the firm and the amount of the claim is significant in relation to the firm's financial resources or its reputation (SUP 15.3.15R);

(d)   a significant breach of a rule or any breach (whether significant or not) of any requirement imposed by the FSMA 2000 or related regulations or orders (SUP 15.3.11R);

(e)　the firm commencing the provision of a new type of product or service (SUP 15.3.8G);

(f)　the firm ceasing to undertake or significantly reducing the scope of a regulated activity or ancillary activity (SUP 15.3.8G); or

(g)　the firm entering into or significantly changing a material outsourcing arrangement (SUP 15.3.8G).

Guidance intended to assist the firm to determine whether disclosure would be appropriate in relation to notification under Principle 11 or SUP 15.3.17R (relating to "significant" events) states that a firm considering whether to notify should have regard to the following relevant factors:

(a)　the size of any actual or potential monetary loss to the insurer or its customers;

(b)　the risk of reputational loss to the insurer; and

(c)　whether the incident or a pattern of incidents reveals weaknesses in the firm's internal controls (SUP 15.3.18G).

9.4.1.4　*Information about the group*
The notifiable events under Principle 11 include relevant events relating to another member of the insurer's group.

Threshold Condition 3 (close links) also reflects the importance for the FSA of obtaining adequate information across a firm's group. Guidance on Threshold Condition 3 states that the factors that the FSA will take into account to determine whether this Threshold Condition is satisfied include whether it is likely that the FSA will receive adequate information from the insurer and those persons with whom the insurer has close links to determine whether the insurer is complying with regulatory requirements and standards and to identify and assess the impact on the regulatory objectives (COND 2.3.3G).

A direct insurer's duty to report significant transactions entered into with a related undertaking, a participating undertaking, a related undertaking of a participating undertaking or a natural person holding a participation in the direct insurer or any of the aforementioned undertakings, in accordance with the provisions in Chapter 10 IPRU(INS) implementing the EC Directive on Insurance Groups, is another example.

9.4.2　*Enforcement*

From N2, the FSA's wide-ranging powers of investigation and enforcement include the power to:

(a) require firms and certain other persons to provide particular information or documents to it (Section 165, FSMA 2000);

(b) require a firm to commission a report on a particular matter from a "skilled person", such as an actuary, accountant or person with technological skills (Section 166, FSMA 2000);

(c) appoint an investigator to conduct a formal investigation in certain circumstances in accordance with directions received from the FSA and to issue a factual report thereon (Section 170, FSMA 2000). The investigator is then entitled to obtain relevant documents from third parties who hold them, to require an explanation of documents, to obtain a warrant to enter and search premises and to bring proceedings against a relevant person who does not comply (Sections 175–177, FSMA 2000);

(d) take disciplinary action against a firm, which can include issuing a public censure or imposing a fine on the firm (Sections 205 and 206, FSMA 2000). The FSA may also vary a permission granted to a firm by imposing limitations, restrictions or requirements on it (Section 45(1), FSMA 2000) or (presumably only in extremely severe cases) cancel permission (Section 45(2), FSMA 2000);

(e) impose a restitution order requiring a firm to compensate investors who have suffered losses from its breach or pay out profits arising from such breach, or apply to the court for the granting of such a restitution order (Sections 382–386, FSMA 2000);

(f) apply for an injunction to prevent a firm from committing regulatory breaches, to require it to remedy those breaches or mitigate their effect or to freeze a firm's assets (Sections 380 and 381, FSMA 2000);

(g) impose sanctions on approved persons in certain circumstances, for example:

(i) publicly censuring or fining an approved person who has either breached a Statement of Principle or been knowingly involved in a regulatory breach by the firm (Section 66, FSMA 2000);

(ii) withdrawing approval from an approved person who is no longer considered fit and proper to prevent him from continuing to carry on the relevant controlled function (Section 63, FSMA 2000); or

(h) impose a prohibition order to prevent any person who is considered not to be fit and proper from being involved in the financial services sector (Section 56, FSMA 2000).

9.5 Rules relating to the long-term insurance fund and transactions with connected persons

Chapter 3 of the IPRU(INS) contains certain prudential rules which apply to long-term insurers in relation to the allocation and application of assets and liabilities of the long-term insurance business, arrangements to avoid unfairness between the insurer's funds, the adequacy of assets and premiums, and restrictions regarding transactions with connected persons. These are briefly summarised below.

9.5.1 Separation of long-term insurance business assets and liabilities

Long-term insurers must maintain a separate internal fund for their long-term insurance business. A long-term insurance fund can, if appropriate, be divided into separate sub-funds for different types of long-term insurance business, so that it becomes a "fund of funds". Only assets and liabilities attributable to the insurer's long-term insurance business can be allocated to the long-term insurance fund. Other assets and liabilities must be allocated to the shareholders' fund.

An insurer's segregation of its long-term insurance business assets and liabilities is reflected in its internal accounts and in the statutory returns filed with the FSA. Rule 3.1(1) (previously Section 28, ICA 1982) provides that insurers must maintain a separate account for each type of business and the receipts of each kind of business must be entered in the account maintained for that business. Insurers must maintain such accounting and other records as are necessary for identifying the assets representing the long-term insurance fund (IPRU(INS) 3.1R(2)). More difficult to attribute may be general overhead expenses and liabilities relating to borrowings. On a winding up of a long-term insurer, the creditors of its long-term insurance business are entitled to participate in the assets of the long-term insurance fund(s) in priority to other creditors of the insurer. It can be important therefore for creditors (other than policyholders) to specify whether sums due to them are due from the long term fund or other funds of an insurer.

The determination of which assets in the insurer's accounts are attributable to its long-term insurance business and should therefore be identified as representing the insurer's long-term insurance fund or funds is largely an actuarial matter. An obvious example is the premium income derived from that business. Liabilities which should be allocated to the long-term insurance fund are those liabilities of an insurer arising under or in connection with its long-term insurance business (IPRU(INS)

Ann 11.1). This includes liabilities arising from deposit-back arrangements with a reinsurer (whereby an amount is deposited by the reinsurer with the cedant).

9.5.2 Limitation on use of assets in the long-term insurance fund

Assets in the long-term insurance fund can be used only for the purposes of the long-term insurance business (IPRU(INS) 3.2R, similar to previous Section 29, ICA 1982).

Rule 3.2R(1) provides that long-term insurance business assets cannot be transferred out of the long-term insurance fund so as to be available for other purposes of the insurer except where the transfer constitutes reimbursement of expenditure borne by other assets (in the same or preceding financial year) in discharging liabilities wholly or partly attributable to long-term insurance business. Money from an insurer's long-term insurance fund must not be used for the purposes of other business of the insurer notwithstanding its subsequent repayment out of the receipts of that other business (IPRU(INS) 3.2R(5)).

Two exceptions to this rule are set out in rule 3.2(2) and (4). Rule 3.2(1) does not prevent:

(a) an insurer from exchanging, at fair market value, long-term business assets for other assets of the insurer; and
(b) the transfer out of the fund, where appropriate, of excess assets established by an actuarial investigation of the long-term insurer in accordance with rule 9.4.

Rule 3.2(6) provides that a long-term insurer must not declare a dividend at any time when the value of the long-term business assets (as determined in accordance with the Valuation of Assets Rules) is less than the amount of the long-term insurance business liabilities (as determined in accordance with the Determination of Liabilities Rules). Unlike Section 29 ICA 1982, rule 3.2(6) does not prevent a parent company of an insurer from declaring dividends in similar circumstances. However the FSA has indicated that regulations under Section 142, FSMA 2000 may (eventually) apply to restrict a parent undertaking of an insurer from doing anything to lessen the effectiveness of rule 3.2(6) or other rules in Part 1 of Chapter 3, IPRU(INS).

9.5.3   Arrangements to avoid unfairness

Rule 3.5 provides that a long-term insurer must have adequate arrangements in place for securing that transactions affecting its assets (other than transactions outside its control) do not operate unfairly between the long-term insurance fund or funds and other assets of the insurer, or between "identified funds" comprising receipts of a particular part of its long-term insurance business which can be identified as such by virtue of accounting or other records maintained by the insurer. This is similar to the provisions previously contained in Section 31A, ICA 1982.

9.5.4   Adequacy of assets

Pursuant to rule 2.3(1) (previously Section 35A, ICA 1982), a UK insurer must secure that:

(a)   its liabilities under contracts of insurance written by it (other than liabilities in respect of linked benefits – *see* 9.6 below) are covered by assets of appropriate safety, yield and marketability having regard to the classes of business carried on; and

(b)   its investments are appropriately diversified and adequately spread, and excessive reliance is not placed on investments of any particular category or description.

9.5.5   Adequacy of premiums

Before entering into a long-term insurance contract, a UK insurer must satisfy itself that the aggregate of the premiums payable under the contract and the income which will be derived from them, and other resources of the UK insurer which are available for the purpose, will be sufficient, on reasonable actuarial assumptions, to meet all commitments arising under or in connection with the contract (IPRU(INS) 3.5AR(1), previously Section 35B, ICA 1982). Rule 3.5A(2) provides that the insurer must not rely on other resources for this purpose in such a way as to jeopardise its solvency in the long term.

9.5.6   Restriction on transactions with connected persons

Rule 3.4 sets out restrictions on transactions by a long term insurer with connected persons which are similar to those previously set out in Section 31, ICA 1982. The rule provides that a long-term insurer must not enter into, and must take steps to ensure that any subordinate company does not enter into, certain transactions with connected persons if, at the time of the transaction (or had the transaction been entered into), the aggregate value of assets and the amount of liabilities attributable to that and other restricted transactions already entered into exceeds five per cent of the total amount standing to the credit of the insurer's long-term insurance funds.

The transactions in question are:

(a)   transactions entered into by the insurer where:
    (i)   a connected person will owe it money,
    (ii)   the insurer acquires shares in a company which is a connected person, or
    (iii)   the insurer undertakes a liability to meet an obligation of the connected person or to help the connected person meet such obligation; and
(b)   transactions entered into by a subordinate company of the insurer where:
    (i)   the insurer or a connected person will owe money to the subordinate company,
    (ii)   the subordinate company acquires shares in the insurer or a connected person, or
    (iii)   the subordinate company undertakes a liability to meet an obligation of the insurer or a connected person or to help the insurer or connected person meet such obligation. This restriction does not apply to the subordinate company, however, if it is a long-term insurer and the right to receive money would constitute a long-term asset, the acquisition would be made out of its long-term insurance fund, or the liability would fall to be discharged out of its long-term insurance fund.

As defined in rule 3.4, "connected person" includes:

(a)   a controller of the insurer;
(b)   a company controlled by the insurer or by another person who controls the insurer; or
(c)   a director, or the wife, husband or minor son or daughter of such director.

"Control" includes:

(a)   control of 15 per cent or more of the voting shares in the insurer or any of its parent companies; or

(b)   the ability to direct or instruct directors of the insurer or any parent company of the insurer.

"Subordinate company" includes a company where the insurer or another subordinate company of the insurer holds more than half in nominal value of its equity share as part of its long-term assets and such shareholding confers on the insurer (or its subordinate company) to appoint or remove a majority of the directors and more than 50 per cent of the voting power.

9.6   Linked long-term contracts

A linked long-term contract is one where benefits payable to the policy-holder are wholly or partly linked to the value of (or income from, or fluctuations in the value of) specified underlying assets or indices (IPRU(INS) 2.3(4)R). Long-term contracts linked to the value of assets, referred to as "property-linked contracts", can be either directly linked to the value of a specified asset or group of assets, or linked to the value of notional units in a fund comprising assets (e.g. an internal fund of the insurer), in which case the insurance contract is referred to as "unit-linked".

Linked long-term contracts are subject to specific rules, particularly in relation to:

(a)   the types of the assets or indices that are "permitted links" used to determine the amount of the linked benefit; and

(b)   the types of assets that may be held to match liabilities in respect of linked benefits and the insurer's obligation regarding "close-matching" of such assets and liabilities.

9.6.1   Permitted links

Linked benefits can be determined only by reference to property or indices which are permitted links described in Appendix 3.2 IPRU(INS), which is similar to Schedule 10 to the Insurance Companies Regulations 1994.

9.6.1.1   Types of links permitted
Property classified as a permitted link includes:

(a) cash;
(b) listed and unlisted securities that are readily realisable;
(c) land in the EEA, the US and certain other states, and certain loans
     secured by mortgage or charge on land in such states;
(d) certain approved government securities;
(e) loans to or deposits with approved credit institutions, approved
     financial institutions or approved investment firms;
(f) derivative contracts but only if they are "permitted derivative
     contracts" (described in more detail below);
(g) units in a fund falling within the UCITS Directive or in certain
     collective investment funds where units are realisable and the price
     at which units are bought and sold is published regularly; and
(h) units in other notional or real funds comprising assets that are
     themselves permitted links, if under the insurance contract either:
     (i)   the fund is to be managed wholly by insurer, or
     (ii) the insurer assumes responsibility to the policyholders for any
           acts or omissions of the fund manager as if they were acts or
           omissions of the insurer.

An index is a permitted link if it is an approved index, which means that
it must be:

(a) an index which is published at least once every week, based on
     constituents which are themselves assets which are permitted links,
     and calculated independently on a basis made available to the
     public;
(b) a national index of retail prices issued by the government in the
     EEA or certain other states; or
(c) an index based on certain listed securities, income derived
     therefrom or cash as constituents in respect of which a derivative
     contract is listed.

9.6.1.2 Certain restrictions
Rule 3.7(3) specifies some additional restrictions in relation to permitted
links. For example:

(a) Benefits payable under any linked long-term contract must not be
     determined by reference to unlisted securities, units in a collective
     investment fund (that does not fall within the UCITS Directive) or
     loans or deposits with approved credit institutions, financial insti-
     tutions or investment firms if the value of the securities, units, loans
     or deposits is itself determined, wholly or partly, by the value of
     assets which are not themselves permitted links. For example,

applying this "look-through" approach it would not be permitted to link benefits under a linked long-term contract to the value of units in a hedge fund that:

    (i)   invests in derivative contracts or other assets that are not permitted links, or

    (ii)   invests in other unregulated funds which themselves comprise investments that are not permitted links.

(b)   Not more than 10 per cent in aggregate of the property-linked benefits under any policy can be determined by reference to the value of unlisted securities.

(c)   Not more than 10 per cent in aggregate of the property-linked benefits under any policy can be determined by reference to the value of units in a collective investment fund (that is not regulated under the UCITS Directive), unless the insurance contract has been marketed in accordance with any legal restrictions which apply to the marketing of the corresponding collective investment fund.

(d)   Any asset listed in Part I of Appendix 3.2 IPRU(INS) which has the effect of a derivative contract cannot be a permitted link unless it has the effect of a permitted derivative contract.

9.6.1.3 *Permitted derivative contracts*

As mentioned above, derivative contracts may be permitted links only if they satisfy certain conditions and can therefore be classified as "permitted derivative contracts". The conditions, which are similar to the conditions applicable to determine whether a derivative contract is an "approved derivative contract" to which a value can be attributed under the Valuation of Assets Rules, may be summarised briefly as follows:

(a)   The derivative contract is either listed on a regulated market or has been entered into with an "approved counterparty". Approved counterparties include "approved credit institutions" and investment firms permitted in the EEA, pursuant to provisions implementing the Investment Services Directive, to enter into unlisted derivative contracts as principal. It should be noted that a bank (even if established in the US) is an "approved credit institution" only if it is recognised or permitted to carry on banking activities in an EEA state. Furthermore, subsidiaries of an approved counterparty are not approved counterparties unless they are themselves EEA authorised banks or investment firms.

(b)   The insurer reasonably believes that the derivative contract may be readily closed out. This means that the insurer cannot reasonably foresee any circumstances in which it would need to close out part or all of the derivative contract at a few days' notice and would not be able to do so.

(c)   The derivative contract is "covered", that is, if the Valuation of Assets Rules applied to the contract, it would not require a significant provision to be made in respect of it pursuant to rule 5.3.

(d)   The derivative contract is held (or has the effect of a derivative contract held) in connection with property for the purpose of reducing investment risk or efficient portfolio management.

(e)   The derivative contract has a prescribed pricing basis and is based on underlying assets which are themselves permitted links, an index of such assets or an official index of retail prices.

Guidance in respect of the conditions applying to approved or permitted derivative contracts is included in Guidance Note 4.2 "Use of derivative contracts in insurance funds".

Further guidance on permitted links and other aspects of linked long-term contracts is set out in Guidance Note 4.4 "Linked contracts".

9.6.2   *Close-matching and adequacy of assets*

Liabilities in respect of linked benefits that are not covered by contracts of reinsurance must be covered by assets described in rule 3.7 (permitted links).

Rule 2.3(2) provides that insurers offering linked long-term contracts must secure that, as far as practicable, their liabilities in respect of linked benefits are covered as follows:

(a)   if benefits are linked to the value of units in an undertaking for collective investments, in transferable securities or of the value of assets continued in an internal fund, by those units or assets; or

(b)   if benefits are linked to a share index or other reference value not mentioned in (a) above, by units which represent the reference value, or by assets of appropriate safety and marketability which correspond, as nearly as may be, to the assets on which that reference value is based.

9.7   With-profits policies

With-profits policies are essentially policies that entitle the holder to share in the profits (and possibly the losses) of the insurer. The regulation of the with-profits industry is being comprehensively reviewed in the context of the FSA's With-Profits Review. This section describes certain features of with-profits policies and outlines the current regulatory regime and current proposals for change.

9.7.1 Features of with-profits policies

With-profits policies permit holders to participate in equity and property markets while in principle reducing the investment risk to some extent by the application of "smoothing" against any extreme volatility in such markets. At the same time, a holder's entitlement to participate in the profits of the insurer can carry with it a significant business risk. For example, if the policy entitles the holder to share in the profits of all long-term business carried on by the insurer, its benefit entitlement may be affected by any losses incurred within such business, e.g. costs in connection with a misselling review and compensation payments or the cost of maintaining reserves to cover guaranteed options. With-profits policies are generally considered more appropriate for longer-term investments as benefits payable on early surrender or transfer of the policy will usually be reduced by the application of early surrender penalties.

Participation rights vary from policy to policy but typical features include one or more of the following:

(a) The policyholders are entitled to specified benefits when the policy terminates on a specified date or event. Typically the specified events include death (this is the life insurance element of the policy), retirement (e.g. in the case of a pensions policy) or other specified maturity date(s). For example, it is common in the case of "with-profits bonds" for the policies to specify dates occurring five or 10 years after the issue of the policy. The benefits will typically include a guaranteed amount and discretionary amounts comprising discretionary bonuses during the life of the policy and a terminal bonus.

(b) With-profits policyholders may share in one or more sources of profits, such as:
  (i) profits accumulated within the insurer's with-profits fund or within certain of its with-profits funds or sub-funds;
  (ii) profits from other insurance business of the insurer, such as non-profits business; and/or
  (iii) potentially any distribution of the inherited estate of the insurer.

Each policy has an "asset share" in the with-profits fund(s) based on the amount of premiums paid in, the investment return and the expenses incurred. The entitlement to a share in profits of any category of with-profits policyholders is realised through the declaration by the insurer from time to time of bonuses. These include regular bonuses (also called "reversionary bonuses"), usually declared on an annual basis and added to the value of the policy, and a terminal bonus declared shortly prior to the maturity or termination of the policy. Special bonuses may also be declared, for example, upon a distribution of part of the inherited estate.

(c)   The amount of the terminal bonus is calculated by the insurer on the advice of the appointed actuary and is in principle the amount required to bring the total pay-out to the policyholder up to fair value of the policy, taking into account a participation in appropriate profits and losses, after smoothing, and the previous bonuses declared.

(d)   The application of a "smoothing" mechanism by the insurer to ensure that the calculation of the amount payable to the policyholder protects him from the extremes of fluctuations in the property and equity markets, in which most with-profits funds invest primarily. The smoothing mechanism applied varies from insurer to insurer.

(e)   If the holder surrenders or transfers the policy before the maturity date, the amount of the benefit payable on surrender or transfer will usually be at the discretion of the insurer. There will not usually be any minimum guaranteed amount and the insurer has discretion as to whether to pay any terminal bonus at all and whether to apply smoothing. The insurer will usually exercise its discretion to pay a terminal bonus, but a market value reduction (or "MVR") may be applied to the amount that would otherwise be payable to the policyholder.

With-profits policies can take various forms, including:

(a)   a conventional with-profits policy, which entitles the holder to a share of the profits of the insurer's with-profits fund and where benefits include a guaranteed amount, the addition of regular bonuses and a discretionary terminal bonus;

(b)   a unitised with-profits policy, where premiums are invested in a segregated with-profits fund or a fund or sub-fund(s), and possibly other funds of the insurer and a number of notional units in the fund(s) is allocated to each policy. The units are usually entitled to a share of the distributed surplus within the fund.

Unitised policies facilitate investment in different funds, for example partial investment in the with-profits fund and partial investment in other unit-linked funds offered by the insurer, through a single policy. They may also allow switching between funds. Regular bonuses are announced on a prospective basis (with the actual amount added possibly being higher or lower than indicated at the outset), whereas in conventional policies they are declared retrospectively. The minimum guaranteed amount under a unitised policy is usually the number of units allocated to the policy at the current unit price (this is also referred to as "the face value" of units).

A unitised with-profits policy, especially if under the contract terms the policyholder only participates in investment return, can be very similar to a unit-linked policy. However, in the case of a unitised with-profits policy, smoothing will usually be applied to reduce fluctuations in the market value of the underlying assets and corresponding units. Unit-linked policies do not involve any smoothing.

Variations on the above include:

(a)   a with-profits bond, which is a single premium, whole life policy with no defined maturity date other than death. Benefits are in the form of a cash sum equivalent to a surrender or withdrawal from the policy;

(b)   an endowment policy, typically entered into for the purpose of repayment of a mortgage or securing payment of a sum on retirement, having a longer term to a maturity date on which a cash sum benefit will become payable if the policyholder has not previously died or surrendered the policy; and

(c)   a with-profits annuity, involving the addition of profit-related payment to each annuity payment.

The FSA's publication *A Description and Classification of With-Profits Policies* (FSA, October 2001) sets out detailed descriptions of the types of with-profits policies and their common features.

9.7.2   Current regulation of with-profits policies

Before N2, the exercise of discretion by an insurer's directors in the operation of with-profits funds was restricted, to some extent, by the rules relating to the segregation of assets of the long-term business and rules regarding sound and prudent management, implicitly including the obligation to take into account the specialist advice of the appointed actuary. It was also affected by pragmatic considerations such as, in the case of decisions relating to the declaration or payment of bonuses, maintaining a competitive position among other providers, and, in the case of distributions from the inherited estate, the estimated amounts required by the company for working capital and future reserves.

Most important, however, was the generally recognised requirement that the insurer satisfy the reasonable expectations of its current and future policyholders of "PRE".

9.7.2.1   PRE and customers' interests
The concept of PRE was not defined in the ICA 1982 and, while referred to in the judgments rendered in *Equitable Life Assurance Society* v *Hyman*, (2000) 3 All ER 951 and *Axa Equity & Sun Life Assurance Society Plc: in Re Axa Sun Life Plc* (TLR, 19 December 2000), was never given a comprehensive meaning. In the *Axa* case the High Court, referring to the House of Lord's decision in the *Equitable Life* case, confirmed that:

> "PRE results from a number of different sources and will vary from company to company. It is the collective reasonable expectations of the policyholders of a company as a class. . . . Those sources include the company's promotional material, the provisions of its articles, the past practice of the company, in particular its bonus policy and the current practice of the insurance industry generally."

As a consequence of PRE, the practice of declaring high bonus rates for a number of years, for instance, may lead to policyholders' reasonable expectations that similar rates will be declared for following years.

The FSMA 2000 and the Handbook no longer refer to the concept of PRE. The FSA has indicated that the concept of PRE has been replaced by Principle 6 (customers' interests), found within the Principles for Business module of the High-Level Standards block of the Handbook. Principle 6 states that a firm must pay due regard to the interests of customers and treat them fairly. No guidance has been issued on how this Principle will apply specifically to the operation of a with-profits fund. Further clarification on how the "customers' interests" concept will apply as a replacement for PRE is to be considered as part of the FSA's With-Profits Review.

9.7.2.2   Rules 3.2 and 3.3

The IPRU(INS) contains rules relevant to the declaration of bonuses.

Rule 3.2(2) confirms that the excess of assets exceeding the liabilities attributable to the long-term insurance business, as established by an actuarial investigation (referred to in rule 3.3 as the "established surplus") can, in certain circumstances, be transferred out of the long-term insurance fund.

Rule 3.3 provides that an insurer cannot, unless it discloses its intention to the FSA and publishes a statement to that effect, allocate a share of the established surplus in a given period to a category of with-profits policy-holders (by payment of a bonus to them, declaration of a reversionary bonus in their favour or making a reduction in the premiums payable by them) if that share is lower than a "relevant minimum" level. A proposed share allocation will be lower than the "relevant minimum" if it is the less than the proportionate share of the current established surplus equivalent to the previous distribution by more than 0.5 per cent of the current established surplus.

Rule 3.3(3) provides that if the proposed allocation is less than the relevant minimum level, the insurer must:

(a)   notify the FSA of its proposed allocation below the minimum level;
(b)   not earlier than 14 days after notification to the FSA, publish a statement explaining the allocation it proposes to make and the reasons for it in the London, Edinburgh and Belfast Gazettes and in two national newspapers; and
(c)   allow a period of not less than 56 days to elapse before it makes the allocation.

9.7.3   Equitable Life and proposals for future regulation

9.7.3.1   Equitable Life

The situation which led to Equitable Life's closure to new business and to its subsequent compromise proposal to with-profits policyholders is a good example of what can happen when the operation of with-profits business does not run smoothly. It resulted in the commissioning of the Baird Report and the FSA report on The Future Regulation of Insurance and was one of the factors that led to the Tiner Project, including the With-Profits Review.

Equitable Life, a mutual which wrote both with-profits and non-profits business, acknowledged in 1995 that it would be unable to continue to pay benefits under certain with-profits policies written between 1957 and 1988 which gave holders the option to receive an annuity at a fixed guaranteed rate (or "GAR"). At the time the GAR policies were issued, the GARs offered were lower than market annuity rates. However, because of changing market circumstances, from 1995 to 1998 the GARs previously promised to GAR policyholders were consistently higher than current market annuity rates, with increasing margins between the two.

The Baird Report refers to several factors that rendered the existence of these unquantifiable GAR liabilities of particular problematic significance to Equitable Life. First, the GAR policies represented a much bigger proportion of its business than was the case with other insurers. Second, Equitable Life had a history of providing a full distribution of its profits as bonuses to its with-profits policyholders and did not therefore maintain a large inherited estate. Thirdly, as a mutual, it did not have any shareholders to draw on for additional funding. Equitable Life therefore sought to resolve the issue by adopting a differential bonus policy which reduced the level of terminal bonus payable to any GAR policyholders who exercised their GAR option, thereby equalising the benefits payable to those policyholders and holders of policies that did not have the GAR option.

Following policyholder complaints, the matter was eventually brought before the House of Lords. In July 2000, the House of Lords issued a ruling (*see Equitable Life* case cited above) confirming that the differential terminal bonus practice was a breach of contract, as the GAR policies required Equitable Life to pay GAR policyholders the same terminal bonuses as had been paid to non-GAR policyholders.

In December 2000, having failed to secure a buyer for its business, Equitable Life announced that it would stop writing new business with immediate effect. In November 2001, it made a compromise proposal to its with-profits policyholders whereby broadly an additional bonus was promised to GAR with-profits policyholders in exchange for their giving up their GAR options and to non-GAR with-profits policyholders in exchange for their agreeing not to pursue misselling claims. At the time of writing, the FSA had issued a statement confirming its approval of the compromise proposal, policyholders voted in favour of the proposal and the scheme was to be approved by the High Court. However, Equitable Life was still facing legal actions from policyholders.

259

9.7.3.2 *Proposals for future regulation*

The Baird Report and the FSA's report on The Future Regulation of Insurance and recent issues papers circulated as part of its With-Profits Review allude to the following unsatisfactory aspects of current regulation of with-profits policies:

(a) Directors of the insurer have almost unfettered discretion, and little or no accountability to policyholders, in relation to the operation of the insurer's with-profits fund(s). In particular, decisions on the following elements of a with-profits policy all depend on the exercise of the directors' discretion:
   (i)   the declaration and amount of regular bonuses;
   (ii) the amount of terminal bonuses;
   (iii) how to smooth investment return;
   (iv) the mix of assets in which the with-profits fund invests;
   (v)   whether and when to distribute any part of the inherited estate; and
   (vi) amounts payable on early surrender or transfer, including whether to apply an MVR in relation to the guaranteed amount or terminal bonus.
   As part of its With-Profits Review, the FSA intends to produce issues papers on "Governance of With-Profits Funds and Discretion & Fairness".

(b) The limit on the directors' discretion resulting from the concept of PRE is not considered in the Baird Report to be effective. The Baird Report criticises the reliance formerly placed on a vague concept like PRE. In relation to the replacement of the concept of PRE by that of "customer interests", the Baird Report recommends that the FSA continue its ongoing work on clarifying the meaning of "customer interests". The FSA's proposed measures should be included in the issues paper on "Discretion & Fairness" to be issued as part of the With-Profits Review.

(c) Directors rely on the insurer's appointed actuary, who has a professional duty to advise the directors of his interpretation of PRE, but in this respect the Baird Report recommends that appointed actuaries be subject to independent external reviews. It also suggests that it may be inappropriate, as is currently often the case, for appointed actuaries to sit on the board of the insurer.

(d) The Baird Report's findings included the fact that the FSA needed to be more informed about the affairs of the insurers that it regulates and worrying trends in the insurance industry, if it is to be able to regulate efficiently and in a timely manner. As part of its recommendations, the Baird Report suggests that regulatory returns include more detailed information about the insurer's with-profits fund(s) than is currently included.

(e) Recent research by the FSA shows that policyholders do not understand with-profits policies, and in particular the nature of the risks involved, due to the complexity and opacity of the products and the lack of any post-sale disclosure regarding continuing performance. The Baird Report recommends more disclosure to customers at the point of sale and, following the issue of the policy, ongoing disclosure to policyholders about the performance of the with-profits fund. There is also a suggestion that insurers' regulatory returns should be easily accessible, for example by being available on the FSA website (although this could raise issues given the potential confidentiality or market sensitivity of certain information in the return). As part of its With-Profits Review, the FSA intends to publish an issues paper on "Disclosure to Customers and Regulatory Reporting".

9.8 The inherited estate

9.8.1 What is the "inherited estate"?

Over the years, an insurer may accumulate assets in its long-term insurance fund(s) which exceed the amount required to be maintained to meet the liabilities of its long-term insurance business, including liabilities which arise from the duty to treat customers fairly in making and setting discretionary benefits. Such accumulated excess assets, to the extent that they have not been distributed and have been retained within the long-term insurance fund, are generally referred to as the inherited estate of an insurer (sometimes called the "orphan estate").

The accumulated excess assets comprising the inherited estate should not be confused with the "excess assets" over regulatory capital; the inherited estate represents the excess over and above any regulatory capital and other assets required to be maintained in the long-term insurance fund to satisfy policyholders' interests (previously, policyholders' reasonable expectations) in respect of the insurer's ability to continue to declare and pay appropriate bonuses under with-profits policies and to apply appropriate smoothing.

The inherited estate is derived mainly from retained investment return on past and present with-profits policyholders' premiums, profits that have arisen from past surrenders or transfers, and possibly past injections of capital from shareholders or the explicit reinvestment of shareholders' dividends.

The inherited estate provides working capital for the long-term insurer. It enhances investment flexibility by enabling the insurer to invest a higher proportion of assets in the long-term insurance fund in higher risk (and higher return) investments such as equities. It can also facilitate the smoothing of a fund and provide a cushion against unexpected adverse events or to develop new business.

By the 1990s several long-term insurers in UK had accumulated significant inherited estates and there was increasing interest in clarifying the respective interests of shareholders and policyholders in the inherited estate. Questions arose in connection with:

(a)   The "attribution" of the inherited estate –this refers to the proportionate ownership, by policyholders and shareholders of the insurer, of the inherited estate, while held within the long-term insurance fund. The attribution determines the entitlement that policyholders and shareholders have in relation to any future distribution of any part of the inherited estate. In the case of an insurer which is a mutual, policyholders as a general rule hold an interest in 100 per cent of the inherited estate, as there are no shareholders. For certain insurers which are proprietary companies, the articles of association and other relevant documents do not clearly establish policyholders' and shareholders' respective shares and the attribution of the inherited estate can be difficult to determine, although a starting point would be the ratio at which profits are generally divided between shareholders and policyholders.

(b)   The "distribution" of the inherited estate – if the insurer, on actuarial advice, considers that retention of any part of the inherited estate is no longer necessary, that part of the inherited estate may be available for release. Any distribution of the inherited estate involves a consideration by the insurer, on the advice of its actuary, of the competing interests of shareholders and past and present policyholders and future business requirements. Relevant issues include:

   (i)   the extent to which shareholders should be free to transfer funds out of that part of the inherited estate that is attributed to them;

   (ii)   the extent to which declared distributions to policyholders are fair, as one generation of policyholders may be benefiting from accumulated surplus earned during a previous generation of policyholders, possibly at the expense of such future generations.

(c) The "re-attribution" of the inherited estate – in recent publications, the FSA refers to the process whereby shareholders of an insurer seek to buy out policyholders' present rights to any future distribution of the inherited estate as the "re-attribution" of the inherited estate. Recently, Axa obtained court approval (*see* the *Axa* case cited above) in the context of a business transfer scheme under Schedule 2C to the ICA 1982, to a proposal whereby the company bought out with-profits policyholders' interests in future interests in return for special bonus payments, a capital injection and special arrangements providing for limitations on amounts that could be extracted by shareholders in future years and continued monitoring of the fund to ensure that the arrangement continued to protect policyholders' reasonable expectations.

9.8.2 *Current regulation of the inherited estate*

The IPRU(INS), like the ICA 1982 before it, does not contain many provisions specifically covering the inherited estate. "Inherited estate" is not defined in the FSMA 2000 or the Handbook.

The determination of what part of the long-term insurance fund constitutes the inherited estate, the attribution of the inherited estate, what distributions may be made and what re-attribution is possible are all subject to the insurer's duty to pay due regard to the interests of customers and treat them fairly (Principle 6 or, previously under the ICA 1982, policyholders' reasonable expectations). The relevance of PRE, which is discussed in further detail in 9.8.2 above, arises implicitly in view of the FSA's powers of intervention in the event that Principle 6 is contravened. The role of PRE was established in practice and was formally acknowledged in the ministerial decrees issued by the DTI in the 1990s, in response to applications by insurers for a clarification of the attribution of the inherited estate. More recently it has been confirmed in the *Axa* case.

In relation to the attribution of inherited estate, the DTI ministerial decrees and the *Axa* case confirm that:

(a) Ownership of surplus essentially depends on PRE, which in turn is influenced by a range of factors including the fair treatment of policyholders vis-a-vis shareholders, any statements of the company as to its bonus policy and the entitlement of policyholders to share in profits (e.g. in the insurer's articles of association or in company literature, history and past practice of the insurer and general practice within the industry).

(b) It is common practice to make distributions to policyholders and shareholders in the proportion 90: 10 and it is therefore presumed that a 90: 10 ratio should be used as the ratio of attribution between policyholders and shareholders, with shareholders receiving up to, or exactly, one-ninth of the value of profits distributed by way of bonuses to policyholders, unless there is clear evidence, based on the company's circumstances (e.g. the terms of its articles of association), statements or practice, that a different proportion is appropriate.

(c) Even if a surplus is derived from sources other than policyholder investments (e.g. if it arises from shareholder funding), there is a presumption that the established ratio should be used as the basis of attribution between policyholders and shareholders, unless there is clear evidence that a different proportion was appropriate in respect of the surplus arising from time to time from some particular part of the business.

In certain cases it can be established that the ratio should be 100: 0, where 100 per cent of the distributed profits are allocated to with-profits policyholders. For example, unitised policies participating only in investment returns within a ring-fenced with-profits fund will often be written on a 100: 0 basis. The bonus distribution is, however, limited to surplus within the fund. The shareholders receive profits on such business by way of charges on premiums or through a defined annual management charge.

9.8.3   Proposals for future regulation

Once the Integrated Prudential Sourcebook comes into force (not expected to be before 2004), there could be further codification of the principles applicable to inherited estates. Current consultation on the Integrated Prudential Sourcebook sets out proposals that include new rules restricting the purposes for which surpluses in with-profits funds may be applied, a codification of the presumption of 90: 10 attribution and the presumption of attribution by reference to the source from which surpluses arose (*see* Consultation Paper 97, Integrated Prudential Sourcebook, FSA, June 2001).

As part of its With-Profits Review, the FSA has published an issues paper on the process for attribution and re-attribution of inherited estates (*Process for Dealing with Attribution of Inherited Estates*, FSA, October 2001).

The issues paper identifies two points as problematic:

(a)   even though attribution or re-attribution of the inherited estate essentially involves a determination or negotiation respectively of the competing interests of shareholders and policyholders, the current processes for attribution or re-attribution do not involve any formal requirement for a negotiator on behalf of policyholders; and

(b)   attribution and re-attribution exercises are complex and opaque to policyholders and there is a lack of transparency of the process and details of the relevant negotiations.

The questions being consulted on include:

(a)   Whether the process of attribution of an inherited estate should either:
   (i)   remain as is, but with greater disclosure to policyholders, or
   (ii) be replaced by a new process involving either the FSA, the independent actuary or other independent expert or a third party as an active negotiator on behalf of the policyholders, or
   (iii) be replaced by a new process involving formal prior consultation with policyholders; and

(b)   Whether further transparency could be achieved through a process initiated by an initial confidential approach to the FSA followed by stages involving formal publicity requirements, including for example an initial statement of intent, regular progress reports and detailed communication of the agreed position or formal offer.

Other related measures being considered include amending current reporting requirements to ensure that annual returns provide more transparent disclosure of the financial condition of with-profits funds.

Chapter 10

Conduct of Business of Life Assurance Companies

Philip Skerrett

Partner

Stephanie Fuller

Associate
The City Law Partnership

The Conduct of Business Sourcebook ("COBS" or "COB" as it is more commonly known) has arisen from the FSA's aim to produce a "consolidated set of rules which is for purpose from N2". It represents an amalgamation of the existing Self Regulatory Organisation ("SRO") rulebooks, together with some legislative provisions originating from, for example, the Insurance Companies Act 1982. It should be read in conjunction with the handbook produced by the FSA and the 11 Principles of Business published by the FSA. COBS was produced after a lengthy consultation process and a number of consultation papers, in particular CP45 and CP57, were produced. If there is any doubt as to the effect of a Rule a study of the consultation papers may assist in defining the aim of the FSA.

COBS replaces the various rulebooks produced by previous regulators and integrates the conduct of business and customer assets sections. COBS, along with the provisions of the Financial Services and Markets Act 2000 ("the Act"), took effect on N2. It codifies existing practice and introduces certain new concepts such as real-time and non real-time promotions. There is an extensive definition section in the last part of COBS which is helpful in understanding the Rules.

The FSA have taken care with the design of COBS to aid ease of use and it is set out in such a way that there are Rules which are in "black letters" and plain rules of evidential value and guidance. The latter, though helpful, are not an absolute safe haven and by following them may only "tend" to show compliance rather than guaranteeing compliance.

10.1 Transitional provisions to lighten the compliance burden on firms caused by the introduction of COBS

The Transitional Rules are in three forms:

(a) Extra Time Provisions ("ETPs") which give firms additional time from commencement (i.e. midnight on 30 November 2001) until 30 June 2002. These provisions do not apply to ex Section 43 firms (i.e. those firms whose activities have been an exempted person under Section 43 Financial Services Act 1986 ("the 1986 Act") ("Section 43 firms")) who have until the expiry of 12 months following commencement to complete their preparations for the impact of certain provisions in COBS.

(b) Technical Timing Provisions ("TTPs") which give relief from certain provisions in COB that require firms to fulfil obligations to customers at periodic intervals (e.g. periodic disclosure of soft commission, periodic statements). TTPs postpone the impact of these provisions in relation to periods at that span N2.

(c) Timeless (Saving) Provisions ("TSPs") which give firms relief for an indefinite period after N2 from certain provisions in COB, relating mainly to terms of business and client agreements and for client classification. These TSPs allow firms to continue to use or rely upon documentation of compliance work that was undertaken in accordance with previous regulator rules in relation to existing clients at N2.

10.1.1 Extra Time Provisions

10.1.1.1 ETP 1

ETP1 is the rule of transitional relief and provides that a pre-N2 firm (i.e. a firm who was authorised to carry on investment business by virtue of its membership of IMRO, PIA or SFA, or was authorised directly by the FSA under the 1986 Act or an employee of such firm, including appointed representatives) will not contravene any of the provisions labelled ETP1 in the transitional rules table to the extent that on or after commencement it is able to demonstrate that it has complied with the corresponding rule of its previous regulator or where applicable with the relevant former statutory requirement.

Please note that the definition of "pre-N2 firm" does not include an ex-Recognised Professional Body (RPB) firm or an ex-Section 43 firm in relation to its Section 43 business. The guidance under these rules puts the onus on the firm to satisfy itself that it has complied with the corresponding rule of its previous regulator, but to benefit from the relief that rule must be substantially similar to the provision in COBS to which it relates. Helpfully, the FSA have compiled tables of derivations indicating the rules that correspond with the provisions in COBS. This means that where necessary a firm should treat the previous regulator's rules as modified to ensure that they can operate effectively notwithstanding the Act.

10.1.1.2 ETP2
This relates to financial promotion and provides that a firm will not contravene the provisions labelled ETP2 in the COBS Transitional Rules table to the extent that on or after the commencement it communicates a non real-time financial promotion which, as to it's content, complies with the corresponding rules of its previous regulator and which, for that purpose, had been approved by the firm as complying with the corresponding rules before commencement.

10.1.1.3 ETP3
This rule relates to client classification – but only to a client of a pre-N2 firm which the firm had classified as an expert private client before commencement.

Under the transitional provision such client may be treated as a private customer or an intermediate customer until expiry of the transitional period (30 June 2002), by which time the client must be classified in accordance with COB 4.1.

The guidance notes point out that the provisions only comply to existing clients. COB 4.1 will apply in full to any new clients.

10.1.1.4 ETP4
This relates to ex Section 43 firms in relation to their Section 43 business. For existing clients, the firm may treat them as a market counterparty until the expiry of the transitional period (i.e. 30 November 2002) by which time the client must be reclassified in accordance with COB 4.1.

10.1.1.5 ETP5
This provisions relates to client assets.

An "approved bank" in COB 9 must be treated as if it were reference to an institution which satisfied the definition of "approved bank" under the rules of the firm's previous regulator. Similarly, "custodian" in COB 9 must be treated as if it were reference to "custodian" as defined in the previous regulator's rules.

10.1.1.6   ETP6
This provision relates to client money and provides that the firm need not comply with provisions labelled ETP6 in the Transitional Rules table until the date of expiry of the transitional period.

10.1.1.7   ETP7
Similar provisions apply to ex Section 43 firms in relation to client money, but of the transitional period is only 12 months following commencement. The ex Section 43 firm during that period must continue to comply with the requirements of the grey paper (Version June 1999) published by the FSA relating to segregation of money and other assets belonging to counterparties.

10.1.1.8   ETP8
This transitional provision relates to information about the firm. Written material produced before commencement will not contravene the new provisions to the extent that the firm is able to demonstrate on or after commencement that it provided information about itself in accordance with the corresponding rule of its previous regulator.

This provision does not apply to firms' appointed representatives (as defined under Section 44 of the 1986 Act).

10.1.2   Technical Timing Provisions

10.1.2.1   TTP1
In relation to periodic disclosure of soft commission, a pre-N2 firm will not contravene the transitional rule to the extent it is able to demonstrate that the periodic disclosure given (in relation to the period in which N2 falls) is in accordance with the corresponding rule of its previous regulator.

10.1.2.2   TTP2
Similar provisions apply under TTP2 with profit guides produced by pre-N2 sum for the financial year in which N2 falls.

10.1.2.3   TTP3

Periodic statements produced for the period in which N2 falls will not contravene the transitional rules providing they are in accordance with the corresponding rules of the pre-N2 firms' previous regulator.

10.1.3   Timeless (Saving) Provisions

10.1.3.1   TSP1

Under TSP1 a pre-N2 firm will not contravene the relevant provisions in the transitional rules to the extent that it is able to demonstrate that it has carried out the confirmation exercise in COB 3.6.1R (confirmation of compliance) for an investment advertisement issued or approved before commencement in accordance with the corresponding rules of its previous regulator. This provision applies indefinitely.

10.1.3.2   TSP2

This provision relates to terms of business and client agreements and provides that a pre-N2 firm will not contravene the relevant transitional rules to the extent that it is able to demonstrate that it has continued to use or rely upon terms of business (including a client agreement) given to or made with the client before the end of the transitional period in accordance with its previous regulator's rules. However, if the basis on which that firm conducts or proposes to conduct its designated investment business changes after commencement in a way not covered in the original terms of business and where the original terms allow the firm to amend its terms without the customer's consent, then the firm must provide the clients with amended terms of business in accordance with the new COBS 4.2.13R.

In addition, a pre-N2 firm must as soon as practicable after N2 take reasonable steps to ensure that a private customer to whom it provided the terms of business or client agreement is notified in writing of matters set out in COBS 4.2.15 e (2) (21) and (22).

10.1.3.3   TSP3

A pre-N2 firm will not contravene the relevant transitional rules to the extent that it is able to demonstrate on or after N2 that it continued to use or rely upon a record of a private customer's financial circumstances made in accordance with the previous regulator's rules, and in doing so had regard to the guidance set out in COBS 5.2.6G.

This relief will apply indefinitely providing there is no relevant change in the customer's personal and financial circumstances.

10.1.3.4 TSP4

This provision provides that a pre-N2 firm may rely upon a suitability letter, risk warning or disclosure given to a customer in accordance with its previous regulator's rules in relation to a transaction or series of transactions executed or arranged before the expiry of the transitional period.

10.1.3.5 TSP5

This provision relates to scheme documents for an unregulated collected investment scheme. Again, a pre-N2 firm may rely upon a scheme document provided to a participant before the expiry of the transitional period in accordance with its previous regulator's rules.

10.1.3.6 TSP6

A pre-N2 firm will not contravene any of the relevant provisions in the transitional rules to the extent that it can demonstrate that on or after commencement it has continued to use or rely upon a valid notice given to or valid notice or consent obtained from, a client or counterparty in accordance with its previous regulator's rules or, where applicable, the relevant format statutory instrument in relation to an investment agreement concluded before expiry of the transitional period.

10.1.3.7 TSP7

This provision preserves the Financial Services (Cancellation) Rules and Financial Services (Non-Life Cancellation) Rules 1997 in respect of investment agreements (as defined under Section 44 of the 1986 Act) entered into before commencement.

10.2 Application of COB

10.2.1 *General application to firms*

COB applies to every firm apart from the following:

(a) COB 9 (Customer Assets) does not apply to an incoming EEA firm which is an EEA firm which is exercising, or has exercised, its right to carry on a regulated activity in the UK. An EEA firm is, unless it has its head office in the UK, *inter alia* an undertaking pursuing the activity of direct insurance (within the meaning of Article 1 of the First Life Directive or of the First Non-Life Directive) which has received authorisation under Article 6 from its Home State regulator.

An EEA State is defined as a State which is a contracting party to the agreement on the European Economic Area ("EEA") signed on 2 May 1992, as it has effect for the time being. As at January 2001 the following are EEA States: Austria, Belgium, Denmark, Finland, France, Germany, Greece, Iceland, Ireland, Italy, Liechtenstein, Luxembourg, the Netherlands, Norway, Portugal, Spain, Sweden and the UK;

(b) for a firm which is a UCITS qualifier, which includes an operator, trustee or depository under a scheme recognised under Section 264 of the Act and an authorised person as a result of paragraph 1(I) of Schedule 5 (Persons Concerned in Collective Investment Schemes) to the Act (but note that the provisions of COB 3 apply);

(c) COB does not apply to an investment company with variable capital (an "ICVC").

COB 6.7 (Cancellation) confers rights on customers to rescind agreements with, or withdraw offers from, firms in respect of particular regulated activities or non-regulated activities or, in the case of COB 3 (Financial Promotion), in relation to particular kinds of promotion. Most of COB applies to regulated activities conducted by firms which fall within the definition of designated investment business. In relation to deposits, pure protection contracts and general insurance contracts, COB has only limited application. The scope of the regulated activities to which COB applies is determined by the description of the activity as it is set out in the Regulated Activities Order (the Financial Services and Markets Act 2000 (Regulated Activities) Order 2001.

COB 3 (Financial Promotion) is available for nationals of EEA States (other than the UK) wishing to take advantage of Article 37 of the Financial Promotions Order or Article 17 of the Financial Services and Markets Act (Promotion of Collective Investment Schemes) (Exemptions) Order 2001.

10.2.2 *General application to activities*

COB applies to firms with respect to the carrying on of all regulated activities (except to the extent that a provision of COB provides for a narrower application), and non-regulated activities to the extent specified in any provision of COB.

In COB the term customer is defined as a client who is a private customer or an intermediate customer, but not market counterparties. The FSA has endeavoured to make it clear in the relevant provisions whether it applies to private customers, intermediate customers or both.

10.2.3 General application in respect of territory

The territorial scope of COB as a whole is laid out in a table set out at COB 1.4.3.R. The territorial application of financial promotion rules is laid out in a table set out at COB 3.4.2.R. These tables show clearly the application of COB to activities carried out by amongst others overseas firms with or without branches in the UK.

10.2.4 Application to Occupational Pension Schemes firms ("OPS firms")

COB applies to OPS activity undertaken by an OPS firm which is a firm carrying on OPS activity for an Occupational Pension Scheme and is also:

> "either a trustee of the Occupational Pension Scheme in question; or a company owned by the trustees of the Occupational Pension Scheme in question; or
> a company which is an employer in relation to the Occupational Pension Scheme in question in respect of its employees or former employees or their dependants, a company within the group which includes such an employee or is an administering authority subject to the Local Government Superannuation Regulations 1986."

The above also applies to any firm which has satisfied the requirements set out above at any time during the last 12 months including those who cannot comply with these requirements because of a change of control or ownership of the employer during that period. References to customer in this connection refer to the OPS or welfare trust in respect of which the OPS firm is acting, which means that any information required to be supplied under any COB rules must be provided to, or have consent obtained from, each of the trustees of the OPS or welfare trust in respect of which that firm is acting.

10.2.5 Appointed representatives

COB does not apply directly to a firm's appointed representatives, but:

> "a firm will always be responsible for the acts and omissions of its appointed representatives in carrying on business for which the firm has accepted responsibility (Section 39.3 of the Act)." (COB 1.7.1)

It is clear that anything done or omitted to be done by a firm's appointed representative (as defined in COBS) will be treated as having been done or omitted by the firm.

10.3 Rules which apply to all firms conducting designated investment business (COB 2)

These rules apply to firms communicating information to a customer in the scope of, or in connection with, their designated investment business. They do not apply to a firm communicating a financial promotion in circumstances in which COB 3 (Financial Promotion) applies. The purpose of COB 2 is to restate part of Principle 7 (Communication with Clients) that relates to communication of information as a separate role. It enables a customer, who is a private person, to seek redress under Section 150 of the Act to recover loss resulting from a firm communicating information, in the course of designated investment business, in a way that is not clear, fair or is misleading.

It is a fundamental principle that when a firm communicates information to a customer the firm must take reasonable steps to communicate in a way which is clear, fair and not misleading (COB 2.1.3). In considering what is reasonable a firm must have regard to the customer's knowledge of the designated investment business to which the information relates. Communication includes all communications with customers, for example customer agreements, periodic statements, financial reports, telephone calls and any correspondence which is not a financial promotion (*see* COB 3 below).

10.3.1 *Inducements and soft commission*

The rules in COB 2.2 relate to inducements and soft commissions and apply to a firm when it carries out designated investment business with or for a customer. Principles 1 and 6 require a firm to conduct its business with integrity, to pay due regard to the interests of its customers and to treat them fairly. COB 2.2 sets out to ensure that a firm does not conduct its business in a way that will conflict with its duty to its customers. COB 2.2.3 is designed to prohibit the offer, solicitation or acceptance inducements. It may be a defence for a firm to show that it could not reasonably have known of an associate giving or receiving an inducement. A firm should never direct business to another person on the instructions of an associate if this is likely to conflict with the interests of its customers (COB 2.4).

275

There are further restrictions in relation to the sale of packaged products set out in COB 2.2.5 qualifying the rule under COB 2.4. If any of these matters are contravened then it will be relied upon by the FSA as tending to establish breach of the rule set out in Rule 2.2.3.R (Prohibition of Inducements). It will be incumbent on the firm to show that it is not in breach of this rule.

The FSA have set out guidelines in relation to indirect benefits given in relation to packaged products. Subject to the duties which a firm owes to its customer, the FSA will not regard a firm as being in contravention of COB 2.2.3.R (Prohibition of Inducements) if it receives any of the indirect benefits set out in the guidelines in COB 2.2.6.

A product provider is permitted to assist an independent intermediary to promote its packaged products to enhance the quality of the service to the customer. However, any such assistance must not be such as to prejudice such independent intermediary's ability to act independently, in particular, to give advice on, and recommend, products available in the market. COB 2.2.7 sets out in detail the kind of benefits which, in the FSA's view, a firm can give and receive without contravening COB 2.2.3. They include matters such as literature, stationery, articles, financial promotions, seminars, data links, information, training, travel etc.

A firm must not deal for a customer, either directly or indirectly, through any intermediary, under a soft commission agreement unless the requirements set out in COB 2.2.8.R are complied with. It is suggested that a firm should select a soft commission intermediary who is able to show independence in the marketplace to avoid conflict with COB 2.2.8 provided that such intermediary does not deal exclusively with one market maker. A firm may be able to meet the requirements of COB 2.8.8. if it is able to monitor the individual transaction prices obtained by the intermediary and has taken reasonable steps to ensure that the intermediary has complied with its best execution obligation provided the soft commission intermediary is part of an "integrated house". Where an intermediary is only partly remunerated then COB 2.2.10 sets out guidance as to how the commission element should be calculated.

COB 2.2.12 permits firms to accept goods and services supplied under a soft commission agreement in certain circumstances relating to investment management, custody, valuation etc. Examples of such goods and services are research, analysis, market pricing, electronic information systems, telephone lines, seminar fees, publications etc. Examples of items that the FSA does not regard as relevant to the provision of services

are set out in COB 2.2.14; these include travel, accommodation, enter-
tainment, word processing, accounting programs, computer hardware,
rental of standard office equipment, employees' salaries, direct money
payments etc.

A firm has a duty under COB 2.2.16 to disclose to a customer that a
member of its group has a soft commission agreement with another
person with which the customer may deal together with details of the
group's policy relating to soft commission agreements. Such policy
should explain generally why the group has these arrangements. It
should be noted that it is acceptable to make a general disclosure that
soft commission agreements may be in place. In addition under COB
2.2.18, where a firm knows that such arrangements are in place, then it
must provide each relevant customer at least once a year with information, including *inter alia* the percentage paid under soft commission
agreements, the value and summary of goods and services received, a
list of intermediaries and total commission paid. It must also supply the
customer with an explanation of the firm's policy on soft commissions
and if there is a material change in the policy an explanation of such
change immediately it is made. A firm need not make the periodic disclosures required by COB 2.2.18 if the customer is habitually overseas
and has requested the firm not to do so, or if the firm has information
which makes it reasonable to assume the customer does not want the
information. A firm is required to keep records of all periodic reports sent
to customers for three years, and of all disclosable commission and
benefits given to independent intermediaries for six years.

10.3.2 Reliance on others

Principle 2 requires a firm to conduct its business with due skill, care and
diligence. COB 2.3 deals with the extent to which this can be delegated
to others.

> "A firm will be taken to be in compliance with any of the COB rules
> that requires a firm to obtain information to the extent that the firm
> can show that it was reasonable for the firm to rely on information
> provided to it in writing by another person." (COB 2.3.3)

A firm must take reasonable steps to establish that the other person
providing written information is both independent of the firm and
competent. Failure to take such steps may be taken by the FSA "as
tending to establish contravention of COB 2.3.3" whereas compliance
with the steps can be relied on as "tending to establish" compliance with

277

COB 2.3.3. A firm may generally rely on information supplied in writing by an unconnected authorised person, a professional firm or an exempt professional firm unless they are or ought to be aware of any facts that would give reasonable grounds to question the accuracy of any such information. A firm may rely on others supplying information to a customer so long as they take reasonable steps to establish that it is being supplied.

10.3.3 Chinese Walls

COB 2.4.4 sets out provisions for the control of information held by a firm which might lead to a conflict of interest as set out in Principle 8. In certain circumstances a firm may establish and maintain arrangements (Chinese Walls) requiring information held by it in one part of its business. Conformity with COB 2.4.4.R will be relevant in providing a defence against proceedings under Section 397(2) or (3) of the Act, an FSA enforcement action under Section 150 and also an allegation of market abuse.

10.3.4 Exclusion of liability

Where a firm makes any written or oral communication to a customer while conducting designated investment business then it must pay due regard to their interests and treat them fairly. It is not fair for a firm to exclude its liabilities to its customers arising under the Act or the regulatory system (COB 2.5.3). It may exclude other duties owed to customers only if it is reasonable to do so (COB 2.5.4).

10.4 Financial promotion

10.4.1 Application

The rules in COB 3 which relate to financial promotion apply to every firm to which COBS applies save for a firm which communicates or approves the content of a financial promotion solely for:

"(a) a deposit; or
(b) a general insurance contract, pure protection contract or re-insurance contract" (COB 3.2.3)

where only certain parts of COB 3 apply. The rules relating to financial promotion are detailed and lay great emphasis, as do many other rules, on packaged products.

10.4.2   *Purpose*

Section 21(1) of the Act imposes a restriction on the communication of financial promotion by unauthorised persons. A person may not communicate an invitation or inducement to engage in investment activity (as defined in Section 21(8), (9) and (10) of the Act) unless the person is an authorised person or the content of the communication is approved by an authorised person. An authorised person is defined under Section 31 of the Act. If the communication originates outside the UK the restrictions only apply if the communication is capable of having effect in the UK and, for non real-time financial promotions, directed at persons in the UK. Exemptions to the restriction created by Section 21(1) of the Act are contained in the Financial Promotion Order and set out at COB 3 Annex 1G.

10.4.3   *Communications covered*

COB 3 applies when a firm communicates a financial promotion or approves a financial promotion which another person communicates. There is no restriction on the type of communication, it applies to printed advertising, radio broadcasts, personal visits, telephone calls, e-mails, digital television etc. including solicited and unsolicited communi-cations. COB 3.3.2 sets out some examples of financial promotion including written product brochures, general advertising (including broadcast advertising), mailshots, telemarketing contacts (including call centres) contact with customers whether written or oral, sales aids, presentations to private customers, tip-sheets etc.

10.4.4   *Real-time and non real-time promotion*

COB 3.5.4 draws a distinction between real-time and non real-time financial promotions. A real-time financial promotion is communicated in the course of a personal visit, telephone conversation or other interactive dialogue. A non real-time financial promotion is a financial promotion which is not a real-time promotion and includes a "financial promotion communicated by letter, e-mail or contained in a newspaper, journal, magazine, or other periodical publication, website, television or radio programme or teletext service" (COB 3.3.4).

It includes a communication to more than one person, if it is communicated by way of a system that in normal course creates a record or it is made by way of a system that does not require an immediate response. Other statutes and regulations, other than those set out in COBS, relating to financial communications may apply (some of these are referred to in COB 3.3.5.3).

10.4.5 Financial promotion

The financial promotion rules do not apply to a firm in relation to a financial promotion of the kind listed in COB 3.5.2 unless it is an unregulated collective investment scheme when COB 3.11 applies, or if the firm approves the financial promotion when COB 3.12.4 applies. Some of the exemptions are set out in COB 3.5.3 and include correspondence written specifically for a customer, a company's annual report and accounts (other than ICVCs, Open-ended Investment Companies and Unit Trusts), image advertising, and financial promotions sent only to investment professionals.

Under COB 3.6.1 and 3.6.2 a firm must, before a financial promotion is communicated or approved, ensure it complies with the financial promotion rules. A confirmation must be given by a person or persons with the appropriate expertise before communicating or approving a non real-time promotion. A firm must withdraw the financial promotion or its approval if, after confirmation or approval, it becomes aware that a financial promotion no longer meets the requirements of the financial promotion rules. A firm may delegate to a third party with the appropriate expertise the duty of carrying out the confirmation exercise, but the responsibility remains with the firm. The FSA will expect firms to monitor financial promotions as part of a firm's routine compliance monitoring; it suggests that a "review date" be established for each financial promotion (COB 3.6.4). If a firm becomes aware that customers may have been misled by a financial promotion it is suggested strongly that it should consider contacting the relevant customers. If a firm communicates a non real-time financial promotion that has been produced by another person it will not contravene any rules provided that it takes care to abide by the criteria set out in COB 3.6.5.

10.4.6 Records

"A firm must make and retain an adequate record of each financial promotion which it has confirmed as complying with the non real-time financial promotion rules. The record should be retained for the following periods:

(i)   indefinitely in the case of a record relevant to a pension transfer, pension opt-out or Freestanding Additional Voluntary Contribution "FSAVC";

(ii)   six years in the case of a record relevant to a life policy or pension contract or stakeholder pension scheme;

(iii) three years in any other case." (COB 3.7.1)

References to these periods occur throughout COBS and apply wherever records are required to be kept. Any record in relation to a financial promotion should contain those matters set out in COB 3.7.2, in particular the name of the individual who confirmed that the financial promotion complied or approved it, the date of confirmation or approval, a copy of the final proof version, details of the medium used and evidence supporting any material factual statement. A firm should, if practicable, keep a copy of the published version of the financial promotion.

10.4.7   Content of financial promotions

COB 3.8, which deals with the form and content of financial promotions, applies to the communication and approval of financial promotions and sets out the conditions relating thereto. COB 3.8.2 to 3.8.17 apply to the communication and approval of non real-time promotions. COB 3.8.18 to 3.8.22 apply to the communication of real-time financial promotions.

> "A firm must ensure that a non real-time financial promotion which it communicates or approves contains its name (and, if different, the name of the provider whose product is being promoted) and either an address or a contact point from which an address is available." (COB 3.8.2.R)

The name displayed in the non real-time financial promotion may be a trading name or a shortened version of the legal name of the firm (subject to requirements of other legislation such as the Companies Act). Except for a direct offer financial promotion it is not a requirement that a financial promotion communicated or approved by a firm (or its appointed representative) name the FSA or its regulator. However, if a firm does, in an effort to comply with COB 3.8.4.R (*see* below), choose to name the FSA as its regulator and the financial promotion refers to matters not regulated by the FSA it should also make it clear that those matters are not regulated by the FSA.

10.4.8   Form and content of financial promotions

In respect of any non real-time financial promotion which a firm communicates or approves, it must be able to show that it has taken reasonable steps to ensure that it complies with the Principle that it is clear, fair and not misleading. If it includes a comparison or contrast it must ensure that the financial promotion abides by the rules set out in COB 3.8.4. It must not create confusion in the marketplace between the firm itself and a competitor, nor discredit or denigrate the trade marks, trade names, other distinguishing marks, investment services, activities or circumstances of a competitor, nor take advantage of the reputation of a competitor. It is important that a firm takes all reasonable steps to ensure that in any financial promotion which it communicates or approves, the promotional purpose is not in any way disguised or misrepresented. Any opinion that is expressed must be honestly held and any comparison or contrast must be presented in a fair and balanced way which is not misleading and includes all factors which are relevant to the comparison or contrast. It must not contain any false indications in particular as to the firm's independence, resources or scarcity of any investment advice. There must be no reference to approval by the FSA unless the FSA has approved it in writing (this is to avoid any implication that such communication has been approved by the FSA) (COB 3.5). Any omission which renders the financial promotion unclear, unfair or misleading is a breach. Further it must not be assumed that customers necessarily have an understanding of an investment or service being promoted. If a financial promotion is specially designated for a target collection of private customers who are reasonably believed to have particular knowledge of the investment or service being promoted, then it should make this clear. It should be noted that the use of the word "guarantee" in promotions should be avoided except in relation to life policies providing guaranteed benefits or deposits. The provisions of COB 3.8.7 should be considered before any reference is made to a guarantee.

10.4.9   Words and phrases in promotions

There are certain words and phrases that may not be used as their use may not meet the Principle of being clear, fair and not misleading. An example is a statement such as "no initial charges" or "no entry or redemption charges" where the bid price is not the same as the offer price (i.e. there is a spread) unless the statement is suitably qualified with information about the additional costs of investment. Other instances of words and phrases not to be used are set out in COB 3.8.7(3). It is important to note that in relation to a quotation of opinion it should be a fair representation and, where an opinion is quoted, any connection of the holder of the opinion to the firm should be made clear.

10.4.10   *Promotions of investments*

A firm must, in respect of any financial promotion which it communicates or approves and which identifies and promotes a specific investment, include a fair and adequate description of the nature of the investment, the commitment required and the risks involved. In particular, firms should avoid failing to describe any benefits under a life policy which are not fixed. Any financial promotion should give a fair and balanced indication of the requirements set out in COB 3.8.8.

If a financial promotion gives information about past performance of an investment fund it must comply with COB 3.8.10. The purpose of this rule is to prevent promotion of investment in such a way as to induce a customer to believe that any previous periods of favourable performance will necessarily be repeated in the future and to encourage firms to draft warnings that are tailored to fit the design for financial promotion and the audience to which they are primarily directed. COB 3.8.11(2) sets out certain activities which might mean that a financial promotion does not meet the Principle of being clear, fair and not misleading. Some of the examples quoted are an unfair comparison with the performance of another type of investment, the selection of an inappropriate or irrelevant investment period, the selection of an unreasonably short time period or the selection of inconsistent time periods for a range of funds. There are special provisions relating to the euro (COB 3.8.11(3)) and the relationship between the performance of with-profit contracts and unitised contracts (COB 3.8.11(4)).

10.4.11   *Previous performance*

> "A firm must include, in any financial promotion directed at a private customer which refers to past performance, information about the performance of the investment which covers at least the previous five years (or a whole period if the investment has been offered for less than this), ending with the date of confirmation of compliance (or as near as is reasonably practicable)." (COB 3.8.12)

The information provided should refer, where appropriate, to such matters as an offer to bid basis, comparison with any index, movements in the price of units etc. It should be noted that if a single pricing basis is used then there must be an allowance for charges. If pricing policy has changed then the information should show adjustments in pricing to reflect change in pricing methods. No information relating to past performance must be presented by a firm in such a way that it constitutes a projection of future performance or value (COB 3.8.14). Specific rules relating to life policy projections are set out in COB 6.6 and are dealt with in 10.7 below.

10.4.12   Real-time financial promotions

Under COB 3.10.2 unsolicited real-time financial promotions are prohibited, other than exempt financial promotions or where there is an existing customer relationship where the customer envisages receiving unsolicited real-time financial promotions. Many solicited real-time financial promotions will be exempt financial promotions and therefore outside the scope of the financial promotions rules. COB 3.8.19 which deals with real-time promotions applies only to solicited real-time financial promotions which are not exempt financial promotions and unsolicited real-time financial promotions within COB 3.10.2.

Detailed requirements for a communication to a private customer are set out in COB 3.8.19 including the question of unsocial hours, appointments, customer checks, advisers, call-centre operators and introducers. It applies to all forms of real-time financial promotion with customers including face-to-face and telephone financial promotions. With regard to telemarketing campaigns a firm must take reasonable care to make and retain certain records which should include any scripts that are used.

10.4.13   Direct offer life policy promotions

The promotion of life policies is exempt from the rules relating to direct offer financial promotions under COB 3.9.2(5)(b) as it is covered by COB 3.9.18. Any direct offer financial promotion which promotes a life policy must state which benefits are fixed amounts and what those amounts are, and which benefits are not fixed amounts. A direct offer financial promotion is a non real-time financial promotion which contains an offer by a firm to enter into a controlled agreement with anyone who responds to the financial promotion, or an invitation to the public to make an offer to the firm to enter into a controlled agreement and specifies the manner of response or includes a form for any such response.

10.4.14   *Direct offer financial promotions*

A firm must not communicate or approve a direct offer financial promotion inviting investment in a broker fund unless the firm itself has adequate evidence to suggest that the investment may be suitable for the customer at whom the promotion is directed (COB 3.9.5). The requirements for direct offer financial statements are set out in detail in COB 3.9.6 to 3.9.17 dealing with charges and expenses, commission, execution only and fluctuation investments. Any direct financial promotion must comply with these and other sections of COB 3.9.

A direct offer financial promotion must include a summary of the taxation and/or taxation consequences of an investment for a prospective customer (COB 3.9.19). Such summary must include the assumed rate of taxation and a warning that rates and bases of taxation can change. If tax reliefs are referred to then detailed mention should be made of the application and value of such reliefs. Similarly, use of the phrase "free from tax liability" or something similar should be avoided unless a statement is made in accordance with paragraph (4) of COB 3.9.20. If a direct offer financial promotion has cancellation rights then they must be set out clearly, in particular if there may be a shortfall on cancellation. Any direct offer financial promotion offering income withdrawals must include explanations relating to the erosion of capital, that investment returns may be lower and that annuity rates may be lower when an annuity is purchased (COB 3.9.29).

10.4.15   *Unsolicited real-time promotions*

> "An unsolicited real-time financial promotion is a real time financial promotion which is not made in response to an express request from the recipient." (COB 3.10.1)

Such a promotion must not be communicated to a private customer unless it falls within the exemptions of COB 3.10.2.

10.4.16   *Financial promotion by an overseas person*

COB 3.12.1 sets out certain restrictions on communications or approvals issued by a firm which identify and promote specific investments that may lead to an overseas person carrying on designed investment business with or for a private customer who is in the UK. The rules in COB 3.13.2, COB 3.13.3 and COB 3.13.4 set out the requirements for statements to be made relating to overseas life offices which have no establishment in the UK, or financial promotions for an overseas life office which is authorised in certain territories, and where a financial promotion relates to a life policy with an overseas life office but does not name the overseas life office. In particular the FSA is concerned to see that any prospective policyholder is aware that they will not be protected by the Financial Services Compensation Scheme and that the life office is not supervised by the FSA. As always, any statements made must be clear, fair and not misleading, and providing the rules set out in COB 13 are adhered to then any such promotion by an overseas life office will comply with the rules.

10.4.17   Internet and electronic media

Any material which meets the definition of a financial promotion, including any video or moving image material incorporated in any site containing a financial promotion, should comply with the rules set out in COB 3.14. Real-time financial promotions can be promoted using the internet and other electronic media as can non real-time financial promotions where the customer chooses from a list of investment services by completing a contract via a direct offer financial promotion in a similar way to browsing through a leaflet rack. E-mails, material displayed on a website, and sound and television broadcasts are non real-time financial promotions. COB 3.14.5 sets out specific guidance for firms wishing to use the internet and other electronic media including the use of application forms. The main exemptions contained in the financial promotion order are set out comprehensively in Annex 1G to COB 3.

10.5   Accepting customers

10.5.1   Client classification

Under COB there are now three categories of customer – intermediate customers, market counterparty and private customers.

COB 4.1 requires clients to be classified where the firm is intending to conduct, or is conducting, designated investment business for a client. Designated investment business is defined in COB and includes dealing and arranging deals in investments, advising on investments, pension transfers and opt-outs.

An intermediate customer is defined in COB and includes local or public authorities, substantial companies and partnerships, trusts and certain special-purpose vehicles. Certain intermediate customers may "opt up" to market counterparty status. However, except in the case of local or public authorities, in order to "opt up" they must meet specified asset thresholds.

Market counterparty is likewise defined in COB and includes governments of any country or territory, central banks or monetary authorities, and other UK and overseas authorised firms. However, another authorised firm or overseas financial services institution may "opt down" to intermediate customer status when dealing with a market counterparty in order to protect underlying customers.

A private customer as defined in COB as someone who is not a market counterparty or intermediate customer. The definition includes individuals both in this country and overseas and regulated collective investment schemes or its trustees. A private customer may "opt up" to intermediate customer status (but not to market counterparty status) as having sufficient experience and understanding to be classified as an intermediate customer. The firm must give a written warning to the client of the protection he will lose under the regulatory system, and the client must have sufficient time to consider the implications of the revised classification before giving his formal consent.

Any private client who is classified as an intermediate customer (or intermediate customer classified as a market counterparty) must have the classification reviewed at least annually by the firm unless no designated investment business has been conducted in that year, in which case the review may be deferred until the next piece of business is conducted.

10.5.2 Terms of business and customer agreements

Principle 7 of the FSA's Principles for Business "Communications with Clients" requires a firm to pay due regard to the information needs of its clients and to communicate information to them in a way which is clear, fair and not misleading. This is referred to in the guidance notes (COB 4.2.3).

A private customer must be provided with a firm's terms of business before any designated investment business is conducted (COB 4.2.4). The exceptions to this rule are where the customer has made an oral offer to enter into an ISA agreement or a stakeholder pension scheme, in which case the terms of business must be provided within five business days of such an offer. Where the customer is an intermediate customer the terms of business must be provided within a reasonable period of the firm beginning to conduct designated investment business for that customer. Definitions of "Terms of Business" and "Customer Agreement" appear in the definitions sections of COBS.

The guidance notes (COB 4.2.5) acknowledge that some information required for the terms of business will not be known at an early stage and may be provided later. For example, a firm will not necessarily know a private customer's investment objectives without undertaking "know your client" checks.

A customer agreement is required with a private customer where the firm is:

(a)   managing investments on a discretionary basis;
(b)   conducting a transaction in a contingent liability investment;
(c)   undertaking stock lending activity or underwriting (except in respect of a life policy),

unless that customer is habitually resident outside the UK and the firm has taken reasonable steps to establish that the customer does not want to enter into a customer agreement.

The table under COB 4.2.1 also sets out designated investment business to which the terms of business and customer agreement requirements do not apply. It includes, for example, a direct offer financial promotion when the customer enters into the transaction as a result of that direct offer, and execution only transactions with or for a private customer (except in a contingent liability investment).

A firm must ensure its terms of business (and the customer agreement) set out in adequate detail the basis on which the designated investment business is to be carried out (COB 4.2.9). A table within COB 4.2 sets out the general requirements for the contents of the terms of business, such as when and how the terms are to come into force, the regulator's details, the customer's investment options, how the firm is to be paid, the right to withdraw, the client's understanding of risk and termination. Additional contents are required in respect of discretionary management of investments.

A firm must give at least 10 business days' notice to a customer of any amendment to its terms of business unless it is impractical in the circumstances to do so (COB 4.2.12). Finally, a firm must make and retain a record of all terms of business (and any amendments) for the following periods:

(a) indefinitely in the case of a pension transfer, a pension opt-out or free-standing AVC;
(b) six years for a life policy, pension contract or stakeholder pension scheme; and
(c) three years in any other case.

Note these time periods run from the date on which the customer *ceases* to be a customer of the firm (COB 4.2.13).

10.6   Advising and selling

10.6.1   *Polarisation and status disclosure*

COB 5.1 relates to a firm when it gives advice to a private customer on packaged products. The FSA have made it clear that they have placed an emphasis on packaged products. The section gives support to Principles 6 and 7 which require firms to have due regard to the information needs of their customers and to treat them fairly. When advice is given about packaged products it is important that a private customer is always clear whether a firm, its advisers or representatives will act solely in the customer's interests or whether the range or advice offered by the firm will be constrained by the nature and number of the firm's commercial relationships. Accordingly the rules and guidance in COB 5.1 give effect to this regulatory policy on polarisation which, in relation only to packaged products, requires the firm to act either:

(a) independently from the customer; or
(b) on a tied basis where advice is restricted to the range of products available from one particular firm or from a collection of firms, including the provider firm, which are allied together as a marketing group.

The rules set out in COB 5.1 are to give effect to this policy of polarisation and in particular require firms to disclose the polarised status to customers in clear and non-misleading way. A provider firm must take reasonable steps to ensure that neither it nor any of its employees or representatives gives advice to a private customer concerning the purchase of a packaged product unless the product is issued by the firm itself or by another member of its marketing group. This does not inhibit the sale by a provider firm of packaged products issued by firms which do not belong to the firm's marketing group, where the sale does not involve the provision of advice to a private customer. A provider firm may sell such packaged products on an execution only basis.

A provider firm must take reasonable steps to ensure that neither it, nor any of its employees, representatives or introducers says or does, or omits to say or do, anything which might lead a private customer reasonably to believe that it is in a position to advise or procure advice on packaged products other than those of its marketing group. A provider firm must also take reasonable steps to ensure that its representatives are able to sell each type of packaged product issued by its marketing group. When a firm offers different versions of a type of product for sale through different sales channels, whether or not there is a differential price between those channels, each of its representatives should, in accordance with COB 5.9.9.R, be in a position to sell at least one version of each type of product in the firm's product range.

COB 5.11 provides that a provider firm must take reasonable steps to ensure that its representatives:

(a) are not likely to be influenced by the structure of their remuneration to give unsuitable advice to a private customer; and
(b) do not refer private customers to an independent intermediary in circumstances which would amount to the provision of inducement under COB 2.2.3.R (prohibition of inducements).

A provider firm must take reasonable steps to ensure that each of its appointed representatives complies with the requirements in COB 5.1.4 (COB 5.1.12).

The FSA have published a Consultation Paper (CP121) entitled *Reforming Polarisation: Making the Market Work for Consumers*, which, as its title suggests, is aimed at reforming the principle of polarisation. The FSA does not believe that polarisation is delivering 'sufficient consumer benefits to justify it as a continuing intervention in the market". The proposal put forward in the Consultation Paper is that polarisation should be abolished and new disclosures should be made by the providers to the consumers. The proposals are based on extensive research carried out on behalf of the FSA which has stiffened its resolve to see that the proposals come into effect. It is not likely that the FSA will roll back the proposal though they want the industry to engage in a constructive debate.

Therefore, practitioners should note that whilst this section of COBS holds good at present it is likely to be substantially revised. The present timetable suggests that the proposals will come into effect in Easter 2003 but that assumes that there is no slippage in the process. As a further Consultation Paper with rules attached will have to be published, it is highly likely that the process will be delayed. It is to be hoped that the FSA will co-ordinate the abolition of polarisation with other proposed changes to the regulatory regime so that the industry can adopt all the changes at one time rather than piecemeal.

10.6.2   *Independent advice*

An independent intermediary (including its appointed representatives) must, in relation to advice given about packaged products, act in the best interests of its customers. It must not enter into commercial arrangements with other persons which might be likely to adversely affect its ability to provide advice on packaged products on an independent basis (COB 5.1.13). Private customers must be informed on a timely basis whether any advice which a firm gives about packaged products will be independent or restricted to the packaged products of one product provider or marketing group, or given for the purposes of managing a portfolio with discretion (COB 5.1.4). A provider firm must take reasonable steps to ensure that its introducers and representatives, when first contacting a private customer, state the name of the firm and identify themselves as an introducer or representative of the provider firm or its marketing group and make it clear that the firm provides advice only on the packaged product of the provider firm or its marketing group (COB 5.1.15). Likewise when an independent intermediary makes first contact with a private customer it must take reasonable steps to ensure that its financial advisers (including appointed representatives) state the name of the firm and make it clear that the firm provides independent advice. If the first contact is by electronic means every firm should ensure that a message specifying the firm's polarisation status is prominently displayed at the outset of any presentation or series of screens (COB 5.1.18). A provider firm must ensure that it has not communicated or approved a financial promotion for a packaged product unless it has disclosed in the communication that the firm is only able to advise private customers on the packaged products of the firm or of its marketing group save where it is only an "image" financial promotion (i.e. a promotion which does no more than promote a firm's image). If a promotion only includes general references such as life assurance, savings or pensions, this does not need to include a status disclosure statement.

10.6.3   Know your customer

The rules in COB 5.2 apply to firms that give personal recommendations concerning designated investments to a private customer, or act as investment manager for a private customer, or arrange a pension opt-out or pension transfer from an Occupational Pension Scheme for a private customer. It only relates to relationships with private customers and does not apply to execution only transactions for private customers. When a firm provides limited advice to a private customer the firm should not treat any resulting transaction as an execution-only one (COB 5.2). The purpose of the know your customer rule is to support Principle 9 which requires a firm to take reasonable care to ensure the suitability of its advice and discretionary decisions. In order to comply with this principle a firm should obtain sufficient information about its private customer to enable it to meet its responsibility to give suitable advice.

> "Before a firm gives a personal recommendation concerning a designated investment to a private customer it must take reasonable steps to ensure that it is in possession of sufficient personal and financial information about that customer relevant to the services that the firm has agreed to provide." (COB 5.2.5)

If a firm advises a private customer or exercises a discretion for a private customer on a continuing basis then it should keep its information about that customer under regular review. If a firm acts for a private customer on an infrequent basis it should undertake such review when that customer seeks advice. If a private customer does not want to provide such relevant personal and financial information then a firm must not provide the services described in COB 5.2.5 without advising the customer, prior to the provision of such services, that the lack of the relevant information may affect adversely the quality of the services to be provided. The firm should consider sending written confirmation of that advice and whilst this is not a requirement of the FSA it would certainly show compliance with the rules relating to the retention of records and therefore is recommended. A table set out in COB 5.2.11.G provides detailed guidance on the process of collecting personal and financial information.

10.6.4   Record keeping

Under COB 5.2.9 a firm must make and retain a record of private customers' personal and financial circumstances and the record must be retained for a minimum period after the information obtained in accordance with the following:

"(i) indefinitely for a record relating to a pension, transfer, pension opt-out or FSAVC;
(ii) six years for a record relating to a life policy or pension contract; or
(iii) three years in any other case." (COB 5.2.9)

In the case of a pension opt-out or a pension transfer from an OPS for a private customer on an execution only basis, the record must show that no investment advice was supplied to such private customer (COB 5.2.10).

10.6.5 *Suitability*

Principle 9 requires a firm to take reasonable care to ensure the suitability of its advice and discretionary decisions. COB 5.3 amplifies this requirement and sets out the rules relating to suitability. COB 5.3 applies to a firm when it makes a personal recommendation concerning a designated investment to a private customer; or when it manages the assets of an occupational scheme or a stakeholder pension scheme; or promotes a personal pension scheme by means of a direct offer financial promotion to a group of employees. It does not apply to a firm in respect of a direct offer financial promotion except in respect of promotion of a personal pension scheme. COB 5.3.3 reminds firms of the requirements of COB 3.9.7 under which any direct offer financial promotion must state that a private customer should contact the firm or an independent intermediary if the firm does not offer advice or if he is in doubt about the agreement offered to him. A firm must take reasonable care to ensure the suitability of its advice following the guidelines in COB 5.3.4.

10.6.6 *Requirements for suitability*

A firm must make sure that whilst conducting designated investment business it does not make a recommendation to a private client unless such recommendation is suitable for the private client, taking into account the facts disclosed by that party and other relevant facts known or which ought to be known by the firm about the customer. (COB 5.3.5)

Under COB 5.3.6 if a provider firm makes a personal recommendation to a private customer to buy a packaged product it must (except where COB 5.3.8 applies) take reasonable steps to ensure that the recommended packaged product is the most suitable of those available from the marketing group. Also, no recommendation must be made by it if there is no suitable packaged product available from within the marketing group. A firm may satisfy this rule by referring a private customer to an independent intermediary provided it does not do so in contravention of COB 2.2 (inducements and soft commission). COB 5.3.8 provides that *inter alia* one packaged product will not be more suitable than another merely because it is available at a more favourable price through an alternative distribution channel, or on special terms offered by the provider firm, and its availability is restricted.

As mentioned previously, the FSA is concerned with regard to the promotion of packaged products and in particular their suitability. Under COB 5.3.9 an independent intermediary must not make a personal recommendation to a private customer to buy a packaged product if he is aware or ought to be aware of a generally available packaged product which will be more appropriate to the needs and circumstance of the private customer. Nor must he do so if the packaged product is issued or operated by a connected person when he ought to be aware of another generally available packaged product which could equally satisfy the needs and circumstance of the private customer. An independent intermediary must have regard to the packaged products available from the market as a whole and if he does not have such knowledge he may well be in breach of COB 5.3.9.

10.6.7 Suitability of managers and other specific requirements

Under COB 5.3.12:

> "a firm that manages the assets of an Occupational Pension Scheme or Stakeholder Pension Scheme must take reasonable steps to ensure the suitability of specific transactions and of the investment portfolio under management with regard to the investment objective specified in the portfolio mandate."

Other specific requirements for suitability are referred to in COB 5.3.13 and relate to pension transfers, pension opt-outs, group pension schemes, FSAVCs, stakeholder pension schemes, income withdrawals etc. They are set out in more detail COB 5.3.20, COB 5.3.21–COB 5.3.27, COB 5.3.28 and COB 5.3.29. There is a comprehensive suitability guidance table in COB 5.3.29.

10.6.8 Suitability letter

There is a requirement for a suitability letter to be issued by a firm if it has made a personal recommendation to a private customer and that private customer:

(a) buys, sells, surrenders, converts, cancels or suspends premiums for or contribution to a life policy or a stakeholder pension scheme;
(b) elects to make income withdrawals;
(c) acquires a holding in or sells all or part of a holding in a scheme; or
(d) enters into a pension transfer or pension opt-out from an OPS (COB 5.3.14).

A suitability letter is also required if a personal recommendation is made by a firm to buy or sell shares or units in a regulated collective investment scheme when the firm is acting as an investment manager for a private customer.

One of the terms of the suitability letter referred to in COB 5.3.14 must state why the firm has concluded that the transaction is suitable for the customer having regard to his personal financial circumstances and must contain a summary of the main consequences and any possible disadvantages of the transaction (COB 5.3.16). COB 5.3.16 also sets out certain conditions relating to FSAVCs and COB 5.3.30 provides guidance generally on the contents of suitability letters. A suitability letter must be provided by a firm to a customer where the firm has issued a life policy or stakeholder pension scheme when, or as soon as possible after, the transaction is effected (COB 5.3.18). If the cancellation rules of such scheme require notification of the right to cancel then the suitability letter must be provided no later than the issue of the post-sale notice of the customer's right to cancel. The requirement to provide a suitability letter does not apply in certain circumstances set out in COB 5.3.19 which relate mainly to persons resident in another EEA State or outside EEA States and for increases to existing contracts with a single premium or regular premium. COB 5.3.20 deals with the suitability of broker funds and imposes duties on firms to take account of the various criteria set out in the rule. The firm must provide the customer with a suitable alternative recommendation if the broker fund arrangement is no longer appropriate.

10.6.9 Suitability of pension transfers and opt-outs

Where personal recommendations about a pension transfer or pension opt-out are made on the firm's behalf by an individual who is not one of its pension transfer specialists, the firm must already have established procedures for checking:

(a)   the individual's compliance with the firm's procedure;
(b)   the correctness of the application of the transfer value analysis system where applicable;
(c)   the merits of the proposed transaction; and
(d)   the suitability of the recommendation.

Any such recommendation must be assessed by one of the firm's designated pension transfer specialists (as defined) to ensure that the procedures have been followed (COB 5.3.21).

Under COB 5.3.22 a firm must ensure that a transfer value analysis is carried out before it makes any recommendations to a customer to transfer out of a defined benefits pension scheme. A transfer value analysis is an analysis performed to make a comparison between the benefits which are likely (on reasonable assumptions) to be paid under an OPS and the benefits afforded by a personal pension or a pension buy-out contract. A copy of the analysis must be delivered with the key features document or otherwise provided to the customer before he gives consent to the application to transfer. Further, the firm must take reasonable steps to ensure that the customer understands the analysis, drawing attention to factors which do and do not support the recommendation to transfer. A key features document contains information about a life policy or scheme or stakeholder pension scheme, and is required to be produced in the form specified in COB 6.1 (packaged products and ISA disclosures) to COB 6.5 (content of key features and important information; life policy schemes, ISA, cash deposit components and stakeholder pension schemes).

> "A firm must provide a projection of the possible future benefits of the proposed individual pension contract before it makes any personal recommendations to a customer to opt out or transfer from an occupational scheme.
> 1. The format and nature of the benefits given in the projection must so far as possible be the same as those which apply under the occupation pension scheme of which the customer is or is eligible to become a member.
> 2. If it is not possible for the benefit shown as projection to replicate those of the occupational pension scheme an explanation must be given.
> 3. If the customer has expressed an interest when changing the structure of his eventual benefits, an additional projection may also be prepared on that basis." (COB 5.3.23)

This rule is to enable any proposed transfer to be assessed by the customer. In addition, any suitability letter issued by a firm relating to a personal recommendation to opt out or transfer from an occupational pension scheme must include a summary of the disadvantages as well as the advantages of such a course of action. In the case of a pension opt-out the suitability letter must contain a financial analysis explaining the decision to opt out. This is based on the Principle of it being clear, fair and not misleading.

In the event that a private customer does not accept the advice of the firm and, contrary to such advice, instructs the firm to arrange a pension opt-out or pension transfer, the firm must keep "a clear record" of the firm's advice that the private customer should not proceed with the pension opt-out or pension transfer, together with a copy of the customer's specific instruction to proceed with the transaction. It must also make clear in writing to the private customer that the firm's advice is that the private customer should not proceed with the pension opt-out or pension transfer (COB 5.3.25). Every six months the firm must notify the FSA in writing of the number of such opt-outs and transfer transactions it has handled during the previous six months and it must also supply at quarterly intervals the details set out in COB 5.3.26 in respect of the preceding quarters. Any records of these notifications should be kept indefinitely; as should any records for private customers of every pension transfer, pension opt-out or free-standing additional voluntary contribution arranged, whether advised or not (COB 5.3.27).

In the event that a firm is promoting a personal pension scheme including group personal pension schemes by means of a direct offer of financial promotion to a group of employees the firm must be satisfied, on reasonable grounds, that the pension scheme is likely to be at least suitable for the majority of the employees as a stakeholder pension scheme and must record why it thinks the promotion is justified (COB 5.3.28). COB 5.3.29 sets out in table form the suitability guidance requirements which should be consulted by all firms before issuing any such suitability letters.

10.6.10   *Customers' understanding of risk*

COB 5.4 relates to the conduct of designated investment business with or for a private customer. The purpose of the section is to reinforce Principle 7 which requires a firm to pay due regard to the information needs of its clients and communicate information in a way that is clear, fair and not misleading. In addition, Principle 9 requires a firm to take reasonable care to ensure the suitability of its advice and discretionary decisions. The FSA wishes to ensure that a firm takes reasonable steps to ensure that a private customer understands the nature of the risk inherent in certain transactions. Therefore, under COB 5.4.3 the FSA has set out a requirement for risk warnings to be issued to private customers and COB 5.4.6 to COB 5.4.10 relate to risk warnings in respect of various investments.

10.6.11 Information about the firm

COB 5.5 again relates to firms that conduct designated investment business with or for private customers and sets out the information which is required about such firms. When a firm conducts designated investment business it must take reasonable steps to ensure that a private customer is given adequate information about the firm and any relevant agent of the firm. The information must include such matters as identities, status, or relationship with the firm of the employees and other agents with whom the customer may have contact, and also the fact that the firm is regulated or authorised by the FSA (COB 5.5.3). This requirement is not necessary for private customers who have been given the information on a previous occasion provided that information is still up to date. There is a table, relating to written communication, in COB 5.5.4 which sets out in detail the requirements of the information to be included in any written communication.

In the event that a firm conducts designated investment business from an office of its own or of an appointed representative outside the UK with or for a private customer who is in the UK, then it must make a written disclosure of such fact to the private customer. It should be made clear that in some or all respects any regulatory system applying, including any compensation arrangements, will be different from that applying in the UK. The statement should also include the protections or compensation available or otherwise under any other system of regulation. A firm must not make an introduction or make arrangements or give advice with a view to another person conducting designated investment business with or for such a private customer, as envisaged above, unless the firm has made an appropriate disclosure and is also satisfied that the private customer will be dealt with in an honest and reliable way (COB 5.5.7). If a firm makes a communication to a private customer outside the UK in connection with business conducted outside the UK and indicates it is an authorised person, it must also where relevant and with equal prominence make the disclosures made in COB 5.5.7 referred to above (COB 5.5.8).

10.6.12   *Excessive charges*

Principle 6 requires a firm to pay due regard to the interests of its customers and treat them fairly. Part of the FSA's efforts to ensure compliance of this principle is that under COB 5.6 charges which a firm makes to its private customers must not be excessive (COB 5.6.3). The firm has an obligation to disclose to a private customer the charges that the firm intends to make under COB 5.7. In determining whether a charge is excessive the firm should consider the amount of its charges for the services or products in question compared with the charges for similar services for products in the market. It should also consider the degree to which the charges are an abuse of the trust that the customer has placed in the firm together with the extent that they have been disclosed to him (COB 5.6.4).

10.6.13   *Disclosure of charges, remuneration and commission*

COB 5.7 sets out to adhere to Principle 7 whereby a firm is required to pay due regard to the needs of its clients and to communicate information to them in a way that is clear, fair and not misleading. COB 5.7 ensures that a private customer is made aware of the cost to him directly or indirectly of financial services so that he is better able to make informed choices. Accordingly, before a firm conducts designated investment business with or for a private customer it:

> "must disclose in writing to that private customer the basis or amount of its charges for conducting that business and the nature or amount of any other income receivable by it or to its knowledge by its associate and attributable to that business." (COB 5.7.3)

The firm may make such disclosures either in its terms of business, or in a customer agreement, or in a separate written statement and the disclosures should include any product related charges that are deducted from the private customer's investment. In the case of a packaged product then compliance with COB 6.2 will reveal product related charges and expenses in the key features document or in the minimum information that the firm is required to provide to private customers. A broker fund adviser disclosure must include any fees payable by a provider firm to the adviser or any associate in accordance with that activity.

When effecting a transaction in a life policy with or for a private customer:

"a firm must disclose to that private customer in cash terms any remuneration payable by its associates to its employees or agents or any remuneration or commission receivable by it in connection with the transaction"

and also must do so if requested by the customer. In determining the amount to be disclosed a firm must put a proper value on the cash payments benefits and services which it provides to its employees and agents in connection with the transaction. Compliance or non-compliance with COB 5.7.E may be relied on by the FSA in establishing whether or not there has been compliance with COB 5.7.

There is an exception to the rule of disclosure where the firm is acting as investment manager, and that is where the transaction is effected for a private customer who is habitually resident overseas or the packaged product is a life policy and the private customer is not present in the UK at the time the application is made. COB 5.7.9 permits a relaxation of the rule on disclosure where a customer is supplied with key features and the amount or value of the remuneration or commission is disclosed within five days of effecting the transaction. COB 5.7.15 sets out in detail the method of calculating remuneration and COB 5.7.16 sets out the content of the wording of remuneration and commission disclosure statements.

10.6.14 Customers introduced to clearing firms by introducing brokers and overseas introducing brokers

COB 5.8 sets out guidance in relation to firms acting as a clearing firm to which an introducing broker or an overseas introducing broker introduces a transaction for its customers. The purpose of the guidance is to adhere to Principle 1 which requires a firm to conduct its business with integrity, and Principle 6 which requires the firm to pay due regard to the interests of its customers and treat them fairly. The purpose of the rules set out in COB 5.8 is to ensure that the customer is aware of the nature of the services that the clearing firm will be providing to the customer and that only those services but not those of the overseas introducing broker will be regulated under the Act.

10.6.15 Information about stakeholder pensions

Where a firm provides the promotion about stakeholder pension schemes to a group of five or more employees at a meeting which has been sponsored by one or more employers, that information must be given by an adviser appointed by the firm to give advice to private customers on packaged products (COB 5.9).

10.7 Product disclosure and the customer's right to cancel or withdraw

10.7.1 *Packaged product and ISA disclosure*

COB 6.1 applies to firms:

> "which sell, recommend or arrange for the sale of a packaged product to a private customer or to the trustees of an occupational pension scheme or to the trustee or manager of a stakeholder pension scheme or which manages, sells or personally recommends a cash deposit ISA to a private company or which affects, personally recommends or arranges for a variation of a life policy for a private customer or which affects, personally recommends or arranges income withdrawal through a private customer."

The purpose of this Rule is to amplify Principle 7 which requires the firm to pay due regard to the information needs of its customers. As mentioned previously, the FSA are concerned about packaged products and wish to ensure that private customers are supplied with information which will highlight particular packaged product features. They require this to be achieved in a way which will enhance the private customer's ability to make a comparative analysis of different packaged products. Under COB 6.1.4 there is a requirement on a product provider or stakeholder pension scheme manager in the case of a packaged product to produce key features which comply with the requirements of COB 6.

In these cases the requirement of COB 6.1.5 is that any key features or information document must be produced in writing, whether in printed hard copy or in electronic format, to at least the same quality and standard as the associated sales or marketing material being used by the firm to promote the packaged product. It must also be separate from any other material given to the customer, unless it is produced for stakeholder pension schemes in which case it may be included as part of another item of sales or marketing material but only if the key features or information document appears with due prominence. Under COB 6.1.6 rules are laid out as to the requirements of firms to comply with regard to the quality of paper, type size and use of colour printing. It is made clear that where key features are permitted to be included within

301

another item, the need for due prominence is unlikely to be satisfied if they are hidden away at the end or are produced in such small type that their impact on the reader is likely to be materially less than other parts of the document or series of screens (COB 6.1.6).

10.7.2 Provision of key features

Key features, required to be provided to a private customer under COB 6.2 and COB 6.4, must be provided by the firm in writing and are also subject to the rules relating to financial promotion set out in COB 3, in particular the keeping of records. When a firm first sells, personally recommends or arranges the sale of a life policy to a private customer a firm must, subject to COB 6.2.9, provide the private customer with appropriate key features before the private customer completes an application for the policy (COB 6.2.7). The key features are set out in COB 6.5 (*see* below). This rule does not apply to a product provider when its life policy is sold on the personal recommendation of, or arranged to be sold by, an independent intermediary or marketing group associate. It also does not apply to a firm where the private customer is to acquire a life policy without making a written application, but the firm must instead ensure that it gives an adequate oral explanation of the main features of the policy and must give or send the private customer appropriate key features within five business days of the date on which the sale, recommendation or arrangement was made (COB 6.2.9). This permits life policies to be sold quickly when speed is essential, say at the end of a tax year and the transaction is effected by telephone. COB 6.2.11 sets out what an adequate oral explanation should include. COB 6.2.12 deals with changes in key features where they have already been provided by a firm to a private customer.

In the event that any changes occur, the firm must ensure that the private customer is provided with revised key features unless it is only the amount of the premium that is to change, or the amount of any commission or remuneration payable is reduced or a rider benefit is added, removed or amended. This permits simple changes to be made before a private customer commits himself without further packaged product disclosure information being provided. Changes in the amount of premium alone (of whatever size) will not require revised key features if the underlying purpose of the proposed contract is unchanged. It should be noted that in the case of a change of packaged product a revised key features document would be required. If key features have been provided to a private customer and the terms of the proposed life policy are materially altered after the private customer completes an application form, then the firm must ensure that the private customer is provided with written details of the changes as soon as practicable and offered revised key features (COB 6.2.14). Incidentally, COB 6.2.15 defines material change and in particular mentions that an increase of premium of less than 25 per cent is not material.

10.7.3 Variations to existing life policies

Where a policyholder applies to vary a life policy issued on or after 1 January 1995, or is recommended to do so, and the variation of the policy gives rise to a right to cancel under COB 6.7.7 (*see* below), a document containing the information required under COB 6.5 relating to the nature of the life policy etc. must be provided to the policyholder by the firm personally recommending, arranging or effecting the variation before it is put into effect. This rule can be complied with if a complete set of new key features is communicated to the policyholder. The key features could just relate to the increase in benefits or could illustrate a "before and after" situation.

In the case of a policy issued before 1 January 1995, if this is varied and the variation of the policy gives a right to cancel under COB 6.7.7, infor-mation must be given to the policyholder by the firm that is personally recommending, arranging or effecting the variation before it is put into effect. The firm must believe on reasonable grounds that the information given is sufficient to enable the customer to understand the consequences of the variation (COB 6.2.18). The requirements relating to variation of life policies do not apply to a product provider when the variation of its life policy is effected on the personal recommendation of or is arranged by an independent intermediary or marketing group associate. In the event that a private customer is to vary a life policy without making a written application, the firm must ensure that it gives adequate oral explanation of the variation and must give or send the private customer the information required (depending on whether it is a policy issued before or after 1 January 1995) within five days of the variation being effected (COB 6.2.19). It is worth noting that there is no requirement for key features to be provided for a new life policy or a variation to an existing policy if the policyholder is habitually resident in EEA State other than the UK or is habitually resident outside the EEA and the private customer is not present in the UK.

10.7.4 Schemes

Under COB 6.2.22 if a firm sells, personally recommends or arranges for the sale of a scheme to a private customer the firm must provide the customer with key features for the scheme before he completes an application for the scheme holding. If the customer is to acquire the scheme without making a written application, then it is sufficient if the firm gives an adequate oral explanation of the main features of the scheme holding to the private customer and the key features are sent to the customer within five business days of the date on which the sale, recommendation or arrangement was made. This rule applies not just to new purchases but also to any recommendation or application to transfer the value of a particular fund within a scheme to a different fund within the same scheme. Where a private customer has responded to a direct offer financial promotion, the mailing package or direct offer financial promotion should have included example based key features. Any oral explanation of the information required by COB 6.2.22 should include *inter alia*:

(a)   the name of the scheme;
(b)   the scheme's aims;
(c)   amounts to be invested;
(d)   risk factors;
(e)   the charges that the customer will have to bear;
(f)   a summary of the reasons for any recommendation; and
(g)   if appropriate, the commission or remuneration which would be paid to the adviser or representative.

COB 6.2.22 does not apply if the firm is a UK firm and the obligation arises from business carried on in another EEA State under an EEA right, or at the time the customer signs the application he is habitually resident outside the EEA and is not present in the UK. It also does not apply if the scheme holding is purchased by a private customer on an execution only basis or if purchased on behalf of a private customer by an investment manager. COB 6.2.24 sets out further exemptions to the rule in COB 6.2.22, and COB 6.2.25 provides that COB 6.2.22 does not apply when the scheme holding is sold on the personal recommendation of, or arranged to be sold by, an independent intermediary or marketing group associate.

10.7.5 Post-sale confirmation in respect of life policies

If a life policy which is a packaged product is sold by a firm, then a post-sale confirmation must be issued by the firm. It is not necessary for a life office to issue post-sale confirmation in respect of schemes or pure protection contracts or stakeholder pension schemes (COB 6.3.2). Once again the FSA is concerned to regulate packaged products. When a private customer buys a life policy which is a packaged product or varies such an existing life policy and the variation gives rise to cancellation under COB 6.7.7 (which relates to the rights to cancel an investment agreement in various circumstances) then COB 6.3.3 applies. The life office must send to (or in the case of an industrial assurance policy, must either give or send to) the private customer information required by COB 6.5.15 to COB 6.5.19, COB 6.5.23 to COB 6.5.28 and COB 6.5.38. These relate to examples of projections, descriptions of policies, tables and deduction summary, commission and remuneration. This rule does not apply to the exceptions set out below in COB 6.3.6. Any post-sale confirmation may be provided in a printed hard copy and sent through the post direct to the private customer. In the case of industrial assurance policies the post-sale confirmation may be delivered by the firm's representative rather than sent by post. If a private customer has approached the firm through electronic media then the post-sale confirmation may be provided by the same means. Note, however, that electronic messages should only be used where the private customer expects to communicate in this way. Under COB 6.3.5 any post-sale confirmation required must be sent or given to the private customer no later than the issue of any cancellation notice or, if such notice is not required, as soon as is reasonably practicable after the contract is effected.

COB 6.3.6 sets out various exemptions to the rule relating to post-sale confirmation. No post-sale confirmation is needed if the circumstances contained in COB 6.3.6 pertain. These are *inter alia* that the life office has taken reasonable steps to determine that the life policy:

(a) is purchased on behalf of a private customer by an investment manager;
(b) is purchased by the trustees of an OPS;
(c) is purchased by the trustees or manager of a stakeholder pension scheme:
(d) was issued before 1 January 1995 and is being varied.

Neither is confirmation needed if at the time the customer signs the application for the new life policy he is habitually resident in an EEA State other than the UK or outside the EEA and is not present in the UK.

10.7.6   Key features relating to special situations

Key features are required to be provided to a private customer in writing under the terms of COB 6.4.1 which relates to occupational pension schemes, self-invested personal pensions, income withdrawals, cash deposit ISAs, traded life policies and stakeholder pension schemes.

In relation to packaged products sold to trustees of defined benefit occupational pension schemes, no key features need to be supplied. However, if a firm provides packaged products, whether life policies or schemes, to the trustees of money-purchase occupational pension schemes then key features need to be provided. If a firm sells, recommends or arranges the sale of a new group or master life policy, the first of a series of individual life policies or the first units in a particular scheme to or for the trustees of a money-purchase occupational pension scheme, it must provide the trustees with key features (COB 6.4.4). In these circumstances the firm must treat the trustees in the same way as they would treat private customers. The firm must ensure that the key features are made available to the trustees to enable them to distribute them to all scheme members at the outset of the scheme and also for any members that may join the scheme subsequently. These requirements also apply to main scheme benefits and to any additional voluntary contributions where members" benefits are linked to earmarked segments of life policies or schemes. It should be noted that the definition of money-purchase occupational schemes includes executive pension plans, small self-administered schemes that provide money-purchase benefits, and additional voluntary contribution schemes. Group personal pension schemes are not deemed to be occupational pension schemes and the rule under COB 6.4.4 does not apply to them. It is therefore necessary that a firm should provide each person who is offered membership of a group personal scheme with key features under COB 6.1 and COB 6.2. The purpose behind the rules under COB 6.4 is to give any prospective scheme members access to information about the occupational pension scheme to enable them to make comparisons with alternative personal investments.

In the case of self-invested personal pension schemes, if a firm sells, recommends or arranges a packaged product to or for a member, prospective member or trustee of a self-invested personal pension scheme then key features must be provided both to the member and the trustee. In these circumstances trustees are treated the same as private customers.

In the case of income withdrawals, if a firm personally recommends, arranges or effects income withdrawals for a private customer then key features must be provided to the customer before he signs any form of application or authority electing to make those withdrawals whether or not the election is made with advice or on an execution-only basis. Key features are also required under rules COB 6.2.7 and COB 6.2.22 when an existing life policy is to be endorsed or when an existing scheme holding is to be used. However, it should be noted that the rules COB 6.4.11 and COB 6.4.12 override any other requirements of COB in relation to income withdrawal. Under COB 6.4.11 if a private customer makes a series of elections in a period of 12 months to make income withdrawals, the firm that is recommending, arranging or effecting the elections may provide one combined set of key features for those elections or it may provide separate sets of key features for such election if they relate to life policies and schemes. Under COB 6.4.12 at intervals of no longer than 12 months the product provider must give the customer information that will enable him to review his elections, and the provider should inform the private customer how to obtain advice in respect of income withdrawals and should emphasise that it would be in his best interest to take such advice.

In the case of stakeholder pension schemes, before a private customer completes an application for the scheme the firm which is selling or recommending it must provide the customer with key features. If a firm proposes to deal with a private customer over the telephone for the purposes of providing information through a decision tree about stakeholder pension schemes, it may only do so if it has adequate evidence to show that the private customer has access to a copy of the decision tree during the conversation. Decision trees are contained in COB 6.5.5. If a firm has contacted a customer by telephone it must take the customer through the decision tree process and if the customer does not have a copy of this they must make sure that he is sent one before taking him through the decision process by way of a follow-up telephone call.

These rules do not apply to a stakeholder pension scheme manager when its stakeholder pensions scheme is sold on the personal recommendation of, or arranged to be sold by, an independent intermediary or marketing group associate, unless the intermediary or associate is also the manager of the stakeholder pension scheme (COB 6.4.18). Key features must be provided to the trustees or a manager of a stakeholder pension scheme when a firm sells or recommends the sale of a new group or master life policy. In these cases the firm must treat the trustees and managers as private customers. The guidance in COB 6.4.20 suggests using a range of representative actual or hypothetical scheme members (covering, for example, different ages, sex and salaries) so that the trustees or manager can assess the effectiveness of an investment for scheme members.

If a firm provides a private customer with information through a decision tree which relates to membership of a stakeholder pension scheme but does not actually give advice or make a personal recommendation, then the firm must provide the customer with a written notice. Such written notice must be provided by the firm no later than the issue of the post-sale notification of the private customer's right to cancel under the cancellation rules. It must also confirm that no advice has been given, that the private customer has decided that the stakeholder pension is appropriate as a result of the answers he has given to the questions posed in the decision tree, and must include a copy of the decision tree which indicates the answers which the private customer has given. COB 6.4.24 suggests that after a customer gives information through a decision tree but before he completes his application, a firm could satisfy the requirement to provide key features by providing an adequate oral explanation about the main features of the stakeholder pension scheme, provided written key features are then sent along with a copy decision tree referred to above within five business days.

10.7.7 Content of key features and important information relating to life policies, schemes and stakeholder pension schemes

A firm must ensure that any key features it produces for a packaged product (other than a stakeholder pension scheme) include the information required in the table set out in COB 6.5.11. Also it should follow the order shown and be divided by appropriate and prominent subheadings some of which are described within the rules. The rules in relation to ISA cash deposits and traded life policies are contained in different sets. Those key features relating to stakeholder pension schemes are, in addition, subject to the subheadings set out in COB 6.5.11 and they must include the application information specified in COB 6.5.12–COB 6.5.40. Under COB 6.5.3 a firm may amend or adapt the prescribed content and format requirements which are set out in COB 6.5, but it must demonstrate that this is necessary to reflect the terms and nature of a particular product. If the rules in COB 6.5 do not apply then a firm may give the relevant information using its own words and style. A firm does have a discretion where it offers more than one scheme to choose whether to produce separate key features for each scheme or to produce a single key feature to cover a range of funds.

10.7.8   Stakeholder pension scheme decision tree

Under COB 6.5.5 there is no obligation on a firm to supply a decision tree where it has personally recommended a stakeholder pension scheme to a private customer. It may wish to supply a copy of any decision tree used as part of the advice process along with a mandatory suitability letter. If a firm knows that a certain decision tree or trees will not be relevant then it can omit them and include only the relevant decision tree/s. The guidance set out in COB 6.5.7, which applies where the decision trees are within the key features or are used separately, states that where the employment status of the customer is known then firms are permitted to issue one decision tree consisting of the introductory text and the relevant version of the flow chart. In other circumstances the introductory text and the three versions of the flow charts (for employed persons, the self-employed and those not in employment) should be included. There is limited scope to adapt the decision trees and the only adaptations that really are readily approved are those suitable to branding the decision tree in the corporate image of the firm to reflect the design of its stakeholder pension scheme promotional material. However, the text and general design should follow the prescribed content and format. The guidance note mentions that the FSA publishes its own version of the decision trees and states that firms must consider them as examples of acceptable design. The guidance note in COB 6.5.10 sets out those adaptations which are permitted and those which are not. In relation to the information which has to be supplied, COB 6.5.11 sets out in the table the appropriate provisions of COB relating to the information to be supplied. Under COB 6.5.12 a firm must include a specific heading "Key features of the [name of life policy/scheme/ stakeholder pension scheme]".

Under COB 6.5.13 a firm must describe the nature of the life policy or scheme or stakeholder pension scheme with a heading which contains reference to "its aims", "your commitment to your investment" and "risk factors". In relation to the risk factors a firm must give a brief description of the factors which may have an adverse effect on performance or are otherwise material to the decision to invest. The guidance under COB 6.5.14 sets out the relevant information which might be included under risk factors, such as:

(a)   whether the value of the capital and any income might fluctuate;
(b)   the risk that the value of an investment might fall before notice of cancellation is given and therefore the original investment may be less;

(c) risk relating to the underlying assets of a packaged product;
(d) risk relating to the markets in which the investment will be made;
(e) risk relating to capital erosion, volatility, market value adjustments;
(f) potential problems with an investment in a property in respect of liquidity, broker funds etc.

Under COB 6.5.15 a firm must include a projection which illustrates to the private customer the principal terms of the proposed transaction where the proposed transaction is for a life policy or a scheme. Such projection only relates to schemes with either an election to make income withdrawals or where the customer's primary objective is to acquire a specified sum of money on a specified date or death, or an annuity of a specified amount payable as from a specified date.

In respect of stakeholder pension schemes, a specimen projection will have been included within the decision tree, therefore the rule under COB 6.5.15 does not require projections to be included within the key features. Any projections which are included must comply with COB 6.6 relating to projections using the lower, intermediate and higher rates of return set out COB 6.6.15.

Under COB 6.5.19 a life policy projection within key features must be specific to the private customer, calculated on the basis of his age, sex, the sum assured, the premium and other principal factors of the proposed life policy. Such projection is not necessary if such policy is a single-premium life policy, or the premiums do not exceed £120 per annum, or the total premiums are less than £1,000, or the key features are part of a direct offer financial promotion. If in relation to the latter no customer specific projection is included, a projection must be provided which typically represents the type of business which the firm conducts in relation to the life policy in question. Any projection within key features must be based on either the actual amounts which the customer is proposing to invest or the amounts which typically represent the type of business which the firm conducts. The rules under COB 6.5 are intended to enable a private customer to make an informed decision based on the relevant information. Under COB 6.5.20 this information must be set out in the form of questions and answers describing the principal terms of the life policy, scheme or stakeholder pension scheme. The guidance note set out in COB 6.5.21 sets out the relevant information which must be supplied to the private customer and includes matters such as details of any endowment which is being used to repay an interest only mortgage, the consequences of making a life policy paid up or taking a contribution holiday etc. In the case of a personal pension scheme, an indication of the general availability of stakeholder pension schemes and the default investment option offered under the stakeholder pension schemes regulations must be included.

Under COB 6.5.23, which relates to life policies which have a surrender value, a firm must include the contents of the tables set out in COB 6.5.24 unless it is a without profits life policy of which the benefits, except on surrender or variation, are guaranteed benefits or it is a life policy for a term not exceeding five years (COB 6.5.28). When completing the table set out in COB 6.5.24 a firm must include all the matters set out in COB 6.5.25 which relate to the proper calculation and information that is to be supplied in the table. This table will not apply to a life policy which will never have a surrender value, but a warning must be given in the key features, instead of the table, headed "WARNING – this policy has no cash-in value at any time". COB 6.5.27 sets out the information which must appear in conjunction with the tables relating to deductions. Specific wording is set out and must be followed. The calculations relating to "total actual deductions to date" and the "effect of deductions to date" are covered by COB 6.5.29 which sets out the precise manner in which they must be calculated. In relation to schemes, the table set out in COB 6.5.31 relating to charges and expenses affecting an investment must be followed. COB 6.5.32 sets out in detail how the table must be completed and COB 6.5.33 to COB 6.5.35 set out the manner of calculation of deductions.

In respect of stakeholder pension schemes, a statement must appear specifying the annual charge as a percentage of the value of the funds accumulated giving a monetary example relating to the valuation of the fund at £500 and at £7,500. The wording set out in COB 6.5.37 is specific and must be followed.

Under COB 6.5.38 specific wording is required relating to commission and remuneration for life policies, schemes and stakeholder pension schemes. It is essential that the name of the adviser to whom the commission or remuneration (if any) is to be paid is given.

COB 6.5.40 sets out a long list of information which is required in key features applying to life policies schemes, regulated collective investment schemes, ISAs and stakeholder pension schemes. These requirements are all mandatory and must be carefully followed. The information relating to the requirement for cash deposit ISAs, friendly society tax exempt policies, traded life policies and broker funds is set out in COB 6.5.41 and COB 6.5.42.

The post-sale confirmation relating to life policies which have to be given to private customers must include the information set out in COB 6.5.15 to 6.5.19 (which relates to examples), COB 6.5.23 to COB 6.5.28 (which relates to tables and deduction summaries) and COB 6.5.38 (which relates to commission and remuneration). It must also include a statement relating to the advisers in the following form: "a person who advised you about this policy represents only [name of firm or, if appropriate, marketing group]".

Under the terms of the Third Life Directive, which relates to the information to be supplied, the statement must be in the official language of the appropriate EEA State of Commitment set out in the table in COB 6.5.49 which gives guidance as to which is the appropriate state.

10.7.9 Projections

10.7.9.1 Preparation

COB 6.6 is again one of the rules arising from Principle 7 which imposes an obligation on a firm to pay due regard to the information needs of its clients and to communicate information to them in a way which is "clear, fair and not misleading". Any projection must follow this Principle. It should be prepared on the basis of uniform and consistent rates of investment terms and should not be prepared on the basis of "wholly speculative forecasts" as to potential value of future benefits. Any projection prepared by a firm must ensure that private customers purchasing a life policy, scheme or stakeholder's pension scheme receive appropriate information about possible future returns from their investment in a manner which is clear, fair and not misleading.

10.7.9.2 Rules

There are a large number of rules set out in COB 6.6 relating to the requirements of projections. It is only possible in this Chapter to touch on the principal ones. It is a general rule that a firm must not provide a projection for a life policy, scheme or stakeholder pension scheme unless the projection is calculated and presented in accordance with the rules in COB 6.6 (COB 6.6.4). These rules do not apply in respect of a projection issued by a firm where it relates to benefits payable under a defined benefit occupational pension scheme unless they are money-purchased benefits and comply with COB 6.6.5. If an investment is in a higher volatility fund then a firm must not provide a projection of possible investment returns. A higher volatility fund is one that relates to geared futures and options schemes, or a geared security scheme, or a warrant scheme. If a projection is issued by an independent intermediary it must not only comply with the rules in COB 6.6 but it must also ensure that a projection given to a particular customer is relevant to that customer's circumstances.

10.7.9.3 Tables
Any document containing a projection must include the information relating to key features and set out in the example, tables, deduction summary, and commissions and remuneration statements set out in COB 6.5. Under COB 6.6.9 a firm may provide a generic projection for illustrative purposes in certain circumstances if it is based on a single rate of investment return. This rule sets out the requirements for such a projection.

10.7.9.4 Rates
In relation to pension projections, COB 6.6.10 and COB 6.6.11 set out the future rates of return, salary rates, and increases and inflation which may be used to determine the level of contributions and also the criteria which must be used for the purposes of comparison in an appropriate personal pension. It is important to note that the FSA have set down strict wording to be used in these circumstances. In addition the guidance note states that where a State Earnings Related Pension Scheme (SERPS) is used there should be a comparison using real rates of return of the benefits being given up and the relevant contract. Under COB 6.6.13 criteria for projections relating to a personal pension or a stakeholder pension scheme with income withdrawals are laid out. Any such projection must include *inter alia* the initial amounts of minimum and maximum income as specified in the current tables published by the government actuary for income withdrawals, a statement of the assumed initial level of income and the assumed basis for future years. It must also include a schedule headed "What the benefits might be" which shows the amount of income and the fund at each or every third anniversary, statements relating to open market values and annuities at age 75 and statements relating to the amount of annuity that could be secured using an immediate annuity rate available in the market. Any such projection must also be based on the assumption that the current rate of gilt index yield will continue to apply in projecting amounts of a minimum and maximum income throughout the term of the projection (COB 6.6.13).

10.7.9.5 Statement
Any document which contains a projection must include the appropriate statements set out in COB 6.6.16 to COB 6.6.18. Under rule 6.6.14(2) a statement may be altered if a firm has reasonable grounds to believe that it is not wholly appropriate to the contract in question, but the

alterations must not reduce the significance or impact of the statement. As usual, the FSA requires that any statement accompanying a projection must be in a type size no smaller or less prominent than that used for the projected value. These statements must accompany any projection for a life policy or scheme except a generic projection or a protected rights annuity projection. The statements which must accompany projections of life policies, schemes or stakeholder pension schemes are set out in the table contained in COB 6.6.16 and must be followed absolutely unless in accordance with COB 6.6.14(2) the firm believes on reasonable grounds that it is not wholly appropriate to the contract in question. No alteration must be made which reduces the significance or impact of the statement. COB 6.6.17 sets out the statements which must accompany generic projections and COB 6.6.18 sets out statements to accompany projections for a projected rights contract. As stated elsewhere in COB, a record must be kept of any projection that is supplied to a customer and it must be retained for the usual minimum periods (i.e. six years in the case of a record relevant to a life policy, pension contract or stakeholder pension scheme; indefinitely in the case of a record relevant to a pension transfer or pension opt-out and three years in any other case).

10.7.9.6   Key terms
There are several key terms used in this section of COB and the definitions are set out in COB 6.6.22 to COB 6.6.33. The type of terms defined are "adjusted premiums", "charges and expenses", "contract period", "cost of risk benefits", "relevant contribution", "relevant premium", "relevant premium or contribution for protected rights annuities" and "relevant rate of return".

10.7.9.7   Calculation criteria
COB 6.6.34 to COB 6.6.37 deal with the calculation of projections and set out the criteria for such calculations. The criteria include, for example, that future benefits payable under life policies or stakeholder pension schemes must be calculated by reference to the relevant premium for that policy or stakeholder pension scheme. Also any relevant premium must be accumulated subject to charges and expenses and the cost of risk benefits. Allowances may be made where a customer has exercised or is intending to exercise an option to effect a partial surrender of a policy, but no allowance must be made for income withdrawals, surrenders or lapses. Calculations relating to future benefits under a scheme are made in accordance with COB 6.6.36. The general rules applying to a calculation of projections are set out in COB 6.6.37 and deal *inter alia* with projections being rounded down to not more than three significant

figures, increasing projections to the guaranteed amount if they are less than the amount guaranteed under the life policy or scheme and, where the customers indicate an intention to increase the premium, permitting the calculation to make allowance for such increase in premium.

10.7.9.8 Surrender and transfer values

Any projections of surrender values or transfer values must comply with COB 6.6.38 which imposes the obligation on the firm making the projection of such surrender or transfer value to use the intermediate rate of return appropriate to its category of business. If the firm reasonably expects the rate to overstate the potential of the contract then a lower rate of return must be used and disclosed; likewise if the customer requests a lower rate to be used, in which case this fact must also be disclosed. Any projection of a surrender or transfer value must also make allowance for partial surrenders where the contract permits this and the customer has exercised this option or indicated his intention to do so. Allowance must also be made for the firm's surrender value basis and must reflect the current approach of the firm towards applying penalties on surrender including less than full credit for accrued terminal bonuses, specific penalties or exit charges. In the situation where bonus rates apply to with profit contracts, the firm must ensure that the bonus rates supported by the relevant premium are assumed to apply throughout the term of the contract.

10.7.9.9 Annuities

Projections relating to annuities must show annuity values based on the higher and lower rates of return set out in the tables in COB 6.6.7 to COB 6.6.52. They must make allowances for mortality or morbidity together with charges and expenses. A projection of an annuity with less than one year to maturity is calculated on the basis of the firm's current immediate annuity rates and, if a firm does not offer annuities but issues a projection for a contract the proceeds of which are to be applied to purchase an annuity, the firm must use annuity rates no more favourable that those currently being used in the open market for a similar projection. COB 6.6.40 provides for projections in relation to immediate annuities and states that a uniform rate of continuous change in annuity must be determined for each rate of return whilst making allowances for mortality appropriate to the class of customer and charges and expenses.

10.7.9.10 Retirement funds

COB 6.6.41 refers to the calculations relating to retirement funds for a protected rights annuity under an appropriate personal pension scheme or stakeholder pension scheme. It must be calculated by accumulating the relevant contribution less charges and expenses at the two relevant rates of return as set out in COB 6.6.52. Any calculation of annuity arising from the retirement fund must be calculated using the higher and lower rates of return set out in COB 6.6.51, making allowance for the mortality appropriate to the class of customer, charges and expenses and the relevant rate of increasing payment. COB 6.6.42 gives additional projection for pension contracts or stakeholder pension scheme where the maturity period is five years or less. In these cases any calculation may use the intermediate rates of return specified in COB 6.6.51 or may use a current annuity rate calculated at a rate no higher than that specified in COB 6.6.51. However, if a firm is providing projection of its own annuities it must use it own annuity rates. In relation to a single-premium contract, projections may be calculated on the basis that the premiums are regular premiums if it is not given on a misleading basis and the firm is bound unconditionally to accept all single premiums which may be paid by the customer under the contract (COB 6.6.43). In relation to with profits endowment business and with profit whole life assurance business, COB 6.6.44 and COB 6.6.45 set out the allowance for the cost of risk benefits and the rates or rates of bonus which must be applied under these policies. If a contract has a reviewable administration charge then a firm must make allowance for increases in administration charges on a basis which is fair and reasonable and takes into account the firm pricing policy. Any increases must be assumed at the rate set out in the table in COB 6.6.47 relating to administration charges reviewed in line with price increases and administration charges reviewed in line with earnings increases.

10.7.9.11   Extra benefits
In relation to contracts which provide the benefits or extra premiums for additional underwriting risks, then any projection must comply with COB 6.6.48 which sets out details of the rider benefit or the extra premium charged in the case of, say, an impaired life or hazardous pursuit. If a deduction is made from the actual premium for a rider benefit or an increased underwriting risk then this sum must be quoted in any projection.

10.7.9.12   Rates of return
The tables in COB 6.6.50 to COB 6.6.52 set out the rates of return assumptions used in particular contracts. These must be used when calculating any projection save that "reduced rates of return must be used if the firm expects the rates in the tables to overstate the investment potential of a contract", if reduced rates of return are requested by a customer they must be used and if reduced rates are used they must be disclosed in the

document containing the projection. It should be noted that the rates of return used in COB 6.6.50 to COB 6.6.52 are compounded annually and allow for inflation. Under COB 6.6.55 to COB 6.6.62 the rules are set out as to the calculations affecting deductions to be provided within the key features for all types of life policies and schemes. The basic calculation relating to the reduction in yield for such matters as charges and expenses are set out in COB 6.6.55 and COB 6.6.56. An alternative calculation method for the reduction of yield in a life policy which may be used at a firm's discretion is set out fully in COB 6.6.57. In respect of a protected rights annuity, the effects of charging expenses may be calculated assuming that premiums will continue to be paid after the first year. Any reduction in yield on the effect of charges and expenses must be expressed to the nearest tenth of one per cent.

10.7.9.13   *Multiple funds*
COB 6.6.60 deals with unit linked contracts where there is more than one fund. In this case the effect of charges and expenses must be calculated separately in relation to each such fund and must be shown in the information required within key features. In considering a unitised with profits fund, any calculation relating to that fund must be made on the with profits expenses basis. If, in looking at the various funds, two or more of the calculations of the charges and expenses on those funds would produce results that are similar so that one could be regarded as representative of the other, then only one figure need be shown, providing it is clear that it is a representative figure. If a contract has a regular and single premium element in it then any reduction in yield should be calculated separately for the regular premium and for the single premium and shown in the information sheet.

10.7.9.14   *Scheme charges*
COB 6.6.65 to COB 6.6.79 set out rules and guidance on how to calculate charges and expenses for schemes and in particular COB 6.6.65 to COB 6.6.69 provide rules and guidance for authorised unit trusts and other recognised collective investment schemes. COB 6.6.65 sets out arguments on the assessment and apportionment of expenses which are described as "all explicit charges and expenses and includes all other deductions and expenses which will or may bear upon the fund". It is important to note here that reference is made to the Statements of Recommended Practice issued by the FSA. These will normally provide a suitable starting point for any assessment of the level of charges and expenses. It is permissible to express such expenses as an annual percentage charge against the fund. The FSA is again keen to see where packaged products are used that schemes are looked through to ensure that all charges and

expenses which the customer will or may bear are included as there may be an abatement to avoid double charging. If a document refers to an investment in a number of trusts, those charges and expenses applicable to the trusts selected by the customer may be used. If this is not practicable it will be permissible for the firm to disclose the charges and expenses of a representative unit trust. This will normally be one that is most likely to be selected by the customers to whom the material is issued (COB 6.6.66).

10.7.9.15 *Expenses*

Guidance is set out in COB 6.6.67 as to the type of investment expenses that a firm should take into account in making their calculations. It is emphasised that this is not comprehensive and it is in addition to explicit charges. If there has been any variation in costs then this is covered under COB 6.6.68 which provides that the adjusted expenses should be expressed as a proportion of the relevant fund which is the average size of the fund for the period of the report (unless such a figure would be misleading, when a fair estimate of the size of the relevant fund must be used). These expenses must be reviewed whenever there are material changes and in any event at least once a year (COB 6.6.69). COB 6.6.76 to COB 6.6.78 set out examples to assist in understanding the method of calculating the reduction in investment return. It should be noted that these figures are representative and should not be regarded as indicative of likely levels of charges and expenses to be expected. COB 6.6.79 sets out a specimen table of how the effects of charges and expenses should be presented. The formula for calculating the factors for converting a retirement fund into an annuity are set out in a table in COB 6.6.81, and COB 6.6.80 deals with the basis of certain assumptions used in the calculation. COB 6.6.82 deals with the definitions in the formulas set out in the table in COB 6.6.81. COB 6.6.83 sets out the allowance for expenses, COB 6.6.84 sets out the mortality rates to be used and COB 6.6.85 sets out the formulas for mortality functions calculated in the table set out in COB 6.6.81.

10.7.9.16 *Pension transfer value*

COB 6.6.87 to COB 6.6.93 deal with the calculation of a pension transfer value analysis. They show how it should be prepared and state that it should provide a comparison between the potential benefits available to the customer from an OPS and the potential benefits that would be available to him under a personal pension or buy-out contract. The fundamental rule is that the basis for any pension transfer value analysis must be clear, fair and not misleading. COB 6.6.87 sets out the information that must be analysed and which would be relevant to the customer's circumstances. COB 6.6.88 sets comparisons that must be put to the customer to enable him to make an informed choice. Some of the items that the analysis must contain are statements of rate of return, early retirement and a statement of the value of the benefits payable on the death of the customer. There are also special provisions where the period before the benefits are assumed to commence is less than one year. In all cases a statement of the assumptions used must be provided which complies with the requirements of COB 6.6.90 which relate to the required assumptions (COB 6.6.89). The required assumptions set out in COB 6.6.90 must be made for the purposes of the required calculations and may only be varied to incorporate more cautious assumptions. It deals with a case where an annuity interest rate different from the FSA annuity rate is used and also where an occupational pension scheme has a record of discretionary increases in pension. The assumptions to be made in COB 6.6.90 are set out in a table in COB 6.6.91. COB 6.6.92 deals with the method of calculation of Target Benefits.

10.7.9.17 *Assumptions*
Any analysis must contain *inter alia* a list of all the main assumptions made for the purpose of the analysis set out consecutively and with equal prominence, a warning as to the difference between the amounts of benefits, a description of any differences in the dates at which the pensions become payable, and warning of any shortfall in the value of the death benefit (COB 6.6.93).

10.7.10 *Cancellation and withdrawal*

10.7.10.1 *Application*
COB 6.7 applies to product providers, insurers, deposit taking firms or stakeholder pension scheme managers (i.e. the firms responsible for issuing life policies, selling units, issuing long-term insurance contracts, accepting deposits for ISAs, or acting as managers of stakeholder pension schemes). It deals with the rights which customers have either to cancel agreements into which they have entered or to withdraw any offer before an agreement is commenced. Also it specifies stakeholder pension scheme agreements which the customers have a right to cancel, those EIS, ISA or PEP agreements in which the customers have the right to withdraw, and long-term insurance contracts under which the customers have a right to cancel and also those which they do not. The rules under COB 6.7 have been extended so that any customer has the right to withdraw in respect of defined benefits (or finally salary) pension transfer.

10.7.10.2 Cancellation substitute

If a firm chooses, it can offer the right to cancel certain policies with a procedure referred to as a cancellation substitute. If the firm does not offer the option of a cancellation substitute it has to offer cancellation. The FSA have made the cancellation substitute available as they have considered that it is very difficult for a post-sale cancellation to work effectively in the case of pension transfers as there is considerable difficulty in putting the customer back into his original position. In COB 6.7 Part 5 there is a table summarising the application cancellation and withdrawal rights and the maximum period of reflection. The whole basis of COB 6.7 is to back up Principle 6 which requires the firm to pay due regard to the interests of its customers and to treat them fairly. It has been deemed appropriate that in certain circumstances customers who enter into an investment agreement shall be entitled to a period of reflection during which they can decide whether or not to proceed with the purchase. A customer who is an individual has the right to cancel an investment agreement in a large number of circumstances set out in the tables in COB 6.7, and in this regard the trustees of an OPS or the trustees of managers of a stakeholder pension scheme are treated, so far as necessary, as an individual customer for the purposes of the cancellation rules and have the same right to cancel as an individual customer. Therefore, if trustees purchase life policies or schemes as investments of their pension schemes, individual members of stakeholder pension schemes have the right to cancel initial membership of the scheme and may in some cases vary their contribution. The responsibility for ensuring compliance with the cancellation rules is with the product provider or the manager of a stakeholder pension scheme. COB 6.7.10 sets out the time periods within which the right of cancellation must be exercised.

10.7.10.3 Stakeholder pensions

COB 6.7.2 provides that the cancellation rules shall apply to a customer who is an individual who has entered into an investment scheme for a stakeholder pension scheme. Providing the customer has made clear his intention to make regular contributions then only the first contribution to such a scheme will attract cancellation rights. It is recommended that the disclosure of the option to make regular contributions take place in the key features. An individual customer's intention to make regular contributions could be evidenced by a direct debit mandate or instructions to an employer to deduct regular contributions from salary. COB 6.7.14 sets out the circumstances in which a customer who is an individual has the right to withdraw an offer to enter into certain agreements following investment or a pension annuity or a pension transfer.

10.7.10.4 Tables

The table in COB 6.7.15 sets out the rights to cancellation and should be read in conjunction with the note set out in COB 6.7.16. The tables relating to cancellation of non-life agreements are set out in COB 6.7.17 to COB 6.7.19.

10.7.10.5 Voluntary cancellation and variations

If under the COB rules a firm has removed the right to cancel an investment agreement but voluntarily gives the customer the right to cancel in any event, the agreement is treated as if it were cancellable. The guidelines also state that if there is any doubt as to whether an investment agreement or the circumstance of the purchase bring it within the COB rules then the agreement should be treated as if it were cancellable. Likewise, if a firm sends a pre-sale notice or post-sale notice where it is not obliged to do so under the COB rules then it will be assumed to have voluntarily granted the customer a right to cancel. If a variation to a life policy, pension contract or stakeholder pension scheme occurs then a firm must give a customer (who is an individual) the right to cancel in the circumstances set out in COB 6.7.23. Variations covered in COB 6.7.23 include increases in premiums which are substantial (an increase of more than 25 per cent), the imposition of additional obligations on the customer or where the increase represents the proceeds of a pension transfer. The right to cancel only applies to the variation of the contract and not the original contract (COB 6.7.24). The guideline in COB 6.7.25 states that there is no right to cancel where the variation results in an increase in a premium or payment of £25 or less. The rule in respect of variations does not apply where an increase results from a "pre-selected option". This is because the pre-selected option will have been agreed with the customer at the outset.

10.7.10.6 Electronic communication

Where electronic communication is involved, cancellation or withdrawal may be accepted by the firm by electronic means provided the firm can demonstrate that the customer wished to communicate electronically. Any time limits laid down under COB rules are based on calendar days (excluding public holidays) and are calculated by reference to the day after the date on which the agreement is concluded.

10.7.10.7 Time of cancellation and notices

A firm must give a customer notice of the right to cancel both before the agreement is concluded (a presale notice) and after the agreement has been concluded (a post-sale notice). If the customer is a trustee who is believed to act on behalf of individual beneficiaries then the post-sale notice must be sent to not only the trustee but also the beneficiary or purchaser. A presale notice must contain at least a summary of the information required in a post-sale notice (COB 6.7.32). A post-sale notice has to be in writing; given to the customer after the agreement is concluded; sufficiently clear, prominent and informative to enable the customer to exercise the right to cancel to the extent required; and accompanied by a slip or form to enable the customer to exercise the right to cancel (COB 6.7.34). A post-sale notice must be sent by post or electronically if appropriate. The form and content of a post-sale notice is set out in COB 6.7.36 which deals with the fact that there is an agreement, there is a right to cancel the agreement, the duration of the rights, steps the customers must take, the consequences of cancellation and other matters. The requirements in respect of post-sale notices relating to ISAs are set out in COB 6.7.37. If a post-sale notice forms part of another document then the firm must ensure that the presence of the post-sale notice is drawn to the customer's attention and must feature the words set out in COB 6.7.40. If a firm fails to send a post-sale notice then a customer may cancel the agreement at any time within two years of the agreement and will not be liable for any shortfall. A notice of cancellation is required to cancel the agreement and is valid if sent by post or in any other manner that the firm has told the customer is acceptable. The notice of cancellation will be valid if it is served on the firm or its appointed representative or agent of the firm with authority to accept notice on the firm's behalf. A firm must treat any notice of cancellation sent by prepaid post as being served on the date it was posted (COB 6.7.44). Unless the firm has clear written evidence to the contrary, it must treat the date cited by the customer as being the date when the notice was posted or otherwise sent. In accordance with the other provisions of COB relating to record keeping, any notice of cancellation of withdrawal which has been served on a firm must be kept for the same period as stated in other matters relating to record keeping. A firm is not bound to accept a notice of cancellation (if it has sent a post-sale notice) if the notice of cancellation is served later than the period specified for that agreement in COB 6.7.10. Also it need not accept a notice of cancellation in respect of pension annuity if the life assured under it has died before notice is given. In the case of joint policyholders, the cancellation by one of several policyholders is valid if that person has the right to cancel, irrespective of whether the policyholder is exercising that right alone or jointly on behalf of all the policyholders (COB 6.7.50).

10.7.10.8 *Result of cancellation*
In exercising the right of cancellation a customer is deemed to withdraw from the investment agreement and the entire agreement or, if applicable,

the variation is rescinded. If a customer has exercised the right to cancel under COB 6.7.7 the firm must pay to the customer any sums which he has paid to the firm in connection with the agreement, and the firm receives any property that has become the customer's under the agreement plus any sum which the firm has paid under the agreement. In the case of a pension transfer or a pension annuity, the payment is made not to the customer but for the benefit of the customer (COB 6.7.52). As the sums due both to the customer and firm are simple contract debts each party has the right of set off against the other. In the event that between the entry into the agreement and the end of the cancellation period the market falls, the firm is entitled to charge to the customer for the market loss that the firm would incur cancelling any investment agreement (COB 6.7.54). COB 6.7.55 gives a worked example of the process relating to shortfall, and exceptions to shortfall are set out in COB 6.7.56. The table in COB 6.7.7 deals with investment agreements which are subject to shortfall and the table in COB 6.7.58 sets out the method of calculation of such a shortfall.

10.7.11   With profits guide

10.7.11.1   Application
COB 6.9 relates to life offices which issue with profits life policies. The purpose of rule 6.9 is once again to enforce the firm's obligations under Principle 7 which requires the firm to pay due regard to the information needs of its customers and communicate with them in a way which is clear, fair and not misleading. It is deemed desirable in the case of with profits policies for customers and their advisers to have additional information available to them in order that they can better understand how the life office is likely to make decisions concerning distribution of profits and the declaration of bonuses.

10.7.11.2   With profits guide
Every firm which issues with profit policies must produce a with profits guide, where the firm is a life office (other than a friendly society), a directive friendly society that is carrying on long-term insurance business (other than industrial assurance business) or a friendly society which issues Holloway sickness policies. If details of the fund's expenses and asset distribution are not published elsewhere at least annually then, in accordance with COB 6.9.4, a firm must within eight months of its financial year end produce a separate and self-contained guide for each with profits fund that it maintains. It must also revise any such guide as soon as reasonably practicable after a change in the circumstances of or effecting the with profits fund which would cause the guide to become

misleading or incomplete. It must also ensure that each guide is consistent with the information contained in its annual prudential regulatory returns and contains the information set out in COB 6.9.6 dealing with the contents of with profit guides. If a life office is asked to supply a with profits guide for a fund that it maintains, it must do so free of charge. It must be the latest version unless a specific earlier version has been requested (COB 6.9.5).

10.7.11.3   Contents

COB 6.9.6 sets out the contents of with profit guides which must contain headings tables and information subscribed in the table set out in COB 6.9.7. The lettered sections and tables must appear in the order set out in the tables in COB 6.9.7 but the information may be provided in a different order. Prescribed text set out in COB 6.9.7 must be used, with any text in brackets being replaced by appropriate text applicable to the firm and the with profits policies to which the guide relates, and it must be modified if the firm considers it inappropriate to the fund or the aspects of it being explained. A firm is permitted to omit or alter the lettering and numbers of the headings, sections and paragraphs. The guidance notes must not be included. In preparing information for inclusion in a with profits guide a firm must have regard to any relevant guidance published by the Institute of Actuaries or the Faculty of Actuaries or both jointly. The table set out in COB 6.9.7 relating to the form of the with profits guide is comprehensive and detailed and must be followed absolutely unless variations are permitted under COB 6.9.6.

10.8   Conflict of interest and material interest

10.8.1   Dealing and managing

10.8.1.1   Conflicts of interest

Principle 8 imposes an obligation on service to manage contracts of interest in a fair manner. If a firm has a conflict of interest between itself and a customer or between one customer and another, COB 7.1.1 requires the firm to pay due regard to the interest of each customer and manage the conflict of interest fairly. COB 7.1.3 imposes an obligation of fair treatment in that a firm should not "knowingly advise or deal in the exercise of discretion, in relation to a transaction unless it takes reasonable steps to ensure fair treatment for the customer" (COB 7.1.3). The guidance sets out the steps that a firm may take to deal with a conflict of interest by either disclosing the interest to the customer, relying on a policy of independence, relying on Chinese Walls, or declining to act for a customer.

10.8.1.2   Broker funds
Most of this section relates to dealings on behalf of customers, but it is important to note that in relation to broker fund advisers COB 7.1.10 applies whereby a broker fund adviser, acting for a private customer, must obtain an acknowledgment from the private customer stating that he, the private customer, understands the nature of the firm's dual role as adviser to the private customer and adviser to the life office or operator of the fund in question (COB 7.1.10).

10.8.1.3   Churning
COB 7.2 deals with churning and switching. The guidance in COB 7.2.2 points out that Principle 6 requires a firm to pay due regard to the interests of its customers and to treat them fairly and, therefore, a firm should not "churn" a customer's account (i.e. enter into transactions with unnecessary frequency having regard to the customer's agreed investment strategy). A firm should not switch a private customer with or between packaged products unnecessarily having regard to what is suitable for that customer. At all times customers" interests are paramount.

10.8.1.4   Best execution
COB 7.5 deals with the best execution rule. This follows Principles 2 and 6 which require a firm to act with due skill, care and diligence and to have due regard to the customer's interest. The purpose of COB 7.5 is to set out standards for the firms when executing current customers" orders and designated investment. This does not apply to the purchase of a life policy or the purchase or sale of units in a regulated collective investment scheme from the operator of that scheme. It does apply if the customer is the trustee of an occupational pension scheme or an OPS collective investment scheme, or is a trustee of any other trust to the extent that the firm acts as a permitted third party. COB 7.5.5 sets out the rule relating to best execution. This rule states that reasonable care must be taken by a firm to ascertain the price which is the best available for the customer order in the relevant market at the time for transactions of the kind and size concerned, and the firm should execute the customer order to a price which is not less advantageous to the customer. COB 7.5.6 sets out the standard applicable to a firm taking "reasonable care" and deals *inter alia* with matters such as the disclosure of charges and commission.

10.8.1.5 Lending

COB 7.9 covers lending to private customers which would include lending to policyholders based on the surrender value of their policies. COB 7.9.3 sets out restrictions on lending to private customers and includes the fact that the firm has made and recorded an assessment of the private customer's financial standing based on information disclosed by that customer. It also has to take reasonable steps to ensure that the arrangement for the loan and the amount concerned are suitable. The private customer has to give his written consent to both the maximum amount of the loan and the amount or basis of any interest or fees to be levied in connection with the loan. COB 7.9.7 again requires a record to be kept and this must be retained for three years from the date on which the loan arrangement ceases.

10.8.2 Reporting to customers

COB 8.1 imposes an obligation on firms to confirm transactions in designated investments for customers. However, the rules do not apply when:

(a) the designated investment is a life policy or a personal pension contract; or

(b) an arrangement is in place for the customer to make a series of payments for the purchase of units in a regulated collective investment scheme;

(c) or a firm has been requested by the customer in writing not to supply confirmation.

A firm which is not an OPS firm may only rely on the exceptions in COB 8.1.6 if it provides periodic statements to its customers containing the information set out in the table in COB 8.2.10.

10.9 Operators of collective investment schemes

10.9.1 Application

COB 10.1 applies to firms which are operators of collective investment schemes, and the table in COB 10.1.2 sets out the types of firms and the sections of COB 10 which apply. It should be noted that operators are also required to comply with the other relevant provisions of the FSA Handbook including:

- principles for business;
- senior management arrangements;
- systems and controls;
- financial promotion;
- holding of clients' money;
- the collective investment schemes sourcebook; and
- money laundering.

The purpose of this Chapter of COB is to take into existence other legislation and rules that apply to operators and to adapt them or to supply them so that conflicts between the rules and duplication of rules are avoided. It also modifies the operation of certain COB rules.

10.9.2 Tables

The application of the general COB rules for operators of collective investment schemes are set out in a table in COB 10.2.5.

10.9.3 Scheme documents

The table in COB 10.6.8 sets out the content of scheme documents which are required in relation to under-regulated collective investment schemes. Reference should be made to the Collective Investment Scheme sourcebook in dealing with this matter. Operators of unregulated collective investment schemes must provide periodic statements which contain adequate information on the value and composition of the portfolio of the scheme, and the full details of what should be contained in these periodic statements is set out in COB 10.7.7 to COB 10.7.10.

10.10 Trustee and depository activities

10.10.1 Applications

COB 11 applies to depositories which include trustees of authorised and unauthorised unit trust schemes as well as depositories of ICVCs. Trustees are defined as any trustee firm which carries on an activity as a trustee but does not include OPS firms. It is acknowledged in the guidance to COB 11 that there is an overlap between these definitions and, for example, a trustee of an authorised unit trust scheme is both a trustee firm and a depository. It is also pointed out that a trustee firm will include the firm acting as a personal representative. Trustee firms may include individuals who require authorisations and who are within the definition of a trustee firm. Also included are partnerships where the partnership requires authorisation. It is pointed out in COB 11.1.8 that the rules in COB 11 are in addition to any other duties or powers imposed or conferred upon a trustee by the general law and do not qualify or restrict these duties or powers that the general law imposes (COB 11).

A depository must treat any regulated collective investment scheme of which it is a depository as a private customer for the purposes of the COB rules. In respect of an unregulated collective investment scheme of which it is a depository, the scheme is treated as an intermediate customer. In relation to polarisation COB 11.3.1 provides that a trustee firm must not arrange for the purchase of a packaged product unless the trustee firm has taken reasonable steps to ensure that the packaged product will secure the investment objectives of the trust of which it is a trustee at least as well as any other generally available packaged product of which it is or reasonably should be aware.

10.10.2   Tables

COB 11.4 sets out in a table the rules which apply to depositories, and COB 11.5 sets out the COB rules which apply to a trustee firm which is not a depository.

10.10.3   Permitted third parties

A trustee firm may not appoint a permitted third party ("PTP") unless it could not reasonably be expected to discharge the responsibility itself. Any such appointment or delegation must be made in writing and describe in detail the regulated activities to be carried on by the PTP and state that the arrangement is a PTP arrangement for the purposes of COB 11.6. The PTP must undertake in writing to the trustee firm to comply with all the rules related to the regulated activity, and also the PTP must be an appropriate person to perform the regulated activity.

10.10.4   Trustee

Where a trustee firm has appointed a PTP in accordance with COB 11.6, a trustee will not be responsible for compliance by the PTP with any rules relating to any regulated activity which the PTP carries out on behalf of the trustee firm. This means that the trustee firm is not liable for the acts or defaults of the PTP in respect of the regulated activities concerned. A trustee firm must notify the FSA within 14 days of it delegating any regulated activity to a PTP and the notification must include the identity of the PTP (COB 11.6.6). It is pointed out in the guidance in COB 11.6.9 that the rules permitting the use of PTPs do not absolve the trustee firm from the need to comply with restrictions on delegation derived from trust law or from a trust instrument. Also, the rules do not affect the trustee's firm's position under the general law including the law of agency. Any PTP appointments must be recorded and the record must be kept for three years.

10.10.5 Proper advice

Under COB 11.8 a trustee firm must obtain and consider proper advice when it intends to exercise its power of investment except where there are reasonable grounds for not doing so (COB 11.8.1). Proper advice is defined as advice from a person who is able to give it competently. It is not necessary to obtain this proper advice where there are reasonable grounds not to do so, for example if the trustee firm is itself appropriately qualified to make the particular investment decision. Under COB 11.8.5 a trustee firm must follow the proper advice received unless it is reasonable for it not to do so. Any proper advice which is obtained must be recorded and such records must be retained for three years from the date on which the advice is received.

10.11   Breach of the Rules

A breach of the Rules of COB will be dealt with under the Act and could lead to the payment of compensation to a customer and/or fines levied by the FSA on the firm in breach. The indications are that after the transition period, the FSA will take a hard line on breaches of the various Code Books that it produces.

The FSA has produced an enforcement manual which sets out the new enforcement powers derived from the Act. These powers are wider than any single body had under the previous regime. The FSA has exclusive powers to obtain information relating to rule breaches ranging from informal requests for information through to formal enquiries and formal investigations.

The FSA's enforcement powers include the imposition of a fine on or the public censure of a firm. The powers also extend to approved persons for "misconduct" where that person has been knowingly concerned in the firm's breach. The policy on circumstances in which the FSA will seek a fine or the factors it will take into account appear in Chapter 13 of the

Enforcement Manual. In addition, the FSA can impose a restitution order to require a firm to compensate investors who have suffered losses from its breach.

The above are just a few examples of the enforcement powers which may apply in the event of a breach of COB.

10.12   Conclusion

The COB Rules have been produced by the FSA with a view to "providing firms with sufficient flexibility to develop new products, services and delivery mechanisms". In order to maintain this flexibility the FSA intends to be responsive to market developments. For example, at the time of writing the Baird Report on the handling of the Equitable Life problem by the FSA has just been published; this may well lead to regulatory changes of various procedures. The FSA has stated that it intends to exercise its powers under the Act to modify its rules, or grant waivers from them, if they are putting unnecessary constraints on innovation. Therefore, it is essential for practitioners in the life industry to monitor and be aware of any amendments or changes that the FSA makes from time to time.

Chapter 11

The Regulation of Friendly Societies

John Gilbert
Partner
Lovells

11.1   The nature and types of friendly societies

Although friendly societies resemble mutual insurance companies in many ways, they are a fundamentally different type of legal entity which, until N2, were also regulated by different regulators (i.e. the Friendly Societies Commission in relation to prudential regulation, and the Chief Registrar of Friendly Societies in relation to the registration of rules), operating under different statutes and rules. N2 saw the disappearance of the separate regulators for friendly societies. Nevertheless, friendly societies continue to be subject to their own distinct regulatory regime with their own interim prudential sourcebook. Furthermore, the constitutional differences which derive from their separate legal status still remain and the FSA, as successor to the Friendly Societies Commission, has taken on the function of superintending the constitutional affairs of friendly societies. This means that the FSA has even wider responsibilities in relation to friendly societies than in relation to other firms that it regulates.

The modern form of friendly society has been in existence for a little over 200 years. Until the advent of the Friendly Societies Act 1992, all friendly societies were unincorporated associations without a separate legal personality. Although the Friendly Societies Act 1992 prohibited the formation of new unincorporated friendly societies, it did not require existing societies to incorporate and the majority of friendly societies therefore remain unincorporated. They are usually referred to as "registered societies" and this term will be used for them in this Chapter. As unincorporated associations, registered societies cannot themselves own property. The assets of registered societies are therefore held by trustees on behalf of the membership. Registered friendly societies are specifically included in the categories of legal entities which can meet the threshold conditions for the grant of permission under paragraph 1(1) of Schedule 6 to the Financial Services and Markets Act 2000 ("FSMA") and fall within the definition of "firms" for the purposes of the FSA's rules.

Registered societies may take the form of "orders", that is societies with separately registered branches. Orders are relatively rare and their special regulatory position under the FSMA 2000 and the FSA's rules will not be considered further in this Guide.

The FSA rules distinguish between directive friendly societies (i.e. those to which the EC Insurance Directives apply – broadly, societies carrying on long-term business whose annual gross premium income equals or exceeds €500,000 or societies carrying on general business whose annual gross premium income equals or exceeds €1 million) and non directive friendly societies. Although there are a large number of non-directive friendly societies still in existence, all of which are registered societies, they are, by definition, small and are disregarded in this Guide.

Since the coming into force of Part II of the Friendly Societies Act 1992 on 1 February 1993, it has been possible for friendly societies to incorporate and since that date all new friendly societies have been required to be formed as incorporated societies. As at 31 March 2001 there were 40 incorporated societies. These are mostly the larger societies but there are still some very significant registered societies (for example, the Ancient Order of Foresters Friendly Society and the Independent Order of Odd Fellows Manchester Unity Friendly Society each have over £100 million under management and around 100,000 members).

Like all modern bodies corporate, incorporated friendly societies derive their legal existence from statute and their capacity and powers are defined by statute. In the case of incorporated friendly societies the relevant statute is the Friendly Societies Act 1992. It is important to note that the Companies Acts have no relevance to incorporated friendly societies (except to the extent that the decisions of the courts on provisions of the Companies Acts may apply to analogous provisions in the Friendly Societies Act 1992).

Finally, it should be mentioned that until N2 the Chief Registrar of Friendly Societies was responsible for the registration not only of friendly societies but also of industrial and provident societies and certain working men's clubs as well a miscellaneous collection of cattle insurance societies, benevolent societies and old people's home societies. This responsibility has also been taken over by the FSA under Part XXI of the FSMA 2000. Although the involvement of the Chief Registrar of Friendly Societies in their registration has often led to this hotchpotch of other societies being confused with friendly societies (and the confusion has not been helped by certain provisions of the Friendly Societies Act 1974 applying to some of these types of societies), these bodies are not friendly societies and any regulated activities they may undertake fall outside the scope of this Chapter.

11.2   Sources of law

The Friendly Societies Act 1974 has been substantially repealed and amended. However, the remaining provisions contain the principal source of law on the constitution, powers and registration of registered friendly societies.

Before N2 the Friendly Societies Act 1992 had two principal functions:

(a)   as the statute governing the corporate existence and administration of incorporated friendly societies and containing miscellaneous provisions relating to both incorporated and registered societies; and

(b)   as the statute governing the prudential regulation of both incorporated and registered societies.

The matters dealt with in relation to the corporate existence, administration and miscellaneous matters are:

(a)   the formation, constitution, capacity and powers and winding up of incorporated friendly societies (Part II);

(b)   the internal management and administration of both incorporated and registered societies (Part III);

(c)   accounting matters and audit (Part VI);

(d)   the handling of disputes (Part VII); and

(e)   amalgamations and portfolio transfers (Part VIII).

Other parts of the Friendly Societies Act 1992 dealt with the prudential supervision of societies' insurance business (for example, Part I dealt with the establishment of the pre-N2 regulator, the Friendly Societies Commission; Part IV dealt with the authorisation of friendly societies to conduct insurance business; and Part V dealt with actuarial matters, the criteria of prudent management and the powers of the Friendly Societies Commission to investigate societies and to intervene in their affairs).

Most, but not all, of these regulatory provisions were repealed on N2 but there remains some overlap between sections of the Friendly Societies Act 1992 which relate to what may broadly be described as "regulatory" matters which have not been repealed on the one hand and new provisions under the FSMA 2000 and the FSA's rules on the other hand (for example, those relating to accounting records and systems of business control under Section 68, Friendly Societies Act 1992 and under IPRU(FSOC) 3.1 discussed in 11.4.5 below).

In considering the regulation of friendly societies it is therefore necessary not only to look at the FSMA 2000 and the FSA Handbook, but also to consider whether any provisions of the Friendly Societies Act 1992 (or any subordinate legislation made under the 1992 Act) are relevant either because of some constitutional limitation on friendly societies or because of some residual regulatory provision. To complicate matters further, the Financial Services and Markets Act 2000 (Mutual Societies) Order 2001 (SI 2001/2617) contains substantial amendments to the Friendly Societies Acts 1974 and 1992 and disapplies a large number of provisions which escaped repeal in the FSMA 2000. The amendments made under the Financial Services and Markets Act 2000 (Mutual Societies) Order 2001 are thus in addition to the amendments to both Acts contained in Schedule 18 to the FSMA 2000 and the repeals of parts of both the Friendly Societies Act 1974 and the Friendly Societies Act 1992 contained in Schedule 22 to the FSMA 2000. It would have been far less confusing if all these amendments and repeals had been enacted by a single piece of legislation and kept in the same place.

Friendly societies, as authorised persons under the FSMA 2000, are subject to the general rules of the FSA to the extent that they are relevant to friendly societies' business, in the same way as insurance companies. However, by virtue of paragraph 1.1(a) of the *Interim Prudential Sourcebook for Insurers* ("IPRU(INS)"), that sourcebook does not apply to friendly societies. Also, the regime for insurance business transfers under Part VII of the FSMA 2000 does not apply to friendly societies (case 1 of subsection 105(3) of the FSMA 2000). The regime for business transfers by friendly societies (known as "transfers of engagements") is dealt with in further detail in 11.8 below.

A separate interim prudential sourcebook (part IPRU(FSOC) of the FSA Handbook) applies to friendly societies. This largely reproduces, with some amendments, the repealed sections of the Friendly Societies Act 1992 which contained regulatory provisions and certain practice notes from the series of "Commission Practice Notes" issued by the Friendly

Societies Commission under the Friendly Societies Act 1992 between 1992 and N2. Therefore, many of the features of the separate regulatory regime for friendly societies, which distinguished the regulatory treatment of friendly societies from that of insurance companies, have been preserved under the FSA Handbook and will remain in place until the interim prudential sourcebooks are replaced by the proposed *Integrated Prudential Sourcebook* embodying a risk based regime of prudential supervision for all regulated bodies as envisaged in the FSA's consultation paper CP31, "The FSA's Approach to Setting Prudential Standards", published in November 1999.

Before N2 the Friendly Societies Commission issued guidance to friendly societies under the series of Commission Practice Notes (referred to above) and a series of Chief Executive Letters. These were originally included as FSA guidance in the first draft of the *Interim Prudential Sourcebook for Friendly Societies* issued for consultation in January 2000, but most were dropped from the final version of IPRU(FSOC) which came into effect on N2. Nevertheless, the pre-N2 guidance has become part of the regulatory ethos for friendly societies (both on the part of societies themselves and on the part of regulators) and may continue to influence societies' behaviour and regulators' decisions after N2. Certain other Commission Practice Notes have been incorporated as annexes to IPRU(FSOC) where they have the status of guidance issued by the FSA under Section 157 of the FSMA 2000. These annexes cover:

(a) officers' liability insurance;
(b) accounting records, systems of control and inspection and report, and systems of control over investments;
(c) margins of solvency and the minimum guarantee fund;
(d) exemptions from triennial valuations; and
(e) the use of derivative contracts by directive friendly societies.

11.3   The constitution of friendly societies – general

An incorporated friendly society may only be established for the limited purposes ("purposes" being the friendly society equivalent to the "objects" of a company formed under the Companies Acts) set out or referred to in Section 5 of the Friendly Societies Act 1992, and a registered society may only remain registered for the purposes referred to in Section 7(1)(a) of the Friendly Societies Act 1974. The purposes of an incorporated friendly society are set out its "memorandum" (the equivalent of a company's memorandum of association) and the manner in which it is administered is set out in its "rules" (the equivalent of articles of association). Registered friendly societies have a single constitutional document, known as the society's "rules", dealing with both purposes and administration.

The principal purposes, for both incorporated and registered societies, are the carrying out of the insurance and other activities set out in Schedule 2 to the Friendly Societies Act 1992 (discussed in 11.4.1 below). In addition, incorporated friendly societies may:

(a)   include within their purposes social or benevolent activities under Section 10 of the Friendly Societies Act 1992 (*see* 11.4.2 below);
(b)   undertake group insurance business under Section 11 of the Friendly Societies Act 1992 (*see* 11.4.3 below);
(c)   undertake reinsurance under Section 12 of the Friendly Societies Act 1992 (*see* 11.4.4 below); and
(d)   control or jointly control bodies corporate under Section 13 of the Friendly Societies Act 1992 (*see* 11.4.5 below).

As is the case with companies incorporated under the Companies Acts, the Friendly Societies Act 1992 draws a distinction between the purposes for which an incorporated friendly society exists and the powers by which it may carry out its purposes. The powers available to incorporated friendly societies are considered in paragraph 11.5 below.

The memorandum and rules of an incorporated friendly society are binding on the members and officers of the society and on all persons claiming on account of members or under the society's rules, all of whom are deemed to have notice of the provisions of the memorandum and rules. Third parties are not bound by the permitted capacity of societies or by any limitation on the powers of the committee of management. Sections 8 and 9 of the Friendly Societies Act 1992 contain protections for third parties dealing with incorporated friendly societies in good faith analogous to the protections for third parties dealing with companies under Sections 35 and 35A of the Companies Act 1985. The burden of proving that an act was beyond the capacity of the society or outside the powers of the committee of management lies with the person making the allegation. However, there is no provision equivalent to Section 35A(2)(b) of the Companies Act 1985 under which a person is not to be regarded as acting in bad faith by reason only of knowing that an act is beyond the powers of the directors of a company. Under Section 9(7) of the Friendly Societies Act 1992 an act by the committee of management of a friendly society which is beyond its powers may be ratified by members in general meeting if the act was within the capacity of the society but acts which are outside a society's purposes cannot be ratified. Thus, the law on the purposes and powers of an incorporated friendly society resembles the common law position on the objects and powers of companies prior to the amendments made by the Companies Act 1989.

11.4 The purposes of friendly societies

11.4.1 Principal purposes

Although they may carry out other activities, friendly societies must carry out at least one of the activities set out in Schedule 2 to the Friendly Societies Act 1992. In the case of incorporated friendly societies, these activities must be "carried on by the society with a view to the provision, for its members and such persons connected with its members as may be prescribed by its rules, of insurance or other benefits" (Section 5(2)(b)(i) of the Friendly Societies Act 1992). With the exception of group insurance business (which is discussed below), friendly societies are thus required only to insure members and persons connected with them (typically family members). Although there does not appear to be any justification for this view in the legislation, the Friendly Societies Commission took the view that the corollary also applied (i.e. that the only persons who could become members of incorporated friendly societies were persons who receive, or were eligible to receive, benefits from the society). In particular, it indicated that it would not be prepared to permit an incorporated society to amend its rules to allow persons who were clients of the society's subsidiaries to become members of the society unless they also undertook a permitted activity with the society itself. Whether the FSA will continue to take the same view remains to be seen.

The principal activities set out in Schedule 2 to the Friendly Societies Act 1992 include various classes of long-term and general insurance business. It should be noted that the classes of insurance business permitted for friendly societies are more restrictive than those permitted for insurance companies under Schedule 1 to the Financial Services and Markets Act 2000 (Regulated Activities) Order 2001. For long-term business (Head A in Schedule 2 to the Friendly Societies Act 1992) the only classes omitted are classes VIII (collective insurance) and IX (social insurance), which are of scant relevance to UK insurers in any event. However, for general business (Head B in Schedule 2 to the Friendly Societies Act 1992), most of the classes available to general insurance companies are unavailable to friendly societies, leaving only classes 1 (accident), 2 (sickness) and 3 (miscellaneous financial loss) available to friendly societies which carry out general business.

It should be noted that although the range of insurance business open to friendly societies themselves is limited, groups headed by incorporated friendly societies may carry out the full range of long-term and general business permitted under the Financial Services and Markets Act 2000 (Regulated Activities) Order 2001 through subsidiaries which are insurance companies. Although the Friendly Societies Act 1992 speaks, somewhat curiously, of the purposes for which a friendly society may be *established*, the same limitations will apply to any amendments to the purposes of an existing friendly society.

Unlike the corresponding schedule to the Financial Services and Markets Act 2000 (Regulated Activities) Order 2001 (Schedule 1), Schedule 2 to the Friendly Societies Act 1992 includes among the permitted purposes of friendly societies certain non-insurance activities. Head C of Schedule 2 allows payments to be made "for the relief or maintenance of any person during sickness or when in distressed circumstances" and to meet funeral expenses, whether or not a contract to provide these benefits constitutes insurance business. (The only activity under Head C which is regulated under the Financial Services and Markets Act 2000 (Regulated Activities) Order 2001 is flat-rate benefits business.) Head D of Schedule 2 allows discretionary benefits to be paid for education, for relief and maintenance during sickness, unemployment or "distressed circumstances" and also for the payment of funeral expenses. Heads C and D of Schedule 2 to the Friendly Societies Act 1992 also apply to registered societies by virtue of Section 7(1)(a) of the Friendly Societies Act 1974 in the same way as they apply to incorporated friendly societies.

11.4.2 Social and benevolent activities

As well as having the capacity to take part in these specific activities, incorporated friendly societies are also given the capacity under Section 10 of the Friendly Societies Act 1992 to include among their purposes the carrying on of any "social or benevolent activity" which is not inconsistent with the other purposes of the society. "Benevolent activity" is widely defined to mean the making of donations, the raising of funds, or any other activity carried on for a charitable purpose or for any other benevolent purpose.

Section 10 of the Friendly Societies Act 1992 applies only to incorporated societies, although registered societies do commonly undertake social and benevolent activities. Indeed, such activities are a large part of the rationale of certain registered societies. Registered societies are unincorporated associations of natural persons and therefore do not need statutory powers to undertake each of their activities in order that those activities should be intra vires.

11.4.3 Group insurance business

Under Section 11 of the Friendly Societies Act 1992 incorporated friendly societies are permitted to carry out group insurance business. Group business is an exception to the rule under Section 5(2)(b)(i) of the Friendly Societies Act 1992 that friendly societies must carry out their insurance and other activities with a view to providing benefits to members and persons connected with members. Participants in a group scheme need not be members of the society but the society may (but is not obliged to) allow for a representative of the group to be a member of the society. Friendly societies are subject to a rule prohibiting voting rights being weighted according to the amount of subscriptions (see paragraph 5 of Schedule 12 to the Friendly Societies Act 1992), which may be construed as preventing the representative of a group scheme having any more votes than ordinary members – although it should be possible, if so desired, to avoid this effect by careful drafting.

The parties for which group schemes can be established are employees of a particular employer and other groups prescribed in regulations made under Section 11(7) of the Friendly Societies Act 1992. To date, the only groups prescribed in regulations (The Friendly Societies (Group Schemes) Regulations 1993 (SI 1993/59) are sports clubs and clubs for the provision of recreation or other leisure time activities.

Section 55 of the Friendly Societies Act 1992 gives the FSA powers of intervention if it believes that the group insurance business conducted by a friendly society is disproportionate to the other activities of the society.

Registered friendly societies are also able to undertake group business under Section 65A of the Friendly Societies Act 1974, which is substantially the same as Section 11 of the Friendly Societies Act 1992. Groups prescribed under Section 11(7) of the Friendly Societies Act 1992 are valid for registered societies by virtue of Section 65A(8) of the Friendly Societies Act 1974. Section 55 and paragraph 5 in Schedule 12 to the Friendly Societies Act 1992 apply to both registered and incorporated friendly societies.

11.4.4 Reinsurance

A further purpose of incorporated friendly societies is the reinsurance of risks insured by another friendly society. In order to conduct reinsurance business a friendly society must obtain the approval of its appropriate actuary and ensure that the risks reinsured are of a class or part of a class which the society itself carries on. Registered friendly societies are also permitted to reinsure risks underwritten by other friendly societies (whether registered or incorporated) under part 23A of the Friendly Societies Act 1974. It is important to note that in both cases inward reinsurance may only be carried out for risks underwritten by another friendly society and not for risks underwritten by an insurance company. However, incorporated friendly societies are permitted under Section 16 of the Friendly Societies Act 1992 to provide a wide range of services to their subsidiaries and jointly controlled bodies including "the use of services", "grants of money" and "guarantees for the discharge of their liabilities". These powers allow incorporated friendly societies to provide services to their subsidiaries with similar commercial effects to reinsurance services. However, see the commentary on rule IPRU(FSOC) 1.3(1) in paragraph 11.6 below in relation to the requirement for payment for these services not to be on a commercial footing.

11.4.5 Control or joint control of bodies corporate

Incorporated societies may also take part, as one of their purposes under Section 13 of the Friendly Societies Act 1992, in forming, acquiring or holding "controlled bodies" (also referred to in the legislation as "subsidiaries") and "jointly controlled bodies" (i.e. joint ventures with other organisations). The purposes of forming, acquiring or holding subsidiaries or jointly controlled bodies must be specifically adopted by incorporated friendly societies in their memoranda. The adoption (and any amendment to) the relevant purpose must be by special resolution as required by Section 13(6) of the Friendly Societies Act 1992. All other amendments to a friendly society's constitution may be made in the manner set out in the society's constitution (i.e. usually by ordinary resolution – *see* paragraph 11.7 below). Until N2 the Friendly Societies Act 1992 contained strict limitations on the activities of a subsidiary or jointly controlled body of an incorporated friendly society, the jurisdictions in which such bodies could be incorporated, the structure of a group headed by an incorporated friendly society, and the persons with whom jointly controlled bodies could be held.

The test of "control" in Section 13(9) of the Friendly Societies Act 1992, as supplemented by Schedule 8, is the same as the test used in the definition of subsidiary in Section 736, Companies Act 1985. A similar test applies to "joint control", which arises where an incorporated friendly society and any other person together have control "in pursuance of an agreement or other arrangement between them". This means that most joint venture agreements and any investment in a company subject to a shareholders' agreement will be caught as an investment in a "jointly controlled body". However, investments in limited partnerships would not normally be caught (even if the limited partnership itself is a body corporate) unless the friendly society invests through a corporate vehicle or the friendly society or one of its subsidiaries controls the general partner.

The powers of the FSA in relation to groups consisting of incorporated friendly societies and their subsidiaries is distinguished from the regulation of groups headed by a company formed under the Companies Act by the power of the FSA under Section 54 of the Friendly Societies Act 1992 to intervene if it appears to the FSA that the activities of subsidiaries of the society (or of bodies jointly controlled by it) "are or may become disproportionate" to those of the friendly society group as a whole. In these circumstance, the FSA has power to direct the society to take steps to ensure that the activities cease to be or do not become disproportionate, or to dispose of the offending subsidiary or jointly controlled body or to wind it up. These apparently draconian powers, which also were vested in the Friendly Societies Commission before N2, have never been used. The friendly societies movement did ask the government to consider repealing them under the FSMA 2000 at the same time that they requested the repeal of the other limitations on subsidiaries. However, the government declined to repeal Section 54, which suggests that these powers are regarded as an important tool for the regulation of friendly societies and that the FSA may consider invoking them in the future.

A further distinguishing feature is that by virtue of Section 68(10) of the Friendly Societies Act 1992, the requirements of Section 68 with regard to accounting records apply equally to subsidiaries and jointly controlled bodies as they do to friendly societies themselves regardless of whether the subsidiaries carry on regulated activities. The requirements under Section 68 were significantly modified on N2 by the removal of references to systems of business control and systems of inspection and report, and do not now impose significantly greater burdens with regard to the keeping of accounting records than apply to companies under the Companies Act 1985. The former Section 68 requirements on systems of business control and inspection and report have been reimposed on friendly societies and registered branches under IPRU(FSOC) 3.1, but not in relation to subsidiaries or jointly controlled bodies. As a result of these changes, friendly societies are still required under Section 68(11) of the Friendly Societies Act 1992 to send the FSA a statement of their compliance with the requirements of Section 68 (which will include a statement in respect of their subsidiaries even if the subsidiaries undertake no regulated activities). Section 68 statements must be submitted within six months of the beginning of each financial year. (Since friendly societies are required by Section 118 of the Friendly Societies Act 1992 to have financial years which are coterminous with calendar years, this means by 30 June each year.) The former requirement which applied pre N2 under Section 79 of the Friendly Societies Act 1992 for auditors of friendly societies to report on compliance with Section 68 has been disapplied under Article 13(1) of the Financial Services and Markets Act 2000 (Mutual Societies) Order 2001. Although it did reappear in the version of IPRU(FSOC) published by the FSA as late as July 2001, it has also been deleted from the final text of IPRU(FSOC) which came into force on N2.

11.5 The powers of friendly societies

While the purposes available to incorporated friendly societies may be restricted when compared with the objects available to companies incorporated under the Companies Acts, incorporated friendly societies may adopt wide-ranging powers. These powers fall into a number of distinct categories:

(a) the power to undertake various miscellaneous activities set out in Schedule 5 to the Friendly Societies Act 1992 (*see* 11.5.1 below);

(b) the powers which incorporated friendly societies may adopt under Section 7(3) of the Friendly Societies Act 1992 which are specifically referred to in Part II of that Act (*see* 11.5.2 below);

(c) the "catch all" power in Section 7(4) of the Friendly Societies Act 1992 to do anything else which is "incidental or conducive" to the carrying out of the society's purposes or to the activities in Schedule 5 – subject always to the other provisions of the Friendly Societies Act 1992 and the society's memorandum and rules. This "catch all" power does not have to be specifically adopted by a friendly society, but most incorporated friendly societies do refer to it in their memoranda and rules.

The specific powers which may be adopted under Section 7(3) may only be exercised for the carrying out of the society's purposes and the "catch all" power also relates only to actions for carrying out the purposes of the society or for carrying out activities which fall within Schedule 5.

There are no equivalent provisions to the powers of incorporated friendly societies in the Friendly Societies Act 1974 in relation to registered societies. Registered societies, as unincorporated associations of natural persons, have unlimited legal capacity and powers and therefore do not need powers to be granted to them by statute.

11.5.1 *Power to undertake various miscellaneous activities*

Section 7(2) of the 1992 Act gives incorporated friendly societies power to undertake a number of miscellaneous activities set out in Schedule 5 of the Friendly Societies Act 1992. These consist of:

(a)   the acceptance of contributions and deposits from members to establish a fund out of which loans can be made to members;
(b)   the establishment of funds to purchase government securities on behalf of members;
(c)   the investment of funds in housing associations;
(d)   the accumulation of surplus contributions from members on which the society may pay interest; and
(e)   the making of subscriptions to hospitals, infirmaries and other charitable or provident institutions so that members of the society may enjoy the benefits provided by the institution.

Finally, Schedule 5 also permits incorporated friendly societies to contribute to the funds, and take part in the government, of any other friendly society (whether incorporated or not).

Although these activities might appear to be purposes, they are omitted from the list of purposes in Section 7(2) of the Friendly Societies Act 1992 and are referred to in that section as "powers". This appears anomalous in that these activities cannot be undertaken in order to carry out the society's purposes as required for other powers by Section 7(3). However, this appears to have been recognised by the reference to Schedule 5 activities in Section 7(4).

11.5.2   *Part II, Friendly Societies Act 1992 powers*

Section 14 of the Friendly Societies Act 1992 confers general investment powers on incorporated friendly societies, including the power to invest in land, other securities or other investments which are permitted for trustees. These powers are conferred on all incorporated friendly societies and need not be specifically adopted in a society's memorandum or rules. In addition, any society carrying out regulated activities may adopt whatever wider investment powers it thinks fit.

Section 15 of the Friendly Societies Act 1992 confers on incorporated friendly societies the power (again, without specifically adopting the power in its memorandum or rules) to acquire and hold land for operational purposes or for the operational purposes of a subsidiary or jointly controlled body and also to dispose of such land or otherwise to deal with it.

Section 16 of the Friendly Societies Act 1992 allows incorporated friendly societies to provide services to subsidiaries or jointly controlled bodies and also to make payments towards the discharge of the liabilities of subsidiaries (but not those of jointly controlled bodies). The services permitted under Section 16 are the making of loans of money (with or without security and whether or not at interest), the use of services or property (whether or not for payment), grants of money (whether or not repayable) and guarantees of the discharge of their liabilities. The Friendly Societies Commission has accepted that the employment by an incorporated friendly society of staff who are engaged wholly or partly on the business of subsidiaries falls within the meaning of the use of services for the purposes of Section 16. However, the services of staff (and any other services provided under Section 16) must be provided on an "at cost" or less basis (but not at a profit) to avoid a breach of what is now IPRU(FSOC) 1.3(1) (*see* 11.6 below).

A further permitted activity for incorporated societies is the making of loans to members under Section 17 of the Friendly Societies Act 1992. Although this power applies only to incorporated societies, the language of Section 17 betrays its 19th century origins. The section permits an incorporated society to:

> "advance to a member of at least one full year's standing any sum not exceeding one half of the amount of an assurance on his life, on the written security of himself and two satisfactory sureties or, in Scotland, cautioners for repayment."

The requirement for two sureties makes this power difficult to use in practice and the need for it must be questionable since the amount advanced is limited to one half of the amount which would be payable to the member's estate on death under a contract of life assurance in any event. The ability to make advances to members is attractive to many societies and some societies have considered making advances through separate subsidiaries or setting up somewhat artificial arrangements whereby the requirement to provide guarantees is satisfied by the members' entitlement to payment of life assurance proceeds being assigned to trustees who in turn provide guarantees to the society.

Like the "power" to undertake the various miscellaneous activities set out in Schedule 5, the power to make loans to members appears to be more a "purpose" than a "power". However, it does not appear in the list of purposes contained in Section 7(2) and therefore would appear to be subject to the restriction in Section 7(3) that it should only be exercised for the carrying out of the society's actual purposes. It is difficult to see how this might ever be achieved.

11.6   Combinations of business

Friendly societies are subject to a restriction on the combination of their insurance business with other activities under the equivalent of what used to be Section 16 of the Insurance Companies Act 1982 and Section 38 of the Friendly Societies Act 1992. These restrictions, as they apply to friendly societies, are now contained in IPRU(FSOC) 1.3(1) which states: "A directive friendly society must not carry on any commercial business in the United Kingdom or elsewhere other than insurance business and activities directly arising from that business."

This prohibition applies to "commercial business" whereas the old Section 16 prohibition applied to "any activities". The IPRU (INS) prohibition has now been conformed with the "commercial business" prohibition for friendly societies. The Friendly Societies Commission interpreted the phrase "commercial business" to mean "profit-making activities". These might include:

(a)   the various social and benevolent activities permitted for incorporated friendly societies under Section 10 of the Friendly Societies Act 1992;

(b)   the miscellaneous activities permitted for incorporated friendly societies under Schedule 5 to the Friendly Societies Act 1992;

(c) the provision by both incorporated and registered societies of contractual benefits under Head C and discretionary benefits under Head D of Schedule 2 to the Friendly Societies Act 1992; and

(d) in the case of incorporated societies only, the provision of support services for subsidiaries either at cost or at a price less than cost and loans to members under Section 17 of the Friendly Societies Act 1992.

The comments above apply equally to registered societies, although it should be noted that not all registered societies are directive friendly societies to which IPRU(FSOC) 1.3(1) applies. The activities of registered friendly societies are limited to the activities specified in Schedule 2 to the Friendly Societies Act 1992 by virtue of Section 7(1)(a) of the Friendly Societies Act 1974.

The prohibition on the combination of long-term business with general business (except classes 1 and 2) under AUTH 3.12.4G applies equally to friendly societies as it does to insurance companies.

11.7   The management and administration of friendly societies

The management and administration of a friendly society is entrusted to a committee of management which fulfils similar functions to the board of directors of a company. Indeed, a number of societies refer to their committee of management as a "board" and to the individual committee members as "directors". Section 27 of the Friendly Societies Act 1992 requires each society (registered as well as incorporated) to have a committee of management with at least two members. Guidance issued by the Friendly Societies Commission in CPN 1992/2 (paragraph 12) suggested that the Commission would favour a maximum number of between five and 11 depending on the size of the society and the nature of its business. Although this particular guidance has not (unlike other Commission Practice Notes) been reissued as guidance in IPRU(FSOC) and therefore ceases to apply on N2, there is no reason to think that the FSA would depart from it.

Material relating to the regulation of committees of management is contained in Section 27 and Schedule 11 to the 1992 Act. The "approved persons" rules discussed in Chapter 3 also apply to committee members, subject to certain exemptions for "small friendly societies" discussed below. Although a detailed description of fiduciary duties is outside the scope of this Chapter, it should be noted that in addition to the statutory provisions and FSA rules, the common law rules on directors' fiduciary duties are thought to apply equally to members of the committee of management of a friendly society as they do to directors of a company, as the committee of management stands in the same fiduciary relationship to the members of the society as the directors of a company do to the members of the company.

The requirements of Section 27 and Schedule 11 to the Friendly Societies Act 1992 contain a more restrictive regime for the appointment of committee members than applies to the directors of a company. A friendly society may regulate the appointment and retirement of committee members as it sees fit through its rules subject to the general requirements of the FSA Handbook and the following additional overriding provisions:

(a)   a committee member cannot be elected or re-elected if he has passed the age of 70 unless his election has been approved by resolution of the committee and the reasons for the committee's approval of his eligibility have been notified to members eligible to vote on his election;

(b)   a person who is a member of the committee of management or is nominated for election or co-option onto the committee must give 28 days notice to the society before he becomes 70 years old;

(c)   committee members must retire at the fifth annual general meeting following the date of their election and, if over 70, at each annual general meeting;

(d)   the committee of management may co-opt members but they must pass a "fit and proper" test (this requirement remains as a separate statutory requirement for friendly societies in parallel with the requirements of the FSA Handbook) and cannot be co-opted if they have been proposed for election to the committee during the previous 12 months and the motion to elect them has been defeated.

Societies may adopt in their rules an age below 70 for the purposes of the tests described in paragraphs (a) to (d) above but not a higher age.

The legislation on dealings between directors of building societies and their societies are applied to friendly societies under Part II of Schedule 11 to the Friendly Societies Act 1992 with minor variations. This is broadly similar to the legislation on dealings between directors and companies under Part X of the Companies Act 1985. It should be noted that Section 63 of the Building Societies Act 1986 on the disclosure of interests in contracts and other transactions (which applies to friendly societies by virtue of paragraph 9(1)(b) of Schedule 11 to the Friendly Societies Act 1992 and largely replicates the provisions of Section 317 of the Companies Act 1985) does not prevent a director from forming part of the quorum or voting on a contract in which he is interested so long as he declares his interest. It is commonplace for the articles of association of companies to give directors a specific power to do so in order to exonerate them from any breach of their fiduciary duties which may otherwise occur. The model memorandum and rules for friendly societies published by the Registry of Friendly Societies shortly after the enactment of the Friendly Societies Act 1992 contains prohibitions against committee members forming part of a quorum or voting on matters in which they are interested – a considerably stricter rule than that which applies to insurance companies. The Friendly Societies Commission did indicate that it would not be prepared to countenance the registration of rules which varied from the model by permitting committee members to participate in committee of management deliberations on contracts to which they are party. It remains to be seen how the FSA will react on this issue.

The approved persons regime under the FSA Handbook applies to members of the committee of management who have "governing functions" for the purposes of SUP 10.4. SUP 10.6.26 recognises a separate "controlled function" for the members of the committee of management of a non-directive friendly society. SUP 10.6.28 allows the possibility for the committee of management of a non-directive friendly society to delegate responsibility for the society's regulated activities to a single individual to whom it is reasonable to delegate that responsibility, in which case the members of the committee of management will no longer have the responsibility themselves for the purposes of the FSA Handbook. The individual to whom the responsibility is delegated need not be a member of the committee of management but will, of course, himself need to be an approved person.

The only officers that an incorporated friendly society is required to have are a chief executive and secretary (under Section 28 of the Friendly Societies Act 1992) and these offices may be held by the same person. Section 28 of the Friendly Societies Act 1992 applies equally to registered societies but registered societies are required, in addition, to have one or more trustees under Section 24 of the Friendly Societies Act 1974. The trustees will hold the assets of a registered society and, typically, under the rules of the society they will be the persons entitled to sue, or liable or be sued, on behalf of the society.

Certain decisions may be reserved under the rules or by statute for the members of the society in general meeting. Friendly societies have unusually wide scope to determine themselves under their rules which matters do require reference to a general meeting (for example, friendly societies may amend their memoranda and rules by any procedure set out in the rules) although most do so by ordinary resolution (requiring a simple majority of the votes cast) at a general meeting. Some matters are required by statute to be approved by a special resolution (requiring a minimum notice period of 14 days and approval by *not less than* 75 per cent of the votes cast, in contrast to the requirement for *more than* 75 per cent of the votes cast for special resolutions of companies). The principal regulatory matters which require members' approval by special resolution are referred to in the relevant paragraphs of this Chapter.

11.8 Mergers and transfers of engagements

Friendly societies fall outside the regime for portfolio transfers under Part VII of the Financial Services and Market Act as described in Chapter 6. This perpetuates the situation pre N2 where transfers by friendly societies were not subject to Schedule 2C to the Insurance Companies Act 1982. The procedure for portfolio transfers by friendly societies (known as "transfers of engagements") both pre and post N2 is set out in Part VIII of the Friendly Societies Act 1992 and Schedule 15 to that Act. These provisions apply to both registered and incorporated societies. Broadly speaking, the procedure is similar to the procedure which applies to insurance companies with the preparation of an independent actuary's report and a circular to members, but there are important differences. It is beyond the scope of this Guide to set out the full procedure for friendly society transfers but the principal differences between the friendly society procedure and the procedure for insurance companies are as follows:

(a)   Insurance business transfers under Part VII of the FSMA 2000 are required to be implemented by a court order. Transfers of engagements of friendly societies are implemented through the FSA confirming an "instrument of transfer of engagements" after considering any representations made to it by interested persons. The instrument of transfer then takes effect upon registration with the FSA. (See Section 86 and Schedule 15 to the Friendly Societies Act 1992.) The apparent duplication between confirmation and registration derives from the pre N2 regime when the two processes were carried out by different bodies: confirmation by the Friendly

Societies Commission and registration by the Chief Register of Friendly Societies.

(b) An insurance business transfer or transfer of engagements *to* a friendly society must be approved by the transferee friendly society by special resolution as well as by the transferor. There is no equivalent requirement in Part VII of the FSMA 2000 or in the previous regime under Schedule 2C to the Insurance Companies Act 1982 – although it was relatively common for portfolio transfers under schedule 2C to be put to members of both the transferor and the transferee insurance companies for approval.

Where the transferor and the transferee are both friendly societies, the FSA has power under Section 86(3)(b) of the Friendly Societies Act 1992 to waive the requirement for a special resolution of members of the transferee and allow the transfer of engagements to proceed on the basis of a resolution of the transferee society's committee of management. Section 86(8) of the Friendly Societies Act 1992 requires inward transfers to a friendly society from a person which is not a friendly society to be approved by a special resolution of the transferee friendly society, but there is no power for the FSA to grant exemption from this provision. [At the date of writing, the Chapter of the FSA Handbook dealing with insurance company and friendly society business transfers is still in draft form. However, the draft rules contained in the consultation paper CP110 contain guidance (paragraph 18.4.11G) on the circumstances in which the FSA proposes to use its discretion to allow a transferee friendly society to approve a transfer by resolution of the committee of management. The factors which the FSA will take into account are whether the transfer will be in the interests of the members of both societies and whether the transfer will require a "change of policy" by the transferee society. Clarification has been sought in the consultation process as to what the FSA means by a "change of policy" – it is not immediately obvious. Paragraph 18.4.11G also states that the FSA is unlikely to exercise its discretion unless the transferee is significantly larger than the business to be transferred. This is more flexible than the 10 per cent rule of thumb previously operated by the Friendly Societies Commission.]

In addition to transfers of engagements, Part VIII of the Friendly Societies Act 1992 also provides a mechanism for friendly societies to amalgamate and to convert into companies. An amalgamation of two friendly societies (whether incorporated or registered) can take place under Section 85 of the Friendly Societies Act 1992 and requires a similar procedure of:

(a)   consultation with the FSA;
(b)   the preparation of an actuary's report;
(c)   a circular to members;
(d)   confirmation of an instrument of transfer by the FSA after members and others concerned have had an opportunity to make representations; and
(e)   the registration of the successor society.

Any successor to two amalgamated societies, even if both were registered societies, must be an incorporated friendly society.

Section 90 of the Friendly Societies Act 1992 confers on the FSA power to direct a friendly society to transfer all or part of its engagements to another friendly society or to another body if the FSA considers that the transferor society is unable to manage its affairs satisfactorily in relation to the relevant business and the transfer would be expedient to protect the interests of members of the society. In the case of a compulsory transfer under section 90, the proposed transferee is required, whether or not it is a friendly society, to approve the inward transfer by special resolution. However, section 90 also gives the FSA power to consent to approval being made by a resolution of the "committee of management of the transferee", which implies that the draftsman was thinking of friendly society transferees. How this might work with a non-friendly society transferee has never been tested in practice.

Section 91 of the Friendly Societies Act 1992 contains a mechanism for friendly societies to convert into companies. Although conversions of friendly societies into companies have taken place under similar provisions in predecessor Friendly Societies Acts, no societies have taken advantage of this mechanism in recent years. The mechanism again involves a circular to members, a special resolution of the society to convert and the process of confirmation by the FSA. HM Treasury has taken over the powers formally vested in the Friendly Societies Commission to make regulations in relation to the conversion of friendly societies into companies. To date, this power has not been exercised either by the Friendly Societies Commission or by the Treasury.

It should be noted that the FSA has considerable flexibility under Section 89 of the Friendly Societies Act 1992 to modify the requirements for transfers of engagements *by* friendly societies (but not for transfers of engagements or insurance business transfers *to* friendly societies). The powers allow the FSA to waive the requirements for a special resolution by the transferor society and to modify the requirements to circularise members under Schedule 15. However, these powers may not be exercised so as to allow a friendly society to approve a transfer of engagements by less than a majority of those voting (or to require more than three-quarters of those voting to approve a transfer of engagements). The power may only be exercised upon application by at least 100 members of the society (or, if fewer, by 10 per cent of the entire membership).

Certain societies have adopted special rules in relation to transfers of engagement and conversions into companies. These rules include a minimum period of membership before members may vote on resolutions (including resolutions to approve transfers or conversions) and requirements for a minimum turn-out on resolutions to transfer engagements or to convert, analogous to the minimum turn-out requirements which automatically apply to building societies under Schedule 2 to the Building Societies Act 1986.

11.9 Disputes and arbitration, disciplinary powers

Friendly societies are required under Section 80 of the Friendly Societies Act 1992 to include within their rules a mechanism whereby disputes with members and certain other persons or bodies can be referred to arbitration with the alternative, if all parties to the dispute consent, to refer the dispute to the county court (or to a sheriff in Scotland). This requirement has been preserved notwithstanding the establishment of the Financial Ombudsman under Part XVI of the FSMA 2000. Friendly societies fall within the compulsory jurisdiction of the Financial Ombudsman under DISP2.1. Friendly societies are also required to comply with the complaint handling procedures for firms under DISP1. Section 80(1A) of the Friendly Societies Act 1992 (inserted by the Financial Services and Markets Act 2000 (Mutual Societies) Order 2001) states that the arbitration mechanism is without prejudice to a complainant's right to refer complaints to the Financial Ombudsman.

The FSA has specific disciplinary and enforcement powers in relation to friendly societies under the Friendly Societies Act 1992 in addition to the powers that it has under the enforcement Chapter of the FSA Handbook. These powers are:

(a)   a power to apply to the High Court for the winding up of a friendly
      society under Section 52 of the Friendly Societies Act 1992 if the FSA
      has reason to believe:
      (i)   that the society is carrying out activities which are not
             permitted under the Friendly Societies Act 1992 or the
             Friendly Societies Act 1974;
      (ii)   that the society is not carrying out any of the activities referred
             to in Schedule 2 to the Friendly Societies Act 1992 (as to which,
             see 11.4.1 above); or
      (iii) that it is failing to comply with the laws relating to insurance
             in any EEA Member State other than the UK;
(b)   the power to issue directions in relation to disproportionate
      activities of subsidiaries under Section 54 of the Friendly Societies
      Act 1992 referred to under 11.4.5 above;
(c)   the power in relation to disproportionate group business under
      Section 55 of the Friendly Societies Act 1992 referred to in 11.4.3
      above;
(d)   the power to direct a society to transfer its engagements to a third
      party under Section 90 of the Friendly Societies Act 1992 referred
      to in 11.8 above.

Section 58A of the Friendly Societies Act 1992 (inserted by Article 13(1)
of the Financial Services and Markets Act 2000 (Mutual Societies) Order
2001) applies the system of warning notices and decision notices under
Part XXVI of the FSMA 2000, mutatis mutandis, to any actions taken by
the FSA under Sections 54, 55 or 90 of the Friendly Societies Act 1992.
There is also a right to refer any decision notices issued by the FSA in
respect of these matters to the Financial Services and Markets Tribunal
under Part IX of the FSMA 2000. Parts IX and XXVI of the FSMA 2000
do not apply to applications for winding up under Section 52 of the
Friendly Societies Act 1992 as such applications must be made to the
High Court.

Index

NB: All references are to chapter number followed by paragraph number, for example, 8.2.3.3 refers to Chapter 8, paragraph 2.3.3.

best execution rule,
conduct of business 10.8.1.4
birth assurance 1.3.1
'black letters',
conduct of business 10
'blended rate',
stamp duty 6.7.9
bodies corporate, control,
friendly societies 11.4.5
branches, establishment
approved persons regime 5.9
changes in details
EEA firms 5.4.2
general 5.4.1
UK firms 5.4.3
consequences 5.6.2
EEA firms, in UK 5.3.2–5.3.4
EU legislation, implementation in UK
5.2
'general good', conditions imposed by
host Member State
background 5.7.1
case law 5.7.3
examples 5.7.4
FSMA, under 5.7.2
interpretation 5.7.3
typical FSA conditions 5.7.5
general requirements, procedure
EEA firms 5.3.2
UK firms 5.3.5
insurance passport *see* **insurance
passport**
procedure
authorisation, cancellation of
qualification for 5.3.9
consent notice 5.3.3, 5.3.6
EEA firms, branches in UK 5.3.3
'establishment conditions' 5.3.3
general requirements 5.3.2, 5.3.5
notice of intention 5.3.6
notification requirements 5.3.1
UK firms, in EEA states 5.3.6
validity of policies 5.3.8
reinsurance
Reinsurance and Retrocession
Directive (1964) 5.8.1
Third Insurance Directives,
application of 5.8.2

UK regime, other EEA states
compared 5.8.3
right of, versus freedom to provide
services
analysis 5.6.1
consequences 5.6.2
interaction 5.6.1
transitional provisions 5.5
UK firms, in EEA states 5.3.5–5.3.8
see also **services, cross-border
provision of**
broker funds,
conduct of business 10.8.1.2
brokers
introducing 10.6.14
regulatory return, users of 4.2.4.2
business revenue forms,
regulatory return 4.2.3.2

**CALA (Contracts (Applicable Law) Act
1990)** 7.4, 7.4.3, 7.4.4
calculations, solvency requirements
composite insurers 4.3.3.3
free asset ratios 4.3.3.5
general business 4.3.3.1
long-term business 4.3.3.2
parent undertaking solvency margin
4.3.3.4
cancellation of insurance policies
'cold calling' 7.1
conduct of business
cancellation substitutes 10.7.10.2
COB, application of 10.2.1, 10.7.10.1
electronic communication of
cancellation 10.7.10.6
notices 10.7.10.7
result of cancellation 10.7.10.8
stakeholder pensions 10.7.10.3
tables 10.7.10.4
time of cancellation 10.7.10.7
variations to policies 10.7.10.5
voluntary cancellation 10.7.10.5
'cooling off' period, following 7.1
electronic communication 10.7.10.6
EU directives 7.1
form of notice 7.1.1
'investment agreements' 7.1
notices 10.7.10.7

consent notices *continued*
  services, cross-border provision of
    5.3.7
contracts of insurance
  derivative 4.2.3.4, 4.6.1.5, 9.6.1.3
  linked *see* **linked contracts**
  long-term 7.5.2
  regulation 1.3.5
  see also **choice of law, insurance
    contracts**
**controlled functions, insurance
  companies**
  AP regime, 'controlled function' test
    5.9, 9.2.3
  significant influence 3.2.3.2
  specification 3.2.3.1
  threshold conditions 2.7.9
controllers,
  Threshold Conditions 2.7.10
**controllers, requirements imposed
  upon**
  acquisitions 3.1.2.1
  approval 3.1.1
  improperly acquired shares 3.1.2.2
  increases in control 3.1.2.1
  reductions in control 3.1.2.3
'cooling off' rights 7.1
Corporate Authorisation Department
  2.8.1, 2.8.4
Council Directives,
  motor insurance 8.1.1
counterparty exposure of insurers,
  FSA guidance 4.6.1.1
Court of Session, procedure in 6.4.13
CPR (Civil Procedure Rules) 1998
  legal expenses insurance 8.3.2
  portfolio transfers
    court applications 6.4.5
    scheme report 6.4.6
**Credit and Suretyship Insurance
  Directive (1987)** 1.3.11
Critical Illness Cover (CII) 8.2.1, 8.2.3.3
customers
  acceptance of
    client classification 10.5.1
    customer agreements 10.5.2
    terms of business 10.5.2
  client classification 10.1.1.3, 10.5.1

  intermediate 10.5.1
  lending to 10.8.1.5
  market counterparty 10.5.1
  private 10.5.1
  reporting to 10.8.2
  risk, understanding of 10.6.10

**Dear appointed actuary/Dear Director
  letters** 4.7.5
DEC (Decision-Making Manual),
  statutory sources, authorisation of
    insurers 2.1
Decision Making Manual, 5.3.7
decision tree,
  stakeholder pensions 10.7.6, 10.7.8
Deduction and Aggregation Method,
  parent undertaking solvency margin
    4.5.2.1
definitions/interpretations
  advertisements 7.2.1
  authorised agent 5.6.1
  authorised person 2.2
  co-insurance policy 1.3.10
  commercial business 9.2.5
  common ownership 6.7.13.3
  connected person 9.5.6
  contract of general insurance 2.3.3.1
  contract of long-term insurance
    2.3.3.1
  contractually based investments
    2.3.4.1
  controlled investments 7.2.3
  controller 2.7.10, 3.1.1
  EEA State 6.2.3, 10.2.1
  export credit insurance 8.4.1
  financial supervision 4.1.1
  home state regulator 2.11.2
  inherited estate 9.8.1
  insurance business transfer scheme
    6.2.1
  investments 7.1.1
  mandatory rules 7.4.3
  parent undertaking 4.5.2.2
  participating undertaking 4.5.2.2
  RMM (required minimum margin)
    4.3.2
  transfer 6.2.7
  treaty firms 2.11.2

solvency requirements *continued*
parent undertaking solvency
margin 4.3.3.4
MGF (minimum guarantee fund)
4.3.2
RMM (required minimum margin)
4.3.2–4.3.3.3
SRO (Self Regulatory Organisation)
prudential regulation, long-term
insurance 9.1.1
rulebooks 10.0
stakeholder pensions
advising and selling 10.6.15
cancellation of insurance policies
10.7.10.3
decision tree 10.7.6, 10.7.8
disclosure requirements 10.7.7
product disclosure 10.7.6
regulated activities 2.3.3.2
stamp duty 6.7.9
general insurance business 6.7.13.5
standards, high-level
SYSC (senior management
arrangements, systems and
controls) 3.2.4.1
see also **APER (Statements of
Principle and Code of Practice
for Approved Persons)**
'state of the commitment',
meaning 6.4.4
**Statement of Best Practice for Critical
Illness Cover**, ABI 8.2.3.3
Statements of Principle, APER *see*
**APER (Statements of Principle
and Code of Practice for
Approved Persons)**
Statements of Recommended Practice,
scheme charges 10.7.9.14
statutory notices,
compulsory information given to
policyholders 7.5.1
subrogation rights,
compensation, motor insurance 8.1.3
suitability of advice *see* **advising and
selling**: suitability
**Supervision Manual (SUP), FSA
Handbook**
AP regime, applicable firms 3.2.2.1

appointed actuaries, regulation of
long-term insurance 9.2.4
changes in details, notification
requirements 5.4.3
controlled firm, requirements
imposed on 3.1.3
FSA, duty to inform 9.4.1
notifiable events 9.4.1.3
Part IV Permissions, variation or
cancellation of 2.9, 2.9.1
passport rights, exercise of 5.3.5
powers of FSA 4.7.3
prudential categories 2.6.4
risk assessment 2.6.5
services, cross-border provision
5.3.7
specification of controlled functions
3.2.3.1
statutory sources, authorisation of
insurers 2.1
supervisors, company and lead 4.7.4
surrender values,
projections of 10.7.9.8
switching,
conduct of business 10.8.1.3
Switzerland,
insurance passport application
5.1.6
**SYSC (senior management
arrangements, systems and
controls)**
audit functions 2.7.8
business strategy 2.7.8
compliance and oversight function
2.7.8
delegation of activities 2.7.8
disaster recovery plans 2.7.8
high-level standards 3.2.4.1
management information 2.7.8
prudential regulation, long-term
insurance 9.3.3
record keeping 2.7.8
resources, adequacy of 2.7.4
threshold conditions 2.7.8
systems and controls, FSA guidance
general business claims provisions
4.6.1.2
investments of insurers 4.6.1.1